ESTATE PLANNING 2023

The School of Law
University of California, Los Angeles, and
California Continuing Education of the Bar

CEB®

Library of Congress Catalog No. 82-64082

Printed in the United States of America
ISBN 978-0-7626-3307-4
ISBN Series 0-88124-183-0
ES-31605

CEB Advisory Board 2023–2024

UCLA-CEB
Estate Planning Institute
—————— Advisory Board ——————

Contents

Preface

These materials were prepared for the 45th Annual UCLA-CEB Estate Planning Institute, presented April 20–21, 2023, in California via Livestream Webinar.

The University of California, Los Angeles, School of Law, and Continuing Education of the Bar wish to express deep appreciation to the Institute's distinguished faculty for participating in the Institute and preparing these materials.

The success of the annual Institute is the result of the generous participation of these nationally known experts and the continued efforts of the Advisory Board, chaired by Monica Dell'Osso and Paul Gordon Hoffman.

Due to the ongoing COVID-19 pandemic, the Estate Planning Institute was livestreamed for the fourth straight year and numerous practitioners successfully attended online. A special thank you to John Wuopio and Carmen Roberson for their invaluable efforts to ensure the smooth transition from live venue to livestream. Continuing Education of the Bar also thanks Bruce Last, Geoff Moore, John Wuopio, Carmen Roberson, Casey Hatton, Kate Murphy, and Norman Valera for their help with the Institute.

The Institute serves as a forum for experienced attorneys and tax specialists to work together in analyzing and examining the complex issues of planning for substantial estates. The Institute further serves to provide authoritative information on aspects of estate administration, statutory and case law, pending legislation and how it affects estate planning practice, and other issues of concern to experienced estate planning attorneys.

CEB Content Attorney Bruce Last and Legal Content Specialist Norman Valera contributed to this book. Darma DeMarco handled production editing. Composition was performed by Ann Becker.

Philip Weverka
Manager
Content Development

Casey Hatton
Director
Content Operations

About the Authors

JAY D. ADKISSON is a managing partner of Adkisson Pitet LLP and is admitted to practice in Arizona, California, Nevada, Oklahoma, and Texas. A 1988 graduate of the University of Oklahoma College of Law with honors, and a member of the Oklahoma Law Review, Jay has twice been an expert witness to the U.S. Senate Finance Committee and is the Forbes.com writer on wealth preservation issues. He has served as an ABA Advisor to the drafting committees of the Uniform Voidable Transactions Act, the Uniform Protected Series Act, the Uniform Registration of Canadian Money Judgments Act, and the Uniform Public Expression Protection Act. He has also served as the Chair of the American Bar Association Committees on Captive Insurance and Insurance and Financial Products. His books include Asset Protection Concepts & Strategies (McGraw-Hill 2004), Adkisson's Captive Insurance Companies (iUniverse 2007), the Charging Order Practice Guide (Am.Bar.Assoc. 2018), and Anti-SLAPP Law Modernized: The Uniform Public Expression Protection Act. Jay is an honorary member of the California Association of Judgment Professionals, and a Hall of Fame member of the National Association of Estate Planning Councils. His law practice is primarily in the area of creditor-debtor litigation, including the attack and defense of sophisticated asset protection structures, plus some limited consulting in the area of asset protection planning. He is the author of chapter 2.

DR. GERRY W. BEYER joined the faculty of the Texas Tech University School of Law in June 2005 as the first holder of the Governor Preston E. Smith Regents Professorship. Prof. Beyer previously taught as a professor at many other law schools, including Boston College, Boston University, The Ohio State University, Southern Methodist University, The University of New Mexico, Santa Clara University, St. Mary's University, and La Trobe University (Australia). Prof. Beyer is admitted to practice in Texas, Illinois, Ohio, and before the U.S. Supreme Court and the U.S. Court of Appeals for the Armed Forces. Prof. Beyer received dozens of outstanding and distinguished faculty awards, including the Chancellor's Distinguished Teaching Award and the Outstanding (Law) Researcher Award. A recognized expert in estate planning, Prof. Beyer presents dozens of CLE presentations each year for bar associations, universities, and civic groups. In recognition of his efforts, the National Association of Estate Planners & Councils inducted him into the Estate Planning Hall of Fame, and the Real Estate, Probate, and Trust Law Section of the State Bar of Texas awarded him the Distinguished Probate Attorney Lifetime Achievement Award. Prof. Beyer is the author of numerous books and articles on estate planning, including a treatise on Texas wills law, an estate planning law school casebook, and the Wills, Trusts, and Estates volume of the Examples & Explanations, and is the Editor-in-Chief of the REPTL Reporter, the official journal of the Real Estate,

Probate and Trust Law Section of the State Bar of Texas. He has won three awards from the American Bar Association's Probate & Property magazine, and is one of the most downloaded law authors on the Social Science Research Network. Prof. Beyer mentors students and various law school organizations, regularly participates in pro bono activities, and is the advisor for the Estate Planning and Community Property Law Journal, the Black Law Students Association, and the Estate and Property Law Society. Prof. Beyer received his J.D. from The Ohio State University (summa cum laude) and his LL.M. and J.SD. from the University of Illinois. He is a member of the Order of the Coif, an Academic Fellow and Regent of the American College of Trust and Estate Counsel, a member of the American Law Institute, and was appointed by the Uniform Law Commission as the Reporter for the Uniform Electronic Estate Planning Document Act. He is a co-author of chapter 7.

CYNTHIA "CINDY" D. BRITTAIN, Karlin & Peebles, LLP, Los Angeles, has decades of experience advising high-net-worth and ultra-high-net-worth individuals and families on domestic and international income and estate tax planning strategies, as well as philanthropic endeavors. Her practice offers significant cross-border expertise for families whose members are multinational and whose companies have a global footprint. She frequently helps clients navigate complex issues relevant to international and domestic wealth and asset transfer, as well as assisting with pre-immigration planning and international corporate tax matters. Her extensive experience with the cross-border regulatory laws that affect U.S. domestic planning and U.S. tax compliance under the various voluntary disclosure regimes enables her to help clients avoid negative consequences and minimize tax implications. Over the course of her distinguished career, Cindy has worked with clients in Brazil, Saudi Arabia, Dubai, London, Hong Kong, Mainland China, India, and the United States. She takes a personal approach to advising large global families, working closely with each family member to obtain a comprehensive understanding of values and dynamics to ensure that unique personal and business goals are accounted for and achieved. Cindy also provides hands-on guidance for financial institutions and corporate trustees who work with international clients, advising on global enforcement initiatives relevant to companies, CPA firms, and law firms that handle international clients. Infrastructure for the U.K. Criminal Finances Act of 2017, trust registration obligations within European Union countries, and domestic planning taking into account Brussels IV are just some of the foreign rules that cross the Atlantic and impact planning and protocols here in the United States, and Cindy is a frequent speaker on the application of these rules. She is the author of chapter 9.

KALYANI CHANDRA was hired as an Estate and Gift tax attorney with the Internal Revenue Service in Oakland 15 years ago. For 11 years, she examined estate and gift tax returns before becoming the group manager for the Los Angeles and Hawaii areas. Since

January 2023, she has been the Acting Technical Advisor to the Chief of Estate and Gift Tax. She is the author of chapter 5.

HON. REVA G. GOETZ (RET.) is a full time neutral at JAMS and has successfully mediated and arbitrated hundreds of estate/probate/trust and family law matters. Her vast experience includes high-value trust, sensitive conservatorship and family matters for high-profile individuals, as well as complex trials as a judge pro tem. She also serves as a court reference, appointed by the court for accounting trials and as a discovery referee, and selected for all purposes as agreed to by counsel. Previously, Judge Goetz served as a judicial officer for 25 years, which included splitting her time between probate and family law assignments. During her time in probate court, she heard hundreds of contested cases, including those with high-value trusts, high-profile conservatorships, undue influence and capacity issues, elder abuse, highly complex accountings, and surcharge petitions. While serving on the family law court, Judge Goetz handled complex dissolutions, addressing issues such as characterization of property; separate and/or community property; high-profile individuals; complex child custody matters, including those involving children with special needs and difficult custodial schedules; business and asset valuations; and support issues. She is a co-author of chapter 3.

LAURELLE M. GUTIERREZ, McDermott Will & Emery LLP, San Francisco, has a diverse practice representing high-net-worth and ultra-high-net-worth individuals and their families with respect to all aspects of income, gift, estate, and generation-skipping wealth-transfer tax planning, as well as trust and estate administration. She is a certified specialist in Estate Planning, Trust and Probate Law by the State Bar of California Board of Legal Specialization. Ms. Gutierrez has been named one of the Best Lawyers in America every year since 2013, and in the Private Client Global Elite every year since 2017. She is a co-author of chapter 7.

JOHN A. HARTOG is a principal of Hartog, Baer, Zabronsky & Verriere, APC, a ten-attorney firm in Orinda whose practice is limited to all aspects of trusts and estates law. He focuses his practice on trust and estate planning, administration, dispute resolution, and litigation. Extensively published, he has co-authored three practice guides essential to professionals in the field: California Wills & Trusts (Matthew Bender), California Trust Practice (Matthew Bender), and California Trust Litigation (Matthew Bender). Mr. Hartog is also a legal consultant to the California Wills and Trusts document assembly program. Mr. Hartog is a Fellow of the American College of Trust and Estate Counsel. He is certified by the California Board of Legal Specialization as a specialist in taxation law and in estate planning, trust and probate law. He is past chair of the executive committee of the State Bar of California's Trust and Estates Section, as well as past chair of the Estate Planning, Trust and Probate Law Advisory Commission to the California Board of Legal Specialization. He is a co-author of chapter 3.

PATRICK A. KOHLMANN is the managing partner at Temmerman, Cilley & Kohlmann. Patrick advises individuals and families in all aspects of wealth transfer planning, including tax-advantaged transfers of assets, multigenerational planning, the taxation of trusts and estates, and business succession counseling. Patrick is passionate about the law. He was Chair of the Executive Committee of the Trusts and Estates Section (TEXCOM) of the State Bar of California (now CLA) from 2015–2016, and served on TEXCOM from 2008–2019. He is a Fellow of the American College of Trust and Estates Counsel, was formerly a member of the Judicial Council's Probate and Mental Health Advisory Committee, and has consistently been named a Northern California "Super Lawyer," including recognition as one of the top 100 lawyers in Northern California (2021–2022). Patrick practiced public accounting as a CPA before pursuing a legal career. He is a co-author of chapter 8.

S. ANDREW PHARIES is a partner with Duane Morris LLP in its San Diego office, where he is a member of the firm's Private Client Services Group. Andy practices in the areas of domestic and international estate planning, trust and estate administration and dispute resolution, charitable planning, exempt organizations, and tax compliance and controversy. Andy is a Fellow of the American College of Trust and Estate Counsel (ACTEC) and serves on the Advisory Board for the UCLA-CEB Estate Planning Institute. He previously served as a member and advisor to the Executive Committee of the Trusts and Estates Section of the State Bar of California, where he served as Chair of the Section's Income and Transfer Tax Subcommittee and as Editor-in-Chief of the California Trusts and Estates Quarterly. Andy is a Certified Specialist in Estate Planning, Trust, and Probate Law; he is listed in Best Lawyers in America for Trusts and Estates; and he has been repeatedly named a San Diego and Southern California Super Lawyer in Estate Planning & Probate Law. Andy is a frequent speaker on domestic and international trusts and estates topics and has previously spoken for ACTEC, the UCLA-CEB Estate Planning Institute, the USC Tax Institute, CEB, ALI-ABA, the State Bar of California Trusts and Estates Section, the ABA Real Property, Probate, and Trust Section, the CPA Education Foundation, and various local bar associations and estate planning councils. Andy has also written on various trusts and estates topics in the California Trusts and Estates Quarterly; the Tax Management Estates, Gifts, and Trusts Journal; Probate and Property; and the Matthew Bender Practice Guide, California Trust Litigation. Andy received his B.S. from the University of California, Riverside, and his J.D. from the University of Oregon School of Law, where he served as Editor-in-Chief of the Oregon Law Review. He is the author of chapter 1.

MARK S. POOCHIGIAN, Baker Manock & Jensen, PC, Fresno, practices in all aspects of estate planning, post-death trust and estate administration, trust and estate litigation, and family business planning. Mr. Poochigian is a Fellow of the American College of Trust and Estate Counsel (ACTEC) and is certified by the State Bar of California Board of Legal Specialization as a specialist in Estate Planning, Trust and Probate Law. Mr. Poochigian has served since 2012 as a member of the Executive Committee of the Trusts and Estates Section (TEXCOM) of the California Lawyers Association. Mr. Poochigian has served as the Chair of TEXCOM (2019–2020) and as Editor-in-Chief of the California Trusts and Estates Quarterly (2014–2015). He is a co-author of chapter 3.

BILL SANDERSON, McGuireWoods, Washington, D.C., represents both high-net-worth individuals and families on a variety of sensitive and complex estate and business planning matters. His practice focuses on the areas of estate planning and estate and trust administration. He is a member of McGuireWoods's fiduciary advisory services practice. Prior to completing his law degree at the University of Virginia School of Law, Bill completed coursework at the University of South Carolina School of Law. While attending the University of Virginia, Bill was a member of the Raven Society and the Jefferson Literary and Debating Society. Bill is a Fellow in the American College of Trust and Estate Counsel. Since March 2022, he has served as chair of its Washington Affairs Committee. He is the author of chapter 6.

VIVIAN LEE THOREEN is the executive partner of Holland & Knight's Los Angeles office and chairs the firm's national Private Wealth Services Dispute Resolution Team. She is a litigator and experienced trial attorney whose practice focuses on complex trust, estate, conservatorship, and guardianship matters. She is a Fellow of the American College of Trust and Estate Counsel and served a 6-year term on the California Lawyers Association (formerly the State Bar of California) Trusts & Estates Section Executive Committee (TEXCOM). She is ranked in the Chambers High Net Worth guide both nationally and in California, is named in the The Best Lawyers in America guide, and has been honored by the Los Angeles Business Journal for her trial work. She is a co-author of chapter 8.

PETER M. WALZER is the founding partner of prominent Southern California family law firm Walzer Melcher & Yoda LLP and has been a Certified Family Law Specialist for 35 years. In 2018, he served as President of the American Academy of Matrimonial Lawyers, the largest family law organization in the United States, and is a former president of the Association of Certified Family Law Specialists. He lectures regularly for the State Bar, the University of California, Los Angeles, CEB, ACFLS, AAML, and various other organizations. He is a co-author of chapter 4.

KIMBERLY R. WILLOUGHBY, ESQ., is principal of Willoughby & Associates, a Colorado firm limited to family law, estate planning, and prenuptial agreements. She received her J.D. from the University of Virginia in 1994 and is licensed in Colorado and South Dakota. Ms. Willoughby is a Fellow of the American Academy of Matrimonial Lawyers and past Chapter president. She is also a Fellow of the American College of Trust and Estate Counsel. On the state and national level, she leads committees and speaks frequently to promote collaboration, cross pollination, and education between family law attorneys and trust and estate attorneys. She is a co-author of chapter 4.

1

Current California Developments

S. Andrew Pharies

UCLA-CEB ESTATE PLANNING INSTITUTE

CALIFORNIA DEVELOPMENTS

S. Andrew Pharies
Duane Morris LLP
apharies@duanemorris.com

Wehsener v. Jernigan (2022) 89 Cal.App.5th 1311

California law Applies to Determine Heirship When Facts That Establish Parentage Occurred Outside California

- Decedent died intestate with no close surviving relatives. Litigation involves whether Judy (an alleged cousin) is an intestate heir.

- Judy was taken in by the Decedent's uncle when she was two years old.

- While living in Indiana, the uncle and his wife held Judy out to be their daughter, but they never adopted her.

- Under Indiana law, Judy would not be considered to be uncle's daughter because he never adopted her.

- Under California law, the Uniform Parentage Act (UPA) provides that Judy would be presumed to be uncle's daughter if he took her into his home and openly held her out as his natural child.

- The issue at trial was whether Indiana or California law applied.

- The Probate Court held that California law applies and under the UPA Judy is a child of uncle and an heir of the Decedent.

Wehsener v. Jernigan, cont.

- The Court of Appeal affirmed.

- When determining heirship for a California decedent, California law applies even if the parent-child relationship was formed and existed outside of California.

- Here, Judy was taken in by the Decedent's uncle and held out to be his daughter. Under the UPA, Judy is presumed to be his daughter.

- The objecting party, a cousin of the Decedent, never produced evidence to rebut the presumption. Rather, she argued that the presumption should be rebutted on public policy grounds.

- The Court rejected that argument noting that the UPA provided that the presumption could be rebutted only with clear and convincing evidence.

Estate of Raul Sausedo Franco (2023), Court of Appeal, First District

Application of Marital Presumption to Establish Parentage Bars Child From Claiming Heirship in Biological Parent's Estate

- Marilyn and Frank, Sr., were married. During a period of separation, Marilyn became pregnant by Franco, and Frank Bertuccio was born.

- Marilyn and Frank, Sr., later reunited, and they together with Franco agreed that Bertuccio should be raised as the child of Marilyn and Frank, Sr.

- Bertuccio developed a close relationship with Franco as an adult; Franco referred to him as his son.

- After Franco's death, a dispute arose between Bertuccio and Franco's sister and niece regarding Bertuccio's claim to be Franco's son and heir.

- Probate Court granted a joint motion for summary judgment in favor of Franco's sister and niece. It reasoned that the Marital Presumption of Family Code Section 7540 and *Estate of Cornelious* applied to prevent Bertuccio from being Franco's intestate heir.

Estate of Raul Sausedo Franco, cont.

Application of Marital Presumption to Establish Parentage Bars Child From Claiming Heirship in Biological Parent's Estate

- Court of Appeal affirmed in substance but reversed the granting of the MSJ.

- The Marital Presumption of Family Code Section 7540 provides that a child born spouses who cohabited at the time of conception and birth is presumed to be the child of the marriage.

- *Estate of Cornelious* (1984) 35 Cal.3d 461 provides that if the Marital Presumption applies, then the child is barred from claiming a parent-child relationship with a third party for purposes of intestate succession.

- Here, summary judgment was improperly granted as the Probate Court did not make a finding on whether Frank Sr. and Marilyn cohabited as husband and wife at the time of Bertuccio's conception and birth, which is necessary to apply the Marital Presumption.

Estate of El Wardani (2022) 82 Cal.App.5th 870

Estate Administrators Must Physically Reside in the US

- Husband and Wife retired to Mexico. Husband later passed away.

- Wife was appointed as administrator of Husband's California estate.

- Disputes arose between Wife and Husband's daughter from a prior marriage (Step Daughter).

- Step Daughter sought removal of Wife as administrator based on Probate Code Section 8402(a)(4), claiming she was not a US resident.

- Wife argued her connections to the US made her a resident. These connections included friend, financial accounts, and professional advisors (center of vital interests).

- Probate Court removed Wife as administrator, citing non-residency.

- Court of Appeal affirmed Probate Court's decision.

- Residency for Section 8402(a)(4) equated with domicile; connections to the US alone cannot establish residency.

- Domicile is the physical presence in the US with an intent to remain.

Zahnleuter v. Mueller (2023) 88 Cal.App.5th 1294

Trustee Surcharged for Defending Trust Amendment

- Trust created by Husband and Wife. It contained a no contest clause that allowed the trustee to defend against a contest of the trust instrument or any of its provisions.
- The trust instrument was amended several times. The Third Amendment made material changes, including naming Husband's brother ("Brother") as successor trustee.
- Daughters contested validity of Third Amendment in separate proceedings.
- Brother, as trustee, used trust assets to defend Third Amendment.
- Daughter sought surcharge against Brother for improperly using trust assets to pay his attorneys
- Probate Court granted petition for surcharge against Brother. It found that the terms of the trust instrument allow the trustee to defend the trust instrument but not an amendment to the trust instrument.

Zahnleuter v. Mueller, cont.

Trustee Surcharged for Defending Trust Amendment

- Court of Appeal affirmed the decision.
- Trustee's attorney fees may not be paid from the trust when defending an amendment without proper authorization in the trust instrument itself.
- A challenge to an amendment is a fight between beneficiaries over their rights under the trust. A trustee cannot take sides in that fight.
- By contrast, attorney fees can be paid from the trust when the validity of the trust itself is at stake.
- Takeaway: If you want to give a trustee the power to defend an amendment using trust resources, provide that in the trust and waive duty of impartiality.

Estate of Eskra (2022) 78 Cal.App.5th 209

Rescission of Premarital Agreement Not Permitted When Mistake Cased by Failure to Read Agreement Before Signing

- Husband and Wife signed a premarital agreement waiving rights to each other's separate property.
- Husband died in a car accident without leaving a Will.
- Dispute arose between Wife and Husband's children after his death regarding the enforceability of the agreement.
- Wife claimed agreement should be rescinded due to a mistake of fact – her belief that the agreement applied only to divorce, not death.
- In fact, Husband and Wife agreed that the agreement would apply only in the event of death, and Wife's counsel asked for changes to the agreement to reflect that.
- Husband's counsel made the changes, but they were only to examples and not to the substantive language of the agreement.
- Wife failed to read the revised agreement or consult her counsel before signing. She simply assumed that the changes she requested were incorporated into the revised agreement.
- Trial court denied Wife's rescission claim. Wife bore the risk of her mistake because she did not act with reasonable care.

Estate of Eskra, cont.

Rescission of Premarital Agreement Not Permitted When Mistake Cased by Failure to Read Agreement Before Signing

- The Court of Appeal affirmed the decision.
- Rescission based on unilateral mistake is allowed only when:
    - A party makes a mistake on a basic assumption on which the agreement is made;
    - The mistake has a material effect on the performance of the agreement that is adverse to the mistaken party;
    - The mistaken party does not bear the risk of the mistake; and
    - The effect of the mistake is such that enforcement would be unconscionable.
- Here, the case turns on whether Wife bore the risk of the mistake.
- Under case law, a party who neglects a legal duty bears the risk of the mistake, and failure to read an agreement is a neglect of a legal duty.
- Since Wife failed to read the revised agreement, she bore the risk of the mistake and rescission is barred.

Welch v. Welch (2022) 79 Cal.App.5th 283

Marital Settlement Agreement That Called for Long-Form Agreement Waived Spousal Rights Even Though Long-Form Agreement Not Completed Before Death

- Husband and Wife entered into a marital settlement agreement (MSA) during dissolution proceedings; MSA called for a long-form agreement.

- The MSA did not contain an express waiver of spouse rights to inheritance.

- Disputes arose, and Wife passed away before the completion of the long-form agreement.

- In Wife's probate, Husband took the position that he did not waive his spousal rights under Probate Code Section 141(b) by executing the MSA because it did not include an express wavier.

- Probate Court found the MSA did not waive Husband's spousal rights.

Welch v. Welch, cont.

Marital Settlement Agreement That Called for Long-Form Agreement Waived Spousal Rights Even Though Long-Form Agreement Not Completed Before Death

- Court of Appeal reversed the decision.

- Probate Code Section 145 provides that a waiver of spousal rights can be done through either:
    - An express waiver of rights; or
    - A complete property settlement entered into after or in anticipation of divorce.

- Court of Appeal found that an express waiver requires particularized language, but a complete property settlement does not.

- A complete property settlement is one that is in writing, signed by the surviving spouse, with adequate disclosure of assets and debts, where the parties are represented by counsel, and constitutes a fair disposition of the rights of the surviving spouse.

- Since the MSA met this criteria, it effectively waived Husband's spousal rights even though it did not contact an express waiver.

Parker v. Schwarcz (2022) 84 Cal.App.5th 418

Documents and Communications Are Not "Personal Property" That Can Be Recovered Through A Section 850 Petition

- After a temporary conservatorship was terminated, the conservatee, Parker, filed Probate Code Section 850 petition seeking documents and communications related to the conservatorship estate.

- Probate Court denied the petition, stating that Section 850 applies only when there is a conservator and to recover property belonging to the conservatee.

- Court of Appeal affirmed the decision.

- Purpose of Section 850 is to allow conservators to recover assets that should be part of the conservatorship estate.

- Documents and communications are not "personal property" that can be recovered through a Section 850 petition, as they do not carry the same indicia as real or personal property. Specifically, they have no inherent value to fund the estate or pay down debts and were not previously owned by the former conservatee.

Starr v. Ashbrook (2023) 87 Cal.App.5th 999

Petition Seeking Surcharge Against Trustee for Misuse of Trust Assets Withstands Anti-SLAPP Scrutiny

- Trustee Ashbrook filed a petition for instructions and other litigation adverse the Starr, who was a beneficiary.

- Starr filed a petition seeking surcharge against Ashbrook for wasting trust assets by pursuing a meritless petition and funding litigation against Starr and his brothers.

- Ashbrook filed an Anti-SLAPP motion to strike the petition.

- The Anti-SLAPP statute requires the defendant to establish that the challenged allegations or claims arise out of constitutionally protected activity.

- This case turns on whether the surcharge cause of action arose out of (1) the protected activity of funding and pursuing litigation or (2) the unprotected activity of misusing and wasting trust assets.

- Probate Court denied the Anti-SLAPP motion.

DuaneMorris®
www.duanemorris.com

Starr v. Ashbrook, cont.

Petition Seeking Surcharge Against Trustee for Misuse of Trust Assets Withstands Anti-SLAPP Scrutiny

- The Court of Appeal affirmed.

- For Anti-SLAPP purposes, the focus is on the defendant's alleged activity that gives rise to the asserted liability. If that activity is protected, then Anti-SLAPP may be proper.

- Here, the surcharge cause of action arose out of the unprotected activity of misusing and wasting trust assets, rather than the protected activity of pursuing litigation.

- "Misconduct in the administration of a trust and preservation of trust assets is not action 'in furtherance of the person's right of petition or free speech under the United States Constitution or the California Constitution.'"

DuaneMorris®
www.duanemorris.com

Autonomous Region of Narcotics Anonymous v. Narcotics Anonymous World Services, Inc. (2022) 77 Cal.App.5th 950

Special Interest Standing Does Not Extend to Revocable Charitable Trusts

- Fellowship of Narcotics Anonymous created a revocable trust for its intellectual property, with World Services as the trustee.

- Fellowship is comprised of regional chapters which sends delegates to the World Service Conference.

- Trust allows for revocation by the Fellowship acting through the World Service Conference.

- Autonomous Region of Narcotics Anonymous, a regional chapter, filed a petition against World Services for alleged breaches of trust.

- Autonomous Region of Narcotics Anonymous claimed standing as:

  - A settlor of the trust under and under Probate Code Section 15800; and

  - Under the "special interest" standing doctrine relating to charitable trust (giving beneficiaries standing in certain circumstances).

- Probate Court granted World Service's demurrer without leave to amend.

Autonomous Region of Narcotics Anonymous v. Narcotics Anonymous World Services, Inc., cont.

Special Interest Standing Does Not Extend to Revocable Charitable Trusts

- Court of Appeal affirmed.

- Autonomous Region of Narcotics Anonymous was not a settlor. The Fellowship, acting through the World Service Conference was the settlor.

- Further, unlike with irrevocable trusts, beneficiaries of revocable trusts do not have special interest standing.

- Oversight of a revocable charitable trust can be sufficiently exercised by the party with the power to revoke, without beneficiaries needing standing.

Meiri v. Shamtoubi (2022) 81 Cal.App.5th 606

Probable Cause for a Trust Contest Does Not Exist When Petition is Time-Barred

- Husband and Wife created a standard ABC Trust to be distributed to their four children.

- They amended and restated the trust in order to account for lifetime gifts and loans. The Restatement included a no contest clause.

- After Husband's death, Wife, as trustee, served a Probate Code Section 16061.7 notice on all beneficiaries.

- In response, Daughter filed a petition seeking invalidation of the Restatement. She filed her petition 230 days after receiving notice, exceeding the 120-day contest period.

- Wife's counsel urged Daughter's counsel to withdraw the petition but received no response.

- Probate Court sustained demurrer to the petition, finding it time-barred. It also found that the petition constituted a direct contest without probable cause, enforcing the no contest clause and disinheriting the Daughter.

DuaneMorris®
www.duanemorris.com

Meiri v. Shamtoubi, cont.

Probable Cause for a Trust Contest Does Not Exist When Petition is Time-Barred

- Court of Appeal affirmed.

- Daughter argued that probable cause can be denied only if there is a substantive impediment to relief.

- Both procedural and substantive impediments to relief must be considered in determining probable cause.

- Filing a time-barred petition led a reasonable person to believe there was not a reasonable likelihood of relief being granted, causing a lack of probable cause.

DuaneMorris®
www.duanemorris.com

Bruno v. Hopkins (2022) 79 Cal.App.5th 801

Attorneys' Fees Award For Bad Faith Action to Remove Trustee Can Exceed Share of Trust Estate

- Husband and wife created a trust. Husband was a lawyer and he cobbled together a document with portions handwritten and other typed.

- Trust provided that upon the death of the first spouse, the estate was divided between a revocable Survivor's Trust and an irrevocable Family Trust.

- On death of surviving spouse, two older daughters would receive a pecuniary gift of $200,000 with the residue passing to two younger daughters.

- Husband passed away, and wife became the trustee.

- Wife failed to serve a Probate Code Section 16061.7 notice until several years after Husband's death. By that time, the residue was significantly larger than the pecuniary gifts.

- One of the Older daughters filed a petition to invalidate the trust and remove her mother as trustee.

- Probate Court denied the petition and awarded fees to the wife based on the court's inherent equitable power. It found that petitioner acted in bad faith and ordered the petitioner to be personally liable for the excess fees, as they exceeded her interest in the trust estate.

DuaneMorris®
www.duanemorris.com

Bruno v. Hopkins, cont.

Attorneys' Fees Award For Bad Faith Action to Remove Trustee Can Exceed Share of Trust Estate

- Court of Appeal affirmed Probate Court's decision but disagreed on the legal basis for the fee award. The court's inherent equitable power does not extend beyond the boundaries of the trust.

- However, Probate Code Section 15642 allows a court to order a person seeking removal of the trustee to bear all or any costs of the proceeding if the petition was filed in bad faith and contrary to the trustor's intent.

- No limitation on the court's power to award fees under Section 15642 to a beneficiary's share of the trust estate.

- Here, the Court founds the Probate Court's finding of bad faith was appropriate and removal would be contrary to the trustor's intent.

DuaneMorris®
www.duanemorris.com

Royals v. Lu (2022) 81 Cal.App.5th 328

Pretrial Right to Attach Order Not Appropriate for Punitive Damages

- Father transferred assets from his trust to accounts controlled by Lu, his new wife.

- After Father's death, Royals filed a petition for financial elder abuse against Lu, seeking $1,000,000 of compensatory and treble damages.

- Royals filed an application for pretrial right to attach order (RTAO) seeking to attach $3,000,000 of Lu's assets.

- Lu submitted evidence that Father intended to provide for her and moved assets intentionally.

- Probate Court issued the RTAO without considering Lu's evidence.

- Court of Appeal reversed.

- An RTAO is available for compensatory damages but not punitive damages in financial elder abuse actions.

- Further, Royals' attachment request for compensatory damages did not meet the statutory criteria, as it was not based upon facts within her personal knowledge and did not plead a definite amount of compensatory damages.

Estate of Jones (2022) 82 Cal.App.5th 948

Conditions Precedent and Settlement Agreements

- Father created a revocable trust which he did not amend after marrying Stepmother.

- After Father's death, Daughter became the trustee and sole beneficiary of the trust.

- Stepmother filed a petition under omitted spouse statutes, which was eventually settled. Under the settlement, Trust to pay Stepmother $3,000,000 from the escrow of property sale.

- Court entered a stipulated judgment incorporating the settlement. Later, Property sale fell through, and Daughter never paid Stepmother the settlement amount.

- Stepmother filed a petition to enforce the stipulated judgment.

- Probate Court denied Stepmother's petition to enforce the stipulated judgment on the ground that the settlement unenforceable because the condition precedent (property sale) failed.

Estate of Jones, cont.

Conditions Precedent and Settlement Agreements

- Court of Appeal reversed.

- It found that the promise to pay $3,000,000 and the promise to pay such amount from the sale proceeds were two related but independent promises in the settlement.

- The condition precedent applied to the method of payment, not to the enforceability of the settlement as a whole.

- Conditions precedent are narrowly interpreted. The failure of a condition precedent tied to the method of payment does not necessarily invalidate the enforceability of a settlement agreement.

King v. PG&E (2022) 82 Cal.App.5th 440

Heirs Have Right to Intervene In Wrongful Death Action

- Decedent killed in a helicopter crash in California; probate in Alabama. Decedent's former wife was appointed as personal representative (PR).
- PR filed wrongful death action in California.
- Surviving Spouse (Spouse) filed a motion to intervene as a matter of right.
- Trial court denied Spouse's motion to intervene. No authority supports heir's intervention in a wrongful death action filed by a PR, and the sufficiency of the PR's representation of Surviving Spouse's interests should be adjudicated by Alabama probate court.
- Court of Appeal reversed.
- Spouse, as an heir, has the right to intervene if statutory requirements are met.
- Statutes do not prohibit heir's intervention even if PR's action is pending.
- Spouse's intervention does not violate the "one action" rule.
- California court, not Alabama probate court, should decide PR's adequacy in representing Surviving Spouse's interests.

Estate of Douglas (2022) 83 Cal.App.5th 690

Law Firm's Clerical Error Incorporated Into Order Can Be Corrected Nunc Pro Tunc

- Law Firm ordered to receive statutory fees in a probate estate.
- 2008 judgment named judgment debtor as Audrey (as administrator of the estate).
- 2015 renewal application mistakenly named Audrey without her representative capacity.
- 2020 motion to correct "clerical error" after the 10-year renewal period.
- Audrey and others filed objections arguing the error was not clerical, as it was made by Law Firm, not the court.
- Probate Court granted law firm's motion and amended the renewed judgment *nunc pro tunc*.
- Court of Appeal affirmed.
- Clerical errors may be corrected *nunc pro tunc*, but judicial errors may not.
- Renewing a judgment is a ministerial act, so errors in the judgment are clerical and not judicial.
- Even if the mistake was made by Law Firm, the error was in a court-issued judgment.

Chui v. Chui (2022) 86 Cal.App.5th 929

Minor Has Right To Petition To Removal GAL

- Probate Court appointed Chen as guardian ad litem (GAL) for minor beneficiaries.

- Minor beneficiaries (16 and 17 years old) filed petition to remove Chen as GAL.

- Chen demurred, arguing that minors cannot hire counsel for his removal.

- Probate Court granted motion to disqualify counsel and dismissed the removal petition.

- Beneficiaries appealed and became adults during the appeal.

- Court of Appeal reversed.

- Minors may file a petition for removal of a guardian or conservator under guardianship and conservatorship laws.

- Court held that a minor capable of making informed decisions can petition for removal of a GAL and hire counsel for that purpose.

- GAL's position terminates when the ward reaches the age of majority.

Algo - Heyres v. Oxnard Manor LP (2023) 88 Cal.App.5th 1064

Arbitration Agreement Unenforceable Against Party Presumed Incompetent At Signing

- Cornelio had a stroke, entered a skilled nursing facility (SNF), and signed an arbitration agreement upon admission.

- After Cornelio's death, his successors-in-interest filed an action against the SNF for elder abuse, wrongful death, and other torts.

- SNF filed a petition to compel arbitration, but the trial court denied the petition due to Cornelio's lack of competency to consent to arbitration.

- Court of Appeal affirmed.

- Party seeking arbitration must prove the existence of a valid arbitration agreement.

- Civil Code 39(b) provides guidelines for determining capacity to contract, imposing a rebuttable presumption of unsounds mind if substantially unable to manage financial resources or resist fraud or undue influence.

- The party claiming capacity has the burden rebut the presumption by proving that the person is still capable of contracting despite being unable to manage finances or resist fraud or undue influence.

- Here, evidence showed that Cornelio had deficits in factors set forth in Probate Code Section 811, supporting the trial court's determination of Cornelio's incompetence to enter the arbitration agreement.

White v. Davis (2023), Court of Appeal, Fourth District

Application For Elder Abuse Restraining Order Survives Anti-SLAPP Challenge

- Father had diminishing capacity; New Wife and others influenced him to change his estate plan to disinherit his children.
- Daughter was serving as trustee of Father's trust; New Wife filed a petition to remove her (Removal Petition).
- Daughter applied for an Elder Abuse Restraining Order (EARO) to protect Father from further undue influence attempts. She also applied for a temporary EARO for immediate protection of Father. Trial court denied the temporary relief.
- New Wife filed an anti-SLAPP motion to dismiss the application for an EARO, arguing that the application aimed to thwart constitutionally protected activity – the Removal Petition.
- Daughter urged that the anti-SLAPP motion and application for EARO be heard concurrently so that an appeal by Wife would not keep Father vulnerable during the appeal period.
- Trial court prioritized the anti-SLAPP motion, which it denied. As feared, New Wife appealed with no EARO in place to protect Father.

White v. Davis, cont.

Application For Elder Abuse Restraining Order Survives Anti-SLAPP Challenge

- Court of Appeal affirmed denial of anti-SLAPP motion:
  - Activity to be examined is the one that gives rise to the petition, not the fact of the petition itself.
  - Undue influence of Father gave rise to the EARO; not a protected activity.
  - Estate planning is not a protected activity for purposes of Anti-SLAPP motions (footnote 18).
- However, Court of Appeal reversed with respect to timing of hearings:
  - Lower court abused its discretion by prioritizing the Anti-SLAPP motion over the EARO application.
  - Lower court could have revisited the request for temporary relief and granted it pending resolution of the Anti-SLAPP motion, or decided both requests for relief concurrently.

DuaneMorris®
www.duanemorris.com

Gordon v. Ervin, Cohen & Jessup LLP (2023) 88 Cal.App.5th 543

Estate Planner's Duty to Nonclients

- Client had three sons: Jeffrey, Bruce, and Kenneth. She was close to Kenneth, but did not care for his wife or children.

- Over a ten year period, Client went back and forth disinheriting one or more of Kenneth's children. Ultimately, she instructed her lawyer to create a trust amendment that disinherited all three of Kenneth's children.

- Later, client directed lawyer to form three LLCs for her sons. The LLC agreements contained no provision preventing Kenneth from transferring his LLC interests to his disinherited children.

- After client's death, Bruce sued to the lawyer for legal malpractice, claiming that his failure to structure LLCs to prevent Kenneth from transferring interests to his children harmed him because he would have been the taker in default.

- Trial court granted summary judgment in favor of the lawyer, finding no duty owed to nonclient beneficiaries.

DuaneMorris®
www.duanemorris.com

Gordon v. Ervin, Cohen & Jessup LLP, cont.

Estate Planner's Duty to Nonclients

- Court of Appeal affirmed. A lawyer owes a duty to a nonclient only if:
    - The client's intent to benefit the nonclient is clear, certain, and undisputed.
    - The lawyer fails to do what the client asks.
- Two material limitations on a lawyer's duty to nonclients:
    - No duty if there is any question about what the client's intent is.
    - The lawyer is only obligated to do what the client instructs, and nothing beyond that.
- In this case, the lawyer followed client's instructions. Client's intent regarding the LLCs was not "clear, certain, or undisputed."

Breathe So. Cal v. American Lung Association (2023) 88 Cal.App.5th 1172

Donor Intent Controls As Between Local Affiliate and Statewide Parent Organization

- ALA-LA (affiliate) and ALAC (parent organization) had an affiliation agreement requiring income sharing, including bequests, except for funds restricted by donor in writing (Restricted Funds Exception).
- ALA-LA disaffiliated and became Breathe Southern California (Breathe).
- Consent judgment required continued income sharing for bequests created before or within three months of the financial closing date.
- At issue were three bequests created before December 31, 2015; Breathe claimed they fell under Restricted Funds Exception and didn't share funds with ALAC, leading to a lawsuit.
- Trial Court found in favor of ALAC. It Interpreted Restricted Funds Exception to require "clear language" from donor stating the bequest should not be shared with ALAC.

Breathe So. Cal v. American Lung Association, cont.

Donor Intent Controls As Between Local Affiliate and Statewide Parent Organization

- Court of Appeal reversed.
- Stated donor intent, rather than specific language, should determine whether the Restricted Funds Exception applies.
- The Restricted Funds Exception applies if:
  - Bequest language reflects donor's intent to keep the gift with the affiliate.
  - Restrictive language is incompatible with income sharing.
- In this case, the plain language of the bequests restricts sharing with ALAC:

DuaneMorris®
www.duanemorris.com

AB 1663 - California Conservatorship Reform

- Overhauls conservatorship law, providing more tailored options and allowing conservatees to end unwanted conservatorships.
- Introduces "Supported Decision-Making" (SDM) as a new alternative to avoid a conservatorship.
  - SDM is a support system formalized through an SDM Agreement. Allows the disabled person or elder to maintain autonomy with needed support.
- Makes conservatorships a last resort.
  - Requires a closer examination of alternatives to conservatorship, including list of alternatives considered, details on attempted alternatives, and reasons why they didn't meet conservatee's needs.
  - Creates a conservatorship diversion program in all courts to identify conservatorship petitioner where less restrictive alternatives may be appropriate.
- Makes conservatorships easier to end.
  - Mandates annual provision of conservatee rights by the court.
  - Requires appointment of counsel and scheduling of termination hearings for conservatees who wish to terminate their conservatorship.
  - Allows termination of conservatorships without a hearing if uncontested and both parties agree.
- Gives conservatees a greater say by requiring conservators to consult with and make decisions aligned with

DuaneMorris®
www.duanemorris.com

AB 1716 - Liability For Non-Probate Transferees

- Improves liability rules for transferees who receive property from a decedent's small estate.
  - Prior law imposed a Property Return Procedure by which personal representative could compel transferee from a small estate procedure to return the property to the probate estate to discharge debts or if a non-transferee has a superior right
  - Now, Property Return Procedure is optional for debt satisfaction. Transferee can return the property and not be liable or not return the property and continue to be liable.
  - Mandatory Property Return Procedure still applies when a non-transferee has superior right to the property or in cases of fraud.
- Addresses spousal liability rules for joint tenancy property
  - *Kircher v. Kircher* (2010) 189 Cal.App.4th 1105 interpreted Probate Code Sections 13550 and 13551 to impose liability on surviving spouse who was a joint tenant. This cause spousal joint tenant to have greater liability exposure than non-spousal joint tenants who would not have such liability.
  - This bill overrules *Kircher* so that liability of spousal joint tenant are the same as non-spousal joint tenants.

AB 1745 - Trust Contest Period Clarification

- Trustee must serve notice on beneficiaries under three circumstances as per Probate Code Section 16061.7.
- Under Probate Code Section 16061.7, a trustee is required to serve a notice on beneficiaries under three circumstances:
  - When a revocable trust, or any portion thereof, becomes irrevocable because of the death of one or more settlors or because of the express terms of the trust;
  - Whenever there is a change of trustee of an irrevocable trust; and
  - Whenever a power of appointment retained by the settlor is effective or lapses.
- Notice given when a revocable trust becomes irrevocable must contain a warning about the 120-day contest period.
- Probate Code Section 16061.8 was broader than Section 16061.7. Language stated that a contest had to be brought within the prescribed time when any notice under Probate Code Section 16061.7 is given.
- This bill clarifies that the contest period applies only when the notice is given due to a revocable trust becoming irrevocable.

AB 2338 - Health Care Decisionmakers

- Adds Probate Code Section 4712, which confirms the order of priority for health care decisionmakers if the patient lacks the capacity to make decisions, as follows:
  1. The surrogate designated by the patient pursuant to Section 4711 when they had capacity.
  2. The patient's agent pursuant to an advance health care directive or a power of attorney for health care.
  3. The conservator or guardian of the patient having the authority to make health care decisions for the patient.
- If none of the above designated, a supervising health care provider or designee of the health care facility can choose a decisionmaker on the patient's behalf.
  - Decisionmaker must be an adult who has demonstrated special care and concern for the patient and may be chosen from a list of people, including relatives and a close personal friend.

SB 928 - Public administrator Compensation

- This bill increases the minimum compensation for public guardians who are appointed to administer a decedent's estate from $1,000 to $3,000.

SB 1005 - Power of Partition in Conservatorships

- SB 303 (2019) increased evidentiary and procedural safeguards for selling a conservatee or ward's residence.

- SB 303 did not address procedures for partition actions, even though they often result in a property sale.

- This bill closes the loophole by imposing the same safeguards on a conservator or guardian's proposed partition action as would apply for a sale.

- These safeguards include providing certain information to the court and proving that the partition action is in the best interest of the conservatee or ward by clear and convincing evidence.

SB 1024 - Replacement of Incapacitated or Deceased Professional Fiduciary

- Establishes procedures for handling the death or incapacity of a private professional fiduciary (PPF).
- Allows for the appointment of a Professional Fiduciary Practice Administrator as a temporary PPF through a petition by certain individuals.
  - Notice must be given to all parties entitled to notice of the hearing on the petition for appointment.
  - Temporary appointment of the Professional Fiduciary Practice Administrator terminates 45 days after the order, subject to some exceptions.
  - Administrator must provide written notice to interested parties about the need and process for appointing a permanent successor.
- Court may extend time periods specified in the bill for good cause and if in the best interest of the involved parties.
- Judicial Council must create or revise necessary forms or rules by January 1, 2024.

Corporate Transparency Act

- CTA is a new federal law issued in September 2022 and effective January 1, 2023.
- Create a central registry of beneficial ownership of legal entities and establishes reporting responsibilities.
- Beneficial ownership is "any individual who, directly or indirectly, either exercises substantial control over a reporting company or owns or controls at least 25% of the ownership interests in such reporting company."
  - Could include organizers of companies and beneficiaries of trusts
- CTA requires the following information be reported to FinCEN for each beneficial owner:
  - Full name
  - Date of Birth
  - Address
  - Unique Identifying Number (driver's license, passport) or FinCEN Indentifier.
- Individuals who have substantial control are responsible for reporting – includes trustees.
  - May require reporting information of beneficiaries of trusts.
- Entities created before January 1, 2024, must report by January 1, 2025; thereafter, within 30 days of formation.
- Failure to report leads to severe civil and potentially criminal penalties

CALIFORNIA DEVELOPMENTS
2022-2023[1]

S. Andrew Pharies
Duane Morris LLP
750 B Street, Suite 2900
San Diego, CA 92101
(619) 744-2253
apharies@duanemorris.com

CASE LAW DEVELOPMENTS

TRUST AND ESTATE ADMINISTRATION

Wehsener v. Jernigan (2022), Court of Appeal, Fourth Districted, No. D079623

California law Applies to Determine Heirship When Facts That Establish Parentage Occurred Outside California

- The Decedent died intestate in 2018 with no surviving spouse, issue, parents, issue of parents, or grandparents. Thus, the issue of Decedent's grandparents are his legal heirs.

- Shannon was Decedent's first cousin on the paternal side.

- Decedent's mother had an adopted brother, Charles, who took in Judy when she was abandoned by her natural parents at age two. Charles and his wife held Judy out as their child, but they never adopted her. They all lived in Indiana.

- Judy died in Indiana, and her Indiana personal representative filed an objection to a petition for distribution of Decedent's estate. The representative claimed that Judy was an heir of the Decedent and was entitled to half of the estate.

- The question is whether Judy is Charles' daughter for purposes of intestate succession. If so, she is a legal heir, and the estate is split between Shannon and Judy's estate. If not, then Judy is not a legal heir, and Shannon gets the entire estate.

- The outcome of this issue depends on whether Indiana law or California law applies to determine parentage. If Indiana law applies, then Judy would not be Charles' daughter for purposes of intestate succession. If California law applies, then Judy could be considered Charles' daughter under the Uniform Parentage Act (UPA).

---

[1] These materials cover significant developments in trusts and estate since the 2022 Institute through the beginning of April 2023.

- The Probate Court found that the California UPA applies, and that Charles and his wife held Judy out to be their daughter while residing in Indiana. Thus, Judy is an heir of the Decedent.

- The Court of Appeal affirmed the decision.

- When determining heirship for a California decedent, the laws and policies of California should apply, even if the parent-child relationship was formed or existed outside of California. Thus, California law should apply to determine the legal effect of the relationships that would ultimately bear on the heirship determination.

- Under the UPA, a person is presumed to be the natural parent of a child if the "presumed parent receives the child into their home and openly holds out the child as their natural child." Judy was taken into Charles' home, and Charles held her out as his child. Therefore, Judy is presumed to be Charles' daughter.

- Shannon argued that the presumption could be rebutted on public policy grounds, but the court was unpersuaded. The presumption could only be rebutted by clear and convincing evidence, and it does not say anything about public policy being able to rebut the presumption.

Estate of Raul Sausedo Franco (2023), Court of Appeal, First Appellate District, No. A165840

Application of Marital Presumption to Establish Parentage Bars Child From Claiming Heirship in Biological Parent's Estate

- The case concerns whether Frank G. Bertuccio is an intestate heir of his biological father, Franco.

- Frank Sr. and Marilyn were married in 1957, but Marilyn became pregnant with Bertuccio while dating Franco while she and Frank Sr. were separated.

- Frank Sr., Marilyn, and Franco agreed that Bertuccio should be raised as the child of Frank Sr., and Frank Sr. even paid child support for Bertuccio after their marriage dissolved.

- Bertuccio developed a close relationship with Franco as an adult, who even referred to him as his son.

- After Franco's death, a dispute arose between Bertuccio and Franco's sister and niece regarding Bertuccio's claim to be Franco's son and therefore his heir.

- The Probate Court granted a joint motion for summary judgment in favor of Franco's sister and niece, finding that Bertuccio is not Franco's son for the purposes of intestate succession under the Family Code 7540 marital presumption and the case of *Estate of Cornelious* (1984) 35 Cal.3d 461.

- The Court of Appeal reversed.

- Family Code Section 7540 provides that a child born to spouses who cohabited at the time of conception and birth is presumed to be a child of the marriage (the "Marital Presumption").

- In the *Cornelious* case, the California Supreme Court found that if the Marital Presumption applies, the child is barred from asserting a parent-child relationship with a third party for purposes of inheritance under intestate succession. The Court affirmed that this concept applies here.

- However, the Court found that summary judgment was improperly granted because the Probate Court did not make a finding as to whether Frank Sr. and Marilyn cohabited as husband and wife at the time of Bertuccio's conception and birth, which is necessary to apply the Marital Presumption.

Estate of El Wardani (2022) 82 Cal.App.5th 870

Estate Administrators Must Physically Reside In The US

- Husband and Wife retired to Mexico from San Diego County.

- After Husband's death, Wife was appointed administrator of his California estate.

- Wife and Husband's daughter from a prior marriage (Step Daughter) had a dispute.

- Step Daughter sought Wife's removal as administrator because Wife was not a resident of the US as required by Probate Code Section 8402(a)(4).

- Wife argued that she was a resident of the US because her friends, financial accounts, and professional advisors were in San Diego, and the US was considered her center of vital interests under tax law.

- Step Daughter argued that residency for Section 8402(a)(4) was synonymous with domicile, and the US tax determination of residency should not apply. Wife had permanently moved to Mexico and only came back to the US for visits. Additionally, Wife admitted she intended to move back to the US after the probate administration was over, indicating that she does not now reside in the US.

- The Probate Court removed Wife as administrator on the ground that she is not a US resident.

- The Court of Appeal affirmed the Probate Court's decision.

- The Court of Appeal reviewed statutory history and prior case law, finding that early cases equated residency with domicile, and subsequent recodifications of the law did not render the reasoning of those cases moot.

- The court concluded that "a person is ineligible to serve as administrator who leaves the U.S. and sets up a residence abroad intending to remain indefinitely. Moreover, when a person does not actually live in the U.S., their connections to this country alone cannot establish residency" (for purposes of this case).

Zahnleuter v. Mueller (2023), Court of Appeal, Third District, No. C093909

Trustee Properly Surcharged For Defending Contest Against Trust Amendment Using Trust Assets

- Husband and Wife created a trust. The initial trust instrument included a no contest clause that allowed the trustee to defend, at the expense of the trust estate, any contest of the trust instrument or any of its provisions. It also stated that the defense clause did not apply to any amendment executed after the date of the initial trust instrument.

- The trust instrument was amended twice without making material changes to the dispositive or trustee provisions. The Third Amendment, of which there were two versions at issue, made material changes to both the dispositive and successor trustee provisions, including naming Brother as successor trustee instead of Husband's two daughters with Wife.

- After Husband's death, his daughters contested the validity of both versions of the Third Amendment in separate proceedings.

  - In one proceeding, one daughter contested the first version of the Third Amendment on the grounds of lack of due execution and undue influence. Brother, as trustee, used trust assets to defend the validity of the first version of the Third Amendment. Later, that proceeding was suspended at the request of the parties because of allegations that the drafting attorney may have altered documents after the death of the Decedent.

  - In the other proceeding, the other daughter contested the validity of both versions of the Third Amendment on the ground of lack of due execution. That contest went unopposed and the court invalidated both versions of the Third Amendment.

- One of the daughters brought an action against Brother seeking an accounting and surcharge to compensate the trust for the assets he used to defend the Third Amendment. The Probate Court granted the petition. It found that the express terms of the trust allowed the trustee to defend a contest of the trust but not any amendments to the trust. The court further found that Brother violated his duty of impartiality by favoring beneficiaries who benefited from the Third Amendment over other beneficiaries.

- The Court of Appeal affirmed.

- Brother used trust assets to pursue the interests of the beneficiaries under the Third Amendment over the interests of the beneficiaries under the earlier amendments. The fact that Brother did not have a beneficial interest in the Third Amendment is immaterial.

- If a trustee participates in contest litigation as a neutral party defending the existence of the trust or its assets, then fees can be paid from the trust. Where, as here, the trustee defends an amendment to the trust, the existence of the trust is not an issue and the trustee is taking sides in fight between beneficiaries. Since the trust is not benefited by that litigation, the trustee's attorneys' fees may not be paid from the trust.

- The court acknowledged that a trust can authorize the trustee to defend an amendment, but in this case no such authorization existed.

MARITAL PROPERTY

Estate of Eskra (2022) 78 Cal.App.5th 209

Rescission of Premarital Agreement Not Permitted When Mistake Cased by Failure to Read Agreement Before Signing

- Husband and Wife signed a premarital agreement that waived their rights to each other's separate property.

- Husband passed away in a car accident without leaving a will, and a dispute arose between Wife and Husband's children over the enforceability of the premarital agreement.

- If the agreement was enforceable, Husband's children would receive all of his separate property under the laws of intestate succession. If it was unenforceable, Wife would share in such property under the same laws.

- Wife claimed that the agreement should be rescinded due to a mistake of fact, specifically that the agreement applied only to divorce and not to death.

- Wife's claim was based on the events leading up to the agreement's signing.

- Wife was represented by separate counsel who reviewed a draft agreement prepared by Husband's counsel. Wife's counsel informed her that the agreement applied in the event of both divorce and death, which upset Wife because she and Husband had agreed that it should apply only in the event of divorce.

- Husband and Wife subsequently agreed that the agreement should apply only in the event of divorce, and Wife's counsel conveyed this sentiment to Husband's counsel, who did not take a contrary position. Wife's counsel asked that certain provisions be removed, and informed Wife to come to their office after the agreement was revised for a final review.

- Husband's counsel realized that the language Wife's counsel requested to be removed were only examples and did not affect the agreement's applicability to death. The agreement was revised to remove the examples and provided to Wife's counsel.

- Wife did not go to her counsel for a final review of the agreement and instead went with Husband to sign the agreement without reading it first.

- The trial court found that Wife's rescission claim failed because there was insufficient evidence that Husband encouraged or fostered Wife's mistaken belief that the agreement did not apply at death. The court concluded that Wife bore the risk of her mistake because she did not act with reasonable care when she failed to read the agreement or consult with her counsel after it was revised.

- The Court of Appeal affirmed the trial court's decision.

- Rescission based on a unilateral mistake of fact is allowed only when: (1) a party makes a mistake regarding a basic assumption upon which the party made the contract; (2) the mistake has a material effect on the agreed exchange of performances that is adverse to the mistaken party; (3) the mistaken party does not bear the risk of the mistake; and (4) the effect of the mistake is such that enforcement of the contract would be unconscionable.

- The crucial issue in this case is whether Wife's failure to read the agreement and consult with her counsel caused her to bear the risk of her mistake.

- The California Supreme Court previously found in *Donovan v. RRL Corp.* (2001) that the risk of a mistake must be allocated to a party where the mistake results from that party's neglect of a legal duty.

- The Court also previously found in *Casey v. Proctor* (1963) that failure to read a contract constitutes a neglect of a legal duty.

- Based on these previous rulings, the Court found that Wife neglected a legal duty by not reading the agreement or consulting with her lawyer before signing it, and that such neglect barred rescission of the agreement.

Welch v. Welch (2022) 79 Cal.App.5th 283

Marital Settlement Agreement That Called for Long-Form Agreement Waived Spousal Rights Even Though Long-Form Agreement Not Completed Before Death

- During dissolution proceedings, Husband and Wife entered into a marital settlement agreement (MSA), with both parties being represented by counsel and making disclosures of assets and liabilities to each other. The MSA called for the preparation of a long-form agreement, but it did not include an express waiver of spousal rights.

- Disputes arose over the long-form agreement, with Husband seeking to enforce the MSA and enter his version of the long-form agreement as the court's order. During these disputes, Wife passed away.

- Without knowing about her death, the court granted Husband's petition and entered the long-form agreement as the order of the court. However, this order was later overturned by the Court of Appeal.

- The issue in Wife's probate proceeding became whether Husband waived his rights as a surviving spouse under Probate Code Section 141(b) by executing the MSA. According to Probate Code Section 145, a waiver of spousal rights can be done through either an express waiver of "all rights" or a complete property settlement entered into after or in anticipation of separation or dissolution.

- The Probate Court found that the MSA was not a complete waiver of spousal rights and held that Husband did not waive those rights.

- The Court of Appeal reversed this decision.

- Husband argued that the MSA could not be a complete waiver of spousal rights because it does not identify itself as such. However, the Court of Appeal found that an express waiver requires particularized language to be valid, but a waiver through a complete property settlement does not. Rather, to be an enforceable waiver, the property settlement must be in writing, signed by the surviving spouse (Prob. Code § 142), with adequate disclosure of assets and debts (Prob. Code § 143), representation by counsel at the time of signing the waiver, and a fair and reasonable disposition of the rights of the surviving spouse.

- The Court of Appeal found that the totality of the circumstances indicated that the parties intended the MSA to be a final disposition of property rights and that all conditions for enforceability were satisfied. Therefore, the MSA effectively waived Husband's spousal rights.

LITIGATION

Parker v. Schwarcz (2022) 84 Cal.App.5th 418

Documents and Communications Are Not "Personal Property" That Can Be Recovered Through A Section 850 Petition

- After the temporary conservatorship was terminated, the former conservatee, Parker, filed a Probate Code Section 850 petition seeking all communications and documents possessed by the former conservator, Schwarcz, related to the conservatorship estate.

- The Probate Court denied the petition on the grounds that Probate Code Section 850 can be invoked only when there is a conservator and only to recover property belonging to the conservatee. Here, there is no conservator and the documents sought are not personal property. The court stated that Parker may be able to get the information sought through discovery but not through a Probate Code Section 850 petition.

- The Court of Appeal Affirmed.

- The Court of Appeal affirmed and did not resolve the issue of Parker's standing to bring the petition. The court assumed that Parker had standing as a "claimant."

- The Court then turned to interpreting the term "personal property" in Section 850. It reviewed the legislative history and concluded that the purpose of the statute is to allow conservators the ability to recover assets that should be part of the conservatorship estate by effecting a conveyance of real or personal property.

- The Court found that documents and communications are not "personal property" that can be recovered through a Probate Code Section 850 petition since they do not carry the same indicia as real or personal property. Such items have no inherent value to fund the conservatorship estate or pay down debts, and the documents and communications were not previously owned by the claimant.

Starr v. Ashbrook (2023), Court of Appeal, Fourth District, No. G060597

Petition Seeking Surcharge Against Trustee for Misuse of Trust Assets Withstands Anti-SLAPP Scrutiny

- Starr, a beneficiary of a trust, filed a petition that included a surcharge cause of action against the trustee, Ashbrook, alleging that Ashbrook wasted trust assets by pursuing a meritless petition for instructions and using trust assets to fund litigation against Starr and his brothers.

- Ashbrook filed an Anti-SLAPP special motion to strike the petition in response.

- The Anti-SLAPP statute requires the defendant to establish that the challenged allegations or claims arise out of constitutionally protected activity. This case turns on whether the surcharge cause of action arose out of the protected activity of funding and pursuing litigation or out of the unprotected activity of misusing and wasting trust assets.

- The Probate Court denied the Anti-SLAPP motion, and the Court of Appeal affirmed.

- Case law establishes that a claim arises from a protected activity when the activity itself forms the basis of the claim. The focus must be on the defendant's alleged activity that gives rise to the asserted liability.

- Generally, the pursuit of litigation is a constitutionally protected activity. However, in this case, the waste of trust assets caused the alleged harm, not the filing of the petition itself. "Misconduct in the administration of a trust and preservation of trust assets is not action 'in furtherance of the person's right of petition or free speech under the United States Constitution or the California Constitution."

Autonomous Region of Narcotics Anonymous v. Narcotics Anonymous World Services, Inc. (2022) 77 Cal.App.5th 950

Special Interest Standing Does Not Extend to Revocable Charitable Trusts

- The Fellowship of Narcotics Anonymous created a revocable trust (the "Trust") to hold its intellectual property, with Narcotics Anonymous World Services, Inc. as the trustee.

- The Fellowship is composed of regional chapters of Narcotics Anonymous, which send regional delegates to a biennial conference known as the World Service Conference. The Conference acts on behalf of the Fellowship.

- The Trust allows for revocation by the Fellowship acting through the Conference, meaning the regional delegates can revoke the Trust according to Conference rules.

- The Autonomous Region of Narcotics Anonymous filed a petition against World Services for alleged breaches of trust, but World Services demurred, claiming the petitioner lacked standing.

- The Petitioner claimed standing under Probate Code Section 15800 as a settlor with the power to revoke, and under the "special interest" standing doctrine relating to charitable trusts.

- The Probate Court granted World Service's demurrer without leave to amend, and the Court of Appeal affirmed.

- The Court found that the Petitioner was not a settlor of the Trust, as the Fellowship, acting through the Conference, was the settlor, and the Petitioner, as a component of the Fellowship, could not act on its behalf and revoke the Trust.

- The Petitioner's assertion of special interest standing in a revocable trust was an issue of first impression. The Court concluded that, unlike with irrevocable trusts, a beneficiary of a revocable trust does not have special interest standing since the party with the power to revoke the trust can exercise sufficient oversight over the charitable trust without beneficiaries needing standing.

Meiri v. Shamtoubi (2022) 81 Cal. App. 5th 606

Probable Cause for a Trust Contest Does Not Exist When Petition is Time-Barred

- Husband and Wife were married for over 60 years and had four children.

- They created a standard ABC Trust that would be equally distributed to their four children upon the death of the surviving spouse.

- After the execution of the trust, Husband and Wife made gifts and loans to their children, so they amended and restated the trust to account for those changes. This new version is referred to as the "Restatement," which included a no contest clause.

- Husband passed away in 2016, and Wife became the sole trustee.

- Wife served a Probate Code Section 16061.7 notice to the children, which included a warning that a trust contest had to be commenced within 120 days of the notice or it would be time-barred.

- Daughter filed a petition 230 days after receiving the notice, seeking invalidation of the Restatement on the grounds that Husband lacked competency and was under undue influence.

- Mother's counsel wrote a letter to Daughter's counsel, asking her to withdraw the cause of action seeking invalidation of the Restatement and warning that it could be a violation of the trust's no contest clause. The letter also warned that if Daughter did not withdraw the cause of action, Mother would have to demurrer to the petition.

- Daughter and her counsel failed to respond to the letter and repeatedly failed to appear at hearings, necessitating repeated continuances.

- Mother filed a demurrer to the petition, which the court sustained with prejudice as to the cause of action seeking invalidation of the Restatement on the grounds that it was time-barred. The court sustained the demurrer without prejudice for the other causes of action alleged in the petition, including elder abuse, and gave Daughter leave to amend. Daughter amended her petition, recycling the same allegations of lack of capacity and undue influence while seeking $20 Million in damages for elder abuse and disinheritance of her siblings in lieu of invalidation of the Restatement.

- Mother sought instructions that the cause of action seeking invalidation of the Restatement constituted a direct contest of the Restatement without probable cause.

- The Probate Court found that the cause of action seeking invalidation of the Restatement was a direct contest and that failure to file the petition within the statutorily required 120-day contest period caused a lack of probable cause. Accordingly, the Probate Court ordered enforcement of the no contest clause, causing Daughter to be disinherited.

- The Court of Appeal affirmed.

- Daughter advanced several arguments to support her position that her petition was not time-barred, including the public policy against forfeitures. Her most compelling argument derived from the language of the statute. Daughter pointed to the language of Probate Code Section 21311(b), which limits the probable cause inquiry to showings "that the requested relief will be granted after an opportunity for further investigation or discovery." That language, Daughter argued, requires "any court assessing probable cause . . . [to] look to the 'substance in the matter' rather than procedural impediments to the relief." She argued that since the 120-day limitations period was merely a procedural impediment to relief, failure to satisfy that procedural requirement could not be the sole basis to find a lack of probable cause.

- The Court was unpersuaded by Daughter's argument. Probate Code Section 21311(b) provides that probable cause exists "where 'at the time of filing a contest, the facts known to the contestant would cause a reasonable person to believe that there is a reasonable likelihood that the requested relief will be granted after an opportunity for further investigation or discovery.'" After reviewing the legislative history of the statute, the

Court concluded that both procedural and substantive impediments to relief must be considered in determining whether probable cause exists.

- Here, filing a petition after the 120-day contest period would lead a reasonable person to believe that there was not a reasonable likelihood that the requested relief would be granted. Accordingly, it concluded that filing a time-barred petition caused a lack of probable cause.

Bruno v. Hopkins (2022) 79 Cal.App.5th 801

Attorneys' Fees Award For Bad Faith Action to Remove Trustee Can Exceed Share of Trust Estate

- A husband and wife created a trust, with the husband being a lawyer who drafted it himself. The trust was made up of portions that were typed by various people at the husband's direction and others that were handwritten.

- The trust stated that upon the death of the first spouse, half of the estate would be allocated to a revocable Survivor's Trust, and the other half to an irrevocable Family Trust. Upon the death of the surviving spouse, the two oldest daughters would receive $200,000 each from the Survivor's Trust, with the residue of the Survivor's Trust and Family Trust divided equally between the two youngest daughters. At the time the trust was created, the value of the assets was such that the pecuniary gifts were roughly equal to the residuary gift.

- The husband died and the wife became the trustee. However, she neglected to serve the Probate Code Section 16061.7 notice until several years after her husband's death. By that time, the value of the residuary gift was significantly higher than the value of the pecuniary gift.

- One of the oldest daughters filed a petition seeking to invalidate the trust instrument as a forgery and seeking to remove her mother, who was the trustee. The wife objected to the petition and sought payment of her fees and costs. She advanced three grounds for payment of fees: the court's inherent equitable power, Probate Code Section 15642, and Code of Civil Procedure Section 2033.420.

- After a lengthy trial, the Probate Court denied the petition. As for the wife's request for fees, the Probate Court found there was merit to all three of her arguments but ultimately based its fee award on the court's inherent equitable power. Since the amount of fees and costs exceeded the petitioner's interest in the trust, the court ordered her to be personally liable for the excess. This was done over the objections of the petitioner, who argued that any award of fees and costs must be limited to her share of the trust estate.

- The Court of Appeal affirmed the Probate Court's decision.

- The Court first found that the Probate Court did not have the inherent equitable power to award fees in excess of a beneficiary's share of the trust estate. While the court's equitable power may be exercised to protect the trust, it does not extend beyond the trust's boundaries to enable the court to order a beneficiary to be personally liable for such costs.

- However, the Court found that Probate Code Section 15642 does allow the court to order a person seeking removal of the trustee to "bear all or any costs of the proceeding" if the court finds that the petition was filed in bad faith and that removal would be contrary to the intent of the trustor. The Court found nothing to suggest that the court's power to award fees under Section 15642 is limited to a beneficiary's share of the trust estate, and the legislative history seems to indicate the opposite.

- After reviewing the evidence, the Court found that the Probate Court's finding of bad faith was appropriate and that removal would be contrary to the trustor's intent.

Royals v. Lu (2022) 81 Cal.App.5th 328

Pretrial Right to Attach Order Not Appropriate for Punitive Damages

- During Father's lifetime, he transferred assets from his trust to accounts controlled by Lu, his new wife. He even took out a second mortgage and put the proceeds in those accounts.

- After Father's death, Royals filed a petition for financial elder abuse against Lu, alleging that she unduly influenced Father to remove assets from his trust and give them to her. Royals sought approximately $1,000,000 in compensatory damages and treble damages under Probate Code Section 859.

- Royals also filed an application for pretrial right to attach order (RTAO) seeking to attach around $3,000,000 of Lu's assets on the same day. Lu submitted declarations and documentary evidence showing that Father intended to provide for her after he died and moved assets to her intentionally. Royals filed a demurrer in response to Lu's cross-petition.

- The Probate Court issued the RTAO without considering Lu's evidence.

- The Court of Appeal reversed the decision.

- The Court of Appeal weighed the broad protective and remedial scheme of the elder abuse law against the strict nature and due process concerns of attachment law to conclude that an RTAO is available for compensatory damages but not punitive damages in financial elder abuse actions.

- The Court found that Royals' attachment request for compensatory damages did not meet the statutory criteria because it was not based upon facts within her personal knowledge and did not plead a definite amount of compensatory damages.

Estate of Jones (2022) 82 Cal.App.5th 948

Conditions Precedent Narrowly Interpreted

- Father created a revocable trust which he did not amend after marrying Stepmother.

- After Father's death, Daughter became the trustee and sole beneficiary of the trust.

- Stepmother filed a petition seeking relief under the omitted spouse statutes, which Daughter objected to. They eventually settled, and under the settlement agreement, the trust was to pay Stepmother $3,000,000 as her full and final settlement of her interest in the estate, to be paid out of the escrow from the sale of the property.

- The court entered a stipulated judgment incorporating the settlement.

- At the time of the settlement, the property was in escrow to be sold for $13,600,000. However, after the judgment was entered, the sale of the property fell through, and Daughter never paid Stepmother the amount due under the settlement.

- Stepmother filed a petition to enforce the stipulated judgment, which the court denied, reasoning that the settlement was unenforceable because the condition precedent to settlement, the sale of the property, had failed.

- The Court of Appeal reversed, finding that the promise to pay Stepmother $3,000,000 and the promise to pay from the sale proceeds of the property were two related but independent promises. The promise to pay from the sale proceeds related to the method of payment and was subject to a condition precedent, the sale of the property. It as not a contingent precedent to the enforceability of the settlement as a whole.

King v. PG&E (2022) 82 Cal.App.5th 440

Heirs Have Right to Intervene In Wrongful Death Action

- Decedent was killed in a helicopter crash in California, but his probate was in Alabama and his former wife and mother of his child was appointed personal representative ("PR").

- The PR filed a wrongful death action in California, but Decedent's surviving spouse ("Spouse") filed a motion to intervene as a matter of right, citing the four elements required for mandatory intervention.

- The trial court denied Spouse's motion, stating there was no authority to support an heir's intervention in a wrongful death action filed by the PR and that the sufficiency of the PR's representation of Spouse's interest should be adjudicated by the Alabama probate court.

- The Court of Appeal reversed the decision.

- Spouse, as an heir, is entitled to intervene as a matter of right if she meets the statutory requirements for intervention, and the statutes governing intervention and wrongful death actions do not prohibit an heir from intervening even if an action by the PR is pending.

- The Court further held that Spouse's intervention does not violate the "one action" rule because the defendants will continue to defend a single cause of action in one proceeding which will result in one judgment.

- Finally, the Court held that the California court adjudicating the wrongful death action, not the Alabama probate court, should decide whether the PR will adequately represent Spouse's interests.

Estate of Douglas (2022) 83 Cal.App.5th 690

Law Firm's Clerical Error Incorporated Into Order Can Be Corrected Nunc Pro Tunc

- Law Firm was ordered to receive statutory fees in connection with a probate estate.

- In 2008, a judgment was entered, identifying the judgment debtor as Audrey in her capacity as administrator of the estate.

- In 2015, Law Firm applied to renew the judgment but made an error in naming the debtor in the renewal application, simply naming Audrey instead of identifying her in her representative capacity.

- In 2020, after the 10-year period for renewing judgments, Law Firm filed a motion to correct the "clerical error."

- Audrey and others objected, arguing that it was not a clerical error because it was made by Law Firm, not the court.

- The court granted the motion and amended the renewed judgment nunc pro tunc.

- The Court of Appeal affirmed. Clerical errors may be correct by the court nunc pro tunc, but judicial errors may not be so corrected. Here, renewing a judgment is a ministerial act involving no judicial discretion so an error in the judgment is necessarily a clerical error. Even though the mistake was made by the Law Firm, the error was contained in a court-issued judgment and amending the judgment nunc pro tunc to correct the clerical error was appropriate.

Chui v. Chui (2022) 86 Cal.App.5th 929

Minor Has Right To Petition To Removal GAL

- The Probate Court appointed Chen as guardian ad litem for minor beneficiaries in connection with certain trust litigation. When the minor beneficiaries were 16 and 17, respectively, they filed, through counsel they retained, a petition to review Chen as GAL.

- Chen demurrered to the removal petition on the grounds that the beneficiaries are unemancipated minors and may not hire counsel to seek his removal. He then filed a motion to disqualify the beneficiaries' counsel on the grounds that the minor beneficiaries could not hire counsel and such counsel suffered from a conflict of interest. The Probate Court granted the motion to disqualify counsel and dismissed the removal petition.

- The beneficiaries appealed and both became adults during the pendency of the appeal. Despite reaching the age of majority, Chen continued to act as GAL for the beneficiaries pursuant to orders of the Probate Court.

- The Court of Appeal reversed.

- Looking to the Probate Code provisions for guardianships of the estate and person, as well as conservatorship law, the Court pointed out that under those laws a minor ward or conservatee may file a petition for removal of the guardian or conservator. Reasoning that the same rule should apply in the context of GALs, the court held that a minor capable making informed decisions can petition the court for removal of a GAL. Since a minor may petition for the removal of a GAL, it follows that a minor may hire counsel for that limited purpose.

- Turning to the issue of whether a GAL terminates when the ward reaches the age of majority, the court found that California should follow the rule in other states that a GAL terminates when the ward reaches the age of majority. Accordingly, Chen's position as GAL for the Beneficiaries terminated when the Beneficiaries reached the age of majority and the Probate Court is ordered to terminate the GAL.

Algo-Heyres v. Oxnard Manor LP (2023) Court of Appeal, Second District, No. B319601

Arbitration Agreement Unenforceable Against Party Presumed Incompetent At Signing

- Cornelio had a stroke and entered a skilled nursing facility (SNF), where he remained until his death nine years later.

- At the time of admission, Cornelio signed an arbitration agreement whereby he gave up his right to a jury trial and consented to mandatory arbitration of all claims arising from services provided by the SNF.

- After Cornelio's death, his successors-in-interest filed an action against the SNF for elder abuse, wrongful death, and other torts.

- The SNF filed a petition to compel arbitration. The trial court denied the petition on the ground that Cornelio lacked the competency to consent to arbitration.

- The Court of Appeal affirmed.

- The party seeking arbitration bears the burden of proving the existence of a valid arbitration agreement.

- Civil Code 39(b) provides guidelines for determining the capacity to contract.

- It imposes a rebuttable presumption affecting the burden of proof that a person is of unsound mind if the person is substantially unable to manage his or her financial resources or resist fraud or undue influence.

- When this presumption applies, the party claiming capacity as the burden to prove that despite not being able to manage finances or resist fraud or undue influence, the person is still capable of contracting by virtue of being of sound mind as defined by Probate Code Section 811.

- The evidence showed that Cornelio had deficits in a number of factors set forth in Probate Code Section 811, and substantial evidence supported the trial court's determination that Cornelio was not competent to enter into the arbitration agreement.

ELDER ABUSE

White v. Davis (2023), Court of Appeal, Fourth District, No. E077320

Application For Elder Abuse Restraining Order Survives Anti-SLAPP Challenge

- Father had diminishing capacity, and New Wife, New Wife's children, and various friends went to extraordinary steps to influence Father into changing his estate plan to disinherit his children in favor of New Wife and her children. These steps included isolation, preparing scripts for Father detailing exactly what he should say to his estate planning lawyer, and ignoring various court orders, including a conservatorship, in pursuit of their ends. By the time the case reached the issues addressed in this decision, the case had been heavily litigated in various courts including the Court of Appeal.

- Daughter, was serving as trustee of Father's trust. New Wife filed a petition to remove Daughter as trustee claiming, ironically, that Daughter was committing elder financial abuse by transferring assets to Father's children in the name of saving estate taxes (the "Removal Petition"). Daughter applied for an Elder Abuse Restraining Order ("EARO") to protect Father from the repeated and brazen attempts by New Wife and others to change his estate plan. She also filed an application for a temporary EARO. The first judge to hear the case denied the application for a TEARO and set the matter for a hearing. New Wife disqualified the first judge and filed an anti-SLAPP special motion to dismiss the application for an EARO asserting that the application was aimed at thwarting the constitutionally protected activity of filing the Removal Petition.

- Daughter urged that the anti-SLAPP motion and application for EARO be heard concurrently so that an appeal of a denial of the anti-SLAPP motion would not stay the proceedings relating to the EARO, which would give New Wife and others more time to influence Father. The new judge refused to hear the matters concurrently and set a hearing on the anti-SLAPP motion with the EARO proceeding to following in due course if the anti-SLAPP motion was denied.

- The judge denied the anti-SLAPP motion and, just as Daughter feared, New Wife appealed that denial, leaving Father unnecessarily vulnerable to the alleged influencers.

- The Court of Appeal affirmed in part and reversed in part.

- The Court affirmed the denial of the anti-SLAPP motion. The activity to be examined when determining whether such activity is protected is the activity that gives rise to the petition, not the fact of the petition itself. Here, the activity alleged in the petition involves undue influence of Father, which is not a protected activity. Also, in footnote 18, the Court states that estate planning is not a protected activity for purposes of anti-SLAPP motions.

- The Court reversed with respect to the timing of the hearings. Given the nature of the relief sought in the EARO, which was protecting a dependent adult from financial elder abuse, the lower court abused its discretion by prioritizing the anti-SLAPP motion over the application for the EARO. The lower court could have either revisited the request for temporary relief and granted that pending resolution of the anti-SLAPP motion or decided both requests for relief concurrently.

ATTORNEY MALPRACTICE

Gordon v. Ervin, Cohen & Jessup LLP (2023), Court of Appeal, Second District, No. B313903

Estate Planner's Duty to Nonclients

- A client hired a lawyer to create a trust amendment that disinherited three of her son's children. The lawyer followed the client's instructions.

- Later on, the client directed the lawyer to form three LLCs, which were then given to the client's three sons, including the disinherited son whose children were excluded from the trust.

- The LLCs had no provision that would prevent the disinherited son from transferring his LLC interests to his own children.

- After the client's death, the beneficiaries of her trust sued the lawyer for legal malpractice. The plaintiffs claimed that the lawyer committed malpractice by failing to structure the LLCs in a way that would have prevented the disinherited son from transferring his interests to his children.

- The lawyer filed a motion for summary judgment, asserting that he owed no duty to the plaintiff beneficiaries since they were not his clients. The court agreed and granted the motion.

- The Court of Appeal upheld the decision.

- According to established law, a lawyer owes a duty to a nonclient only if the client's intent to benefit the nonclient is clear, certain, and undisputed, and the lawyer fails to do what the client asks. The lawyer is only obligated to do what the client instructs and nothing beyond that.

- There are two material limitations on the lawyer's duty to nonclients. First, the lawyer owes no duty to the nonclient if there is any question about what "X" is. Second, the lawyer is only obligated to do "X." She is not required to do anything beyond X even if necessary to implement the overall intent of the client.

- In this case, the lawyer did what the client instructed him to do, which was to prepare an amendment to the trust that disinherited the son's children. The lawyer fulfilled his duty to the plaintiffs in doing so. However, the lawyer had no duty to draft the LLCs in a way that would disinherit the disinherited son's children. Client's intent to prevent the disinherited son's children from receiving any shares of the LLC was not "clear, certain, or undisputed."

CHARITABLE GIFTS

Breathe So. Cal v. American Lung Association (2023), Court of Appeal, First District, No. A160785

Donor Intent Controls As Between Local Affiliate and Statewide Parent Organization

- The American Lung Association of Los Angeles County (ALA-LA) was an affiliate of the American Lung Association of California (ALAC). They entered into an affiliation agreement that required sharing of income, including bequests, except for funds restricted from sharing in writing by the donor (the "Restricted Funds Exception").

- ALA-LA disaffiliated and changed its name to Breathe Southern California (Breathe) as part of a restructuring of ALA. A consent judgment required Breathe and ALAC to continue the income sharing arrangement in the affiliate agreement for bequests created before or within three months after the consent judgment's financial closing date.

- The issue is three bequests created before December 31, 2015. One bequest made a gift to the American Lung Association for use in its Los Angeles affiliate. The other two created named funds for the Los Angeles affiliate. Breathe notified ALAC of the bequests but did not share the funds, claiming they fell under the Restricted Funds Exception. ALAC sued, claiming the gifts did not fall under that exception.

- The trial court found for ALAC, interpreting the Restricted Funds Exception to require "clear language" by the donor stating they do not want the bequest shared with ALAC.

- The Court of Appeal reversed, stating that donor intent, rather than specific language, should determine whether the Restricted Funds Exception applies. The Exception applies if the language of the bequest reflects the donor's intent that the gift stays with the affiliate or if the restrictive language is otherwise incompatible with income sharing.

- Here, the plain language of the bequests restrict sharing with ALAC because one bequest made clear that the funds were for the affiliate's use and the other indicated the donors intended to create a single fund.

LEGISLATIVE DEVELOPMENTS

AB 1663 – Conservatorship Reform

- This bill aims to overhaul conservatorship law and provide more options to individuals. It ensures that protective arrangements are tailored to each person's needs and allows conservatees to end unwanted conservatorships.

- The bill introduces "supported decision-making" as an alternative to conservatorship. This process involves supporting an adult with a disability in making life decisions without impeding their self-determination. It is implemented through a Supported Decision Making Agreement as defined in Probate Code Section 21005 and must include a list of areas in which support is needed, areas in which the supporter will provide assistance, and other relevant information.

- The bill requires that petitions for conservatorship must include a list of alternatives considered and why they were not suitable, details on attempted alternatives and their duration, and reasons why they didn't meet the conservatee's needs.

- The court must provide conservatees with a list of their rights on an annual basis.

- If a petition for termination of a limited conservatorship is uncontested and shows that both the conservator and conservatee wish to terminate it and that the conservatorship is no longer the least restrictive alternative, the court may terminate the conservatorship without a hearing.

- If a conservatee communicates their wish to terminate the conservatorship, the court must appoint counsel for them and schedule a hearing for termination if there hasn't been one in the last 12 months or if there is good cause to do so.

AB 1716 – Liability For Non-Probate Transferees

- This bill aims to improve the liability rules for a transferee who receives property from a decedent's small estate.

  o Under previous law, the transferee of property from a small estate was personally liable for the decedent's unsecured debts to the extent of the property received from the decedent. The personal representative could compel the transferee to return the property received from the small estate procedure to the probate estate to discharge the debt against the estate (the "Property Return Procedure").

- o This bill makes the Property Return Procedure optional. Now, the transferee may return the property received through the small estate procedure to the probate estate and not be personally liable, or keep the property and remain personally liable for a share of the decedent's unsecured debts. The bill also clarifies the extent of the transferee's liability.

- o If a non-transferee had a superior right to the property over the transferee, the mandatory Property Return Procedure still applies. If the transfer to the transferee was a result of fraud, the transferee may be liable to the estate for treble damages. However, under this bill, treble damages are to be paid to the person with the superior right.

- This bill also addresses spousal liability rules for joint tenancy property.

- o Previously, *Kircher v. Kircher* (2010) 189 Cal.App.4th 1105 interpreted Probate Code Sections 13550 and 13551 to impose liability on a surviving spouse for spousal property transfers under Probate Code Section 13500, et seq. for all non-probate transfers to the surviving spouse, including joint tenancy transfers. This created an inequitable result for surviving joint tenant spouses, who would be more liable than non-surviving joint tenant spouses.

- o This bill overrules *Kircher* to clarify that the spousal liability provisions of Probate Code Sections 13550 and 13551 only apply to spousal property transfers under Probate Code Section 13500, et seq.

AB 1745 – Trust Contest Period Clarification

- Under Probate Code Section 16061.7, a trustee is required to serve a notice on beneficiaries under three circumstances:

- o When a revocable trust, or any portion thereof, becomes irrevocable because of the death of one or more settlors or because of the express terms of the trust;

- o Whenever there is a change of trustee of an irrevocable trust; and

- o Whenever a power of appointment retained by the settlor is effective or lapses, as provided. (Section 16061.7 (a), (b).)

- The notice given when a revocable trust becomes irrevocable must contain a warning that a contest of a trust could be brought only within 120 days of service of the notice or 60 days from the date a copy of the terms of the trust is delivered within such 120 day period.

- However, Probate Code Section 16061.8 was broader than Probate Code Section 16061.7 since it stated that a contest had to be brought within the prescribed time when any notice under Probate Code Section 16061.7 is given.

- This bill clarifies that the contest period applies only when the notice is given because of a revocable trust becoming irrevocable.

AB 2338 – Health Care Decision-Makers

- Previously, a patient could only designate an adult as a surrogate to make health care decisions by personally informing the supervising health care provider.

- This bill expands the options for designation to include both the supervising health care provider and a designee of the health care facility caring for the patient.

- The bill establishes an order of priority for legally recognized health care decision makers who can make health care decisions on a patient's behalf if the patient lacks capacity.

- The order of priority is (1) the person designated by the patient to the health care provider or health care facility, (2) agent under a health care power of attorney, and (3) conservator of the person.

- If a patient does not have a legally recognized health care decision maker and lacks capacity, the bill specifies related individuals who may be chosen by a health care provider or a designee of the health care facility caring for the patient as a surrogate.

SB 928 – Public administrator Compensation

- This bill increases the minimum compensation for public guardians who are appointed to administer a decedent's estate from $1,000 to $3,000.

SB 1005 – Power of Partition In Conservatorships

- In 2019, the Legislature enacted SB 303, which increased the evidentiary and procedural safeguards for when a conservator or guardian wishes to sell the conservator or ward's current or former place of residence.

- SB 303 requires a conservator or guardian to provide certain information relating to the sale to the court before committing significant resources to the sale, and to prove, by clear and convincing evidence, that the sale is in the conservatee or ward's best interest.

- However, SB 303 did not similarly increase the evidentiary burden or procedures for entering into a partition action for the conservatee or ward's residence, even though partition actions frequently result in the sale of the property.

- This bill aims to close the potential loophole by imposing the same safeguards on a conservator or guardian's proposed action to partition the conservatee or ward's residence as would apply in the context of a sale.

SB 1024 – Replacement of Incapacitated or Deceased Professional Fiduciary

- This bill establishes procedures for handling the death or incapacity of a private professional fiduciary (PPF).

- Effective from January 1, 2024, certain people (conservator, agent under a power of attorney for asset management, trustee, or interested person) may petition for the appointment of a professional fiduciary practice administrator to serve as a temporary PPF.

- All parties entitled to notice must be notified of the hearing on the petition for appointment of a professional fiduciary practice administrator as a temporary successor.

- In each matter for which the professional fiduciary practice administrator was appointed as a temporary successor, their appointment must terminate 45 days after the entry of the order, subject to some exceptions.

- The professional fiduciary practice administrator must provide written notice to all interested parties to inform them of the need and process for appointing a permanent successor.

- The court may extend any of the time periods specified in the bill if it determines that there is good cause and the extension is in the best interest of the applicable minor, conservatee, decedent's estate, or current income beneficiaries under a trust.

- The Judicial Council must create or revise any necessary forms or rules to implement the bill's provisions no later than January 1, 2024.

2

Spendthrift Trusts & Creditor Protection

Jay D. Adkisson

Spendthrift Trusts

In California

Jay D. Adkisson

PITET

Slide 1

Introduction

- Background
  - Creditor-Debtor Litigator 1989-1995
  - Asset Protection Planner 1995-2010
  - Creditor-Debtor Litigator 2010-Present

- The Asset Protection "Fireman"
  - Penetrate Asset Protection Plans
  - Defend Asset Protection Plans

PITET

Slide 2

Introduction

Barry Engel, 1954-2017

Author of the Cook Islands International Trust Act of 1984

Initiated contemporary innovative trust structure planning as we now understand it

PITET

Slide 3

Introduction

- Probate Code 15300 and 15301(a)

  - Only if the trust has a spendthrift provision, then:

  - Until paid to the beneficiary, the beneficiary's interest in income and principal is not:

    - Subject to voluntary or involuntary transfer, or

    - Subject to enforcement of money judgment.

PITET

Slide 4

Introduction

CAVEATS

- Once the distribution is made, it becomes subject to judgment enforcement

- Paying the beneficiary's bills and expenses can be deemed an "imputed distribution"

- Playing games to help a beneficiary/debtor can lead to alter ego challenges

PITET

Slide 5

Preventing Trustee Malfeasance

- Basic Trust

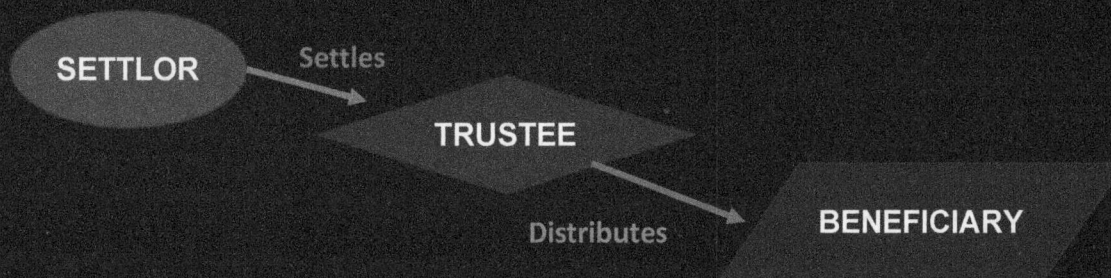

PITET

Slide 6

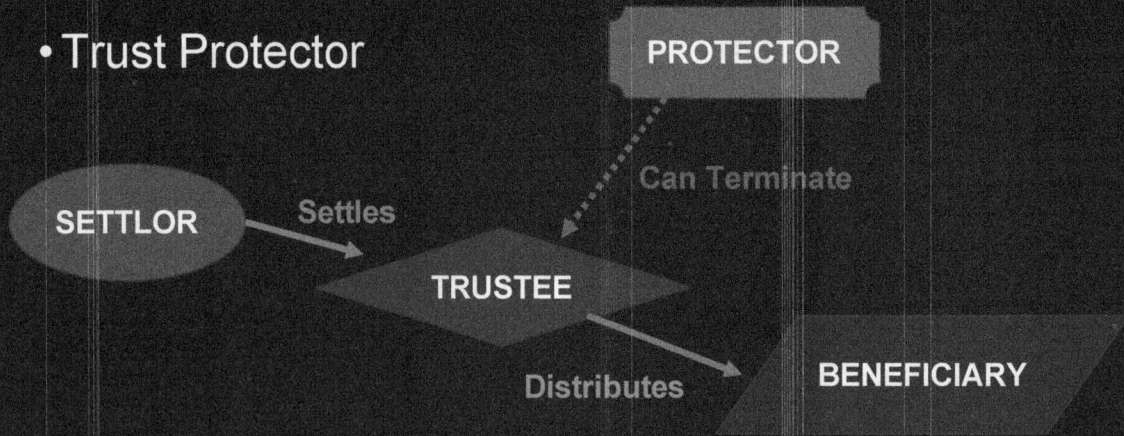

Preventing Trustee Malfeasance

- Trust Protector

PROTECTOR

SETTLOR — Settles → TRUSTEE

Can Terminate

TRUSTEE — Distributes → BENEFICIARY

PITET

Slide 7

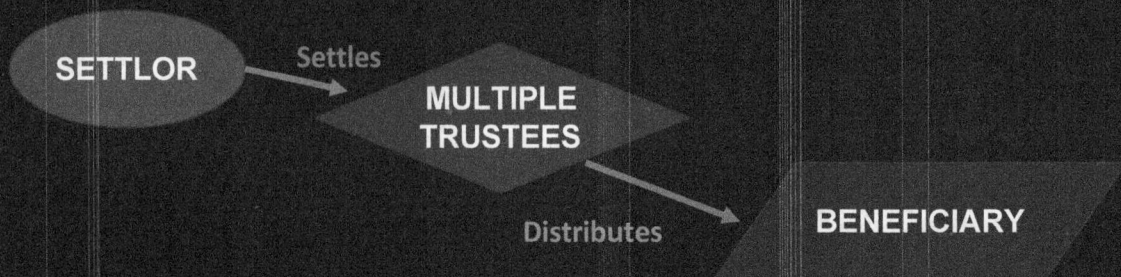

Preventing Trustee Malfeasance

- Internal Limitations

SETTLOR — Settles → MULTIPLE TRUSTEES — Distributes → BENEFICIARY

PITET

Slide 8

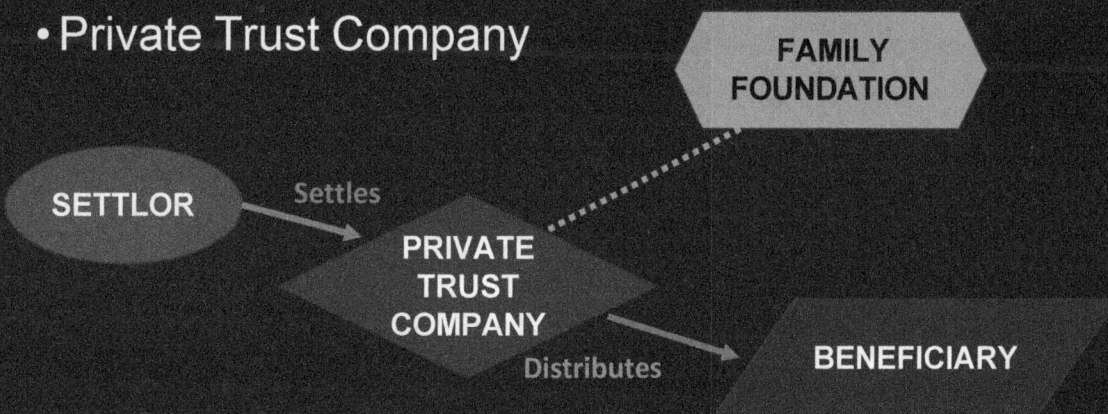

Preventing Trustee Malfeasance

- Structural Limitations

SETTLOR — Settles → TRUSTEE — Distributes → BENEFICIARY

LLC

Trust owns LLC but has no management rights

PITET

Slide 9

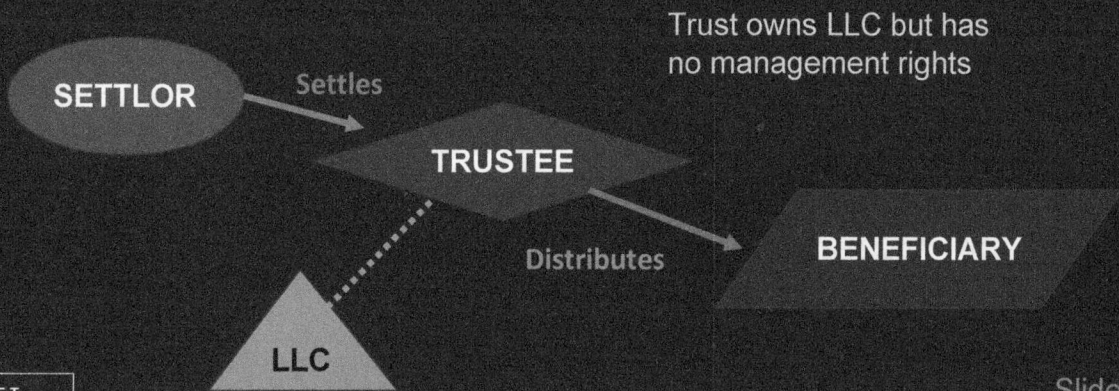

Preventing Trustee Malfeasance

- Private Trust Company

SETTLOR — Settles → PRIVATE TRUST COMPANY — Distributes → BENEFICIARY

FAMILY FOUNDATION

PITET

Slide 10

Internal Creditors Of The Trust

- Probate Code 18004
  - Trust liable for contractual and tort claims
  - Irrelevant whether Trustee is also personally liable

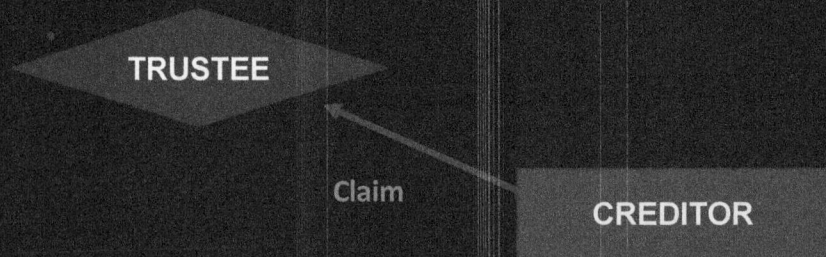

TRUSTEE

Claim

CREDITOR

PITET

Slide 11

Internal Creditors Of The Trust

- Never Mingle Hot Assets And Cold Assets
  - Hot Assets ~ Liability-Producing Assets & Activities
    - Operating Businesses
    - Residential Property With Tenants
    - Commercial Property

  - Cold Assets ~ Benign Assets & Activities
    - Investment Accounts
    - Undeveloped Land (Adequately Insured)
    - Friendly-Occupied Residential Property (i.e., QPRT)

PITET

Slide 12

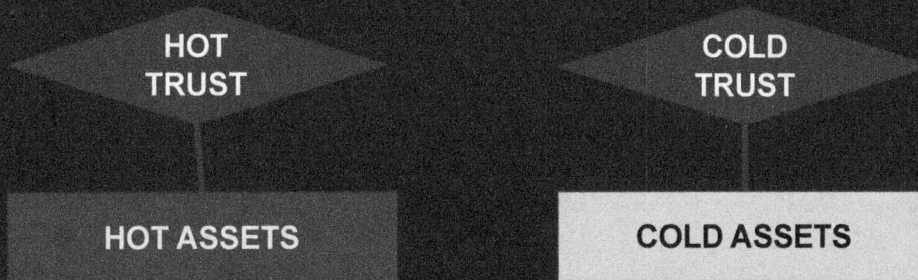

Internal Creditors Of The Trust

Hot Trusts & Cold Trusts

HOT TRUST — HOT ASSETS

COLD TRUST — COLD ASSETS

PITET

Slide 13

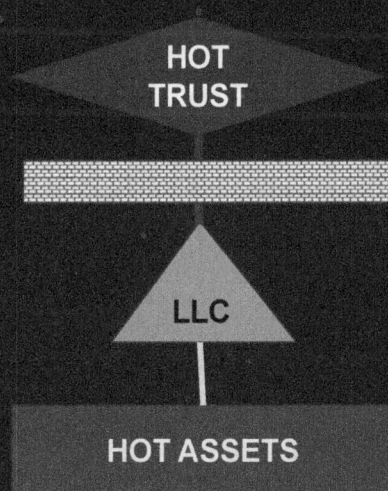

Internal Creditors Of The Trust

Internal Shields

HOT TRUST

Liability shield created by LLC

LLC

HOT ASSETS

PITET

Slide 14

External Creditors

Two classes of creditors:

- Creditors of the debtor as a settlor

- Creditors of the debtor as a beneficiary (who may or may not also be a settlor)

External Creditors

Creditor Of The Debtor As A Settlor

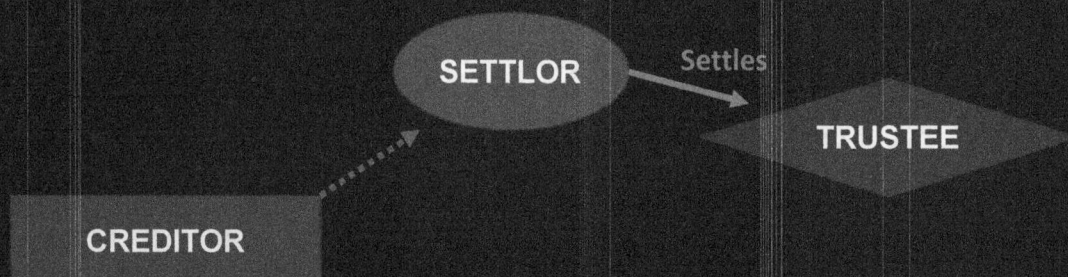

External Creditors

Voidable Transactions (Civ.Code 3439.01 et seq)

Two main tests:

- Intent Test ~ Settlor intended to defeat rights of creditor

- Insolvency Test ~ At time of transfer to trust, settlor was insolvent (or rendered insolvent)

PITET

Slide 17

External Creditors

Fraudulent Transfer Extinguishment Periods
- Generally, four years from date of transfer

- For intent test, also one year from date transfer was or could have been reasonably discovered

- In bankruptcy, 10 years for transfers to "self-settled trust or similar device"

- In bankruptcy, 10 years where debtor has scheduled a federal tax liability

PITET

Slide 18

Self-Settled Trusts

What constitutes a "self-settled trust"?
- Settlor is also a beneficiary of the trust, or

- Sham Trust ~ Trust is managed and revocable by settlor, even if settlor is not a beneficiary
  - *In re Cutter*, 398 B.R. 6, 20 (B.A.P. 9th Cir. 2008).

PITET

Slide 19

External Creditors

Revocable Trusts ~ Probate Code 18200
- If settlor retains the power to revoke in whole or part, then
- Trust property is subject to claims of creditors
- To the extent of
  - The power of revocation, and
  - During the lifetime of the settlor

PITET

Slide 20

External Creditors

Revocable Trusts

Probate Code 18201
- Settlor entitled to all exemptions as if not in trust

Probate Code 19001(a)
- If the trust was revocable at settlor's death, the trust assets are available for claims and expenses of the probate estate (after all other probate assets)

PITET

Slide 21

External Creditors

Creditors Of A Beneficiary

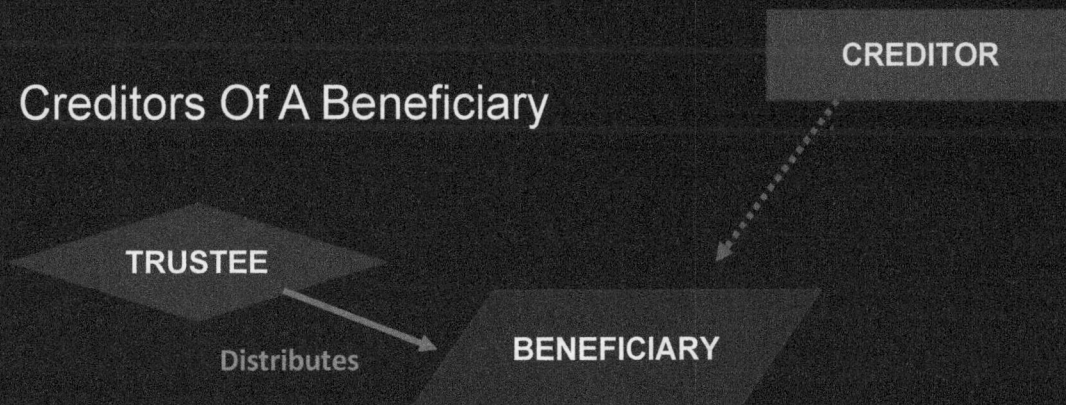

CREDITOR

TRUSTEE

Distributes

BENEFICIARY

PITET

Slide 22

External Creditors

Probate Code 15300 and 15301(a)
- Beneficiary's interest in principal and income is not available to creditors until paid

Probate Code 15302
- Creditor may enforce judgment against education and support payments only after those payments are made to the beneficiary

PITET

Slide 23

External Creditors

Probate Code 15303(a) and (c)
- Creditor may not compel trustee to make a discretionary distribution, even if the trust document provides a standard for making a discretionary distribution

Probate Code 15307
- If the trust either mandates a distribution or the trustee has decided to make a distribution, the creditor can petition under CCP 709.010 for the distribution to go to the creditor.

PITET

Slide 24

External Creditors

Probate Code 15301(b)

- If principal is due to be paid to a beneficiary, the creditor may petition under CCP 709.010 for an order compelling the principal to be paid to the creditor

PITET

Slide 25

External Creditors

Probate Code 15306.5(b)

- Creditor may petition for an order directing that the trustee pay all current and future distributions to the creditor
- Applies to discretionary distributions
- Applies even if trust has spendthrift provision
- But, limited to 25% of the distribution

PITET

Slide 26

External Creditors

Probate Code 15303(c)

- If the trustee has been served with process for a creditor's petition, the trustee will be liable to the creditor for making a distribution.

- True even if the distribution is purely discretionary

PITET

Slide 27

External Creditors

Probate Code 15301(b) vs. 15306.5(b)

- Creditor gets 100% under 15301(b) but must "catch the falling knife"

- Creditor only gets 25% under 15306.5(b) but doesn't have to worry about timing

- Explained in *Carmack v. Reynolds*, 2 Cal.5th 844 (2017)

PITET

Slide 28

External Creditors

Distributions vs. Compensation

- Distributions ~ Creditors can obtain by petition either 25% or 100%

- Compensation ~ Creditor garnishment restricted to 25% of debtor's net disposable income

PITET

Slide 29

External Creditors

Trusts Created To Defeat Creditors

Probate Code 15203
- Trust may not be created for an illegal purpose or against public policy

In re Marriage of Dick, 15 Cal.App.4th (1993)
- Trust created for the purpose of defrauding creditors is illegal and may be disregarded

PITET

Slide 30

External Creditors

Alter Ego Applied To Trusts

- *In re Schwarzkopf*, 626 F.3d 1032, 1038 (9th Cir. 2010); *Greenspan v. LADT, LLC*, 191 Cal. App. 4th 486, 518, (2010).

- Facts and circumstances test

PITET

Slide 31

External Creditors

Alter Ego Applied To Trusts

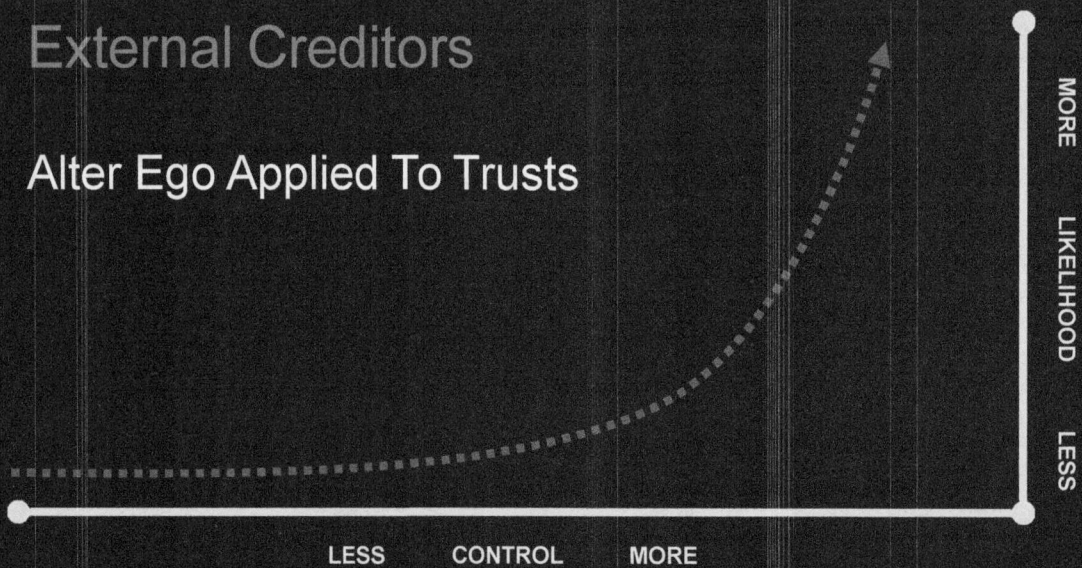

MORE · LIKELIHOOD · LESS

LESS   CONTROL   MORE

PITET

Slide 32

Escape Hatches

• Flight Provisions

• Decanting Provisions

PITET

Slide 33

Escape Hatches

Disclaimers

Probate Code 281
  • Disclaimers are binding upon creditors

Probate Code 283
  • Disclaimers are not voidable transactions

PITET

Slide 34

Escape Hatches

Disclaimers

Probate Code 286
- Disclaimers effective even if spendthrift provision exists

Probate Code 15309
- Disclaimers are not a distribution

PITET

Slide 35

Escape Hatches

Disclaimers

Probate Code 279(a)
- Disclaimer must be made with a reasonable time after
  - Beneficiary has become aware of interest, and
  - The interest has vested
- Presumed reasonable if within 9 months

Probate Code 285
- Disclaimer not effective if beneficiary has already accepted the interest or distribution

PITET

Slide 36

Non-California Asset Protection Trusts

- Foreign Asset Protection Trust (FAPT)

- Domestic Asset Protection Trust (DAPT)

PITET

Slide 37

Non-California Asset Protection Trusts

Foreign Asset Protection Trust (FAPT)

- Operates by brute force: Assets are beyond reach of the U.S. Courts

- Weakness: Repatriation order and contempt remedy

PITET

Slide 38

Non-California Asset Protection Trusts

Domestic Asset Protection Trust (DAPT)

- Operates on premise that the conflict of laws rules of trust jurisdiction will apply.

- Weakness: Courts of non-DAPT states have declined to adopt that conflict of laws position.
  - This results in a self-settled trust with a spendthrift provision that is not enforceable.
  - May also be a trust against public policy in California

PITET

Slide 39

Thank You!

Jay D. Adkisson

jay@apjuris.com

702-953-9617

PITET

Slide 40

Spendthrift Trusts In California

Jay D. Adkisson

Presentation to the 45thAnnual UCLA-CEB Estate Planning Institute, April 20, 2023

Jay D. Adkisson is a managing partner of Adkisson Pitet LLP and is admitted to practice in Arizona, California, Nevada, Oklahoma and Texas. A 1988 graduate of the University of Oklahoma College of Law with honors, and a member of the Oklahoma Law Review, Jay has twice been an expert witness to the U.S. Senate Finance Committee and is the Forbes.com writer on wealth preservation issues. He has served as an ABA Advisor to the drafting committees of the Uniform Voidable Transactions Act, the Uniform Protected Series Act, the Uniform Registration of Canadian Money Judgments Act, and the Uniform Public Expression Protection Act. He has also served as the Chair of the American Bar Association Committees on Captive Insurance and Insurance and Financial Products. His books include Asset Protection Concepts & Strategies (McGraw-Hill 2004), Adkisson's Captive Insurance Companies (iUniverse 2007), the Charging Order Practice Guide (Am.Bar.Assoc. 2018), and Anti-SLAPP Law Modernized: The Uniform Public Expression Protection Act. Jay is an honorary member of the California Association of Judgment Professionals, and a Hall of Fame member of the National Association of Estate Planning Councils. His law practice is primarily in the area of creditor-debtor litigation, including the attack and defense of sophisticated asset protection structures, plus some limited consulting in the area of asset protection planning.

Table of Contents

I.   INTRODUCTION

This presentation considers the spendthrift trust in California as largely viewed from the trust planner's standpoint. While spendthrift provisions are ubiquitous in trust documents, how they function in creditor-debtor litigation is perhaps not well understood. Here we will attempt to demystify the concept for planners.

A spendthrift clause is fundamentally a *restraint on alienation*: A spendthrift beneficiary cannot access, pledge or transfer any rights to trust property or income until the distribution is due or actually made to the beneficiary, and a creditor of a beneficiary likewise cannot enforce a judgment against trust property or income until it is distributed, or a distribution is due. The primary statutory authority for spendthrift trusts in California is found at Probate Code §§ 15300 and 15301(a), as set forth below:

Probate Code 15300.

> Except as provided in Sections 15304 to 15307, inclusive, if the trust instrument provides that a beneficiary's interest in income is not subject to voluntary or involuntary transfer, the beneficiary's interest in income under the trust may not be transferred and is not subject to enforcement of a money judgment until paid to the beneficiary.

Probate Code 15301.

> (a)   Except as provided in subdivision (b) and in Sections 15304 to 15307, inclusive, if the trust instrument provides that a beneficiary's interest in principal is not subject to voluntary or involuntary transfer, the beneficiary's interest in principal may not be transferred and is not subject to enforcement of a money judgment until paid to the beneficiary.

There are two things common to the statutory language of both these sections which requires special emphasis. The first is the phrase "not subject to voluntary or involuntary transfer". The "voluntary" part of this phrase prevents the beneficiary from pledging or hypothecating the beneficiary's interest prior to a distribution. For example, if the beneficiary attempts to use a right to distributions not yet made as security to purchase a house or car, the trustee need not honor the beneficiary's action. Likewise, the "involuntary" part of this phrase refers to actions taken by creditors of the beneficiary, such as to attach (create an involuntary judicial lien upon) or levy upon the trust property and income.

The second critical phrase is "until paid to the beneficiary". A spendthrift protection only protects the trust property and income while it is held in trust and prior to a distribution coming due or being made. Once the distribution has come due or has been made, then the protections of the spendthrift protections terminate at that point. Thereafter, the property is owned by the beneficiary and becomes fair game for creditor enforcement action; if the distributed property or income will be protected from creditors at all, it will be because of something other than the spendthrift provision, such as a statutory creditor exemption (which is outside the scope of this presentation).

II.   TRUSTEE MALFEASANCE

Although not directly germane to the creditor-debtor issues regarding spendthrift trusts in California, it is worth exploring devices that have been created by planners to mitigate the possibility that a trustee would embezzle the trust's assets since those devices have lead to many of the creditor-protective features of modern trusts. To this end, it should be kept in mind that the original so-called "asset protection trusts" (self-settled spendthrift trusts) were formed in offshore jurisdictions following the 1989 adoption by the Cook Islands of the enabling legislation for such trusts.[1]

A.   TRUST PROTECTORS

The office of the trust protector was originally devised for offshore trusts, to qualm the fears of clients that offshore trustees might attempt to embezzle the trust assets. In those early trusts which often featured a joint U.S. and offshore trustee, the trust protector was also used to terminate the U.S. trustee in the event that a U.S. court sought to assert jurisdiction over the trust. Since the trust protector was frequently a U.S. person, great pains were taken to keep the role of the trust protector limited so that the trust protector would not be deemed to be a *de facto* trustee.[2]

The original trust protector had a single power: To discharge the trustee, after which reference to the trust document would be made for the successor trustee. The trust protector gained additional powers, such as to designate a new trustee. Eventually, the trust protector grew into the monster that is found in some trusts today, where the trust protector has so many powers (such as the power to appoint new beneficiaries) that it is difficult to say that the trust protector is other than a trustee.

Used in moderation, and with a person holding the office who is not related or subordinate to any settlor, trustee, or beneficiary of the trust, the office of the trust protector is suitable for use — and should be used — for all but the most simple trusts, including revocable trusts. for There are other potential benefits to the use of trust protectors for asset protection planning that are beyond this discussion.

B.   INTERNAL LIMITATIONS

Trusts may be protected from trustee malfeasance by the uses of various clauses, but also by having multiple trustees, such as an investment trustee, and requiring multiple signatures for certain transactions. Sometimes the settlor or beneficiary is made a limited co-trustee, but this may have negative implications in terms of an alter ego challenge as discussed more fully below. As with trust protectors, the best practice is to not have any trustee who is related or subordinate to a settlor or beneficiary.

---

[1] An interesting history of the Cook Islands asset protection trust legislation is found in the article by David R. McNair, Cook Islands Asset Protection Trust Law, 3 Pepperdine Journal of Business, Entrepreneurship & the Law 321 (2010), as found at https://digitalcommons.pepperdine.edu/cgi/viewcontent.cgi?article=1049&context=jbel

[2] It was also a common practice with the early offshore trusts to require the offshore trustee to sign a resignation form, but with the date left blank, and which resignation form was retained by the settlor. Offshore planning was such a novelty at this time, and offshore frauds so prevalent, that such devices were required to convince the typical plastic surgeon in Wichita to park her $10 million in the Caymans.

C. STRUCTURAL LIMITATIONS

Another way to protect the trust assets is through the use of structural protections. A simple example of this is a trust which owns nothing but membership rights in an LLC (which LLC holds the assets), but the trustee has no management or voting rights in the LLC. Instead, the LLC is managed by somebody else, or perhaps a management company created specifically for that purpose, and has its own internal protections against malfeasance. An ancillary benefit of this arrangement is that it also bifurcates ownership and control of the assets, making an alter ego challenge more difficult.

D. PRIVATE TRUST COMPANY

Another product of offshore planning, also created to protect the trust assets from an errant trustee, is the private trust company. Originally, these were often companies that were formed in Nevis that were owned by a charitable foundation or purpose trust (a form of charitable trust) in variously Liechtenstein or Panama — something which does not have settlors or beneficiaries in the creditor-debtor sense, or even Anglo-American trust law sense. The idea was that the family as a whole would manage the Nevis company, which in turn would be the trustee of various trusts for the benefit of family members.

III. INTERNAL CREDITORS

The term "internal creditors" refers to those creditors who claims have arisen from the operations of the trust, or from trust assets. An example of this would be a trust that owns a rental home and a hot water tank in the home explodes which injures the occupants who then sue the trust for premises liability and negligence.

Sometimes trusts are created for the very purpose of shielding a liability-producing asset from its current owner. To re-use our hot water tank example, say that our client currently owns a rental home and is concerned about such potential liability. The client might set up a trust to hold that rental home and thus shield the client from that potential liability. If a liability does arise, the liability will be to the trustee and not to the client — assuming that the client is not still managing the property and thus risking personal liability for negligence.

However, the trust may be holding other valuable assets in addition to liability-producing assets (so called "hot assets"), and this section discusses how the trust itself may be shielded from such liabilities.

A. TRUST LIABILITY

The trust (in this case, meaning the trustee in his capacity as trustee) is exposed to the liabilities arising from the operations and assets of the trust, per Probate Code § 18004.

Probate Code 18004.

> A claim based on a contract entered into by a trustee in the trustee's representative capacity, on an obligation arising from ownership or control of trust property, or on a tort committed in the course of administration of the trust may be asserted against the trust by

proceeding against the trustee in the trustee's representative capacity, whether or not the trustee is personally liable on the claim.

"The trust estate can be reached for tortious acts of the trustee on behalf of the trust. * * * Hence, a third person with a claim against the trust or trustee may assert the claim against the trust by bringing an action against the trustee in the trustee's representative capacity." *Stoltenberg v. Newman,* 179 Cal. App. 4th 287, 293–94, 101 Cal. Rptr. 3d 606, 611 (2009). The trustee will only be personally liable if personally at fault. *Haskett v. Villas at Desert Falls*, 90 Cal. App. 4th 864, 880, 108 Cal. Rptr. 2d 888, 900 (2001).

B.   HOT TRUSTS & COLD TRUSTS

Because the trust estate may be exposed to liabilities arising from within the trust ("internal liabilities"), it is important that liability-producing assets ("hot assets") not be placed into the same trust as assets not likely to produce a liability ("cold assets"). Hot assets can include real property and active business interests, such as general partnerships. Note that the liability exposure of some hot assets may be reduced, if not practically eliminated, through the purchase of substantial liability insurance. Cold assets are typically cash and financial investments, including life insurance and annuities.

In asset protection planning, where a trust may hold hot assets which cannot be adequately insured, the best practice is to create at least two trusts: A "hot trust" for the potentially liability-producing assets, and a "cold trust" for the benign assets. Often, a vehicle is created whereby cash generated by the assets of the hot trust are then transferred by some mechanism to the cold trust, e.g., the cold trust hold a patent right, which the cold trust leases to a business owned by a hot trust in exchange for a royalty payment.

Note: Attempting to accomplish all asset protection goals with a single trust is perhaps the single most common planning error.

C.   INTERNAL SHIELDS

In addition to insurance, another method to protect some assets of a trust from the liabilities arising from other assets of the trust is to attempt to encapsulate those liabilities and segregate them away from other trust assets through the use of business entities (corporations, LLCs and LPs). In this construct, the trustee owns the equity rights in the business entities, but has no control over those entities (the reason for this design is because of alter ego concerns which are discussed below). The idea is that if a liability does arise from a trust asset, that liability will remained contained in its particular entity and not escape upwards to create liability against the trustee — which would then potentially expose other trust assets to judgment enforcement.

Further, as a backup to the potential failure of a business entity to encapsulate liability, LLCs and LPs are typically used in contrast to corporations, so that a creditor would then be restricted to a charging order against the trustee's interests in other entities that would theoretically limit a creditor to receiving only profit distributions but without an ability to access the assets held by the entity.

IV.   EXTERNAL CREDITORS

A.   CREDITORS OF A SETTLOR

1.   Voidable Transaction

A creditor may seek to set aside a debtor's gift to a trust as a voidable transaction (fraudulent transfer) under Civil Code § 3439.01, *et seq*. Because a gift inherently lacks reasonably equivalent value (REV), such gifts are highly susceptible to being set aside by creditors within the applicable extinguishment periods. These periods are:

- Generally, four years from the date of transfer, § 3439.09(a) and (b);

- For a claim that a debtor had an intent to diminish the rights of any creditor, greater of four years or one year from the date the transfer was or reasonably could have been discovered by the creditor, up to seven years, § 3439.09(a) and (c);

- Ten years in bankruptcy for transfers to a "self-settled trust or similar device" where a debtor had an intent to diminish the rights of any creditor, 11 U.S.C. § 548(e); or

- Ten years in bankruptcy where the debtor scheduled a federal tax liability, *see, e.g.*, *Mitchell v. Zagaroli* (*In re Zagaroli*), 2020 WL 6495156 (Bk.W.D.N.C., Nov. 3, 2020).

Because of these relatively long periods, it is critical that a settlor not settle a trust unless three conditions exist: (1) the settlor is not insolvent, near insolvent, or rendered insolvent by the transfer (excluding from the solvency calculation exempt assets); (2) the settlor not have any significant creditors at the time of the transfer; and (3) the settlor must not have the intent to diminish the rights of any creditors, past, present or future.

The aforementioned conditions are sometimes referred to by the expression "severe clear", *i.e.*, the skies are completely clear of creditors and there are no clouds even on the horizon. Some planners will attempt to document the settlor's condition of solvency and absence of creditors by way of a so-called "Affidavit of Solvency".

2.   Self-Settled Trust

Probate Code 15304.

> (a)   If the settlor is a beneficiary of a trust created by the settlor and the settlor's interest is subject to a provision restraining the voluntary or involuntary transfer of the settlor's interest, the restraint is invalid against transferees or creditors of the settlor. The invalidity of the restraint on transfer does not affect the validity of the trust.

> (b)   If the settlor is the beneficiary of a trust created by the settlor and the trust instrument provides that the trustee shall pay income or principal or both for the education or support of the beneficiary or gives the trustee discretion to determine the amount of income or principal or both to be paid to or for the benefit of the settlor, a transferee or creditor of the settlor may reach the maximum amount that

the trustee could pay to or for the benefit of the settlor under the trust instrument, not exceeding the amount of the settlor's proportionate contribution to the trust.

(c)   For purposes of this chapter, the settlor shall not be considered to be a beneficiary of an irrevocable trust created by the settlor solely by reason of a discretionary authority vested in the trustee to pay directly or reimburse the settlor for any federal or state income tax on trust income or principal that is payable by the settlor, and a transferee or creditor of the settlor shall not be entitled to reach any amount solely by a reason of that discretionary authority.

In a nutshell, here is what § 15304 provides:

The spendthrift clause of a self-settled trust is not enforceable against a creditor of the settlor. § 15304(a), *see also In re Cutter*, 398 B.R. 6, 20 (B.A.P. 9th Cir. 2008), *aff'd*, 468 F. App'x 657 (9th Cir. 2011) ("While California law recognizes the validity of spendthrift trusts, any spendthrift provisions are invalid when the settlor is a beneficiary." *Id.*, at 20). However, the trust shall not be considered to be a self-settled trust if the settlor is a beneficiary of the trust only to the extent of taxes which may be paid or reimbursed. § 15304(c).

If the trust provides for discretionary distributions a settlor/beneficiary, a creditor may reach the maximum amount of the trust that the trustee could distribute to the settlor, but capped by the amount of the settlor/beneficiary's contribution to the trust. § 15304(b).

Note that what constitutes a "self-settled trust" is not *ipso facto* determined by the trust instrument, but rather a court may look to the totality of the facts and circumstances to determine, basically, what is "really going on" in a particular situation:

California law invalidating efforts of a settlor from using a trust to shield property from his or her creditors applies "*even where the settlor is not a nominal beneficiary*, as where a settlor attempts to create a spendthrift trust for the benefit of his or her minor children, to be managed by the settlor and revocable at his or her pleasure." 60 CAL. JUR.3D TRUSTS § 134 (2008)(emphasis added), *citing Sheean v. Michel*, 6 Cal.2d 324, 57 P.2d 127 (1936).

In re Cutter, 398 B.R. 6, 20 (B.A.P. 9th Cir. 2008), *aff'd*, 468 F. App'x 657 (9th Cir. 2011) (emphasis in original) (debtor funded trust for ostensible benefit of his children but was the trustee).

Self-settled spendthrift trusts, a/k/a "asset protection trusts", are further discussed at § VI, *infra*.

3.   Revocable Trusts

Probate Code 18200.

If the settlor retains the power to revoke the trust in whole or in part, the trust property is subject to the claims of creditors of the settlor to the extent of the power of revocation during the lifetime of the settlor.

Probate Code 18201.

> Any settlor whose trust property is subject to the claims of creditors pursuant to Section 18200 shall be entitled to all exemptions as provided in Chapter 4 (commencing with Section 703.010) of Division 2 of Title 9 of Part 2 of the Code of Civil Procedure.

Probate Code 19001(a).

> (a) Upon the death of a settlor, the property of the deceased settlor that was subject to the power of revocation at the time of the settlor's death is subject to the claims of creditors of the deceased settlor's probate estate and to the expenses of administration of the probate estate to the extent that the deceased settlor's probate estate is inadequate to satisfy those claims and expenses.

Probate Code 19002(a).

> (a) Except as expressly provided, this part shall not be construed to affect the right of any creditor to recover from any revocable trust established by the deceased settlor.

The assets of revocable trusts are available to creditor of the settlor during the settlor's lifetime, § 18200, and then upon the settlor's death are subject to claims against the settlor's estate. § 19001(a). However, the settlor's exemptions against judgment enforcement are preserved. § 18201.

Because of this, it is sometimes said that revocable trusts provide no asset protection. This may be true as to the settlor and the settlor's estate, but not as to other non-settlor beneficiaries who do not hold a right of revocation.

B.   CREDITORS OF A BENEFICIARY (INCLUDING A SETTLOR/BENEFICIARY)

This section will consider the scenario the creditor attempts to enforce a judgment against the debtor in the debtor's capacity as the beneficiary of a trust. Note that these same rules apply even where it is the settlor who is the targeted beneficiary.

1.   Creditor Enforcement Against Distributions

Probate Code 15300.

> Except as provided in Sections 15304 to 15307, inclusive, if the trust instrument provides that a beneficiary's interest in income is not subject to voluntary or involuntary transfer, the beneficiary's interest in income under the trust may not be transferred and is not subject to enforcement of a money judgment until paid to the beneficiary.

Probate Code 15301.

> (a)   Except as provided in subdivision (b) and in Sections 15304 to 15307, inclusive, if the trust instrument provides that a beneficiary's interest in principal is not subject to voluntary or involuntary transfer, the beneficiary's interest in principal may not be transferred and is not subject to enforcement of a money judgment until paid to the beneficiary.

> (b)   After an amount of principal has become due and payable to the beneficiary under the trust instrument, upon petition to the court under Section 709.010 of the Code of Civil Procedure by a judgment creditor, the court may make an order directing

the trustee to satisfy the money judgment out of that principal amount. The court in its discretion may issue an order directing the trustee to satisfy all or part of the judgment out of that principal amount.

Probate Code 15302.

Except as provided in Sections 15304 to 15307, inclusive, if the trust instrument provides that the trustee shall pay income or principal or both for the education or support of a beneficiary, the beneficiary's interest in income or principal or both under the trust, to the extent the income or principal or both is necessary for the education or support of the beneficiary, may not be transferred and is not subject to the enforcement of a money judgment until paid to the beneficiary.

Probate Code 15303.

(a)   If the trust instrument provides that the trustee shall pay to or for the benefit of a beneficiary so much of the income or principal or both as the trustee in the trustee's discretion sees fit to pay, a transferee or creditor of the beneficiary may not compel the trustee to pay any amount that may be paid only in the exercise of the trustee's discretion.

(b)   If the trustee has knowledge of the transfer of the beneficiary's interest or has been served with process in a proceeding under Section 709.010 of the Code of Civil Procedure by a judgment creditor seeking to reach the beneficiary's interest, and the trustee pays to or for the benefit of the beneficiary any part of the income or principal that may be paid only in the exercise of the trustee's discretion, the trustee is liable to the transferee or creditor to the extent that the payment to or for the benefit of the beneficiary impairs the right of the transferee or creditor. This subdivision does not apply if the beneficiary's interest in the trust is subject to a restraint on transfer that is valid under Section 15300 or 15301.

(c)   This section applies regardless of whether the trust instrument provides a standard for the exercise of the trustee's discretion.

(d)   Nothing in this section limits any right the beneficiary may have to compel the trustee to pay to or for the benefit of the beneficiary all or part of the income or principal.

Probate Code 15306.5.

(a)   Notwithstanding a restraint on transfer of the beneficiary's interest in the trust under Section 15300 or 15301, and subject to the limitations of this section, upon a judgment creditor's petition under Section 709.010 of the Code of Civil Procedure, the court may make an order directing the trustee to satisfy all or part of the judgment out of the payments to which the beneficiary is entitled under the trust instrument or that the trustee, in the exercise of the trustee's discretion, has determined or determines in the future to pay to the beneficiary.

(b)   An order under this section may not require that the trustee pay in satisfaction of the judgment an amount exceeding 25 percent of the payment that otherwise would be made to, or for the benefit of, the beneficiary.

(c)   An order under this section may not require that the trustee pay in satisfaction of the judgment any amount that the court determines is necessary for the support of the beneficiary and all the persons the beneficiary is required to support.

(d)   An order for satisfaction of a support judgment, as defined in Section 15305, has priority over an order to satisfy a judgment under this section. Any amount ordered to be applied to the satisfaction of a judgment under this section shall be reduced by the amount of an order for satisfaction of a support judgment under Section 15305, regardless of whether the order for satisfaction of the support judgment was made before or after the order under this section.

(e)   If the trust gives the trustee discretion over the payment of either principal or income of a trust, or both, nothing in this section affects or limits that discretion in any manner. The trustee has no duty to oppose a petition to satisfy a judgment under this section or to make any claim for exemption on behalf of the beneficiary. The trustee is not liable for any action taken, or omitted to be taken, in compliance with any court order made under this section.

(f)   Subject to subdivision (d), the aggregate of all orders for satisfaction of money judgments against the beneficiary's interest in the trust may not exceed 25 percent of the payment that otherwise would be made to, or for the benefit of, the beneficiary.

Probate Code 15307.

Notwithstanding a restraint on transfer of a beneficiary's interest in the trust under Section 15300 or 15301, any amount to which the beneficiary is entitled under the trust instrument or that the trustee, in the exercise of the trustee's discretion, has determined to pay to the beneficiary in excess of the amount that is or will be necessary for the education and support of the beneficiary may be applied to the satisfaction of a money judgment against the beneficiary. Upon the judgment creditor's petition under Section 709.010 of the Code of Civil Procedure, the court may make an order directing the trustee to satisfy all or part of the judgment out of the beneficiary's interest in the trust.

Probate Code 15308.

Any order entered by a court under Section 15305, 15306, 15306.5, or 15307 is subject to modification upon petition of an interested person filed in the court where the order was made.

Probate Code 15309.

A disclaimer or renunciation by a beneficiary of all or part of his or her interest under a trust shall not be considered a transfer under Section 15300 or 15301.

Code of Civil Procedure 709.010.

(a)   As used in this section, "trust" has the meaning provided in Section 82 of the Probate Code.

(b)   The judgment debtor's interest as a beneficiary of a trust is subject to enforcement of a money judgment only upon petition under this section by a judgment creditor to a court having jurisdiction over administration of the trust as prescribed in Part 5 (commencing with Section 17000) of Division 9 of the Probate Code. The judgment debtor's interest in the trust may be applied to the satisfaction of the money judgment by such means as the court, in its discretion, determines are proper, including but not limited to imposition of a lien on or sale of the judgment debtor's interest, collection of trust income, and liquidation and transfer of trust property by the trustee.

(c)   Nothing in this section affects the limitations on the enforcement of a money judgment against the judgment debtor's interest in a trust under Chapter 2 (commencing with Section 15300) of Part 2 of Division 9 of the Probate Code, and the provisions of this section are subject to the limitations of that chapter.

The import of these provisions is as follows.

A beneficiary's interest in principal and income is not available to creditors until it is paid if the trust has a spendthrift provision. § 15300 and 15301(a).

A creditor may enforce the judgment against principal due to be paid to a beneficiary if the creditor petitions under CCP § 709.010, and the court in its discretion orders the trustee to pay the principal to the creditor. § 15301(b).

A creditor may enforce the judgment against education or support payments, arising from either income or principal, only after those payments are made to the beneficiary. § 15302.

A creditor may not compel a trustee to pay principal or income to a beneficiary if the trustee has the discretion whether to make such payment. § 15303(a). This is true even if the trust instrument provides a standard for the exercise of the trustee's discretion. § 15303(c).

Unless the trust has a spendthrift provision, the trustee will be liable to a creditor for making a discretionary payment to a beneficiary if the trustee has been served with process in a proceeding under CCP § 709.010 which seeks to reach the beneficiary's interest in the trust. § 15303(b). This is true even if the trust instrument provides a standard for the exercise of the trustee's discretion. § 15303(c).

Even where the trust has a spendthrift provision, a creditor may petition the court for an order directing that a trustee pay the creditor for any and all current and future distributions to the beneficiary from the trust, whether discretionary or not. § 15306.5(a). In this instance, however, the court may not order the trustee to pay creditor for any amount the court determines is necessary for the support of the beneficiary and the beneficiary's dependents, § 15306(c), and the creditor shall only be paid 25% of other distributions. § 15306.5(b).

Even if the trust has a spendthrift provision, if the trust mandates a distribution or the trustee has decided to make a discretionary distribution, a creditor may petition the court under CCP § 709.010 for an order compelling the distribution to go towards satisfaction of the judgment. § 15307.

From the creditor's perspective, what this means is that there is a big difference between two types of distributions:

(1)   A creditor may obtain 100% of a distribution that is already due to be paid, or the trustee has exercised the discretion to make the payment but has not done so yet, per § 15301; and

(2)   A creditor may only obtain 25% of future distributions, per § 15306.5.

Or, to put it differently, if the creditor wants 100% of the distribution, then the creditor should not seek an order as to future distributions under § 15306.5. Instead, the creditor must "catch the falling knife" by obtaining an order under § 15301 as each distribution comes due. *See, e.g., Carmack v.*

Reynolds, 2 Cal.5th 844 (2017) (answering certified question from the 9th Cir. BAP regarding the interplay of §§ 15301 and 15306.5).

Obviously, catching the falling knife of a distribution is easy for a creditor if the distribution is mandatory under the trust document on a particular date. That same trick is, however, all but impossible in the case of a discretionary distribution where as a practical matter the creditor is unlikely to find out about the distribution until it has already been made. This is another reason why it is critically important that trust distributions be purely discretionary.

Note that none of the aforementioned provisions provides any protection to assets which the beneficiary has received; if those assets are protected at all, it will be because of some other creditor exemption under CCP § 704.010 *et seq.*, *i.e.*, once the cash hits the beneficiary's bank account, all of it becomes fair game for creditors unless some other exemption can be established, such as CCP § 704.220 (money in a judgment debtor's deposit account).

The foregoing provisions do make one thing crystal-clear from an asset protection perspective, which is that mandatory distributions are likely to end up 100% in the hands of a creditor, while discretionary distributions are more likely to have only 25% caught by a creditor, and in some instances not caught at all. Moreover, where a beneficiary has a creditor, the trustee may determine to exercise the discretion not to make any distribution at all. Thus, mandatory distributions should be avoided.

A caution is that if the creditor is successful in having a receiver appointed for the beneficiary, the receiver might be able to bring an action against the trustee under particular circumstances to compel the trustee to exercise the trustee's discretion to make a distribution, and per § 15303(d) the foregoing provisions might not act as a check on such an attempt by a creditor.

2.   Distributions Versus Compensation

Generally, wage garnishments by a creditor are restricted to 25% of the debtor's disposable earnings. 15 U.S.C. § 1673; CCP § 706.050 *et seq.*

If the trust owns a business, it might be preferable for the trust to make payments to the beneficiary as compensation for services (presuming this relationship is *bona fide* and not a sham), since the creditor will then be restricted to the 25% of net disposable income.

C.   TRUSTS CREATED TO DEFEAT CREDITORS

In certain circumstances, a court may disregard a trust where the court has concluded that the trust was created to defeat creditors. This line of cases is based on Probate Code § 15203.

Probate Code 15203.

A trust may be created for any purpose that is not illegal or against public policy.

See, e.g., In re Marriage of Dick, 15 Cal. App. 4th 144, 161, 18 Cal. Rptr. 2d 743, 752 (1993) ("It is well-settled that a trust created for the purpose of defrauding creditors or other persons is illegal and may be disregarded." *Id.*, at 15 Cal. App. 4th 161, 18 Cal. Rptr. 2d 752).

Although the settlor may claim that the trust was not created to diminish the rights of creditors but for other purposes — typically estate tax or succession planning — that intent is often belied by documents other than the trust documents, primarily planning memoranda and e-mails between the settlor and trust planning counsel. To this end, note that attorney-client privilege is usually easier for creditors to get around, and thus obtain the planning memoranda and e-mails, than most counsel suspect. *See, e.g., In re Icenhower*, 755 F.3d 1130, 1141 (9th Cir. 2014) (A creditor need make only a *prima facie* showing that a fraudulent transfer has occurred to implicate the crime-fraud exception to attorney-client privilege and thus vitiate the attorney-client privilege).

D.   ALTER EGO — REVERSE VEIL PIERCING — NOMINEE THEORIES

In California, alter ego liability may apply to trusts so as to allow a creditor to reverse-pierce the legal separateness of the debtor and the trustee. *In re Schwarzkopf*, 626 F.3d 1032, 1038 (9th Cir. 2010); *Greenspan v. LADT, LLC*, 191 Cal. App. 4th 486, 518, 121 Cal. Rptr. 3d 118, 143 (2010).

Alter ego challenges have been described to be "like lightning, it is rare, severe, and unprincipled." F. Easterbook and D. Fischel, Limited Liability And The Corporation, U.Chi.L.Rev. (1985). Like lightning, it is difficult to predict when a court may find alter ego. While the court at least notionally looks to the elements of commonality of ownership and commonality of control, in practice a court will look at the totality of the relevant surrounding facts and circumstances to determine whether a relationship is sufficiently close for alter ego liability to apply — basically, a "bad tuna" test where the court determines whether the relationship smells.

The only rational conclusion that we can come to in the area of alter ego challenges as they relate to trusts is this: There is a close relationship to the amount of control exerted by the debtor upon trust assets and the likelihood that the trust will be deemed to be the alter ego of that debtor. The more control that a debtor has over trust assets, the correspondingly more likely it will be that the court will determine the trust to be the alter ego of the debtor, and *vice versa*.

Note that although it has become popular in recent years to add the settlor or a beneficiary to a trust as some sort of limited co-trustee, such as an "investment trustee" or a "distribution trustee", that is precisely the sort of control that increases the chances of a court's alter ego finding. Otherwise stated, the more "strings" that a settlor or beneficiary has over a trust, the more likely that a court may later find it to be an alter ego. Although convenient to, and often desired by, settlors who want to control the trusts assets or activities after they have settled the trust, engaging in that practice is not commensurate with best practices where asset protection is a consideration.

V.   ESCAPE HATCHES

It is impossible to conceive of all the different ways that a particular creditor might attempt to attack a particular trust. Creditor rights attorneys can be very creative and seem to have a special knack for thinking outside the box. At the same time, trust planners can make mistakes, not anticipate certain things, and then of course there are clients and trustees who can make unfortunate decisions. In an attempt to give the trustee some flexibility to deal with the circumstances, certain devices have been created with creditors (of the trust itself, of the settlor, of beneficiaries) in mind.

A.   FLIGHT PROVISIONS

The original asset protection trusts were often domiciled in the offshore jurisdictions where the governments were, at best, sketchy. This gave rise to concerns that the laws of the local government could change unfavorably, or the locale became unsafe for keeping trust property. The answer to these concerns was the so-called *flight clause,* which was a provision in the trust document that allowed the trust to be redomiciled somewhere else.

Later, it was realized that flight clauses might have important uses in the trust dealing with creditors of the settlor or beneficiaries. Here, keep in mind that the typical offshore trust jurisdiction is not required to give full faith and credit to U.S. judgments, but instead a creditor must either identify a treaty through which a judgment can be registered, or else commence an action on the judgment (if not begin the litigation *ab initio* as if there never was a U.S. judgment). Thus, with a flight clause, if a creditor showed up in the jurisdiction where the trust was then located, the trust would be relocated somewhere else, and the creditor would have to start enforcement proceedings anew.

Though flight provisions are best utilized internationally, between jurisdictions that are not required to respect outside judgments, there may be situations where a flight clause may prove to be useful even as to domestic trusts, *e.g.*, the trust has a flaw that creates an exposure under the laws of one state, but not another.

B.   DECANTING PROVISIONS

Another way to move or, effectively, fix an existing trust is by setting up a new trust with the desired features in the desired jurisdiction and decant, or pour over, the property of the existing trust into the new trust. The existing trust must typically, however, have a provision that empowers the trustee to engage in such decanting.

Caution that the decanting of a trust may be a "transfer" for purposes of the voidable transaction laws in particular circumstances. Typically, if a trust has a spendthrift provision, the decanting of the trust will not *ipso facto* create a voidable transaction issue as to the creditor of a beneficiary where that beneficiary had vested right to particular trust property, *i.e.*, the trust is purely discretionary and no decision by the trustee to make any distribution has been made.

C.   DISCLAIMERS

Disclaimers frequently appear in post-judgment enforcement litigation against beneficiaries of a trust or an estate. Generally, disclaimers can be effective in lawfully defeating the enforcement rights of creditors in appropriate circumstances.

Probate Code 275.

> A beneficiary may disclaim any interest, in whole or in part, by filing a disclaimer as provided in this part.

Probate Code 281.

> A disclaimer, when effective, is irrevocable and binding upon the beneficiary and all persons claiming by, through, or under the beneficiary, including creditors of the beneficiary.

Probate Code 283.

> A disclaimer is not a voidable transfer by the beneficiary under the Uniform Voidable Transactions Act (Chapter 1 (commencing with Section 3439) of Title 2 of Part 2 of Division 4 of the Civil Code).

Probate Code 286.

> The right to disclaim exists regardless of any limitation imposed on the interest of a beneficiary in the nature of an expressed or implied spendthrift provision or similar restriction.

Probate Code 15309.

> A disclaimer or renunciation by a beneficiary of all or part of his or her interest under a trust shall not be considered a transfer under Section 15300 or 15301.

A beneficiary may disclaim an interest in a trust (and many other types of interests), Probate Code § 275, and that disclaimer will be binding upon that beneficiary's creditors, per § 281. By statute, the transfer will not be a voidable transaction, § 283, and is not affected by a spendthrift provision or other clause that otherwise restricts the beneficiary from alienating the interest, § 286 and 15309. There are, however, at least two significant restrictions on a beneficiary's use of a disclaimer.

First, the beneficiary must disclaim the interest within a "reasonable time" after the beneficiary acquires knowledge of the interest and the interest has vested. § 279(a). In many cases, the "reasonable time" is presumed to be nine months after the interest has vested, § 279(b), (d) and (e), although this presumption is rebuttable — but the burden of proof is upon the beneficiary. § 279(f).

Second, the disclaimer will not be effective if the beneficiary has already accepted the interest, § 285(a), *e.g.*, the beneficiary cannot accept a distribution from a trust and then disclaim the interest. An excellent discussion of this situation is found in *Patow v. Marshack* (*In re Patow*), 632 B.R. 195 (9th Cir. BAP 2021).

VI.   NON-CALIFORNIA ASSET PROTECTION TRUSTS

This section considers asset protection trusts (self-settled spendthrift trusts) that are formed outside of California for the benefit of California settlors. This is a very complicated area requiring a very extended discussion to be properly understood, so only a cursory top-level summary will be provided.

A.   FOREIGN ASSET PROTECTION TRUST (FAPT)

The Foreign Asset Protection Trust, often known as simply "offshore trusts", are trusts that are created in a non-U.S. jurisdiction that has adopted enabling legislation for self-settled spendthrift trusts, *e.g.*, the Cook Islands, Nevis, the Bahamas, the Cayman Islands, etc.

The FAPT is agnostic to whether the trust technically provides protection to creditors in any U.S. jurisdiction or any particular conflict of laws analysis. Instead, the FAPT provides essentially the brute force protection to assets that the assets are held outside the United States, and by the time of any court action the settlor has migrated away from the U.S. such that the settlor cannot be subject to a contempt remedy which requires the repatriation back to the U.S. of foreign assets. *See, e.g.*, *FTC v. Affordable Media, LLC*, 179 F.3d 1228 (9th Cir. 1999) (offshore trust settlors incarcerated for six months); *Lawrence v. Goldberg (In re Lawrence)*, 279 F.3d 1294 (11th Cir. 2002) (offshore trust settlor incarcerated for 6.5 years).

Offshore trusts can be very effective in the sense that they protect assets in all but the most egregious cases, such as Ponzi schemes or securities fraud. But there is a cost, and that cost is that for an offshore trust to be effective, two conditions much prevail:

(1)   All the trust assets must be held outside the U.S., and

(2)   The settlor/beneficiary must be outside the U.S. when judgment enforcement is ongoing so as to avoid the contempt/repatriation remedy.

Because few people are willing to comply with either, much less both, of these conditions, FAPTs have proven to not be a particularly attractive strategy for most folks. They can, however, be an effective strategy for certain international persons, *e.g.*, a physician from India practicing in the United States who may have international estate planning concerns anyway, is not uncomfortable holding assets abroad, and who would not be too bothered by leaving his U.S. practice and starting over elsewhere should a problem arise.

B.   DOMESTIC ASSET PROTECTION TRUST (DAPT)

In asset protection planning, whatever strategy is the flavor-of-the-day is usually bad for a number of reasons, and for the last few years that has been the domestic asset protection trust. A DAPT is a trust that is formed in a state that has passed enabling legislation for self-settled spendthrift trusts, which is about half the states — but not California.

Unlike an offshore trust, a DAPT formed for a settlor in a non-DAPT state relies on a complex conflict of laws analysis as to why the courts of the non-DAPT state should apply the law of the DAPT state. The problem is that so far the courts of the non-DAPT states have not agreed with this analysis. *See, e.g.*, *Waldron v. Huber (In re Huber)*, 493 B.R. 798 (Bk.W.D. Wash. 2013). *Cf. Toni 1 Trust (Tangwall v. Wacker)*, 413 P.3d 1199 (Alaska 2018).

Another significant problem is that the 2005 changes to the Bankruptcy Code included a new 10-year statute of limitations for fraudulent transfers made to "self-settled trusts and similar devices". 11 USC § 548(e), *i.e.*, if a bankruptcy trustee can prove to the satisfaction of a bankruptcy court that a transfer to a self-settled trust was made either with the intent to defeat the rights of creditors (and what else is asset protection planning?) or while the debtor was insolvent, either situation during the last 10 years, then the transfer to the trust may be avoided for the benefit of the debtor's bankruptcy estate.

C.   ADVANCED ASSET PROTECTION TRUSTS

Suffice it to say that the shortcomings or failures of both FAPTs and DAPTs have infused some planners with the enthusiasm to experiment with other forms of trusts, most notably the Special Power of Appointment Trust ("*SPA Trust*") in which the settlor is not a current beneficiary but who can later "spring" into the trust by way of a power of attorney, the Steve Oshins' Hybrid Trust, as well as Third-Party Settled Trusts and other creations. An examination of those trust forms and ideas are beyond the scope of this discussion, but suffice it to say merely *caveat emptor*. The history of trust planning and creditors has often proven that ideas which sound great in the comfort of the conference room will all too often find their denouement in the crucible of the courtroom.

END.

3

How to Avoid Litigation in the Planning Stage

John A. Hartog
Mark S. Poochigian
Hon. Reva G. Goetz (Ret.)

⚖ CEB®   April 20, 2023

How to Avoid Litigation in the Planning Stage

45th Annual UCLA/CEB Estate Planning Institute

April 20-21, 2023

John A. Hartog
Mark S. Poochigian
Hon. Reva G. Goetz (Ret.)

Speakers

- John A. Hartog | Hartog, Baer, Zabronsky & Verriere, APC
  – jahartog@hbzvlaw.com | 925-253-1717
- Mark S. Poochigian | Baker Manock & Jensen PC
  – mpoochigian@bakermanock.com | 559-432-5400
- Hon. Reva G. Goetz (Ret.) | JAMS
  – rgoetz@jamsadr.com | 213-253-9701

2

Learning Objectives

While no estate plan is guaranteed to be litigation proof, well-crafted and carefully drafted plans can reduce the chance of litigation or otherwise speed resolution and reduce the cost of disputes between fiduciaries and beneficiaries, or between the beneficiaries themselves. This presentation discusses tools, techniques, and practice tips to help you effectively use the planning stage to craft estate plans that avoid litigation.

Agenda

1. Estate Planning Process to Discourage Litigation

2. Drafting Strategies for Various Circumstances
   - Second Marriages and Blended Families
   - Distribution of Specific Assets
   - Choice of Trustee
   - Modifications of Trustee's Liability and Duties
   - Accounting Issues
   - No Contest Clauses
   - The "Bribe Gift"
   - Tax apportionment

3. Pre-Death Strategies
   - Pre-Death Disclosure
   - Pre-Death P.C. 17200 Petition
   - Substituted Judgment – Conservatorship P.C. 2580

4

A True Gift

5

Estate Planning Process

- Know Your Client
- Lifestyle and Prior Estate Plan, if any
- Red Flags in New Plan
    - Significant Changes from Prior Plans
    - Change in Estate Planning Counsel
    - Physical or Mental Impairment
    - Beneficiary Involvement/Participation
    - Family Dynamics
    - Unnatural Dispositive Provisions

6

Second Marriages and Blended Families

- Allocation of Assets to Sub-Trusts
- Surviving Spouse's Ability to Modify His or
  Her Sub-Trust

Distribution of Specific Assets

- *Inter vivos* transfers
  - –Language in trust instrument addressing prior
    transfer
- Post-Death Distributions
- Post-Death Options – valuation and terms

Choice of Trustee

- Importance of WHO shall serve
- Individual vs. corporate vs. private fiduciary
- Single or cotrustees
- Settlor or spouse as trustee
- Beneficiary as trustee
- Successor trustees

Use of Trust Protector

- No California statute (yet)
- Trust terms dictate purpose and powers
- Compensation
- Limiting Trust Protector liability
    - Trust pays for Trust Protector's counsel
- Anyone who holds power over a Trust = Fiduciary compared to Co-Trustee
    - *Crocker Citizens National Bank v. Younger* (1971) 4 Cal.3d 202

Trustee Exculpation and Modification of Duties

- Limitations on Liability/Exculpation Clause
- Modification of Duties
- Accounting issues
  - Waive accountings during Settlor's lifetime
  - Shorten objection period

11

Other Strategies to Minimize Litigation

- Annuities and Gifts in Trust
- Pecuniary Rather Than Residual Gifts
- Tax Apportionment
  - General
  - QTIP Property
  - Other
  - From Where Will Payment Be Made?
  - Exemptions?

12

Deterrents

- No Contest Clauses
- Diminishing Gifts
- Third Party Power of Appointment (the "Bribe Gift")

Preventive Measures

- Disclosure of estate plan to affected persons
  - *Drake v. Pinkham* (2013) 217 Cal.App.4th 400
- Pre-death petition pursuant to Probate Code section 17200 when client is still available to testify
- Substituted Judgment pursuant to Probate Code sections 2580-2586 in conservatorship matters

Q&A

CEB Disclaimer

CEB is a self-supporting non-profit program of the University of California. The program, which provides lawyers with information about the law and the practice of law in California, is administered by an Advisory Board that includes representatives of the University of California and members of the California legal community.

CEB's only financial support comes from the sale of CEB publications, programs, and other products. CEB's publications and programs are intended to provide current and accurate information and are designed to help attorneys maintain their professional competence. Publications are distributed and oral programs presented with the understanding that CEB does not render any legal, accounting, or other professional service. Attorneys using CEB publications or orally conveyed information in dealing with a specific legal matter should also research original sources of authority. CEB's publications and programs are not intended to describe the standard of care for attorneys in any community, but rather to be of assistance to attorneys in providing high quality service to their clients and in protecting their own interests.

How to Avoid Litigation in the Planning Stage

John A. Hartog
Mark S. Poochigian
Hon. Reva Goetz (Ret.)

I.   Introduction.

When an estate plan will provide for unequal distributions, the settlor has a blended family, a caregiver will receive a substantial gift, one or more children are disinherited, or the plan otherwise gives rise to a legitimate fear of future litigation, the estate planner may take prophylactic measures to deter disgruntled beneficiaries from bringing a contest or to prevent the estate plan from being invalidated.

Estate planning for families who own businesses and other significant assets often exposes difficulties rooted in the family's internal dynamics and psychological issues. The very act of estate planning may upset the balance that a family has developed over decades to keep their business functioning. Strong emotions, often suppressed for a lifetime, may emerge when testators contemplate their legacies or beneficiaries contemplate their futures. Death and grief can release suppressed emotions that fuel legal actions by survivors, which in turn can erode the value of the business.

A variety of techniques exist to draft testamentary instruments to inhibit contests, to encourage good behavior or to discourage bad behavior. Having a well-designed estate planning process led by the drafting attorney that is designed to spot areas of potential future disputes and address them in the planning stage can go a long way toward minimizing litigation. Substantively, there are numerous drafting and other strategies available to estate planners to minimize and discourage future litigation over the estate plan. Careful use of these techniques and a thorough understanding of the relevant statutes are integral to successful planning.

II.   Estate Planning Process.

A.   Situation of Attorney.

The estate planning attorney is in a special position of trust and confidence with the client. Preparing an estate plan for a client places the attorney in a unique situation to see behind the proverbial curtain relating to the client's financial situation, family and social life, desires, hopes and fears. The estate planning attorney is sometimes the only person granted such access to the intimate details of the client's life. This responsibility should not be taken lightly; it is a

1

privilege that oftentimes places the estate planning attorney in a unique position to ascertain the client's true wishes, defend and protect the client against fraud and undue influence, and anticipate potential areas of disagreement after the client's death.

B. Know Your Client.

Familiarity of the client by the estate planning attorney enables the attorney to provide the most personalized advice for the client and the client's particular circumstances. Being aware of the client's background and circumstances assists the attorney in crafting an estate plan that is more likely to avoid litigation. In litigation (or even pre-litigation communications intended to avoid litigation), an attorney who conveys a familiarity with and connection to the client will be an effective witness.

Understanding the client's day-to-day living can also provide important insights that enable the estate planning attorney to build in anti-litigation safeguards. For example, the susceptibility of the client to undue influence by a caregiver is often tied to the frequency of the children's visits with the client (more visits by the children tending to reduce the susceptibility of the client to undue influence). Understanding the mechanics of how a client's bills are paid, how the client gets to doctor appointments, to whom the client turns for advice when needed, etc., gives the estate planning attorney an advantage when identifying areas of potential dispute and taking appropriate steps to mitigate them.

C. Red Flags.

"Red flags" may arise that estate planning attorneys must be aware of, and should sometimes give the attorney some pause. "Red flags" range from not very problematic to perhaps significant enough to cause the estate planning attorney to consider declining or terminating a representation. Common fact patterns that may present as red flags include:

1. <u>Wild "swings" or significant changes from prior documents or situation</u>. Of course, it is the client's prerogative to determine the persons who should benefit from the client's estate plan. However, a client's request that their attorney prepare documents that would depart substantially from the client's existing plan should result in "extra caution" by the attorney. For example, when a longtime beneficiary with a close relationship to the client is suddenly proposed to be disinherited in favor of another person with whom the client is not believed to have such an enduring relationship, the estate planning attorney may ask about the proposed change and attempt to understand it.

2. <u>Unnaturalness of dispositive provisions</u>. A client who is unmarried, has no children, and has no close family might very naturally leave their entire estate to friends or charity. However, one might consider it less natural for a client with close relationships with their children to omit distributions to children, and instead provide for substantial gifts to friends or charity, or an entire gift to a new spouse. Unnaturalness is an indicator of undue influence. (*In re Yale's Estate* (1931) 214 Cal. 115, 122.)

3. <u>Involvement of beneficiary in process</u>. Ideally, the estate planning attorney is in a position to conduct their dealings with the client privately and confidentially. However, particularly when it comes to aging or disabled clients, some involvement by the client's trusted family members and friends may be unavoidable. In most cases, the mere fact that the client is driven to the estate planning attorney's office by a child or friend is not troublesome by itself. However, the attorney should be on guard for evidence that the person driving the client to the attorney's office may be in a position of (undue) influence.

4. <u>Physical or mental impairment</u>. A client who is physically or mentally impaired may have a resulting susceptibility to pressure and undue influence. Even when undue influence is not a concern, a client who is heavily reliant upon others for help can be faced with incentives to reward those who provide assistance that should be explored. Some of these incentives are perfectly natural and appropriate, while others can be very unhealthy and lead to conflict.

5. <u>Change in estate planning counsel</u>. A client having terminated their representation by another attorney to engage new estate planning counsel is another potential "red flag." Of course, many attorney-client relationships end completely unremarkably, and the mere fact that the client has changed attorneys should not necessarily arouse suspicion. However, an attorney meeting with a client who has recently terminated a prior relationship with an attorney should at least ask themselves whether there may be more to the story regarding the end of the prior attorney-client relationship. Was the prior attorney so concerned about a potential transaction or dispositive provision that they declined to prepare the requested documents? If so, should the new attorney have similar concerns?

6. <u>Family dysfunction</u>. If the intended beneficiaries of a client's estate plan (often the client's spouse and children) do not get along while the client is alive, it is usually fanciful to think that the client's death and estate administration will serve as a unifying event. Understanding family dynamics and the relationships that are likely to result in conflict after the client's death can inform the attorney in devising strategies to avoid later litigation.

D.   Strengthening the estate plan.

1.   <u>Awareness and impact of "red flags."</u> If a client presents with only one red flag, that often will not be enough to lead an estate planning attorney to decline to prepare documents requested by the client. No "red flag" presents in a vacuum; there is always important context that the estate planning attorney should attempt to observe and take into account.

For example, take a situation where an unmarried client is driven to the estate planning attorney by Child #1, the client explains that they love all three of their children, and requests the preparation of a revocable trust that would leave the assets equally among the three children, and would nominate Child #2 as the successor trustee. Here, the estate planning attorney might reasonably not be troubled by the presence of a potential "red flag," i.e., Child #1's involvement in providing transportation to the client to the meeting.

On the other hand, suppose a paid caregiver for the client schedules an appointment with the estate planning attorney on behalf of the client, the client is driven to the estate planning attorney by a paid caregiver, the client reports wanting to disinherit all of their children without explanation, and the client says that their will should leave everything to the caregiver. Here, the attorney should be sensitive to the presentation of multiple "red flags," and, at a minimum, conduct some further investigation. This investigation will—without attempting to override or force the client's wishes—allow the attorney to assess whether the client's requests are truly volitional, or perhaps the result of some outside pressure.

2.   <u>Detailed interview of client, in private</u>. Estate planning attorneys can "test" a client's stated desires by conducting a detailed interview of the client to understand the client's objectives and to attempt to ascertain the rationale underlying the proposed changes. Testamentary freedom requires that clients be able to put their intentions into effect. Gentle probing from the attorney drafting the proposed documents is an effective way to "test" the voluntariness and rationality of the proposed changes. Often, the colloquy between attorney and client will lead the client to more developed understandings regarding why the client's initial thoughts might not be workable in practice or lead to litigation. Some memorialization of the interview—for example, in notes kept by the attorney or in a confirming letter to the client—will serve to support the attorney's recollection if asked about the matter in subsequent litigation.

3.   <u>Involvement of second attorney in estate planning process</u>. When an estate plan is likely to be attacked based upon lack of capacity or undue influence, consider having a second attorney review the estate plan, hear the client's explanation for it, and counsel the client regarding it. Assuming that the second attorney is another experienced estate planning attorney, this process creates

another witness who can testify after the client's death or incapacity regarding the client's wishes, bolstering the estate plan and discouraging litigation. Under certain circumstances, the Probate Code sets forth a procedure whereby a potentially suspect provision may be reviewed by an attorney who is in a position to counsel the transferor independently and provide a certificate of independent review. (See e.g., Prob. Code §§ 15642, subd. (b)(6)(B), 21384, subd. (a).)

4. <u>Involvement of physician in estate planning process</u>. When a client's capacity to execute estate planning documents is questionable or likely to be questioned, a common practice is for the attorney to encourage the client to see the client's physician contemporaneously with the planned execution of the estate planning documents. This medical review creates a medical record regarding the client's capacity at approximately the time the estate planning documents were signed, and can also have the advantage of providing the estate planning attorney with some assurance that the client is competent to make the changes requested.

5. <u>Lengthen the process</u>. Well-considered decisions are usually better than hasty ones. When a client requests changes that the attorney fears have not been well thought out, the attorney can gently extend the estate planning process. Whereas an attorney might under ordinary circumstances immediately prepare documents upon a client's first request, when the requested documents are problematic or likely to lead to litigation, the estate planning attorney might consider—without compromising the diligence and competence due to the client—attempting to lengthen the usual process by suggesting additional conferences for discussion purposes, taking additional time to gather information, etc. The fit of pique that the client is in when first meeting with the attorney might subside given a couple of weeks for the client to more fully consider their situation.

6. <u>Witnesses</u>. Many clients who understand that their documents may be attacked take solace in knowing that their attorney can act as their "voice" after the client's death, e.g., to testify about the circumstances of the execution of the deceased client's estate planning documents. When litigation is anticipated, it is a best practice for the estate planning attorney to preserve evidence surrounding the execution of the estate planning documents. Having a third party with experience in estate planning present for the explanation of the documents to the client and their execution can be very useful. One easy way of doing this is by having an unrelated third party—for example, a second experienced estate planning attorney or paralegal—participate in the explanation of the documents to the client and the entirety of the document signing meeting, and make a memorandum of the interactions with the client.

III. Drafting Strategies for Minimizing Litigation.

A. Common problem: distribution of specific assets.

1. *Inter Vivos* Transactions, Acknowledge and Credit.

If the testator believes that a particular asset will be the source of the dispute, an *inter vivos* transfer may be an effective method to reduce the potential of post-death litigation. Such transfer can occur by an outright gift, with the will or trust explicitly recognizing the transfer as an advance on the inheritance. A transfer can occur by an *inter vivos* transaction or contract, such as a loan, stock redemption agreement or an option agreement.

a. Advances.

> *EXAMPLE: The settlors acknowledge that they have advanced funds to one or more of their children prior to the execution of this trust declaration, and they may advance funds to their children in the future. The settlors intend to create a written memorandum of those advances and to revise that memorandum as needed. The trustee will take those advances into consideration in determining the share of the trust property that any child or further issue of the settlors is entitled to receive under the provisions of Section **, as follows:*
>
>> *a. The trustee will add the total nominal value of advances to the settlors' children to the trust property available for distribution;*
>> *b. The trust property increased by the amount of such advances will be divided among the settlors' issue in the manner prescribed by Section ** of this declaration; and*
>> *c. Advances that the settlors have made to any child will be deducted from the share of the increased trust property that child or the issue of that child would be entitled to receive.*

b. Loans.

> *EXAMPLE: For the purpose of determining the distribution to KAT or to her issue under this Section, the settlor directs the trustee to add to the total trust assets available for distribution the following amounts:*

> *a.* *Any unreimbursed advances to DAWG, associated with or traceable to the recited Loan Agreement; plus*
>
> *b.* *Interest accrued on any advances to DAWG under the terms of the recited Loan Agreement from the date of the advance to the date of reimbursement, either before or after the settlor's death, if not reimbursed to the settlor during her lifetime.*

2.   Post-Death Distributions and Options.

Many settlors do not wish to part with assets during their lifetimes and only want transfers to be made effective at death. Also, tax considerations frequently militate against *inter vivos* transactions (e.g., where the settlor wishes to transfer appreciated property to the beneficiary but would prefer to wait for the step-up in basis at death). For these and other reasons, *inter vivos* transactions are often undesirable or impractical.

When an *inter vivos* transaction is not a good option, yet the settlor wants a beneficiary to receive a particular item of property after the settlor's death, the simplest approach is for the settlor to require that the property be distributed to the chosen beneficiary after the settlor's death. If the distribution of particular property to a specified child would result in inequality among the settlor's beneficiaries (and if equality is important), or if the settlor wishes for other reasons for the intended recipient to pay something in exchange for receiving the particular property, a common practice is for settlors to give beneficiaries the option to acquire property from their revocable trust after the settlor's death. Well-considered trust provisions, e.g., pursuant to an option, can minimize litigation among the beneficiaries after the settlor's death over one beneficiary's acquisition of certain property.

A frequent area of dispute is valuation. One common approach calls for the purchase price to be equal to the fair market value of the property as determined by an independent appraiser qualified to make such a determination. If this approach is followed, attention must be given to the manner of selection of the appraiser. The trustee could be given discretion to select the appraiser, but this may invite controversy if the trustee is also a beneficiary. For this reason, the attorney should consider naming the appraiser who is to appraise the property in the instrument, with alternate appraisers named in the event that the preferred appraiser is unavailable or unwilling to appraise the property.

Another approach that some practitioners follow is to fix the price at which the beneficiary may acquire the particular asset in the trust instrument. Alternately, the instrument may provide that the beneficiary is to pay the lower of the property's value at the date of the instrument or the date of death. From a litigation-avoidance perspective, this may be an effective technique. However, it also can result in inequality among the beneficiaries, or the property not passing to the intended beneficiary if the fixed price is too high.

When granting options for beneficiaries to acquire property of a trust, other important provisions include the time for the beneficiary to exercise their option and the consequences of a nonexercise, and manner of payment of the purchase price. If the beneficiary will not be able to pay cash for the asset being acquired, the trust instrument should allow the beneficiary's account as a beneficiary to be charged for the property acquired. Allowing the beneficiary to pay the purchase price for the option property with a promissory note (in whole or in part) with predetermined repayment terms is another way of furthering the settlor's intentions while minimizing the opportunity for litigation among the beneficiaries.

> *EXAMPLE: If Child survives the settlor, Child shall enjoy an option to have Blackacre allocated to the share, if any, created for Child under Section ** above. In the event Child exercises such option, Blackacre shall be allocated entirely to the share, if any, created for Child under Section ** above, and Child's share as a beneficiary shall be charged with the fair market value of Blackacre as of the settlor's death, as such fair market value is determined by an independent appraiser experienced in such matters and qualified to make such a determination, such appraiser to be selected by the trustee in the trustee's sole discretion. The fair market value of Blackacre so determined by such appraiser is referred to herein as the "Blackacre Determined Value." Failure by Child to notify the trustee in writing of her exercise of the option granted to her in this Section ** within forty-five (45) days of notification of Child by the trustee of the Blackacre Determined Value shall be treated as Child's nonexercise of such option. In the case of nonexercise by Child of the option granted to her in this Section **, Blackacre shall be distributed as part of the residue of the trust estate.*

> *EXAMPLE: The purchase price to be paid by Child for Blackacre shall be paid by Child by a promissory note (the "Promissory Note") in the amount of the Blackacre Determined Value. The Promissory Note shall (i) have a term of ** years, (ii) bear interest at a rate equal to the applicable Federal rate for a debt instrument having a term of ** years, as defined in Section 1274(d)(1) of the Internal Revenue Code of 1986, as amended, (iii) require annual payments of interest only on the first*

*** anniversaries of the Promissory Note, and (iv) and require that all
remaining principal and accrued by unpaid interest be paid on the **
anniversary of the Promissory Note.*

3. Annuities and Gifts in Trust.

a. <u>GRATS</u>. A strategy that uses lifetime giving while
accomplishing tax planning in a low interest environment is an annuity
stream. A prime example is a grantor retained annuity trust (GRAT).
Because the retained annuity is being valued with a low interest rate, it is
undervalued as an economic matter if the assets are expected to produce a
return in excess of the 7520 rate. Since the GRAT produces a benefit for
family only if the assets produce a total return in excess of the 7520 rate, the
GRAT is a preferred vehicle in a time of low interest rates. The lower the
interest rate, the smaller the annuity needed to result in a zero gift.

b. <u>CLATS</u>. The charitable lead annuity trust produces a
similar benefit when interest rates are low. As with the GRAT, any growth in
the trust in excess of the 7520 rate passes to the non-charitable remainder
beneficiaries at termination of the CLAT free of gift or estate tax.

c. <u>QPRTS</u>. A QPRT offers an alternative to direct gifts of
interests in residential property, either the principal residence or a vacation
home. A QPRT allows the settlor to make a completed gift of the property
while retaining rent free use of it for a period of years. The gift of the
property through a QPRT uses less of the settlor's available gift and estate
tax exclusions than a direct transfer while directing its transfer to the
intended recipient outside of the main vehicle document.

B. Choice of trustee.

The selection of an appropriate trustee or cotrustees and successor
trustees is an important facet of trust planning. Factors that should be considered
include age, health, education, experience, trust purpose, potential tax issues,
relationship to beneficiaries, willingness to serve, and cost. The settlor may also
consider the costs and benefits of individual and corporate trustees.

1. Legal Qualifications.

a. Individual Trustee.

The legal qualifications in California for an individual are minimal:
anyone with the legal capacity to enter into contracts and to hold title to property
may act as a trustee. A person is able to enter into contracts when that person has

reached the age of majority, which is 18 in California. Fam. Code §§ 6500, 6701(b). Residents and nonresidents of California, including nonresident aliens of the U.S., can hold title to real or personal property in California. CC § 671.

b. Corporate Trustee.

Prob. Code § 300 provides that a trust company may be appointed to act as trustee in the same manner as an individual. Prob. Code § 83 provides that trust company means an entity that has qualified to engage in and conduct a trust business in this state. Such entities include trust departments of commercial banks, mutual or stock savings associations, savings and loan associations, savings banks, and nonprofit public benefit corporations. See Fin. Code §§ 106, 107, 1500, 1580.

2. Individual Trustee.

The individual trustee is often a relative, a friend or a financial or investment advisor. Such a trustee's familiarity with the settlor's intent and the beneficiaries may be beneficial for trust administration. On the other hand, such familiarity may lead to favoritism or vulnerability to pressure. Also, the selection of one family member over others may create or aggravate hostilities.

The individual trustee is due reasonable compensation for his or her services. Often, the individual trustee may need to hire agents and advisers to assist him or her in trust administration.

The passage of the Prudent Investor Act ("Act"), effective for all trusts beginning January 1, 1996, codified the "prudent investor rule" and established portfolio administration and management standards for trustees. The Act encourages, may even require, nonprofessional trustees to appropriately delegate to qualified investment professionals. For example, the trustee must establish guidelines by which the trust will be managed. It may be necessary for the trustee to hire an investment consultant to prepare such guidelines, often called an "Investment Policy Statement." The trustee may also have to hire one or more portfolio or money managers who make the day-to-day buy-sell decisions in accordance with such an IPS. See Section II. G. below.

The individual trustee may be required to post a bond to protect the trust against losses from breaches of trust. If, however, the settlor provides that such bond is not required, it may be that the beneficiaries have no recourse against a wayward trustee who is insolvent.

In light of the nonprofessional trustee's potential need to hire various agents to administer the trust and potential risks of favoritism and hostility, the settlor may simply wish to choose a corporate trustee to serve.

10

3.   Corporate Trustee

As in the case of individual trustees, the advantages and disadvantages of appointing a corporate or professional trustee are often the positive and negative aspects of the same characteristic. For example, the size and corporate structure of a professional trustee may be seen as indications of professionalism and neutrality on the one hand and as indications of inflexibility and lack of personal service on the other. Stated in more detail, the advantages of a corporate trustee are its experience and thorough familiarity with trust administration and trust procedures. Having the management of trusts as its full-time business, the corporate trustee necessarily develops a degree of professionalism and sophistication in dealing with such matters that an individual could not be expected to match. The corporate trustee is also neutral in judging competing interests of the trust beneficiaries, and presumably not susceptible to improper pressures by beneficiaries in the administration of the trust. This can eliminate a source of conflict between family members or trust beneficiaries.

A corporate entity can exercise full powers as a trustee without raising potentially dangerous tax issues. The corporate trustee also has a degree of continuity that an individual lacks, which may be important when it is expected that the trust will continue for an extended period of time. Finally, a corporate trustee has qualified with the state to engage in the trust business, and has financial resources to enable it to compensate the trust estate if losses result from its administration.

The disadvantages of using a corporate trustee normally include greater costs. Although it may be possible in particular cases to negotiate some variation from a corporate trustee's standard fee schedules, corporate trustees frequently insist on the payment of minimum fees. Corporate trustees will often refuse to accept "smaller" trusts (defined, not infrequently, as those with less than the minimum in principal value needed to justify the base fee) or show lack of flexibility in agreeing to administer trusts containing assets that may raise any unusual issues of management, including not only business interests but also often parcels of rental real estate.

Corporate trustees also suffer from the perception that large corporations are incapable of rendering truly personal services and that they tend to follow asset management and investment policies that are conservative and simple to administer, whether or not they are necessarily in the best interests of a particular trust. These perceptions may or may not be borne out in specific instances, and the competence and commitment of the corporate trustee's trust department will determine the accuracy of such perceptions. However, professional trustees do suffer from the organizational problems of needing to recruit and retain trust officers and staff of high quality. Further, they often have high turnover in trust officers assigned to each particular trust account.

4. Single Trustee or Cotrustees.

Generally, appointment of cotrustees makes trust administration more cumbersome because all cotrustees may need to be involved in the management and administration of the trust. Probate Code § 15620 provides that "unless otherwise provided in the trust instrument, a power vested in two or more trustees may only be exercised by their unanimous action."

However, cotrustees may be beneficial where such unanimity is desired by the settlor for trust administration or where the appointment of such cotrustees may prevent family conflict.

Other options include (1) the trust instrument clearly delineating different powers to different cotrustees and (2) the appointment of special trustees for certain property or powers.

5. Settlor or Spouse as Trustee.

a. Revocable Trust.

With revocable trusts, it is very common for the settlor to serve as his or her own trustee. Because the trust is revocable, trust assets are basically treated as the settlor's assets for tax purposes and the settlor-trustee has no obligations to the potential remainder beneficiaries.

When spouses create a revocable trust together, often they often serve as cotrustees during their joint lifetimes, with the surviving spouse continuing as sole trustee over certain or all subtrusts after the death of the first spouse to die. The surviving spouse can serve as the sole trustee over any trust which is revocable by the surviving spouse; however, with subtrusts which become irrevocable upon the death of the first spouse to die and are intended to avoid inclusion in the surviving spouse's estate, the surviving spouse's powers as trustee needs to be properly limited if that surviving spouse intends to serve as trustee.

b. Irrevocable Trust.

Often irrevocable trusts are created with certain tax objectives, such as avoiding including the trust assets in the settlor's estate. Income and transfer tax considerations may make it unwise or impossible for the settlor or the settlor's spouse to serve as trustee or cotrustee.

6.   Beneficiary as Trustee.

Generally, a beneficiary may serve as trustee. However, there needs to another beneficiary in addition to the beneficiary serving as the trustee if the trust is irrevocable. If the legal title to the trust property and the entire beneficial interest in the same property become united in one person the trust is terminated under the doctrine of merger. Restatement (Second) of Trusts § 341(1).

It may be unsuitable to name a beneficiary as trustee if the trustee's powers include discretion to distribute principal and income among the beneficiaries. Such a beneficiary-trustee may be subject to a conflict of interest and may be unable to fulfill their duties of loyalty and impartiality. Also, income and transfer tax considerations may make the beneficiary unsuitable as the trustee.

7.   Appointment of Successor Trustees.

Nomination of a successor trustee who shall serve in the event or the refusal, incapacity, or withdrawal of the original trustee is important. If the trust instrument does not name such successor trustee and does not provide for a method of appointing such successor trustee, Probate Code § 15660(c) provides that the vacancy can be filled by a trust company upon the agreement of all adult beneficiaries who are receiving or would be entitled to receive income or principal if the trust were terminated. If such beneficiaries cannot agree, the court may appoint a trustee. Prob. Code §§ 15660(d), 17200(b)(10).

The trust instrument may provide that the trustee may be removed and replaced by someone named in the trust instrument. If the person with the power to remove and replace is the settlor of an irrevocable trust or a beneficiary of any type of trust, such removal and replacement power must be restricted in order to avoid the transfer tax issues.

The insured settlor can retain the power to remove the third party trustee and appoint a successor trustee (individual or corporate) as long as the successor is not related or subordinate to the settlor per I.R.C. § 672(c). This subsection defines as "related or subordinate" the following persons: (i) the settlor's spouse if living with the settlor; (ii) any one of the following: the settlor's parent, issue, or sibling; an employee of the settlor; a corporation or any employee of a corporation in which the stock holdings of the settlor and the trust are significant from the viewpoint of voting control; a subordinate employee of the corporation in which the settlor is an executive. See I.R.C. § 2036(a)(2), 2038 (a)(1), § 2041(a), and § 2042(2).

13

C. Modification of trustee's duties and limiting time to object.

Where a settlor anticipates disputes between the trustee and the beneficiary and wants to give deference to the trustee, there are a number of tools available to the drafting attorney.

1. Exculpatory provisions in general.

Public policy concerns prohibit a settlor from relieving the trustee of all accountability. (*Estate of Ferrall* (1953) 41 Cal.2d 166, 174.) However, subject to some important exceptions, the trustee can be relieved of liability for breach of trust by provisions in the trust instrument. (Prob. Code § 16461, subd. (a).) A provision in the trust instrument relieving the trustee of liability is valid except to the extent it purports to relieve the trustee (1) for breach of trust committed intentionally, with gross negligence, in bad faith, or with reckless indifference to the interest of the beneficiary, or (2) for any profit that the trustee derives from a breach of trust. (Prob. Code, § 16461, subd. (a).) Especially when the settlor has extreme confidence in the fidelity of the trustee and concerns regarding potentially litigious beneficiaries, exculpatory language can disincentivize the beneficiaries from pursuing minor or borderline claims for breach of trust.

> *EXAMPLE: No trustee who was nominated by the trustee shall be liable to any beneficiary of this trust for any act or default of that trustee, or of any other trustee or any other person, unless resulting from that trustee's own willful misconduct, bad faith or gross negligence.*

2. Modifying certain duties of the trustee.

The trustee has a duty to administer the trust according to the trust instrument. (Prob. Code, § 16000.) Some well-known statutory duties imposed upon trustees include the duty of loyalty, the duty to deal impartially with beneficiaries, the duty to avoid conflicts of interest, the duty not to accept adverse trusts, the duty to take control and preservation of trust property, and the duty to make the trust property productive. (See Prob. Code, §§ 16001-16015.) Apart from some duties of trustees that are made non-waivable or non-modifiable by statute, the statutory duties imposed upon trustees do not apply to the extent the trust instrument provides otherwise. (Prob. Code, § 16000.) The attorney drafting a trust instrument should consider the extent to which the trust instrument should modify the default duties imposed on trustees to further the settlor's wishes and avoid litigation. This issue frequently arises in the context of the duties of loyalty, diversification and productivity.

14

Probate Code section 16002, subdivision (a) sets forth the statutory duty of loyalty: "The trustee has a duty to administer the trust solely in the interest of the beneficiaries." It is common for trust instruments to contain some limitations on the trustee's duty of loyalty (e.g., to allow the trustee to lend to the trust or, under appropriate circumstances, to purchase or lease property from the trust). See Drafting California Revocable Trusts (Cont. Ed. Bar 2022) § 17.41 for useful model language for modifying the trustee's duty of loyalty. Absent language in the trust instrument relaxing the trustee's duty of loyalty, a purchase or lease of trust property by the trustee would likely violate the duty.

The trustee has a duty to avoid conflicts of interest. (Prob. Code, § 16004.) However, many settlors nominate trustees with foreseeable conflicts of interest that the settlors intend to authorize. Particularly in the context of family businesses and family-owned farms, the settlors often wish to nominate as trustee the child who is most closely involved in the business or farm. Appropriate trust provisions modifying the duty to avoid conflicts of interest will minimize litigation regarding the administration of the trust.

> EXAMPLE: Conflict of Interest Permissible. Any contrary provision of law notwithstanding, the hiring by the trustee of himself or a related entity to manage the real property that is a part of the trust estate is permissible, and shall not constitute a violation of any duty of the trustee. The foregoing sentence is intended to supersede any contrary duties or obligations placed upon the trustee by applicable law (for example, relating to conflicts of interest), including, without limitation, California Probate Code section 16004, or its successor statute.

The trustee has a duty to diversify the investments of the trust unless, under the circumstances, it is prudent not to do so. (Prob. Code, § 16048.) This duty is frequently implicated where the primary asset of a trust is stock in the family-owned business or family farm.

> EXAMPLE: No Duty to Diversify. Settlors declare that they anticipate that the trust estate will include stock in XYZ Company. One of the primary purposes of the trust is to provide for the continued holding of stock in XYZ Company, regardless of whether it is prudent to do so. Thus, any contrary provision of law notwithstanding, the trustee shall have no duty to diversify the investments of the trust with regard to the stock in XYZ Company and may continue to retain in the trust a concentration of the stock XYZ Company, even if such failure to diversify would be imprudent. The foregoing sentence is intended to supersede any contrary duties or obligations placed upon the trustee by

15

applicable law, including, without limitation, the Uniform Prudent Investor Act (California Probate Code section 16045 et seq.), or its successor statute.

The trustee has a duty to make the trust property productive under the circumstances and in furtherance of the purposes of the trust. (Prob. Code § 16007.) This duty often invites disputes among trustees and beneficiaries, and commonly arises regarding family vacation homes or other real property that the settlors prefer not to develop to its highest and best economic use. The financially successful child who lives far away and owns their own preferred vacation home is unlikely to be satisfied with the trustee's ownership of a family vacation home that is not regularly rented out, and is only used by other family members—especially if the trustee makes use of the vacation home. Settlors who value continued ownership of certain assets over productivity should consider appropriate trust provisions relieving the trustee of the duty of productivity.

> *EXAMPLE: No Duty Make Trust Assets Productive. Settlors are establishing this trust for the primary purpose of holding interests in the family vacation home located at **. The Settlors desire to provide for the availability of the vacation home for family members to enjoy and are not concerned with leasing the vacation home to third parties, even though this tends to make the vacation home a non-productive asset. The Trustee is authorized to continue to hold the vacation home without any obligation to rent it notwithstanding any obligation to diversify or to make trust assets productive. The foregoing sentence is intended to supersede any contrary duties or obligations placed upon the trustee by applicable law, including, without limitation, the Probate Code Section 16007.*

3.   **Shortening time to object to account.**

The statute of limitations for an action by a beneficiary against a trustee for breach of trust is three years. (Prob. Code, § 16460.) The three-year statute of limitations begins to run when the beneficiary receives an interim or final account in writing, or other written report, that "adequately discloses the existence of a claim against the trustee for breach of trust." (Prob. Code § 16460, subd. (a)(1).) An account or report adequately discloses existence of a claim if it provides, "sufficient information so that the beneficiary knows of the claim or reasonably should have inquired into the existence of the claim." (Prob. Code § 16460, subd. (a)(1).) An account or report adequately discloses existence of a claim if it provides, "sufficient information so that the beneficiary knows of the claim or reasonably should have inquired into the existence of the claim. If no written account or report adequately discloses the existence of a claim against the trustee, or if the beneficiary does not receive any written account or report, the three-year statute of limitations begins to run when, "beneficiary discovered, or reasonably should have discovered, the subject of the claim." (Prob. Code § 16460, subd. (a)(2).)

A settlor may limit the trustee's exposure to objections from a beneficiary by requiring the beneficiary to state their objections promptly. A trustee is relieved from liability to a beneficiary unless the beneficiary objects to an account within a specified period, as long as the beneficiary is given at least 180 days to object and other statutory requirements are met. (Prob. Code § 16461, subd. (c).)

D. Reporting and Accounting Requirements.

The general rule under the Probate Code is that the trustee has a general duty to keep the beneficiaries of the trust reasonably informed of the trust and its administration. (Prob. Code § 16060.) On reasonable request by a beneficiary, the trustee is required to report to the beneficiary by providing requested information to the beneficiary relating to the administration of the trust relevant to the beneficiary's interest. (Prob. Code § 16061.) And, the Probate Code imposes a more specific duty to account annually to beneficiaries to whom income or principal is required or authorized in the trustee's discretion to be currently distributed. (Prob. Code § 16062, subd. (a).) However, there is some authority for the principle that remainder beneficiaries may be entitled to particular accounts under those beneficiaries' broader right to receive information relevant to their interest under Probate Code section 16061. (See, e.g., *Esslinger v. Cummings* (2006) 144 Cal.App.4th 517.)

The duty of the trustee to provide requested information to the beneficiary as required by Section 16061 cannot be waived by the settlor, as any such waiver would be against public policy and void. (Prob. Code § 16068.) However, for all trustees other than certain persons described in Probate Code section 21380 (e.g., persons who drafted the instrument, care custodians, etc.), the duty to account can be waived in the trust instrument. (Prob. Code §§ 16062, subd. (e), 16064, subd. (a).)

In appropriate cases, consideration should be given to waiving or modifying the trustee's duty to account to the beneficiaries. At the extreme, the settlor may attempt to completely waive the trustee's duty to account. Or, the settlor may waive the duty to account in a more limited way, e.g., by providing that the trustee is only required to account when requested by a beneficiary, by requiring accounts less frequently than annually, or by limiting the contents required of an accounting. Predictably, despite a waiver of accounting in the trust instrument, "upon a showing that it is reasonably likely that a material breach of the trust has occurred, the court may compel the trustee to account." (Prob. Code § 16064, subd. (a).)

E.   No Contest Clauses.

1.   Sanctioned by Statute.

Probate Code sections 21310-21315 limit the enforcement of no contest clauses to the following three types of contests:

   i.   "Direct contests of protected instruments" brought without probable cause;

   ii.   Pleadings challenging "a transfer of property on the grounds that it was not the transferor's property at the time of the transfer;" and

   iii. Creditor's claims, or actions based on a creditor's claims.

2.   Direct Contests of Protected Instruments.

a.   Definition of Direct Contest.

A "direct contest" is one "that alleges the invalidity of a protected instrument or one or more of its terms," based on one or more of the following grounds:

- Forgery;
- Lack of due execution;
- Lack of capacity;
- Menace, duress, fraud, or undue influence;
- Revocation of a will pursuant to Section 6120;
- Revocation of a trust pursuant to Section 15401;
- Revocation of an instrument other than a will or trust pursuant to the procedure for revocation that is provided by statute or by the instrument; or
- Disqualification under Probate Code Sections 6112, 21350 or 21380.

b.   Test for Probable Cause.

"Probable cause exists if, at the time of filing a contest, the facts known to the contestant would cause a reasonable person to believe that there is a reasonable likelihood that the requested relief will be granted after an opportunity for further investigation and discovery." (Probate Code section 21311(b).)

18

c.   Protected Instruments.

A "protected instrument" is an instrument that contains the no contest clause or "[a]n instrument that is in existence on the date that the instrument containing the no contest clause is executed and is expressly identified in the no contest clause, either individually or as part of an identifiable class of instruments, as being governed by the no contest clause." (Probate Code section 21310(e).)

3.   What is "An Identifiable Class of Instruments"?

Case law has not yet told us what the minimum standard is for expressly identifying one instrument in the no contest clause contained in a different instrument. If the no contest clause in a trust mentions the beneficiary designation for an IRA and that IRA is identified by institution and account number, that would be sufficient. Whether a reference to "all the settlor's IRA beneficiary designations" would suffice is not known. Similarly, we do not know whether a reference to "all beneficiary designations" would be enough.

4.   Later Documents.

One cannot expressly identify an instrument that is not yet in existence, so a trust's no contest clause cannot protect beneficiary designations made after the execution of the trust. Similar logic applies to trust amendments, will codicils and amendments to other instruments protected by the no contest clause.

5.   Problems with No Contest Clauses.

No contest clauses dissuade contestants by threatening them with the forfeiture of their expectancies. A person who is given nothing by an instrument, loses nothing if he contests the instrument. Similarly, a person who expects to receive little from an instrument has little to lose.

Many forms of mischief are not covered by no contest clauses.

F.   Gifts that inspire good behavior.

1.   Forced Election.

A settlor may force a beneficiary to choose between taking the benefits offered in an instrument or pursuing the beneficiary's rights in the property ostensibly subject to the instrument. One spouse may attempt to dispose of more

19

than one half, even up to all, of the property. Such an attempt will be successful, however, only if the dispositive document states the spouse's intention to dispose of more than one half of the property, and only if the surviving spouse acquiesces in the attempt. The right of a surviving spouse to acquiesce (or refuse to acquiesce) in an attempt by the deceased spouse to dispose of more than one half of the community property is often called the "widow's election." The courts have permitted testators to compel the surviving spouse to choose between accepting the benefits given, or pursuing his or her rights in the property subject to the dispositive instrument. (*See Burch v. George* (1994) 7 Cal.4th 246, upholding validity of forced elections when the settlor has expressed the intent to dispose of specific property even when mistaken about the property's character; *See also Estate of Murphy* (1976) 15 Cal. 3d 907.)

> **EXAMPLE:** The settlor left White Acre to her husband and Black Acre to her children. The trust includes a no contest clause as described by Probate Code section 21311(a)(2) and specifically states that, if the husband asserts community property interest in Black Acre, he forfeits his gift of White Acre (and any other gifts under the trust), and will receive only his share of the community property and any of his separate property purportedly governed by the trust.

Depending on the size of an estate, the tax disadvantages of the "widow's election" may be significant. A "forced" or "strict" election can actually result in higher estate taxes in the estate of the deceased spouse by impairing the value of the marital deduction that would otherwise be available for property that passes to the surviving spouse. This result occurs when the deceased spouse's trust requires the surviving spouse to surrender the survivor's interest in the community property in return for a gift from the decedent. The value of the devise to the surviving spouse must be reduced by the value of the community property surrendered. (*See* I.R.C. § 2056(b)(4) value of interest passing to surviving spouse must be reduced by value of obligation imposed on surviving spouse by deceased spouse; *see also* Treas. Reg. § 20.2056(b)-(4)(b), Ex. 3.) The value of the surviving spouse's half of the community property will be subject to estate taxation when the surviving spouse dies under I.R.C. § 2036(a). By contributing the survivor's interest in the community property to a trust in which he or she retained a lifetime income interest, the surviving spouse has made a transfer with a retained lifetime interest (*Gradow v. United States* (Fed. Cir. [U.S. Ct. Cl.] (1990) 897 F.2d 516, 518) Although I.R.C. § 2036(a) allows an exception for property transferred "in a bona fide sale for an adequate consideration in money or money's worth," this exception is not available when the value of the surviving spouse's half is greater than the value of a lifetime income interest in the deceased spouse's half, determined on an actuarial basis according to the surviving spouse's life expectancy (*Gradow, supra,*; *see* Treas. Reg. § 20.2043-1(a).)

20

A taxable gift of a future interest may a l s o occur when the surviving spouse surrenders his or her half of the community property in return for a lifetime income interest in both halves. By accepting only a lifetime income interest in his or her half of the community property, the surviving spouse is giving up the remainder interest in that half. If the value of this remainder interest exceeds the value of the lifetime income interest in both halves of the community property, then the surviving spouse will have made a gift to the extent of the difference [*see Commissioner of Internal Revenue v. Siegel* (9th Cir. [T.C.] 1957) 250 F.2d 339, 349; *Estate of Daisy F. Christ* (1970) 54 T.C. 493, *aff'd on other grounds,* (9th Cir. 1973) 480 F.2d 171]. The surviving spouse also risks having the transfer treated as a taxable gift under Probate Code section 2702.

The following clause may be modified for domestic partners.

EXAMPLE: The trustee may make no distributions to the settlor's spouse until the settlor's spouse has waived in writing any rights he or she may have to the property of the trust estate.

2. Conditional Gifts

A settlor may condition a beneficiary's right to receive or retain a gift upon the beneficiary's written agreement not to contest the estate plan. The trust instrument may require the beneficiary to consent more quickly than the period allowed by Probate Code section 16061.7. Conditional gifts are valid so long as they do not offend public policy. Conditional gift clauses may be adapted to accomplish everything no contest clauses accomplish. (*Burch v. George* (1994) 7 Cal.4th 246, 254, "In essence, a no contest clause conditions a beneficiary's right to take the share provided to that beneficiary under [a will or trust] instrument upon the beneficiary's agreement to acquiesce to the terms of the instrument".)

Whether a court would equate a conditional gift with a no contest clause is unknown. On the one hand, a provision conditioning a gift upon the beneficiary's agreement to forego a contest is analogous to a no contest clause and thus might be unenforceable in circumstances in which the contestant has probable cause to file a direct contest. On the other hand, the law protects testamentary freedom and allows other types of conditional gifts, such as the forced election. (*See* Zabronsky, *From the Ashes: Can No Contest Clauses be Resurrected by Conditional Gifts?* Cal. T.E. Quart, Vol. 14, Issue 3, p. 17 (Fall 2008).)

3. Gifts Conditioned Upon Participating in ADR

In California, a settlor may not require arbitration of disputes over the validity of a testamentary instrument. (*McArthur v. McArthur* (2014) 224 Cal.App.4th 651. *Compare Rachal v. Reitz* (2013) 403. S.W.3d. 840.)

A settlor may, however, condition a gift upon the would-be contestant's participation in mediation. The following examples of mediation clauses were given to the authors by colleagues. The first example requires mediation prior to any litigation of disputes. The second and third examples condition gifts upon mediation as a means to resolve disputes.

EXAMPLE ONE: Paragraph I. Any beneficiary under this instrument who wishes to challenge the validity, construction or effect of all or any portion of this instrument, or who wishes to commence an action against any fiduciary acting hereunder, must proceed as designated in this paragraph or will forfeit his or her interest hereunder as specified in paragraph II. Such individual is hereinafter referred to as the "challenging individual." The challenging individual must agree in writing and in good faith to participate in mediation with the fiduciary acting under this instrument. Any fiduciary that refuses so to agree in writing must cease to act as a fiduciary hereunder. All other persons whose interests hereunder reasonably could be affected by such action must also agree in writing either to participate in such good faith mediation or to be bound by any agreement arising from such mediation. If no agreed resolution of the dispute is reached within six months after the commencement of the mediation or such later period as the parties to the mediation agree in writing, then the challenging individual may assert his or her rights in a duly constituted judicial proceeding in the court which has primary jurisdiction over this instrument. The trustee will be entitled to use the assets of the trust to defend such action; provided, however, that if a court later determines such defense to have been unreasonable, the trustee must reimburse the trust estate for the cost of such defense, including attorneys' fees.

Paragraph II. Forfeiture for Failure to Participate in Mediation. If a challenging individual refuses to participate in the mediation process set forth above and commences an action in any court with respect to any matter relating to the validity, construction or effect of this instrument or complaint against any fiduciary acting hereunder, or if the court determines, based upon clear and convincing evidence, that the challenging individual did not participate in the mediation process in good faith, or if the court determines, based upon clear and convincing evidence, that the challenging individual acted in the pertinent dispute unreasonably or frivolously or in bad faith, the challenging individual will have failed to fulfill a material condition of the gift to that beneficiary, which will result in that beneficiary losing any future benefits of the gift provided for by this instrument.

Paragraph III. Enforceability. If the foregoing provisions contained in this article are held by a court of competent jurisdiction to be invalid, ineffective or otherwise unenforceable, in whole or in part, such provisions will be enforced to the extent held to be valid, effective or otherwise enforceable, and the settlor intends that the Trustees will retain discretion to make distributions to beneficiaries hereunder, and will be entitled not to exercise such discretion in favor of any challenging individual or in favor of any of his or her descendants.

EXAMPLE TWO: Conditional Bequest. A refusal by any beneficiary to mediate in good faith any dispute with the fiduciary will be a failure of a material condition of the gift to that beneficiary, which will result in that beneficiary losing any future benefits of the gift provided for by this instrument.

EXAMPLE THREE: Paragraph I. Conditional Bequest to Child. If, but only if, (1) my child survives me and (2) my child executes, within two months of being advised by my Executor, an acknowledged instrument in writing agreeing, in consideration of the bequest hereby offered to my child, that any challenge my child wishes to make or issue my child wishes to raise relating to the validity, construction or effect of all or any portion of this document or any complaint he may have at any time against any fiduciary acting hereunder will be resolved, as hereafter provided, by mediation and arbitration as provided in paragraph II of this Article, and foregoes any opportunity to make such a challenge, raise such issue or make such complaint before any court or other governmental entity, I give and bequeath to such child the sum of One Hundred Thousand Dollars ($100,000). If my child does not survive me or fails to execute such an acknowledged instrument, this bequest will lapse.

Paragraph II. Terms of Mediation. The mediation that my child must agree to in order to receive the conditional bequest provided for in the foregoing paragraph of this instrument must be by the acknowledged instrument referred to in paragraph I of this Article in which such child agrees to participate in good faith mediation. If no agreed resolution of the dispute is reached within six months after the commencement of the mediation or such later period as the parties to the mediation agree in writing, then the challenging individual may assert his or her rights in a duly constituted judicial proceeding in the court which has primary jurisdiction over this instrument. The trustee will be entitled to use the assets of the trust to defend such action; provided, however, that if a court later determines such defense to have been unreasonable, the trustee must reimburse the trust estate for the cost of such defense, including attorneys' fees. Any fiduciary who refuses to participate in such mediation will cease to act as a fiduciary hereunder.

4. The "Bribe Gift," Using Powers of Appointment to Buy Good Behavior.

No contest clauses penalize very few behaviors and the forfeiture they promise occurs only after trial. Instead of penalizing bad behavior, the "bribe gift" rewards good behavior.

> EXAMPLE: When her relationship with her family was more harmonious, Mom gave her children shares in her closely held business. Her relationship with her children later soured and thinking her children did not "deserve" dividends, Mom began running all of her personal expenses through the business, so it would have no cash to distribute. After doing this for years, Mom learned from her estate planning attorney that her children might have a cause of action against her. Mom intended to leave very little to her children and did not want them to sue her estate after her death.

The power of appointment gift may be structured in either of two ways. In the example below, the expected troublemakers are the takers in default. Structured this way, the powerholder may reward good behavior by doing nothing. Or put differently, to punish trouble, the powerholder must take affirmative action, exercising the power of appointment to direct the appointive property to someone other than the troublemakers. Alternatively, the gift may be structured so that the troublemakers are *not* the takers in default. Structured this way, if the expected troublemakers behave, to reward them, the power holder must take affirmative action.

> EXAMPLE: On the third anniversary of the settlor's death, the trustee must distribute the appointive property as appointed by POWERHOLDER in the exercise of HIS/HER limited power of appointment in accordance with the provisions below.
>
> Appointive property. The appointive property is cash in the amount of Six Hundred Thousand Dollars ($600,000).
>
> Powerholder. The person holding this power of appointment (the "Powerholder") is POWERHOLDER, in HIS/HER individual and not fiduciary capacity. If POWERHOLDER fails to survive the settlor or becomes unable to act, the settlor gives this power of appointment to ALTERNATE POWERHOLDER. If both POWERHOLDER and

24

ALTERNATE POWERHOLDER predecease the settlor or become unable to act prior to exercising this power, this power of appointment will lapse and the trustee must distribute the appointive property to CHARITY. The powerholders have no duty to exercise this power of appointment, no duty to refrain from exercising this power of appointment and no duty to favor any particular person or entity with the exercise or non-exercise of this power of appointment. Although the takers in default of exercise may be beneficiaries of other gifts under this trust, with regard to the appointive property, the powerholders owe the takers in default no duties regarding the appointive property.

Permissible appointees. The class of permissible appointees does not include POWERHOLDER or ALTERNATIVE POWERHOLDER. The class of permissible appointees also does not include the creditors, the estate or the creditors of the estate of POWERHOLDER or ALTERNATIVE POWERHOLDER. All other appointees are permissible.

No deduction for taxes, debts or expenses. The trustee must distribute the appointive property free of any inheritance, estate, succession, or other similar taxes that are payable by reason of the settlor's death, including penalties and interest. The trustee also must distribute the appointive property free of any debts and expenses, including the following: (i) all costs, expenses of litigation, counsel fees, or other charges that the trustee incurs in connection with the determination of the amount of the death taxes, interest, or penalties referred to in the preceding sentence; and (ii) legally enforceable debts, funeral expenses, expenses of last illness, and administration and property expenses.

Method of exercise. POWERHOLDER, or ALTERNATIVE POWERHOLDER, as the case may be, must exercise this power of appointment by delivering a signed and dated writing to the trustee specifying the person, persons, entity or entities to whom or to which the trustee must distribute the appointive property and the amount of appointive property each appointee will receive. The written exercise of the power of appointment must be signed prior to the third anniversary of the settlor's death, but it may be delivered to the trustee before or after that date. Any exercise of the power of appointment will remain revocable by POWERHOLDER, or ALTERNATIVE POWERHOLDER, as the case may be, until the third anniversary of the settlor's death. If not exercised by that date, the power of appointment will terminate upon the third anniversary of the settlor's death.

25

<u>Takers in default</u>. Except as otherwise provided in this section, the trustee will distribute any non-appointed portion of the appointive property to the settlor's issue, by right of representation, such issue to be determined on the third anniversary of the settlor's death as if the settlor had died on that date.

<u>Purpose of power of appointment</u>. The settlor recognizes that in the administration of this trust and the settlor's estate, controversies may arise between the settlor's fiduciary and her children. The settlor believes that avoiding such controversies is in the best interest of the settlor's fiduciary, her family and her beneficiaries. The settlor wishes for the powerholders to use this power of appointment to reduce such controversies. This wish is precatory, not mandatory.

Unlike conditional gifts, which are analogous to no contest clauses, the power of appointment gift is authorized by statute. (Probate Code sections 600 and following.) To be effective, the value of the appointive property must be sufficiently large to motivate the desired behavior. NOTE: The gift will not qualify for the charitable deduction if the taker in default is a charity. (I.R.C. section 2055; Treas. Reg. section 20.2055-2)

5. Pecuniary Gifts.

A settlor can reduce a beneficiary's opportunity to cause trouble by giving a pecuniary amount, rather than a percentage of the residue. The settlor can further reduce the incentive of a beneficiary by expressly waiving the Probate Code section 16340 (b) right to interest on a pecuniary gift if not paid within one year of the date of death. A pecuniary beneficiary does not possess the same rights to accounts, claims of breach of fiduciary duty, and other opportunities for mischief that a percentage recipient does.

G. Tax apportionment.

Tax allocations are one of the most basic and yet most often overlooked parts of an estate plan. The current estate tax and generation-skipping transfer tax rate is 40%, but rates for these taxes were as high as 55% only a few years ago. Combined federal and state income tax rates exceed 43%. Tax liabilities could erode a significant portion of, or eliminate, a beneficiary's inheritance, particularly if the beneficiary has to pay tax for other bequests. Arguably, tax allocation clauses provide the biggest potential liability risk to a planner, because the error can cost millions.

Moreover, it is often easy for a beneficiary to show the tax effects of a particular allocation clause. The beneficiary has the check (or reduction in bequest) to prove it! The beneficiary also may have a simple task of explaining how a different allocation would have saved or reduced the overall tax burden, increased the beneficiary's inheritance, or provided greater equity among a class of beneficiaries than the actual clause.

Estate of Lurie (7th Cir. 2005) 425 F.3d 1021 provides an example of the dangers of ignoring the implications of tax apportionment clauses and electing out of equitable apportionment. In *Estate of Lurie*, the decedent established a revocable trust that provided a gift equal to the minimum amount necessary to avoid estate tax upon his death pass into trust for his wife, in a trust that qualified for the estate tax marital deduction. The residue would pass into a separate trust. The trust instrument stated that the estate tax was to be paid from the trust estate, without apportionment, to the extent the decedent's probate estate was insufficient to pay the expenses. The decedent's estate tax return claimed a marital deduction of nearly $91,700,000 for the gift to the marital trust.

The Internal Revenue Service upon audit determined that separate irrevocable trusts with assets worth in excess of $40,000,000 were includible in the decedent's estate for estate tax purposes. The probate estate was insufficient to pay the resulting estate tax, meaning the decedent's revocable trust estate had to pay the estate tax. Because the residue of that trust was insufficient to pay the estate tax, the gift to the marital trust had to pay the estate tax. The reduction in the marital gift increased the estate tax due, which lead to a decrease in the marital deduction. The net tax due after considering this interrelated calculation was over $12,200,000. Had the tax been payable from the separate trusts, the estate tax savings could have exceeded millions of dollars.

California statutes provide an equitable proration statute for estate tax payments, requiring each beneficiary who receives a taxable bequest to bear a proportional share of the estate tax liability. *See* Cal. Prob. Code § 20100, et seq. A key exception to this pro rata allocation of estate tax is that upon the death of a surviving spouse, property that qualified for a marital deduction under Internal Revenue Code section 2056(b)(7), so-called "QTIP" property, is subject to tax at the top marginal rates. *See generally* I.R.C. § 2207A; Prob. Code § 20110(b)(2). This default rule may be overridden by the decedent in a written instrument disposing of the decedent's property, such as a will trust. *See* Prob. Code § 20110(b)(1).

Many plans take "advantage" of the option out of the default rules and override state law. A decedent's will or revocable trust, or a couple's joint trust, may provide that *all* estate tax is paid by the estate. That allocation may have unintended consequences.

The planner may envision that all the decedent's or couple's assets will pass under those instruments, which may not be the case. Retirement plans, insurance policies, bank accounts, and other assets may pass by contract or beneficiary designation, and the liabilities on those assets may be significant. Shifting the tax burden to the probate or trust estate beneficiaries may deplete their inheritance and provide an unanticipated windfall to the non-probate or trust beneficiaries.

Many individuals' most valuable assets are their retirement plans and insurance policies. If the beneficiaries of those assets are different than the Will or trust beneficiaries, one set of beneficiaries could benefit over the other beneficiaries. While that result may be consistent with the decedent's intent, that result may also arise from a planner's failure to consider the outside assets.

Tax allocations also can have a compounding effect if the marital or charitable bequest has to pay the tax. The estate tax marital or charitable deduction is dependent on the assets passing outright or in trust for the spouse or charity, as the case may be. If that bequest is reduced because of tax liabilities, the deduction is reduced as well. The constant reduction of the deduction due to increase tax creates an interrelated tax that would increase the tax in a significant matter. A recent case from Illinois highlights this danger. *Lurie v. Commissioner* (7th Cir. 2005) 425 F. 3d 1021. As that court decision stated in its opening line, "This case is an example of how the best laid plans of mice and men can often go awry."

An estate must have sufficient liquid assets to pay all taxes, expenses, and allowed debts in full. If the testamentary instrument is to include pecuniary devises, the estate must also have sufficient cash to satisfy those devises. If the estate does not have enough cash to pay all of these obligations, it will be necessary for the executor to sell estate assets to raise cash.

Before drafting any testamentary instrument provision relating to the payment of taxes, expenses, or debts, the attorney and the testator should estimate the estate's cash needs and devise some plan for meeting them. If liquidity may be a problem, life insurance should be seriously considered as a means to satisfy the anticipated cash expenses of the estate. If it is contemplated that property will have to be sold, the plan should take that sale into consideration, and the testamentary instrument should not make special provisions for disposition of the property without sale. In some cases, it may be necessary to plan to raise cash through the sale of business assets. It should be borne in mind, however, that the sale of business assets out of probate rarely brings the best price. Again, the purchase of enough life insurance to cover any anticipated expenses is often the best answer in this situation.

1.   Equitable Proration

a.   Statutory Rule

Rules relating to the proration of estate taxes are set forth in Probate Code §§ 20100-20125. These rules govern the proration of federal and California estate taxes, including interest and penalties on deficiencies. Proration rules relating to generation-skipping transfer taxes are set forth in Probate Code §§ 20200-20225.

The general rule is that estate and generation-skipping transfer taxes must be equitably prorated among the persons interested in the estate. Except as specifically noted in the statute, equitable proration is achieved when taxes are prorated in the proportion that the value of the property received by each person interested in the estate bears to the total value of all property received by all persons interested in the estate. Generally, in the proration of estate tax, estimated future income tax should not be taken into account. *Klein v. Hughes* (2005) 133 Cal.App.4th 121.

The statutory rule requiring equitable proration reflects the public policy that, in the absence of a specific contrary direction from the testator, the burden of estate taxes should be allocated proportionately among the beneficiaries of the estate. *Estate of McManus* (1983) 140 Cal.App.3d 62, 67.

b.   Exceptions to Statutory Rule

The statutory rule of equitable proration is subject to exceptions. First, the statutory rule does not apply when federal law directs otherwise. For example, the Internal Revenue Code provides that the tax on qualified terminable interest property (QTIP) will be at the highest incremental bracket, with the result that other property in the estate is taxed at lower brackets. In this situation, the California proration rule must yield to the federal rule, and the higher tax attributable to the QTIP property should be collected from that property. Similarly, if real property used for farming or business purposes is specially valued under the provisions of I.R.C. § 2032A, the reduction in taxes must be allocated entirely to the person who receives the specially valued property; and, if the property is not used for farming or business purposes for at least 10 years, any additional tax imposed under I.R.C. § 2032A must be imposed on the same person.

Second, the statutory rule does not apply when there are more specific proration rules applicable to income interests in trusts, estates for years, estates for life, and other income interests, or to specially valued farm and business property. If, for example, a trust is created or other provision is made whereby a person is given an income interest, an estate for years, an estate for life, or any other temporary interest in property, the tax on both the temporary interest and the other interests in the property (including remainder interests) must be charged against the corpus of the property, without apportionment between the temporary and other interests.

Third, the statutory rule does not apply if the will or a trust instrument directs that particular property be applied to the satisfaction of a tax or that a tax be prorated in a specific manner. *See Hoover v. Hartman* (1982) 136 Cal.App.3d 1019.

c. Allowances for Credits, Exemptions, and Deductions.

The statutory rules specifically require that "allowances" be made for credits, exemptions, and deductions when taxes are prorated. This requirement means that to the extent any property is subject to a credit, exemption, or deduction, that property is excluded from proration. Thus, the tax liability of the estate will be prorated only against property that is actually being taxed.

In making a proration of the federal estate tax, the statutory rules require that allowances be made for credits allowed for foreign death taxes in determining the federal tax payable and for exemptions and deductions allowed for the purpose of determining the taxable estate. Under this rule, if part of the estate qualifies for the marital deduction or the charitable deduction, that part would not be required to contribute to the payment of estate taxes. *Estate of Silveira* (1983) 149 Cal.App.3d 604, 611.

California's estate tax is entirely dependent upon the federal credit for death taxes paid to a state. Because the federal credit was eliminated effective January 1, 2005, California has had no effective estate tax since then.

d. Right of Reimbursement.

The executor has a duty to recover that portion of the taxes attributable to property that does not come into his or her possession from the persons chargeable with the payment of those taxes under the statutory rules of proration. If, for example, there are assets in an inter vivos trust that are subject to taxation, the executor has a duty to recover the taxes attributable to those assets. However, if the executor cannot collect from any person, the amount not recoverable must be equitably prorated among the other persons interested in the estate who are subject to proration. Any person charged with or required to pay more than his or her proportional share of the taxes because another person has not paid his or her proportional share has a right of reimbursement against the other person. The right of reimbursement can be enforced directly against the person who did not pay his or her proportional share or, in the discretion of the personal representative, it may be enforced indirectly through the personal representative. Either the personal representative or the person who has the right of reimbursement may bring judicial proceedings to compel the reimbursement.

2. Drafting Provisions for Payment of Taxes

a. In General

The general rule of equitable proration of taxes does not apply if the will or a trust instrument directs that particular property be applied to the satisfaction of a tax or that a tax be prorated in a specific manner. Probate Code § 20110(b)(1) specifically provides that the general rule of equitable proration does not apply to the extent the decedent in a written inter vivos or testamentary instrument disposing of property specifically directs that the property be applied to the satisfaction of an estate tax or that an estate tax be prorated to the property in the manner provided in the instrument. Before the adoption of Probate Code § 20110(b)(1), the California Supreme Court held in *Estate of Armstrong* (1961) 56 Cal.2d 796 that, absent a "clear and unambiguous direction" by the decedent of an intention to the contrary, the general rule of equitable proration applies so that the tax burden is equitably allocated among those who are benefitted. In *Estate of Wathen* (1997) 56 Cal.App.4th 48 the court of appeal was asked to apply *Estate of Armstrong* to an ambiguous tax proration clause contained in a will that "poured over" the decedent's property to an inter vivos trust. Although it was clear the will was intended to give directions with respect to tax proration, it was not clear how the directions were intended to apply. One of the beneficiaries under the trust argued that since the proration directions were not clear and unambiguous, *Estate of Armstrong* required the court to apply the general rule of equitable proration and prohibited it from considering extrinsic evidence on the question. The trial court disagreed and admitted extrinsic evidence that the testator-settlor had intended by the will to require all the death taxes to be paid out of the residue of the trust.

The court of appeal agreed with the trial court, holding that *Estate of Armstrong* required the application of the general rule of equitable proration only when the dispositive instrument failed altogether to refer to tax proration. When the existence of a tax proration clause is clear but its terms are ambiguous, it is proper to consider extrinsic evidence to determine the decedent's intentions with respect to proration.

The objecting beneficiary in *Estate of Wathen* offered a second objection to the trial court's ruling on proration. Since the proration clause was in the will and not in the inter vivos trust instrument, the beneficiary argued that the provision had no application to the trust assets. Again the court of appeal disagreed, pointing out that the will and the inter vivos trust instruments were executed on the same day and as part of an "integrated testamentary plan" intended to accomplish the same purpose. Accordingly, both documents had to be considered to determine whether the decedent had expressed a clear direction against statutory proration. When there is an "integrated testamentary plan" consisting of a will and a trust, it is sufficient if the tax proration directions are contained in either document; there is no requirement that they be contained in both.

In many cases, the statutory rule of equitable proration will suit the client's intentions quite well, and it will not be necessary to include a provision varying it. If the client's estate is so small that there is no or only a small likelihood of estate taxes being due, it will rarely be necessary to address the question of proration. However, both the client and the attorney should remember that circumstances may quickly change. An unanticipated inheritance, for example, could increase the client's estate and suddenly make the proration of estate taxes a real rather than a merely theoretical concern.

A will provision dealing with the payment of taxes will not be necessary if all of the testator's assets will pass to one person (such as the testator's spouse). In other cases, it will often be sufficient merely to adopt the statutory proration scheme. Even when assets are to pass to several persons who do not stand in the same relationship to the testator, proration pursuant to the statutory rules will be desirable in many cases, since proration will simply require that each devisee or beneficiary pay his or her proportional share of the total taxes. Finally, many clients may be satisfied with the statutory proration scheme simply because it is easier to understand then other proration plans.

Adoption of the statutory proration scheme can be accomplished either by an express will provision to that effect or simply by saying nothing about tax apportionment in the will. In the interest of drafting clear and complete testamentary instruments that leave nothing to chance, the inclusion of an express provision is probably preferable.

b. Taxes to Which Provision Will Apply

Will provisions respecting the payment of taxes are commonly made applicable to "death taxes." To eliminate any confusion over what is included within that term, it is desirable to define "death taxes" in the will itself.

Death taxes generally include any taxes that are payable by reason of the testator's death and may include state inheritance taxes as well as state and federal estate taxes. Although California no longer imposes an inheritance tax, other states do, and the estate of a California decedent may be subject to such an inheritance tax if it includes property located in another state. If the estate includes property located outside the United States, the death taxes may also include estate or inheritance taxes imposed by a foreign nation.

Before enactment of the Tax Reform Act of 1986, the term "death taxes" was not commonly understood to include generation-skipping transfer taxes. The generation-skipping transfer tax enacted in 1986 is still distinct from the federal estate tax, but generation-skipping transfers that are classified as "direct skips" (such as outright transfers to grandchildren, or transfers to trusts of which all of the beneficiaries are grandchildren) under the current version of the tax may now be taxed at the same time as the testator's estate. In the case of a direct skip from an estate, the executor is liable for the tax and required to file the return. The executor may also be liable for any direct skip occurring at death if the property involved is held in a trust and the total value of the property involved in direct skips with respect to the trust is less than $250,000. Accordingly, some will provisions relating to the payment of death taxes are now drafted so as to include direct skips. A will provision may be made to apply to a direct skip by providing that it includes all death taxes that may be payable by reason of the testator's death but excludes any tax on a generation-skipping transfer that does not qualify as a direct skip. Such a provision will not apply to generation-skipping transfers that qualify as taxable terminations or taxable distributions.

An additional estate tax may be imposed on certain farm or business property specially valued under I.R.C. § 2032A if the property is not used for farming or business purposes for at least ten years after the testator's death. Any additional estate tax due under I.R.C. § 2032A will become due and payable six months after the date the qualified heir disposes of the property or ceases to use it for the qualified use. The qualified heir (or the qualified property), and not the testator's estate, will be liable for payment of any additional tax under I.R.C. § 2032A. Most will provisions respecting the payment of death taxes specifically exclude any additional tax due under I.R.C. § 2032A from their purview, thus leaving the additional tax to be collected from the qualified heir (or the qualified property) as provided in the Internal Revenue Code.

c.   Protecting Marital and Charitable Deductions

A will provision directing that taxes be paid in a certain way or out of a particular fund or property should be drafted with special care if any part of the testator's estate is designed to qualify for the marital deduction or the charitable deduction. The statutory rules for equitable proration require that allowances be made for deductions in prorating the federal estate tax. However, the statutory rules do not apply if the will (or trust instrument) directs that estate taxes be prorated to property in a specific manner.

A will provision requiring the residue of the testator's estate to bear the full burden of the death taxes will almost always be inappropriate if any part of the residue is designed to qualify for the marital or charitable deductions. If the taxes are satisfied entirely out of the residue, the net value of the property passing to the surviving spouse will be reduced, as will the value of the deduction for that property. A will provision requiring the residue to bear the full burden of paying the taxes will also be inappropriate if one or more of the residuary devisees is a charity. Requiring property devised to a charitable devisee to contribute to the payment of taxes will reduce the value of the charitable devise and increase the total taxes on the estate.

Even when all or part of the residue is designed to qualify for the marital deduction or the charitable deduction, a will provision requiring that death taxes be paid out of the residue of the estate may be used if the testator fully understands the tax implications of the provision and, despite those implications, elects to include the provision in the will. There are certain limited circumstances under which a testator may wish to adopt this approach. If, for example, the bulk of the estate is to pass by residuary devise and the testator wishes to make a few tax-free devises of small or modest value to other devisees, the will may require that the death taxes be paid out of the residue, even though the residue is devised to the testator's spouse or to a qualifying charitable organization. If the resulting increased tax burden on the estate is minimal in comparison to the value of the residuary estate, or at least acceptable to the testator, this approach may be used. When these gifts are substantial, however, the attorney should advise the client, before including any such provision in the will, that requiring assets that qualify for the marital deduction or the charitable deduction to pay a portion of the death taxes will increase the overall tax burden on the estate and reduce the net benefits to the marital or charitable devisees. The attorney's advice should be set forth in writing in a letter to the client to guard against the possibility that some person interested in the estate may later charge that the provision was negligently drafted and had the effect of diminishing the value of the residue and increasing the overall tax burden on the estate. If the charitable deduction is important to the testator's overall estate plan, the will should expressly adopt the statutory scheme or require proration from property that does not qualify for the charitable deduction.

In calculating the probable amount of the marital or charitable deduction that will actually be available to the estate, the attorney should bear in mind that the statutory proration rules apply only to federal estate taxes. Liability of the estate for other debts and expenses of administration is governed by the statutory rules of abatement. These rules do not provide for equitable proration, but instead set out a specific order of abatement. The statutory rules governing abatement make no allowances for property covered by the marital or charitable deduction, and so the amount of these devises (and, therefore the available deduction) may end up being reduced, unless the will provides otherwise.

d.   Taxes on QTIP Property.

If the testator's estate will include any QTIP property, special considerations should be given to drafting any will provision governing payment of death taxes. QTIP property is property that was deducted from the gross estate of the first spouse to die under I.R.C. § 2056(b)(7) and that must be included in the estate of the surviving spouse under I.R.C. § 2044(b)(1)(A). When QTIP property is included in the estate of the surviving spouse, the statutes provide that it is to be taxed at the highest incremental rate. However, the testator may vary the statutory rule by a direction in the will (or in a trust instrument).

When QTIP property is taxed at the highest incremental rate, the taxes on other property are reduced. Whether the will should vary the statutory rule taxing QTIP property at the highest incremental rate will depend on the circumstances. In the ordinary case in which the testator's property (both QTIP property and other property) is simply lumped together and divided up among children or other relatives, it is unnecessary to vary the statutory rule because each share will have the same proportion of QTIP and non-QTIP property and therefore will bear a proportionate share of the tax burden. However, if some beneficiaries receive QTIP property and others receive non-QTIP property, or if some receive a higher proportion of QTIP property than others, shares having more QTIP property will be taxed at a higher rate than shares with more non-QTIP property. In this situation, it may be desirable to provide for equitable proration to equalize the tax burden on each share. Although clients are often indifferent on this point, the attorney should nevertheless point it out in appropriate situations.

e.   Taxes on Community Property Interest in Spouse's Qualified Plan Benefits.

Before 1986, the community property interest of a deceased spouse in the surviving spouse's qualified retirement plan was not subject to estate tax in the estate of the deceased spouse. By repealing I.R.C. § 2039(c), the Tax Reform Act of 1986 reversed this rule, thereby causing the community property interest to be included in the nonparticipant spouse's estate. It is not clear whether this interest qualifies for the marital deduction, since an interest will generally qualify for the marital deduction only if it "passes or has passed" from the deceased spouse to the surviving spouse. If the interest qualifies for the marital deduction, then no estate tax problems will arise. If it does not qualify for the deduction, however, the surviving (participant) spouse could be faced with the prospect of paying substantial estate taxes on his or her own retirement benefits. To plan for this eventuality, any will provision respecting the payment of estate taxes should clearly designate the source of those taxes.

f.   Payment From Residue of Estate.

In former times, will provisions respecting the payment of estate taxes often directed that the taxes be paid out of the residue of the testator's estate. A provision requiring that all of the death taxes in the testator's estate be satisfied out of the residue may be appropriate if the will makes a few small devises to friends or distant relatives and leaves the residue of the estate to members of the testator's immediate family. Recognizing that the residuary devisees will receive most of the estate and wishing the recipients of the small devises to receive those devises free of any obligation to contribute to the payment of death taxes, the testator may wish to require that all of the taxes be paid out of the residue.

A provision requiring the residue to bear the full burden of the taxes should be included in the will only if the full ramifications of the provision are clearly understood. First, the testator should be satisfied that the residue will be large enough to bear the full burden of the taxes without unduly impairing the interests of the residuary devisees. Since residuary devisees are often the principal beneficiaries of the testator's bounty, the testator should carefully estimate the total tax burden on the estate and the probable value of the residue before deciding to burden the residue with the payment of all of the taxes. Obviously, the will should not require the residue to bear the full burden of the taxes if the taxes are expected to exceed the value of the residue. The testator should be reminded that the taxable estate may include assets passing outside the probate estate as well as within it. Assets held in joint tenancies, assets disposed of through inter vivos trusts, and the proceeds of life insurance policies may all be taxable for estate tax purposes. The "residue" will consist only of the residue of the testator's probate estate (assets subject to administration in the testator's estate that are not disposed of by specific, general, or demonstrative devises).

Liquidity considerations should play an important part in any plan for the payment of taxes. If the residue is to bear the full burden of the death taxes, the testator should be sure that the residue will include enough cash to discharge all of the taxes (and all of the expenses and debts); or the residue should include assets that can readily be sold to raise sufficient cash. If the testator's cash and readily saleable assets are to be disposed of through non-residuary devises, a provision requiring that all of the taxes be paid out of the residue would seriously disrupt the testator's dispositive plan by forcing the sale of assets that are not readily saleable.

A will provision requiring the residue to bear the full burden of the death taxes will nearly always be inappropriate if any part of the residue is designed to qualify for the marital deduction or the charitable deduction. If the taxes are satisfied entirely out of the residue, the value of the residuary devise will be reduced, the value of the deductions will be diminished, and the overall tax burden on the estate will be increased.

To protect any marital or charitable deduction that may be available in the testator's estate, a will provision directing that death taxes be paid out of the residue may specify that the taxes be paid only from nondeductible assets of the residue. Residuary assets are generally deductible if they pass to charitable devisees or the testator's spouse and nondeductible if they pass to other devisees.

g. Payment of Taxes from Property in Inter Vivos Trust

A will provision requiring that all death taxes be paid out of the assets of an inter vivos trust established by the testator may be appropriate if the bulk of the testator's assets are to be transferred to the trust and the probate estate is to consist of assets of small or merely nominal value. Since planning for liquidity must play a part in any will provision respecting the payment of taxes, requiring an inter vivos trust to bear the full burden of the taxes may make sense when the trust will comprise the bulk of the testator's taxable assets. Such a provision will not make sense, however, if the trust assets are small, or if subjecting those assets to the obligation of paying the taxes would frustrate the purpose of the trust.

If any part of the trust assets are designed to qualify for the marital deduction, a will provision requiring the payment of the taxes out of the assets of the trust may compromise the deduction and increase the overall tax burden on the estate. Similarly, if charitable beneficiaries are to receive assets from the trust, requiring those assets to pay (or to contribute to the payment of the taxes will have the effect of reducing the charitable deduction and increasing the tax burden on the estate. If the testator wishes to preserve the marital deduction or the charitable deduction, it will ordinarily be better not to try to vary the statutory scheme for equitable proration. Under the statutory scheme, property that can be deducted from the gross estate for federal estate tax purposes is not required to contribute to the payment of any death taxes. However, the attorney should bear in mind that the statutory proration rules apply only to federal estate taxes. Liability of the estate for other debts and expenses of administration is governed by the statutory rules of abatement. These rules do not provide for equitable proration, but instead set out a specific order of abatement.

If the settlor's will provides that all taxes are to be paid from the probate estate, but the trust contains a substantial amount of the total estate, the probate estate may be consumed by an unexpectedly larger amount of taxes than anticipated. The result might be that gifts from the probate estate would have to be reduced to pay the taxes, to the detriment of the devisees. This result could be particularly unfair of the devisees under the will are different persons than the beneficiaries of the trust. Another possibility is that the probate estate may contain insufficient assets to pay the taxes. In this situation, an unfair result could occur of the executor had no recourse against the trustee of the trust, especially if the trust instrument does not impose any duty on the trustee. If the trust instrument does not contain such a direction, the trustee may even have a duty to resist any liability for the estate tax burden. It is usually preferable, therefore, to provide that each person or entity receiving property included in the gross estate bear its pro rata share of the tax attributable to the assets held by that person or entity. If the bulk of the assets are in the trust, this language would compel the trustee to pay a fair share of the taxes.

When a will provision is used to require that death taxes be paid out of the assets of an inter vivos trust, it is important to coordinate the provisions of the will and the trust instrument. Careful choice of words and phrases will serve to carry out the testator's interest and avoid potentially costly and time-consuming uncertainties or ambiguities. When ambiguities or conflicts between the will and a trust instrument raise a question as to whether the testator-settlor intended to adopt statutory proration or some other scheme, statutory proration will generally prevail on the basis of public policy.

3. Exemption for Particular Devise

The testator may wish a particular devisee to receive his or her devise free of the obligation to contribute to the payment of any death taxes. A devise of this kind may be appropriate if the devise is relatively small in relation to the total value of the estate. In such a case, the testator may intend that the devisee receive a specified asset (for example, a family heirloom or a work of art) or a specified sum of money without deduction for taxes.

A will provision stating that a devisee is to be free of the obligation to contribute to the payment of taxes will be appropriate only when the testator is satisfied that other assets of the estate are able to bear the full burden of the death taxes. Before any such provision is included in a will, the testator and the attorney should estimate the total tax burden on the estate, the probable value of the property that is to bear the burden of paying the taxes, and the cash or readily saleable assets that will be available for payment. A will provision varying the statutory rules of equitable proration should be included in a will only when the testator and the attorney are satisfied that the provision will not unduly interfere with the testator's overall dispositive plan.

4. Taxes on Property Devised by Codicil

Any scheme the testator selects for payment of taxes is necessarily subject to later change. While intentional changes are rarely the source of difficulty, unintended changes may be. After executing the will, for example, the testator may execute a codicil. The codicil may devise property in such a way that it is unclear whether the scheme for payment of taxes prescribed in the will is or is not intended to cover the devise in the codicil. In *Estate of Steele* (1980) 113 Cal.App.3d 106 the testator executed a formal witnessed will in 1962 and a holographic codicil in 1969. The formal will required that all estate taxes be equitably prorated among the "legatees, devisees, trustees, donees, persons, or beneficiaries sharing my gross taxable estate" as provided by law. The holographic codicil devised the sum of $12,000 a year to a long-time nurse and companion. The court held that the devise of $12,000 a year to the nurse and companion was not subject to the equitable proration scheme set forth in the formal will. It noted that the codicil was executed seven years after the will and pointed to evidence indicating that the testator intended the nurse-companion to receive the full sum of $12,000 per year without deduction for taxes.

A will may anticipate the execution of codicils and include a proration provision specifically including any property devised by codicil in the proration scheme set forth in the will. It may be unwise to do so, however. If such a provision is enforceable, and is not revoked by the codicil or by a subsequent will, it would tie the testator's hands in advance. If it is unsuccessful, it will be a source of dispute among the devisees, and resolution of the dispute may require costly and time-consuming judicial proceedings. In most cases, it will be preferable to deal with the problem of prorating taxes on property devised by codicil if and when a codicil is executed. Whenever possible, every testator should be warned about the dangers of holographic codicils and urged to contact the attorney whenever a change is called for in the will or other estate planning documents.

H.   Amendments that Discourage Contests.

1.   Multiple Amendments, Over Time.

The settlor who expects a beneficiary to contest the trust may amend and restate the trust repeatedly, thereby making it considerably more difficult to invalidate the settlor's plan. Under the doctrine of dependent relative revocation, a will that is revoked by a later will in the belief that the later will is effective remains in effect to the extent that the later will is invalid. (*See Estate of Anderson* (1997) 56 Cal.App.4th 235; *Estate of Cuneo* (1963) 60 Cal.2d 196; *Estate of Salmonski* (1951) 38 Cal.2d 199; *Estate of Robertson* (1968) 266 Cal.App.2d 866.) By analogy, a trust amendment remains in effect to the extent subsequent amendments are invalidated. Additionally, if an amendment were invalidated, its revocation clause would be invalid as well. Using this strategy, several months or weeks after signing the trust instrument that might draw a contest, the settlor would sign another instrument, identical to the prior one.

2. Contestant's Best Gift Is Most Recent.

An even better strategy is to increase the benefit to the would-be contestant, in each successive instrument. For example, the first trust instrument might give the would-be contestant nothing. The first amendment, signed a month or so later, might give the would-be contestant $100,000 and every few months, the settlor might amend the trust to increase the gift by a small amount.

If the settlor anticipates that the would-be contestant might accuse a residual beneficiary of undue influence, this strategy precludes such a challenge. Because each successive gift to the would-be contestant necessarily reduces the residue, the contestant could not prove undue benefit, an element of an undue-benefit challenge.

3. Caregiver's Best Gift Was the First Gift

If the settlor wishes to protect a gift to a caregiver and the gift is larger than the safe-harbor gift described in Probate Code section 21382(e) ($5,000 in most circumstances), the settlor must get a certificate of independent review. (Probate Code section 21384.) Additionally, the settlor might want to use the following strategy. The settlor may amend the instrument in which the gift is made, reducing the amount of the gift in each amendment. Again, because an element of undue influence is the undue benefit the influencer obtains, this strategy would prevent a successful challenge on the grounds of undue influence.

IV. Other Pre-Death Strategies.

A. Disclosure of the estate plan to affected persons.

One tool for attorneys to consider as a means of discouraging litigation is for the testator to share their estate plan with family members while the testator is alive. This strategy runs counter to the typical confidentiality of estate plans until after the death of the testator, but may be useful in appropriate circumstances. Disclosure of the estate plan can have both legal and non-legal consequences that can limit litigation in the future. An otherwise disgruntled child may be less likely to litigate the validity of a trust or amendment when the child was told directly by their parent the instrument represented the parent's true expression of their final wishes. And, an oft-criticized decision may limit a prospective contestant's ability to contest a trust instrument after the settlor's death when the would-be contestant knew of the instrument and the circumstances supporting the contest during the settlor's lifetime. See *Drake v. Pinkham* (2013) 217 Cal.App.4th 400 (suggesting that the equitable doctrine of laches may preclude a beneficiary who had knowledge during the settlor's lifetime of a trust amendment from challenging that amendment after the settlor's death).

B. Pre-death Section 17200 petition.

Among other reasons, a settlor-beneficiary may petition the court to determine the existence of a trust, to determine "the existence or nonexistence of any immunity, power, privilege, duty or, right," to determine "the validity of a trust provision," and for an order, "[a]scertaining beneficiaries and determining to whom property shall pass or be delivered upon final or partial termination of the trust." (Prob. Code § 17200, subds. (a), (b)(2), (b)(3), (b)(4).) A settlor-beneficiary who fears that their trust instrument might be challenged by a disgruntled beneficiary or family member after the settlor's death may essentially force the litigation to occur during the settlor's lifetime by petitioning the court for an order determining the existence of the trust or confirming its validity. An order entered on such a petition after proper notice should protect the trust instrument from a later challenge under the doctrines of res judicata and collateral estoppel.

This strategy is not for everyone. When establishing a trust or making a trust amendment that is expected to be controversial after the settlor dies, many settlors express some version of the "I won't be here anyway" sentiment. For those who are inclined toward this view, voluntarily litigating the validity of their own estate plan will be anathema. However, for clients who are willing to endure potentially bitter litigation during their lifetime in order to minimize future disputes, filing a court petition pursuant to section 17200 can be a valuable tool. First, it makes the settlor available to testify personally regarding their wishes, which can be compelling. Also, the prospect of sitting in the courtroom with the settlor whose trust is being challenged (often the parent of the unhappy beneficiary) may be enough to discourage parties that might otherwise contest from doing so.

For a more thorough discussion of this strategy, see Verriere, Andrew R., "Don't Put Off to Tomorrow What You Can Do Today – Avoiding Post-Death Contests Through Inter Vivos Petitions, *California Trusts and Estates Quarterly*, Vol. 28, Issue 2.)

C. Substituted judgment.

The conservatorship laws establish a framework for substituted judgment petitions: petitions for the court to authorize or direct a conservator to take certain actions on behalf of conservatees. (Prob. Code, §§ 2580-2586.) Among other things, substituted judgment petitions may be used to provide for inter vivos gifts, to create wills, and to make revocable or irrevocable trusts. (Prob. Code, § 2580, subd. (b).)

41

A substituted judgment petition may be filed by, "[t]he conservator or other interested person." (Prob. Code, § 2580.) If the conservatee has capacity to file a substituted judgment position, the conservatee may do so themselves. This strategy has similarities to the pre-death Section 17200 petition discussed above, and perhaps avoids some of the skepticism that some courts have toward pre-death petitions to confirm the validity of revocable trusts. A successful substituted judgment petition results in a court order directing the conservator to enter into the subject estate planning transaction, insulating the transaction from subsequent attack.

4

Premarital Estate Planning & Divorce Awareness Among Estate Planners

Peter M. Walzer, Esq.
Kimberly R. Willoughby, Esq.

Premarital Estate Planning & Divorce Awareness Among Estate Planners

Peter M. Walzer, Esq.
Kimberly R. Willoughby, Esq.

Premarital Agreement Drafting

2

Estate Planning Clauses That Anticipate Divorce

Clients do not always follow the terms of prenup regarding estate planning.

Require amendment to prenup if planning inconsistent with prenup.

Require amendment to prenup if irrevocable trusts are created by the parties during marriage.

Discuss with family lawyer when create irrevocable or joint revocable trust during marriage.

3

Estate Planning Clauses That Anticipate Divorce

- Draft for the ability to transfer assets to accomplish planning and gifting during divorce with ATROs.

- Draft for changing life insurance beneficiaries with ATROs.

- Prenups often terminate rights to inherit if a petition for dissolution is filed. Should this apply only to parties and not 3rd parties? (Guardians, conservators, agents under POAs).

4

Estate Planning Clauses That Anticipate Divorce

- Grey divorce – It's really about adult children and their inheritance.
- Draft so that a spouse does not lose both sets of rights (divorce rights and death rights) if the other spouse dies during a divorce action.

- Draft so that each party waives the right to discovery of value of the assets at time of marriage. (untested in CA).
- Prevents challenging adequacy of disclosures.
- Require written agreement with trustee waiving discovery and prohibiting joinder. Pay consideration for waiver.
- Draft knowing certain descendants may challenge the agreement.

Drafting Tips

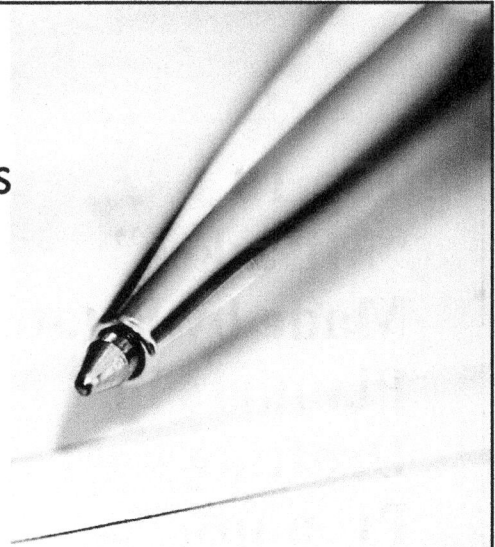

Top 10 "Mistakes" Made by Estate Planners in Drafting Prenups

Waiving spousal support outright (liberal caps on amount with COLA more likely to survive).

Tailoring agreement to death and not divorce.

Not understanding that the agreement may be litigated in another state or that the choice of law clause may not be enforced.

Not addressing dispute resolution.

7

Top 10 "Mistakes" Made by Estate Planners in Drafting Prenups

Not explaining the agreement adequately to the client and advising them of possibility it will not be enforced.

Drafting terms that require the parties to keep track of financial transactions during marriage.

Not adequately protecting separate property.

Not addressing loan proceeds in states where intent of the lender determines character of property.

8

Top 10 "Mistakes" Made by Estate Planners in Drafting Prenups

Making the agreement too complex for the average client to interpret.

Drafting an agreement with too many payments or tasks to complete.

Not addressing the basics of a divorce: temporary support and moving out of the home.

Not insisting that the other party be represented by counsel.

Providing an inadequate disclosure or waiving disclosure (even if permitted by law).

9

Irrevocable Trusts Created and Funded During Marriage: *Ethics*

- Can you represent both parties, if that is what is being requested?
- California Rules of Professional Conduct:
  - 1.4 Communication With Clients
  - 1.6 Confidential Information of Client
  - 1.7 Conflict of Interest: Current Clients
  - 1.9 Duties to Former Clients
  - 1.16 Declining or Terminating Representation

10

Irrevocable Trusts Created and Funded During Marriage: *Covering Yourself*

- Draft clear Engagement Letters.
- Set forth scope of representation and potential conflicts.
- ACTEC Examples of Engagement Letters:
  www.actec.org/assets/1/6/ACTEC_201 7_Engagement_Letters.pdf?hssc=1

11

Irrevocable Trusts Created and Funded During Marriage: *Tips*

- How to be certain both parties are truly informed and consenting?
  - Speak to both parties at the beginning of the representation.
  - Do not assume that emails with a "signature" of both parties is from both parties or was even seen by both parties. Find a work around when the parties use the same email address.
  - Do not assume agreement by both parties unless you hear it directly from both parties.

12

Irrevocable Trusts Created and Funded During Marriage: *The Divorce*

- What do spouses say in the divorce?
  - I never saw that document.
  - He/she always signs docs for me.
  - He/she just shoves the docs under my nose and demands I sign.
  - He/she never gave me a chance to review it.
  - He/she always handled it.
  - I never knew that would be the result.

13

How to Talk to Clients about Divorce

- Consider developing a written, standard advisement for your clients. It might include:
  - Characterization of assets as a result of planning.
  - Control of assets as a result of planning, during marriage and during a divorce.
  - Fiduciary designations and any changes if there is a divorce.
  - Beneficiary designations and any changes if there is a divorce.

14

- The advisement might also include:
  - Ability to unwind planning if there is a divorce, and the (tax) consequences of doing so.
  - Potential effect of planning on potential new spouses/families.
  - Planned use of lifetime exemption amount.
  - Access to property for a new family.

15

Advising Clients Regarding Divorce

Family lawyers often hear, "no one told me that is what would happen if we divorced," or "that is not how my estate planner described the effect of divorce."

Have a family lawyer that can help advise you, because the divorce process and outcomes are driven not just by the statutes.

16

Premarital and Postmarital Agreements

- Before you do your planning, review the premarital agreement:
  - Are there estate planning provisions in the agreement?
  - Are they consistent with the estate plan?
  - Is there an abandonment argument if no consistency?
  - Is a marital agreement required to implement the estate plan?
  - Do you amend the premarital agreement?
- Risks of postmarital agreements.

17

Irrevocable Trusts and Divorce

- Family lawyers love to attack trusts in divorce.
- Keep in mind:
  - Trusts may be interpreted under another state's law.
  - Clients may move to a non community property state.
  - In divorce, the law regarding how to treat a beneficial interest in trust for divorce purposes is NOT trust law.

18

Here are some of the arguments

Irrevocable Trusts and Family Law – What the Family Law Lawyers Say

- Trust interests *are* property for divorce purposes.

- Trust interests *are not* property for divorce purposes.

- A right to income *is* a property interest.

- A right to income *is not* a property interest.

- The trustee *must* be joined in the divorce action.

- The trustee *need not* be joined in the divorce action.

- The trustee *cannot* be joined in a divorce action.

Irrevocable Trusts and Family Law - What the Family Law Lawyers Say

Agreements regarding the trust assets have been made already, and the court cannot change it.

Trust agreements have nothing to do with divorce.

"Irrevocable" means "irrevocable."
There is no such thing as "irrevocable" anymore.

The trust agreement is a sham.

The only interests that need be considered are the interests of the parties before the divorce court.

21

SLATS

- Be vigilant and discuss the potential for divorce.
- Be sure to consider grantor trust/income taxes if there is a divorce, and potential work arounds.
- Consider whether the parties would *want* to preserve a SLAT if there is a divorce.
- Consider the assets used to fund a SLAT.
- Consider the identity of the trustees.
- If retained, consider limiting any substitution powers if there is a divorce.

22

ILITS

- Discuss the potential for a divorce.
- It is very possible that parties will want to keep ILITs in place even if there is a divorce.
- Discuss premium payments if there is a divorce.
- Discuss trustees if there is a divorce.

23

DAPTS

- Effective method of protecting assets.
- Paucity of law interpreting them.
- No requirement that they be disclosed at time of prenuptial agreement signing.
- What if they are created during marriage? Breach of fiduciary duty.
- Advise client of risks of DAPT if there is a divorce.
- Income available to beneficiary may be considered for support.

24

Foundations, DAFs and Inter Vivos Planning for Children

- Talk to clients about how a Family Foundation will be impacted if there is a divorce.
- The family court cannot issue orders around Foundations and DAFs, but clients can be *really* invested in their charitable giving.
- Make sure the Bylaws of Foundation address a divorce.
- Who will remain on the Board? How will Board members be removed or added?
- Discuss how "advice" is given to the sponsoring organization post–divorce.
- Discuss custodians for 529 Plans; discuss custodians of UTMAs.

25

Fiduciary Duties of Spouses

- FC 1100:
  - Restricts gifting of community property personal property for less than fair value without consent of the other spouse.
  - Gives management and control to operator of business, but requires written notice of disposition of most of the personal property in the business.
- Remedies are set forth in FC 1101. Punitive damages are available.
- Spouses have fiduciary duties related to disclosure requirements.

26

Estate Planning In Anticipation of Divorce

- May set negative tone of case which results in award of fees and other unfavorable rulings.
- Questions regarding anticipating divorce – how soon?
- Breach of fiduciary duties/penalties.

27

Estate Planning During Divorce

- What can be done:
  - Modify a will
  - Change powers of appointment
  - Modify MPOA
  - Modify HIPPA releases
  - Modify GPOA
  - Change nominations of fiduciaries

28

Estate Planning During Divorce

- What can be done:
  - Remove and replace trustees.
  - Change disposition of last remains.
  - Create, but not fund, a trust.
  - Revoke a revocable trust, if notice is filed and served before the change takes place.
  - Revoke/eliminate right of survivorship to property, if notice is filed and served before the change took place.

29

What Cannot Be Done

- Create a nonprobate transfer or modify a nonprobate transfer in a manner that affects the disposition of property subject to the transfer, without written consent of other party or order of court.

- Transfer any property, including separate property, without written consent of other party or order of court.

- Change the beneficiaries of any life insurance held for benefit of parties or children.

- Revoke a nonprobate transfer or a right of survivorship to property, without serving a notice of change on other party and filing it.

30

Death During Divorce

- Death ends the divorce court's jurisdiction
  - Except if case has been submitted for decision.
  - Bifurcation of status (see conditions imposed by FC 2337).
  - Joint tenancies automatically severed by status of dissolution.
- Settlement agreements can be enforced as a contract but not a court order.
- Judgment revokes spouse's place in a will and a trust.

31

The End

32

Premarital Estate Planning & Divorce Awareness Among Estate Planners

Peter M. Walzer, Esq.

Walzer Melcher & Yoda, LLC

Woodland Hills, CA

www.walzermelcher.com

Kimberly R. Willoughby, Esq.

Willoughby & Associates

Golden, CO

www.willoughbylaw.com

45th Annual UCLA/CEB Estate Planning Institute

April 20, 2023

I. **Premarital Agreement Drafting**

    A. *Drafting estate planning clauses in premarital agreements that anticipate divorce.*

        1. Premarital agreements that include estate planning often include the following provisions:
            a. A full or partial waiver of rights on death;
            b. A provision for specific gifts or beneficial interests at death;
            c. Life insurance benefits;
            d. Portability; and
            e. Use of marital residence and allowance.

        2. However, clients do not always remember -- or follow -- the terms of a premarital agreement, especially with respect to estate planning.

        3. Draft premarital agreements to require an amendment should parties draft planning that is contrary to or not anticipated by the premarital agreement.

        4. Draft the premarital agreement to require an amendment should the parties create any irrevocable trusts during the marriage. Make sure you talk with a matrimonial attorney before you advise as to the effect of creating an irrevocable or joint revocable trust during marriage because:

            a. The matrimonial attorneys and divorce courts may have a very different argument regarding the effects of the planning on community property;
            b. This area of the law is constantly evolving; and
            c. Courts hearing domestic relations matters do not always fully understand estate planning.

        5. Draft for the ability to transfer assets to accomplish planning and gifting during a divorce irrespective of the Automatic Temporary Restraining Order (ATRO). Draft for the ability to modify life insurance beneficiary designations during divorce irrespective of the ATRO. *Note: the enforceability of such a clause is untested in California.*

        6. Most premarital agreements include a provision that if a divorce action is filed, parties do not receive any death benefits. Consider whether to draft such that this provision is only applicable if the spouse, not a third party, files the action. Specifically, in many states, third parties such as a guardian, guardian ad litem, conservator, or even agent under a power of attorney can

bring the action on behalf of the party. Many "gray divorces" are initiated because adult children are concerned about elderly parents and about their inheritance. Premarital agreements that revoke death benefits if a divorce is pending can incentivize third parties to file for divorce.

7. Draft so that a spouse does not lose both sets of rights (divorce rights and death rights) if the other spouse dies during a divorce action. The spouse should always be entitled to one set of rights.

B. *Drafting general clauses in premarital agreements that keep divorce in mind.*

1. Draft so that each party waives the right to discovery of value of the assets at time of marriage. *Note: the enforceability of such a clause is untested in California.* When premarital agreements are challenged, there is nearly always a challenge to the sufficiency of financial disclosures. It can be extremely difficult to prove values of assets at the time of marriage where more than five years have passed. This fact can give significant leverage to the challenging spouse.

2. Consider having the lesser-moneyed partner enter into an agreement with the trustee of any trusts not to request discovery, not to join the trustee in any action, and not to request court orders distributing any trust property. This agreement should include consideration.

3. Draft keeping in mind descendants that are not joint children, meaning, consider which premarital agreement terms the descendants might want to enforce, and draft to make clear the intent of the parties. For example, if the premarital agreement states that the intent of the parties is to not have any joint/marital/community property, but the parties in fact create such property, ensure there are other provisions that specify that the parties are not precluded from creating that property. Or, if all rights on death are waived, and no specific gifts are required, make sure the premarital agreement calls out that parties may gift to the other at death. Otherwise, descendants may try to claw back property from a spouse after a death.

II. Top "Mistakes" Made by Estate Planners When Drafting Prenuptial Agreements, According to Divorce Attorneys

- Waiving spousal support outright (liberal caps on amount with COLA more likely to survive).
- Tailoring agreement to death and not divorce.
- Not understanding that the agreement may be litigated in another state or that the choice of law clause may not be enforced.
- Not addressing dispute resolution.
- Not explaining the agreement adequately to the client and advising them of the possibility that it will not be enforced.
- Drafting terms that require the parties to keep track of financial transactions during marriage.
- Not adequately protecting separate property.
- Not addressing loan proceeds in states where intent of the borrower determines character of property.
- Making the agreement too complex for the average client to interpret.
- Drafting an agreement with too many payments or tasks to complete.
- Not addressing the basics of a divorce: temporary support and moving out of the home.
- Not insisting that the other party be represented by counsel.
- Providing inadequate disclosure or waiving disclosure.

III. Irrevocable Trusts Created and Funded During Marriage – Keeping Divorce in Mind and Advising Appropriately

A. *Ethical and practical considerations.*

1. Can you represent both parties, if that is what is being requested?

2. Consider California Rules of Professional Conduct:

    a. 1.4 Communication With Clients
    b. 1.6 Confidential Information of Client
    c. 1.7 Conflict of Interest: Current Clients
    d. 1.9 Duties to Former Clients
    e. 1.16 Declining or Terminating Representation

3. Clear Engagement Letters for Joint Representation (Scope and Potential Conflicts).

   a. ACTEC Examples:
   b. Limit the scope of representation.
   c. Be very clear about the identification of the clients.
   d. Explain how conflicts will be identified.
   e. Explain how conflicts will be resolved, to include if the attorney can remain the attorney of one of the clients after a conflict has arisen.
   f. Explain that there is no confidentiality between the attorney and either one of the spouses. Explain that the attorney to be called as a witness.
   g. Explain full transparency with respect to communications, information and documents.
   h. If not representing both spouses but you are communicating with both spouses, prepare a non-representation letter.

4. How to be certain both parties are truly informed and consenting?

   a. Be sure to speak to both parties at the beginning of the representation.
   b. Do not assume that emails with a "signature" of both parties is from both parties or was even seen by both parties. Find a work-around when the parties use the same email address.
   c. Do not assume agreement by both parties unless you hear it directly from both parties.
   d. Educate and advise to the level of the less participatory/sophisticated spouse.
   e. At the time of a divorce, spouses do say:
      i. "I never saw that document."
      ii. "He always signs documents for me, like our tax returns."
      iii. "He just shoves documents under my nose and tells me I have to immediately sign them. He never gave me time to review it."
      iv. "I just let him handle it. I feel so stupid about that."
      v. "I had no idea this would be the effect of those documents."

5. How to talk to clients about a potential divorce.

   a. Consider developing a general advisement, that requires client signatures, for all married clients who are doing any estate planning that could have any impact on a divorce.
   b. The advisement might include:

      i. Characterization of assets as a result of planning.

      ii. Control of assets as a result of planning during marriage and during a divorce.

      iii. Fiduciary designations and any changes if there is a divorce.

      iv. Beneficiary designations and any changes if there is a divorce.

      v. Ability to unwind planning if there is a divorce, and the consequences of doing so.

      vi. Effect on new spouses/families.

      vii. Use of lifetime exemption amount.

      viii. Access to property for new spouses/family.

c. Are you qualified to advise as to what would happen at divorce?

      i. Matrimonial lawyers often hear, "no one told me this is what would happen if we divorced," or "that is not how my estate planner described the effect of divorce."

      ii. Divorce outcomes are driven by:

         A. Statutory law;

         B. Common law; and

         C. What actually happens in the court room and what happens as a practical matter during a divorce.

d. Develop a very good relationship with a very good matrimonial lawyer.

6. Review the premarital agreement, if there was one. If not, also prepare a post-marital agreement.

a. Does the premarital agreement include estate planning provisions? Does the proposed new planning comport with the agreement? If not, will there be an argument that the premarital agreement or parts of it were abandoned?

b. Best practice is to include a marital agreement, or amendment to the premarital agreement, as part of the planning process so that both parties have understood, discussed and agreed on exactly what happens if there is a divorce, including:

      i. Fiduciary roles;

      ii. Beneficial interests;

      iii. Access to principal;

      iv. Access to income;

      v. Characterization of income; and

      vi. Unwinding/decanting.

  c. Be sure the parties' agreed-upon intent regarding what happens if there is a divorce is very clear in the trust agreement for Non-Judicial Settlement Agreement / court purposes.

  d. However, there are risks in using a postmarital agreement to waive property rights, transmute property, and limit spousal support:

    i. The amendment may be treated by the standards of a postmarital agreement, which requires both parties to do a full, fair and reasonable disclosures (with no waiver).

    ii. Postmarital agreements may require consideration. When any interspousal transaction advantages one spouse to the disadvantage of the other, the presumption arises that such transaction was the result of undue influence. *In re Marriage of Delaney* (2003) 111 Cal.App.4th 991. See *In re Marriage of Burkle* [Burkle II] (2006) 139 Cal.App.4th 712. The presumption of undue influence does not apply simply because one spouse received an "advantage" from an interspousal transaction. The 'advantage' which raises a presumption of undue influence in a marital transaction involving a contractual exchange between spouses must necessarily be an unfair advantage.

    iii. It is not clear under California law that spousal support can be limited by a postmarital agreement.

      1. Family Code §1500 provides: "The property rights of spouses prescribed by statute may be altered by a premarital agreement or other marital property agreement."

      2. Pursuant to Family Code §1612(c), spousal support can be limited under a premarital agreement subject to a determination of unconscionablity at the time of trial.

      3. There is no specific provision allowing the limitation of spousal support in postmarital agreements. (Note: there was a limitation of spousal support in *In re Marriage of Burkle* [Burkle II] (2006) 139 Cal.App.4th 712, and the limitation was not challenged on appeal).

7. How matrimonial lawyers will view irrevocable trusts:

  a. Keep in mind a trust may be interpreted in a state other than the state chosen as the choice of law state in the trust agreement.

  b. Keep in mind that if the clients move to another state, it will most likely not be a community property state.

c. Keep in mind that to a great extent, if the parties divorce, the law regarding how to treat a beneficial interest in trust for divorce purposes is family law and NOT trust law.

d. Keep in mind that family law will be applied to the characterization of beneficial interests (property or not property) and that how trust income factors into a divorce may not be determined according to the choice of law designated in the trust.

e. Matrimonial lawyers will argue:

   i. Trust interests are not property for divorce purposes.

   ii. Trust interests are property for divorce purposes.

   iii. A right to income is a property interest.

   iv. A right to income is not a property interest.

   v. The trustee must be joined in the divorce action.

   vi. The trustee need not be joined in the divorce action.

   vii. Agreements regarding the trust assets have been made already, and the court cannot change it.

   viii. Trust agreements have nothing to do with divorce.

   ix. "Irrevocable" means "irrevocable."

   x. "Irrevocable" does not mean "irrevocable."

   xi. The trust agreement is a sham.

   xii. The only interests that need be considered are the interests of the parties before the divorce court.

f. Below is a smattering of somewhat representative trust and divorce cases, but note, "there is no uniform approach applied across jurisdictions" on the issue of whether trust interests are subject to equitable division; rather, courts use a "case-by-case analysis of the facts presented instead of applying a bright line rule based simply upon the provisions contained in the trust agreement." *Guagenti v Guagenti*, 90 N.E.3d 297, 315 (OH App. 2017).

California

Δ   *In re Marriage of Dick*, 15 Cal.App.4th 144 (CA App. 1993): Where husband transferred his assets into a number of off-shore corporations and trusts for purposes of tax avoidance and creditor protection, the transactions must be disregarded. The holding, however, was merely that the trial court had sufficient evidence to determine that the assets in the entities disregarded by the court supported an award of spousal support of $35,000 per month.

Δ   *In re Marriage of De Guigne*, 2002 Cal.App. LEXIS 4034:
True "trust funder" fact scenario wherein neither party worked during the marriage, there was no community property created, and instead the parties' lifestyle was funded with trust income and principal from trusts. The appellate court held that the trial court did not err in awarding support to the spouse significantly in excess of a parent's income in order to meet the best interests of the children, using the statutory "special circumstances" factor.

Δ   *Ventura County Department of Child Support Services v. Brown*, 117 Cal.App.4th 144 (2004):
A court may compel the trustee of a third-party settled, fully discretionary spendthrift trust to pay the beneficiary's child support, as § 15305, subdivision (c) of the California Probate Code allows such orders for public policy reasons and because the trust instrument evidenced the settlor's intent that her grandchildren be supported.

Δ   *In re Marriage of Pallanack*, 2011 WL1459965 (not reported, CA App.):
A court may not direct the trustee of a third-party settled, fully discretionary spendthrift trust to directly pay support, if the trustee did not refuse in bad faith to satisfy a delinquent order.

Δ   *Matter of Cleopatra Cameron Gift Trust*, 931 N.W.2d 244 (SD 2019):
The court considered a third-party settled spendthrift trust for one beneficiary where the divorcing parties lived in CA and the trust was administered in SD under SD law. The court held the trustee could not be ordered by CA family court to make distributions directly to creditor for child support or spousal support obligations. SD determined that CA judgment was not entitled to full faith and credit as it was directly contrary to the SD legislative purposes found in SD domestic asset protection trust law.

New York

Δ   *Reichers v. Riechers*, 267 A.D.2d 445 (NY App. 1999):

The value of Cook Islands trust funded with marital assets was subject to equitable division where funded by husband two years before the divorce was filed.

Δ *Villi v. O'Caining-Villi* 2005 N.Y.Misc. LEXIS 2011(trial court opinion, not selected for publication in official reports):
An irrevocable trust settled by divorcing spouses for the sole benefit of their son was found not to be property available to be distributed as part of divorce unless the party transferring assets to the trust did not have legal authority to do so.

Δ *Spector v. Spector*, 18 A.D.3d 380 (N.Y. App. 2005):
A trial court can order husband to cooperate with wife to dissolve a family trust which was created to defraud wife or at least to make very poor financial decisions.

Δ *Yerushalmi v. Yerushalmi*, 136 A.D.3d 812 (2d Dep't 2016):
The trial court erred when it held that it could not enjoin a spouse from selling the marital residence, which was titled to a QPRT, during the divorce proceedings.

Δ *Markowitz v. Markowitz*, 146 A.D.3d 872 (NY App. 2017):
Assets in ILIT not part of the marital estate where neither husband nor wife has control over the assets.

Δ *Hirsch v. Hirsch*, 148 A.D.3d 997 (N.Y. App. Div. 2017):
The court referred to trusts as husband's "alter ego" since he controlled the assets through his role as investment advisor and his familial relationship with two of the three trustees; additionally, he extensively co-mingled funds between the trusts and his personal and other business accounts. Conveyances to the trusts were deemed fraudulent transfers).

Δ *Trafelet v. Trafelet,* 150 A.D.3d 483 (N.Y. App. 2017):
Husband requested summary judgment excluding self-settled trust from divorce litigation; trial court denied it. The court of appeals affirmed, finding that there were questions of fact regarding the creation and operation of trusts; husband retained substitution powers; a trust protector could terminate trust and distribute

assets to husband's future wife; and current wife claimed she did not know the terms of the trust when created and funded.

Δ   *Oppenheim v. Oppenheim*, 168 A.D.3d 1085(NY App. 2019: The trial court did not err in not distributing the value of an irrevocable trust settled and funded by husband during the marriage where it was not credible that wife was unaware of the planning and there is no evidence of bad intent on the part of husband.

East Coast

Δ   *D.L. v. G.L.*, 811 N.E.2d 1013 (MA App 2004): Trust interests are not marital property where the beneficiary spouse has no "present, enforceable right to use the principal from the trust" because the trustee has "uncontrolled discretion." Additionally, trust interests are not marital property where the beneficiary spouse has to be alive and another person has to be dead at a future date because the interest under these circumstances is too speculative. Finally, trust interests are not marital property where the beneficiary spouse's parent has a power of appointment, making the interest the equivalent of an expectancy under a will.

Δ   *Tannen v. Tannen*, 3 A.3d 1229 (NJ App. 2010): The court considered a third-party settled spendthrift trust that was established and funded during marriage by wife's parents with wife as sole beneficiary and co-trustee. Distributions were made in the sole discretion of trustee but with advisements. The court held that wife's beneficial interest in the trust did not allow her to "tap the income" of the trust, and was not an asset held by her to be considered for support or equitable distribution purposes. Additionally, the court found that trustees cannot be compelled by divorce court to make distributions to a beneficiary. *Note: This case includes an interesting discussion of the differences and applicability of Restatement (Second) of Trusts and Restatement (Third) of Trusts.*

Δ   *In the Matter of Nerbonne*, 2014 WL11643701(NH 2014):

Where husband created and funded a trust with marital property and wherein wife had the power to amend or terminate it for any reason and wife was the trustee and beneficiary, the trust assets are marital property subject to division.

Δ *Pfannenstielhl v. Pfannenstiehl*, 55 N.E. 3d 933 (MA 2016):
A third-party settled discretionary spray trust with 11 beneficiaries and an open class is not property for divorce purposes where the settlor's intent is to benefit generations, even where the trustee is to consider HEMS standard for beneficiary distribution requests.

Δ *Levitan v. Rosen*, 124 N.E.3d 148 (MA App. 2019):
A third-party spendthrift trust for one beneficiary is property for divorce purposes even where the trustee has sole discretion when beneficiary wife had the right to withdraw 5% of principal annually.

Mid West

Δ *Smith v. Smith*, 253 N.W.2d 143 (MN 1977):
A trust beneficiary with a current right to withdraw trust assets and who agreed to satisfy a divorce award with trust assets can be compelled to withdraw assets to satisfy a divorce award, irrespective of spendthrift provisions.

Δ *Loomis v. Loomis*, 158 S.W.3d 787 (MO App. 2005):
ILITs are not marital property even when the asset value was created with marital property).

Δ *Guagenti v. Guagenti*, 90 N.E.3d 297 (OH App. 2017):
A third-party settled irrevocable trust funded during marriage with Husband's family business before a liquidity event does not create marital property even where husband worked in the business all during marriage and the pre-liquidity valuation was about 1/5 of the sale value. *Note: This is one of the very few cases that actually delves into trust and estate practice, and it also illustrates how these cases actually get tried in court.*

Δ *Crawford v. Crawford*, 147 N.E.3d 1047 (IN App. 2020) (unpublished):

A prenuptial agreement is superseded by the creation of a joint trust funded with all assets during the marriage.

Δ *Kim v. Kim*, 150 N.E.3d 1229 (OH App. 2020):
An irrevocable trust funded by husband during marriage with marital assets was marital property subject to division where wife knew nothing about the creating or funding of the trust. The court stated that to hold otherwise would be to allow spouses to deplete the marital estate to their own benefit. Husband was a T&E attorney and had taken out loans against trust assets.

Other

Δ *Dahl v. Dahl*, 345 P.3d 566 (Utah 2015):
Husband and wife took opposing positions on revocability of a trust. Wife argued that under Utah law (state of divorce), trust was revocable and therefore assets remained marital property, while husband argued under Nevada law (situs of trust) that trust was irrevocable and thus assets were not property at all. Wife prevailed due to Utah's public policy protecting spouses and lack of recognition of self-settled trusts as a protection against creditors).

Δ *Sullivan v. Sullivan*, 211 So.3d 836 (AL App. 2016):
The trial court did not err in awarding 25% of beneficiary spouse's actual trust distributions to other spouse where trust income was a major part of parties' income during marriage.

Δ *Vanderlugt v. Vanderlugt*, 429 P.3d 1269 (NM App. 2018):
Assets in an ILIT were not community property, as settlor husband had no beneficial interest, was not a trustee, and otherwise had no control over the trust.

B.   *SLATs*

1. Due in part to the sunsetting of the 2017 Tax Cuts and Jobs Act, spousal limited asset trusts (SLATs) have become the go-to planning device to take advantage of the highest lifetime exemption amount we have ever seen. Estate planners should be vigilant about ensuring that the limited time to take advantage of high exemption amounts does not lead to problems if there is a divorce.

2. Should you identify "spouse" as the current spouse/use "floating spouse" concept?

    a.   Funding SLATs can significantly deplete community property.
    b.   It might make the most sense for an ex-spouse to remain the beneficiary of a SLAT even after divorce. In fact, some planners create SLAT interests as a partial pre-packaging of property to one spouse at divorce.
    c.   SLATs can invite lawsuits by a client who was not fully advised about the consequences of this planning if there is a divorce.
    d.   Grantor may not want secondary beneficiaries to be eligible for distributions after divorce.
    e.   Grantor may not want the new spouse to have SLAT benefits.

3. Specific trust provisions to be addressed there is a divorce.

    a.   Grantor trust status/income taxes.
    b.   Spousal unity rule / §672(e) / §682.
    c.   Work-arounds for current trusts (all of which have problems):
        i.   Repayment of taxes by beneficiary spouse;
        ii.   Repayment of taxes by trustee;
        iii. Swap assets;
        iv.   Decant; or
        v.   Terminate the trust.
    d.   Provisions to consider when drafting for divorce if the spouse is to remain a beneficiary:
        i.   Require that upon divorce, the distributions to the ex-spouse from the SLAT are subject to consent of an adverse party. (However, consider the family dynamics with such a requirement.) Make sure no other provisions of the trust would maintain the grantor status of there is a divorce.
        ii.   Authorize the trustee to reimburse the grantor if grantor is taxed on trust income that is payable to the ex-spouse.
        iii. Consider who the trustee is if there is a divorce.
        iv.   Consider removal/replacement of trustee clauses.
        v.   Consider granting specific Trust Protector powers if divorce.
    e.   Choosing the right assets to fund the SLAT.
    f.   Limiting substitution power (if retained) upon divorce.

C. *ILITs*

1. Generally speaking, irrevocable life insurance trusts (ILITs) are terminated at the time of a divorce. However, there can be very good reasons for maintaining the ILIT after a divorce, and many times, parties are not adverse to an ex-spouse being a beneficiary of the ILIT, particularly if there are joint children, and where the life insurance is term and the ex-spouse can pay the premiums after divorce.

2. When drafting, discuss with clients under what conditions an ex-spouse remain a beneficiary.

3. Discuss whether the ex-spouse could remain a trustee.

D. *DAPTs*

1. Self-settled domestic asset protection trusts (DAPTs) are the most "dangerous" of trusts to create because they can be so effective.

2. There is not much law in the nation regarding DAPTs and divorces. What law there is suggests that these are heavily litigated, and the outcome is not at all sure.

3. A DAPT created just before a marriage as part of premarital planning should be disclosed. However, there is no requirement in most states that they are disclosed.

4. If created during a marriage, consider whether a DAPT is, or could be seen as, divorce planning. If a spouse's beneficial interests automatically terminate at the filing of a divorce action, even if this is a generic clause you use in all trust instruments, will be seen as ipso facto divorce planning.

5. Be extremely clear, in writing, the effect of the creation of a DAPT if there is a divorce.

6. Income available to a beneficiary, regardless of source, will be considered for support.

IV. Foundations, DAFs and Inter Vivos Planning for Children

A. Assets that a couple contributed to a Foundation or a Donor Advised Fund (DAF) are an issue for the couple at divorce. They still see the assets as "theirs." However, because they are not, the court handling the divorce cannot issue orders concerning use of Foundation for DAF assets.

B. Make sure the Foundation's Bylaws address divorce. In particular, can both spouses remain on the Board?

C. As part of this planning, have the parties come to written agreements about how grants are made or "advice" is given, after divorce?

D. Planning for children during marriage should also be discussed in the context of a divorce. In particular, the creation of qualified personal residence trusts should include a discussion about what should happen with the trust if its term is not up when the parties divorce. Estate planning counsel should also discuss how 529 Plans are to be managed if the parents divorce.

V. Fiduciary Duties of Spouses

A. In California, spouses owe each other a fiduciary duty with respect to community property:
   1. Family Code, §721;
   2. Family Code, §1100-1101; and
   3. *In re the Marriage of Simmons*, 215 Cal.App.4th 584, 155 Cal.Rptr.3d 685 (Cal. App. 2013) (fiduciary duties do not apply to nondisclosure of separate property) see also, *In re Marriage of Schleich* 8 Cal.App.5th 267, 213 Cal.Rptr.3d 665 (Cal. App.2017).

VI. Estate Planning In Anticipation of Divorce

A. Planning and the modification of planning before the filing.

   1. "Planning" includes modification of wills, revocable trusts, beneficiary designations, and fiduciary designations; change of situs of trusts; change of trustee.

   2. Allowed, but wise?

3. How close to a filing is "in anticipation of divorce?"

4. No, there should not be gifting right before a divorce. Family Code §1100 – Restrictions on the transfer of property during marriage. Family Code Family Code §1101 – remedies for breach of fiduciary duty.

5. Consequences of planning modifications that are too close to divorce filing.

VII. Estate Planning During Divorce

A. ATROs govern once a divorce action has been filed.

B. What can be done:

1. Modify a will;
2. Change powers of appointment;
3. Modify MPOA;
4. Modify HIPPA releases;
5. Modify GPOA;
6. Change nominations of fiduciaries;
7. Remove and replace trustees;
8. Change disposition of last remains;
9. Create, but not fund, a trust.
10. Revoke a revocable trust, if notice is filed and served before the change takes place; and
11. Revoke/eliminate right of survivorship to property, if notice is filed and served before the change took place.

C. What cannot be done:

1. Changing the beneficiaries of any life insurance held for benefit of parties or children;
2. Transferring any property, including separate property, without written consent of other party or order of court; and
3. Creating a nonprobate transfer or modifying a nonprobate transfer in a manner that affects the disposition of property subject to the transfer, without written consent of other party or order of court.
4. Before revoking a nonprobate transfer or a right of survivorship to property, notice of change must be filed and served on other party.

D. Sanctions/resolutions for doing it anyway.

VIII. Death During Divorce

A. Death before the entry of decree.

1. Death during divorce ends the divorce action. The court no longer has jurisdiction over the divorce and, therefore, no jurisdiction over parties or property.

2. Estate planners and family members are often shocked and dismayed to learn that a person divorcing another will get all of the rights of a spouse if the other spouse dies during the divorce. That includes all rights to jointly titled property, all rights on death, all gifts via estate planning, all property that passes via a beneficiary designation, and the right to dispose of the body.

3. If a party dies after trial and submission of the case to a judge sitting without a jury for decision or after a verdict upon any issue of fact, and before judgment, the court may nevertheless render judgment thereon.Code of Civil Procedure §669.

B. Death after the entry of decree.

1. If the decree has entered, all court orders are still in force after the death, except those that terminate upon a death by the terms of the law, orders or agreements.

2. If the court bifurcates the status of the marriage and issues a decree of dissolution of marriage per Family Code §2337. the family court maintains jurisdiction to divide the marital property. This may be important where there a family code section beneficial to the party asserting a separate property claim, such as under Family Code §2640 which does not apply in probate court. ("… the party shall be reimbursed for the party's contributions to the acquisition of property of the community property estate to the extent the party traces the contributions to a separate property source. The amount reimbursed shall be without interest or adjustment for change in monetary values and may not exceed the net value of the property at the time of the division").

3. Joint tenancy automatically severed by status dissolution. Probate Code §5042.

C. Death after signing a marital settlement agreement and before the entry of decree.

1. Provisions of the agreement can be enforced as a contract, but not a court order.
2. A dissolution judgment revokes a will as to the former spouse's rights. Probate Code §6122.
3. Trust and non-probate provisions for a spouse are also revoked by dissolution or nullity. Probate Code §5600.
4. A dissolution revokes all non-probate transfers in favor of former spouse, **unless**:

   a. there is clear and convincing evidence that decedent intended the contrary;

   b. the court ordered that the non-probate transfer be maintained for the former spouse; *or*

   c. the non-probate transfer is not subject to revocation by transferor at time of death. Probate Code §5600.

Additional Documents

Automatic Temporary Restraining Order

Family Code §2040

(2)(A) Restraining both parties from transferring, encumbering, hypothecating, concealing, or in any way disposing of, any property, real or personal, whether community, quasi-community, or separate, without the written consent of the other party or an order of the court, except in the usual course of business or for the necessities of life, and requiring each party to notify the other party of proposed extraordinary expenditures at least five business days before incurring those expenditures and to account to the court for all extraordinary expenditures made after service of the summons on that party.

(B) Notwithstanding subparagraph (A), the restraining order shall not preclude a party from using community property, quasi-community property, or the party's own separate property to pay reasonable attorney's fees and costs in order to retain legal counsel in the proceeding. A party who uses community property or quasi-community property to pay the party's attorney's retainer for fees and costs under this provision shall account to the community for the use of the property. A party who uses other property that is subsequently determined to be the separate property of the other party to pay the party's attorney's retainer for fees and costs under this provision shall account to the other party for the use of the property.

(3) Restraining both parties from cashing, borrowing against, canceling, transferring, disposing of, or changing the beneficiaries of insurance or other coverage, including life, health, automobile, and disability, held for the benefit of the parties and their child or children for whom support may be ordered.

(4) Restraining both parties from creating a nonprobate transfer or modifying a nonprobate transfer in a manner that affects the disposition of property subject to the transfer, without the written consent of the other party or an order of the court.

(b) This section does not restrain any of the following:

(1) Creation, modification, or revocation of a will.

(2) Revocation of a nonprobate transfer, including a revocable trust, pursuant to the instrument, provided that notice of the change is filed and served on the other party before the change takes effect.

(3) Elimination of a right of survivorship to property, provided that notice of the change is filed and served on the other party before the change takes effect.

(4) Creation of an unfunded revocable or irrevocable trust.

(5) Execution and filing of a disclaimer pursuant to Part 8 (commencing with Section 260) of Division 2 of the Probate Code.

(c) In all actions filed on and after January 1, 1995, the summons shall contain the following notice:

"WARNING: California law provides that, for purposes of division of property upon dissolution of marriage or legal separation, property acquired by the parties during marriage in joint form is presumed to be community property. If either party to this action should die before the jointly held community property is divided, the language of how title is held in the deed (i.e., joint tenancy, tenants in common, or community property) will be controlling and not the community property presumption. You should consult your attorney if you want the community property presumption to be written into the recorded title to the property."

(d) For the purposes of this section:

(1) "Nonprobate transfer" means an instrument, other than a will, that makes a transfer of property on death, including a revocable trust, pay on death account in a financial institution, Totten trust, transfer on death registration of personal property, revocable transfer on death deed, or other instrument of a type described in Section 5000 of the Probate Code.

(2) "Nonprobate transfer" does not include a provision for the transfer of property on death in an insurance policy or other coverage held for the benefit of the parties and their child or children for whom support may be ordered, to the extent that the provision is subject to paragraph (3) of subdivision (a).

(e) The restraining order included in the summons shall include descriptions of the notices required by paragraphs (2) and (3) of subdivision (b).

Example of Waiver of Rights to Trustee

(For use with irrevocable trusts with non-settlor Trustee)

Dear Trustee of the * Trust:

I understand that the Settlor of the Trust has worked and saved to accumulate wealth for the benefit of those named in the Trust instrument, and that therefore s/he does not want what s/he has accumulated to be used for the benefit of anyone other than those s/he intended to benefit. I understand you and Settlor believe that the obligations of a Beneficiary to his or her spouse are the Beneficiary's financial responsibility, not Settlor's, and should be based solely on the Beneficiary's own personal finances and circumstances as if he or she had no beneficial interest of any nature in the assets that Settlor placed into trust.

As such, I hereby irrevocably and permanently waive all rights of any nature I might have or might assert claiming each of the following:

1. A direct or indirect beneficial interest in the Trust principal or income, including any interest awarded by judgment, court order, or other involuntary assignment, other than the beneficial interests specifically conferred upon me personally by the terms of the trust instrument (such as naming me as a Beneficiary by specific reference to my name, or by specific reference as the spouse of a Beneficiary, or by including me as a permissible appointee under a power of appointment);

2. Marital property rights, community property rights, or other direct or indirect ownership interests in the Beneficiary's beneficial interest in the trust;

3. The right to bring proceedings against the Trustee, the Trust estate, or any person or financial institution holding Trust assets seeking to garnish, attach, or otherwise satisfy obligations of the Beneficiary to me arising out of the dissolution of marriage or a probate action; and

4. The right to force the Trustee, Settlor or Beneficiary to provide me or any of my agents with any document or other information whatsoever regarding the Trust, its assets, its income or its distributions.

This waiver of rights runs in favor of the Trustee, the Beneficiary to whom I am married, and all other persons having a beneficial interest in the Trust estate.

_____   _____

Date   Signature

5

IRS & Audits

Kalyani Chandra

Small Business/Self-Employed

Recent Developments in Estate & Gift Tax

Small Business/Self-Employed

Disclaimer

The information presented in this handout from the Internal Revenue Service is for educational purposes only and shall not be cited or relied upon as authority.

2   Recent Developments in Estate and Gift Tax

Recent Guidance

- **Revenue Procedure 2022-32**

  - Effective July 8, 2022

  - Provides a simplified method to obtain an extension of time to make a portability election

  - Executor must file Form 706 within five years of the decedent's death and indicate "FILED PURSUANT TO REV. PROC. 2022-32 TO ELECT PORTABILITY UNDER § 2010(c)(5)(A)" at the top of the return

  - Available only if there was no requirement to file an estate tax return under Section 6018 of the Internal Revenue Code

3   Recent Developments in Estate and Gift Tax

Recent Guidance, continued

- **Proposed Regulations [REG-130975-08] under Section 2053 of the Internal Revenue Code**

  - Published in the Federal Register on June 28, 2022

  - Guidance on the proper use of present-value principles in determining the amount deductible by an estate for funeral expenses, administration expenses, and certain claims against the estate

  - Guidance on the deductibility of certain types of interest expense

  - Clarification of substantiating the value of certain claims

  - Guidance on the deductibility of amounts paid under a decedent's personal guarantee

4   Recent Developments in Estate and Gift Tax

Publication 904

- **Publication 904, Interrelated Computations for Estate and Gift Taxes**
  - Explains and illustrates the methods to use when an interrelated computation is necessary for determining estate or gift taxes
  - Published on September 28, 2022

5   Recent Developments in Estate and Gift Tax

Use of Electronic or Digital Signatures on Certain Forms

- **The IRS is allowing taxpayers to use electronic or digital signatures on certain paper forms that cannot be filed electronically**

  - The policy has been extended through October 31, 2023

  - Form 709, all Form 706-series, Form 1127, Form 4768, and Form 8971 are among the included forms

- **See www.irs.gov/newsroom/details-on-using-e-signatures-for-certain-forms for more information**

6   Recent Developments in Estate and Gift Tax

Electronic Correspondence Tools

- **Electronic Correspondence Tools Include:**
- E-signatures
- E-fax
- Third-party websites such as:
  - Hightail
  - ShareFile
  - Dropbox
- Email encrypted documents
  - See www.irs.gov/help/sign-and-send-documents-electronically for more information

7   Recent Developments in Estate and Gift Tax

Online Submission of Form 2848 and Form 8821

- **On IRS.gov, search "Form 2848" or "Form 8821" and scroll to "Submit Forms 2848 and 8821 Online"**
- **Review the instructions and the FAQs regarding:**
- Electronic signatures
- Authentication
- Secure access
- Form submission
- **You may still submit these forms via fax or mail if you are unable to submit them online**

8   Recent Developments in Estate and Gift Tax

Form 706 Authorization

Part 4—General Information

Note: Please attach the necessary supplemental documents. **You must attach the death certificate.** See instructions.

Authorization to receive confidential tax information under Reg. section 601.504(b)(2)(i); to act as the estate's representative before the IRS; and to make written or oral presentations on behalf of the estate:

Name of representative (print or type)	State	Address (number, street, and room or suite no., city, state, and ZIP code)

I declare that I am the ☐ attorney/ ☐ certified public accountant/ ☐ enrolled agent (check the applicable box) for the executor. I am not under suspension or disbarment from practice before the Internal Revenue Service and am qualified to practice in the state shown above.

Signature	CAF number	Date	Telephone number

- **The authorization on page 2 of the Form 706 is not as expansive as the Form 2848**

- **Form 2848, Power of Attorney, is a more flexible document**

Transcript Delivery Service

- **Transcript Delivery Service is available for Form 706 Estate Tax return accounts**

- **Authenticated and Registered users receive instant account transcripts**

  - Two step process

  - Users may need to re-authenticate their accounts

- **Notice 2017-12 confirms transcripts can substitute for an estate tax closing letter**

- **See www.irs.gov/businesses/small-businesses-self-employed/transcripts-in-lieu-of-estate-tax-closing-letters for more information**

Requesting an Estate Tax Closing Letter

- **New Estate Tax Closing Letter User Fee Regulations were issued effective October 28, 2021**

  - Requests are made through Pay.gov; the fee is $67

- *FAQs on the Estate Tax Closing Letter* **is available on www.IRS.gov providing detailed instructions for requesting an estate tax closing letter on Pay.gov**

  - Go to: www.irs.gov/etcl

- **Not available for Gift Tax Return, Form 709**

- **The closing letter will be prepared and issued to the executor at the address of record and other authorized representatives**

11   Recent Developments in Estate and Gift Tax

Estate and Gift Tax Basics

- **The Federal estate tax is a tax on the transfer of property at death**

- **The Federal gift tax is a tax on the transfer of property by gift during life**

- **Federal gift and estate tax liability is imposed only when the cumulative value of lifetime transfers and transfers at death (less any applicable deductions) exceeds a taxpayer's exclusion amount**

- **The most recent basic exclusion amounts are:**

  - 2021: $11,700,000

  - 2022: $12,060,000

  - 2023: $12,920,000

12   Recent Developments in Estate and Gift Tax

Estate Tax Filing Information

- **The current version of Form 706 was released August 2019 for decedents dying after December 31, 2018**

- **The executor is responsible for filing the estate tax return**

- **The executor may elect portability of any Deceased Spousal Unused Exclusion (DSUE) by timely filing a complete and properly prepared estate tax return**

  - Certain returns filed only to elect portability may report certain assets by using a good-faith estimate of value

- **Review www.irs.gov/businesses/small-businesses-self-employed/filing-estate-and-gift-tax-returns for additional filing information**

13   Recent Developments in Estate and Gift Tax

Gift Tax Filing Information

- **Form 709 is an annual return with a new version released each year**

- **The donor is responsible for filing the return and paying any gift tax due**

- **The return is due April 15th of the year after the gift was made**

- **Review www.irs.gov/businesses/small-businesses-self-employed/filing-estate-and-gift-tax-returns for additional filing information**

14   Recent Developments in Estate and Gift Tax

Extensions to File

IRS

- **Use Form 4768, *Extension of Time To File a Return and/or Pay U.S. Estate (and Generation-Skipping Transfer) Taxes*, to apply for an extension to file a Form 706 and/or pay estate and GST taxes**

  - Automatic 6-month extension to file if Form 4768 is timely filed by the due date of the Form 706

  - Estate tax is due 9 months after death unless an extension to pay is granted

- **Use Form 8892, *Payment of Gift/GST Tax and/or Application for Extension of Time To File Form 709*, if extending only gift tax**

- **Use Form 4868, *Application for Automatic Extension of Time To File U.S. Individual Income Tax Return*, if extending the filing date of both income tax and gift tax**

  - Gift tax is due April 15th of the year after the gift was made

15   Recent Developments in Estate and Gift Tax

Prior Gift Information

IRS

Form 706, Page 2, Part 4, Prior Gift Information

8a Have federal gift tax returns ever been filed?	
If "Yes," attach copies of the returns, if available, and furnish the following information.	
b Period(s) covered	**c** Internal Revenue office(s) where filed

- **Gift tax returns filed by the decedent must be disclosed**

- **You may request return information from the IRS using Forms 4506 or 4506-T**

  - Detailed instructions for completing these forms are provided at www.irs.gov/businesses/small-businesses-self-employed/frequently-asked-questions-on-gift-taxes

16   Recent Developments in Estate and Gift Tax

Gross Estate Tax Computation

Form 706, Page 1, Part 2

1	Total gross estate less exclusion (from Part 5—Recapitulation, item 13)	1
2	Tentative total allowable deductions (from Part 5—Recapitulation, item 24)	2
3a	Tentative taxable estate (subtract line 2 from line 1)	3a
b	State death tax deduction	3b
c	Taxable estate (subtract line 3b from line 3a)	3c
4	Adjusted taxable gifts (see instructions)	4
5	Add lines 3c and 4	5
6	Tentative tax on the amount on line 5 from Table A in the instructions	6
7	Total gift tax paid or payable (see instructions)	7
8	Gross estate tax (subtract line 7 from line 6)	8

- **Gross estate tax is computed using Lines 1 through 8 of Part 2 on the first page of the Form 706**

- **There are worksheets available in the Instructions for Form 706 to assist with Line 4 and Line 7**

  - All gifts since 1976 must be included

  - Line 7 include amounts "paid or payable"

17   Recent Developments in Estate and Gift Tax

Portability

- **The executor elects portability of the Deceased Spousal Unused Exclusion (DSUE) amount, if any, by completing and timely filing Form 706**

- **The executor opts out of electing portability by checking the box in Section A of Part 6 on page 4 of the Form 706**

- **Section B of Part 6 contains "Yes" and "No" checkboxes for the executor to indicate whether any assets of the estate are being transferred to a Qualified Domestic Trust (QDOT)**

  - Note: A portability election may not be made if the decedent was not a U.S. Citizen or Resident at the time of death

- **The executor will use Section C of Part 6 to compute the DSUE amount portable to the surviving spouse**

- **Section D of Part 6 is used to compute any DSUE amount received from a predeceased spouse**

18   Recent Developments in Estate and Gift Tax

Gift Tax Reminders

- **Basic Exclusion is the same as for Estate Tax**
  - $12,060,000 in 2022 and $12,920,000 in 2023
- **Annual Exclusion for certain present interest transfers**
  - $15,000 in 2018-2021, $16,000 in 2022, and $17,000 in 2023
  - $164,000 for gifts to a nonresident, non-U.S. citizen spouse in 2022 and $175,000 in 2023
- **If the donor has DSUE that was received from their last predeceased spouse, it must be used before the donor's own exclusion is applied**

19   Recent Developments in Estate and Gift Tax

Basis Consistency and Reporting

- **Section 1014(f) requires a recipient's basis in certain property acquired from a decedent to be consistent with the value of the property as finally determined for Federal estate tax purposes**
- **Section 6035 requires estates to provide basis information to the IRS and the recipients of certain property acquired from a decedent**
- **Form 8971 and Schedule A are used to satisfy the reporting requirements under Section 6035**

20   Recent Developments in Estate and Gift Tax

Basic Tips for Return Assembly

- **Spiral binding, two and three hole punch document fasteners and/or covers on the return are not necessary and are likely to be removed and destroyed at the Service Center**

- **Exhibits should be indexed and placed at the back of the tax return - not behind each individual schedule**

  - Copies of tax returns filed with Form 706 must be identified as exhibits to the Form 706

- **Include copies of all wills, trusts, disclaimers, agreements, appraisals, and other explanatory documents, referred to in the return or in the supporting documents**

21   Recent Developments in Estate and Gift Tax

Corresponding with the IRS

- **Keep Official IRS Record current**

- **Substantiate person authorized to receive information**

- **File one original Form 2848**

- **Keep CAF current**

22   Recent Developments in Estate and Gift Tax

IRS Tax Help

- **Visit www.IRS.gov and type keywords "estate and gift taxes" to find:**

  - What's New

  - FAQs

  - Pub 559, Survivors, Executors and Administrators

  - Filing Information

- **Consult the Estate and Gift Tax pages on IRS.gov for questions about return accounts, lien discharges, extensions and closing letters**

- **If further assistance is needed, call (866) 699-4083**

23   Recent Developments in Estate and Gift Tax

Questions?

?

24   Recent Developments in Estate and Gift Tax

6

Trust & Estate Scouting Report: Uncovering Tax & Fiduciary Trends to Better Plan & Prepare

Bill Sanderson

Trust and Estate Scouting Report

45th Annual UCLA/CEB Estate Planning Institute

Presented By:

Bill Sanderson, April 21, 2023

McGuireWoods

1

Bill Sanderson

🐦 @thisistherecord

📷 @thisistherecord

McGuireWoods

CONFIDENTIAL

I used to be here...

Now you can find me...

McGuireWoods

This really is where I met my wife...

This is how I started the pandemic...

Time Marches On...

What I'm reading

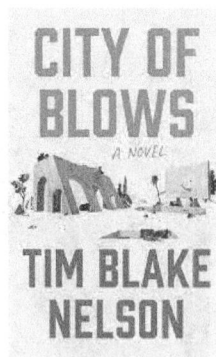

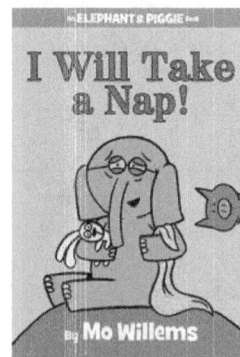

CITY OF BLOWS
A NOVEL
TIM BLAKE NELSON

an ELEPHANT & PIGGIE Book
I Will Take a Nap!
By Mo Willems

And like it or not...

This document is scheduled to be published in the
Federal Register on 02/24/2022 and available online at
federalregister.gov/d/2022-02522, and on **govinfo.gov**

DEPARTMENT OF THE TREASURY

Internal Revenue Service

26 CFR Parts 1 and 54

[REG-105954-20]

RIN 1545-BP82

Required Minimum Distributions

AGENCY: Internal Revenue Service (IRS), Treasury.

ACTION: Notice of proposed rulemaking and notice of public hearing.

SUMMARY: This document contains proposed regulations relating to required

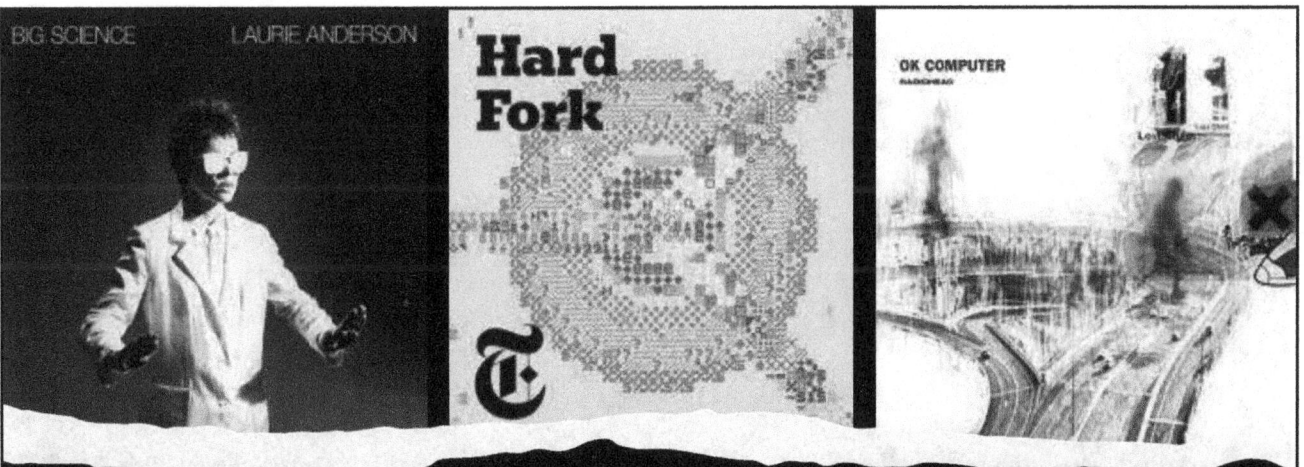

What I'm listening to...

Here's
something
work
related to
listen to...

Christie's

Fair Market Value

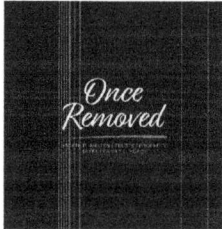

McGuireWoods

Steve Murphy

Once Removed

Trust and Estate Scouting Report

45th Annual UCLA/CEB Estate Planning Institute

Presented By:

Bill Sanderson, April 21, 2023

McGuireWoods

Scouting Report: Legislative and Regulatory Developments

1. **Legislation Affecting the Transfer of Assets During Life and at Death Introduced in the 118th Congress**

435

**United States
House of Representatives
Republican Leadership**

Kevin McCarthy (R) (CA 20)
Speaker of the House of
Representatives

Jason Smith (R) (MO 8)
House Ways and Means
Committee Chair

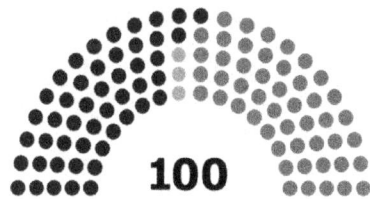

100

**United States
Senate
Democratic Leadership**

Chuck Schumer (D)(NY)
Senate Majority Leader

Ron Wyden (D)(OR)
Senate Finance
Committee Chair

McGuireWoods

Scouting Report: Legislative and Regulatory Developments

1. Legislation Affecting the Transfer of Assets During Life and at Death Introduced in the 118th Congress

7. General Explanations of the Administration's Fiscal Year 2024 Revenue Proposals (March 9, 2023)

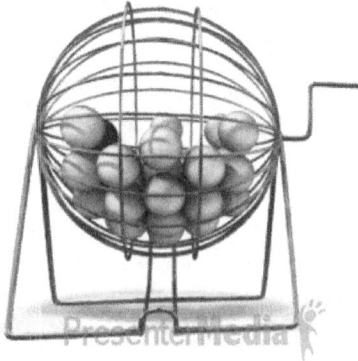

- H.R. 338: Permanently Repeal the Estate Tax Act of 2023

- H.R. 108: Small Business Prosperity Act of 2023

- H.R. 25: Fair Tax Act of 2023

- S. 1108: Death Tax Repeal Act of 2023

McGuireWoods

15

Scouting Report: Legislative and Regulatory Developments

2. Revenue Ruling 2023-06 (March 15, 2023)

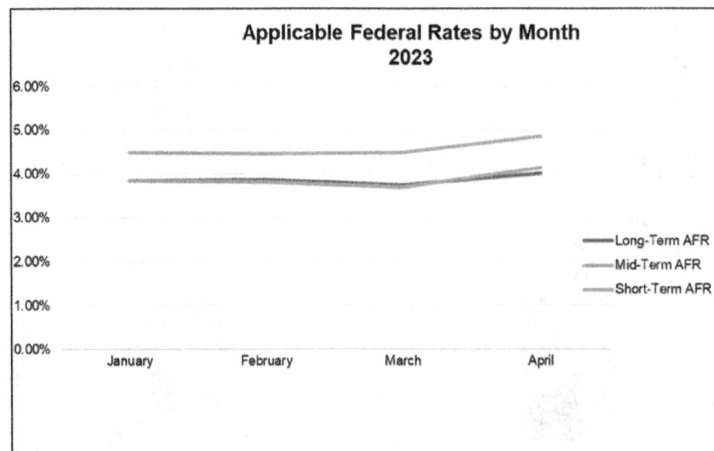

Applicable Federal Rates by Month 2023

— Long-Term AFR
— Mid-Term AFR
— Short-Term AFR

McGuireWoods

Scouting Report: Legislative and Regulatory Developments

2. Revenue Ruling 2023-06 (March 15, 2023)

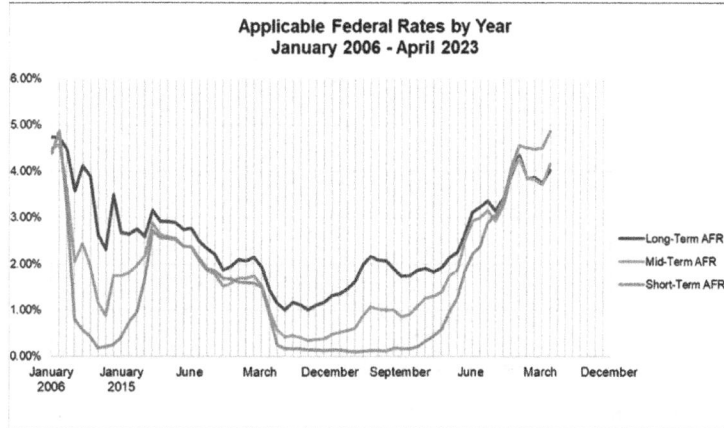

McGuireWoods

CONFIDENTIAL

Scouting Report: Legislative and Regulatory Developments

2. Revenue Ruling 2023-06 (March 15, 2023)

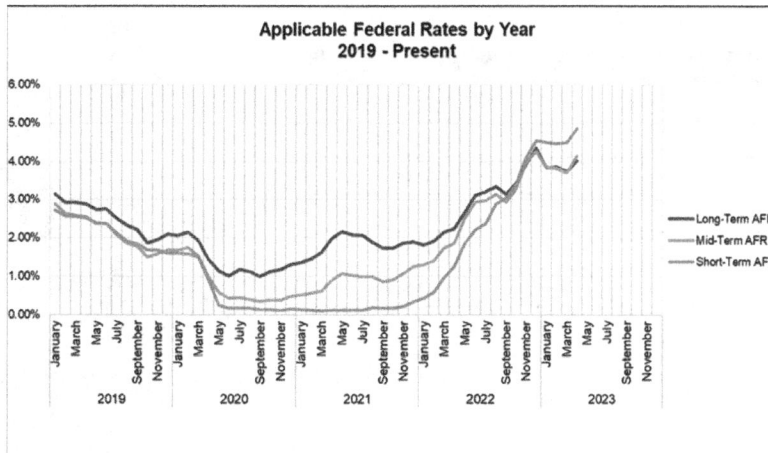

McGuireWoods

CONFIDENTIAL

Scouting Report: Legislative and Regulatory Developments

2. Revenue Ruling 2023-06 (March 15, 2023)

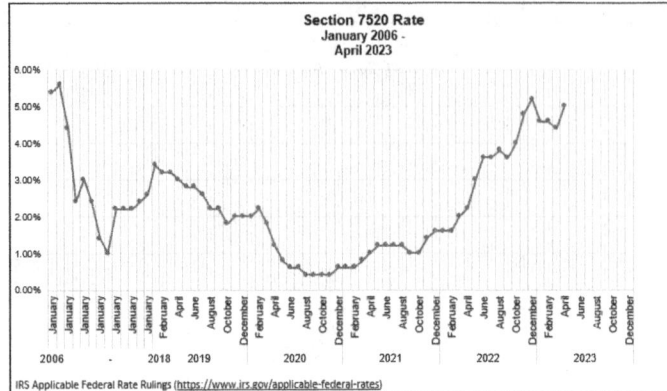

Section 7520 Rate
January 2006 -
April 2023

IRS Applicable Federal Rate Rulings (https://www.irs.gov/applicable-federal-rates)

In general, HIGHER Section 7520 Rates are GOOD for QPRTs, CRATs, and CGAs and BAD for GRATs, CLATs, and private annuities and LOWER 7520 RATES are GOOD for GRATs, CLATs, ad private annuities and BAD for QPRTs, CRATs, and CGAs.

McGuireWoods

CONFIDENTIAL

Scouting Report: Legislative and Regulatory Developments

4. Washington D.C. – Administrative Roundup

IRS Funding Increases by Function	
Enforcement	+$45.6 billion
Operations Support	+$25.3 billion
Business System Modernization	+$4.8 billion
Taxpayer Services	+$3.2 billion
Other	+$0.7 billion
Total	**+$79.6 billion**

Source: https://taxfoundation.org/inflation-reduction-act-irs-funding/; Inflation Reduction Act of 2022, https://www.democrats.senate.gov/07/27/2022/inflation-reduction-act-of-2022.

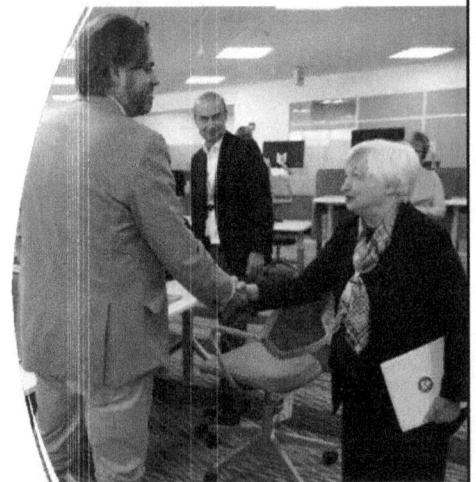

McGuireWoods

20

Scouting Report: Legislative and Regulatory Developments

5. **Revenue Ruling 2023-2 (March 29, 2023)**

   > IRS releases long-awaited guidance confirming that basis "step up" does not apply to assets in an irrevocable grantor trust not included in a decedent's estate.

6. **SEC Amendments to Forms 4 and 5 - 17 CFR Parts 229, 232, 240, and 249 (December 14, 2022)**

   > SEC announces new rules regarding disclosure of gifts of publicly traded securities by "insiders."

McGuireWoods

21

Scouting Report: Charitable Gifts

15. *Hoensheid v. Commissioner*, No. 18606-19, T.C. Memo 2023-34 (March 15, 2023)

   > Tax Court rules against taxpay in assignment of income case; declines to uphold accuracy related penalty.

McGuireWoods

22

Scouting Report: Charitable Gifts

16. PLR 202305017 (February 3, 2023) and PLR 202306011
     (February 10, 2023)

> IRS denies exemption application of proposed organizations.

17. *Calvin A. Lim and Helen K. Chu v. Commissioner*, T.C.
     Memo 2023-11 (January 23, 2023)

> Tax Court hears case of the "Ultimate Tax Plan" involving charitable gift
> of LLC Units.

McGuireWoods

23

Scouting Report: Estate Tax and Estate Inclusion

20. IRS Data Book Statistics for Fiscal Year 2021 (October 2022)

All Estate Tax Returns		
Estate Tax Returns Filed in 2021	**Number of Returns**	**Gross Estate ($000s)**
All Returns	6,158	189,647,122
Under $10 million	532	4,008,485
$10 million < $20 million	3,284	47,162,709
$20 million < $50 million	1,737	50,927,770
$50 million or more	605	87,548,158

Generally, an estate files a Federal estate tax return (Form 706) in the year after a decedent's death. So, in 2021, **most returns were filed for deaths that occurred in 2020**, for which the filing threshold was $11.58 million of gross estate. Because of filing extensions, however, some returns were filed in 2021 for deaths that occurred prior to 2020, for which filing thresholds were lower. There are also a small number of returns filed for deaths that occurred in 2021, for which the filing threshold was $11.70 million.

Source: IRS, Statistics of Income Division
Estate Tax Returns Filed in 2021 by Tax Status and Size of Gross Estate

McGuireWoods

Scouting Report: Estate Tax and Estate Inclusion

20. **IRS Data Book Statistics for Fiscal Year 2021 (October 2022)**

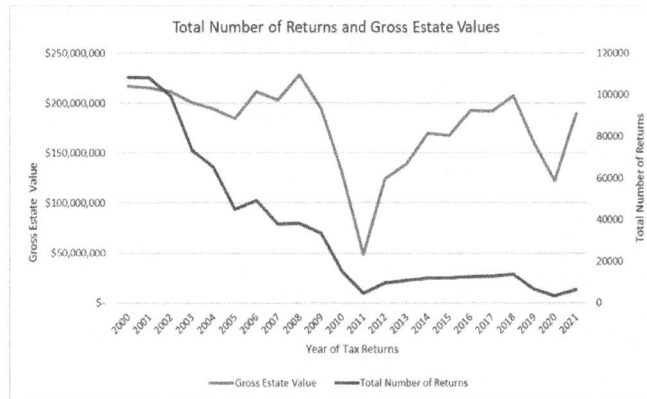

Total Number of Returns and Gross Estate Values

McGuireWoods

25

Scouting Report: Estate Tax and Estate Inclusion

20. **IRS Data Book Statistics for Fiscal Year 2021 (October 2022)**

Taxable Estate Tax Returns		
Estate Tax Returns Filed in 2021	Number of Returns	Gross Estate ($000s)
All Returns	2,584	98,318,430
Under $10 million	233	1,738,376
$10 million < $20 million	1,118	16,434,671
$20 million < $50 million	865	25,504,334
$50 million or more	369	54,641,049

Source: IRS, Statistics of Income Division
Estate Tax Returns Filed in 2021 by Tax Status and Size of Gross Estate

McGuireWoods

Scouting Report: Estate Tax and Estate Inclusion

20. **IRS Data Book Statistics for Fiscal Year 2021 (October 2022)**

All Estate Tax Returns			Returns Reporting: Personal Residence	
Estate Tax Returns Filed in 2021	Number of Returns	Gross Estate ($000s)	% of Total Returns	Gross Estate ($000s)
All Returns	6,158	189,647,122	69%	7,005,971
Under $10 million	532	4,008,485	54%	253,453
$10 million < $20 million	3,284	47,162,709	70%	2,763,776
$20 million < $50 million	1,737	50,927,770	73%	2,304,832
$50 million or more	605	87,548,158	72%	1,683,910

This asset category includes the home identified as the decedent's residence. At most, one item of residential real estate per return is included in this asset category.

Source: IRS, Statistics of Income Division
Estate Tax Returns Filed in 2021 by Tax Status and Size of Gross Estate

McGuireWoods

Scouting Report: Estate Tax and Estate Inclusion

20. **IRS Data Book Statistics for Fiscal Year 2021 (October 2022)**

All Estate Tax Returns			Returns Reporting: Other Real Estate	
Estate Tax Returns Filed in 2021	Number of Returns	Gross Estate ($000s)	% of Total Returns	Gross Estate ($000s)
All Returns	6,158	189,647,122	79%	14,265,395
Under $10 million	532	4,008,485	67%	360,921
$10 million < $20 million	3,284	47,162,709	77%	5,141,619
$20 million < $50 million	1,737	50,927,770	82%	4,388,866
$50 million or more	605	87,548,158	87%	4,373,989

This asset category includes commercial property, undeveloped land, real estate mutual funds (REITs), and residential property other than the personal residence.

Source: IRS, Statistics of Income Division
Estate Tax Returns Filed in 2021 by Tax Status and Size of Gross Estate

McGuireWoods

Scouting Report: Estate Tax and Estate Inclusion

20. IRS Data Book Statistics for Fiscal Year 2021 (October 2022)

All Estate Tax Returns			Returns Reporting: Closely Held Stock	
Estate Tax Returns Filed in 2021	Number of Returns	Gross Estate ($000s)	% of Total Returns	Gross Estate ($000s)
All Returns	6,158	189,647,122	33%	15,830,487
Under $10 million	532	4,008,485	21%	153,494
$10 million < $20 million	3,284	47,162,709	28%	2,816,274
$20 million < $50 million	1,737	50,927,770	37%	3,926,063
$50 million or more	605	87,548,158	53%	8,934,655

This asset category includes the total value of stock held in closely held corporations. Closely held corporations are those whose ownership is concentrated among a relatively small number of owners, and whose stock is not traded publicly.

Source: IRS, Statistics of Income Division
Estate Tax Returns Filed in 2021 by Tax Status and Size of Gross Estate

McGuireWoods

Scouting Report: Estate Tax and Estate Inclusion

20. IRS Data Book Statistics for Fiscal Year 2021 (October 2022)

All Estate Tax Returns			Returns Reporting: Cash	
Estate Tax Returns Filed in 2021	Number of Returns	Gross Estate ($000s)	% of Total Returns	Gross Estate ($000s)
All Returns	6,158	189,647,122	99%	17,251,450
Under $10 million	532	4,008,485	99%	373,154
$10 million < $20 million	3,284	47,162,709	98%	3,924,340
$20 million < $50 million	1,737	50,927,770	99%	4,199,326
$50 million or more	605	87,548,158	99%	8,754,630

This asset category includes all liquid assets, such as actual cash, bank accounts, certificates of deposit (CDs), money market accounts, such as Money Market Deposit Accounts (MMDAs) and Money Market Mutual Funds (MMMFs), and call and sweep accounts held in a brokerage.

Source: IRS, Statistics of Income Division
Estate Tax Returns Filed in 2021 by Tax Status and Size of Gross Estate

McGuireWoods

Scouting Report: Estate Tax and Estate Inclusion

20. **IRS Data Book Statistics for Fiscal Year 2021 (October 2022)**

All Estate Tax Returns			Returns Reporting: Net Life Insurance	
Estate Tax Returns Filed in 2021	Number of Returns	Gross Estate ($000s)	% of Total Returns	Gross Estate ($000s)
All Returns	6,158	189,647,122	37%	1,765,186
Under $10 million	532	4,008,485	31%	48,569
$10 million < $20 million	3,284	47,162,709	38%	835,029
$20 million < $50 million	1,737	50,927,770	37%	441,830
$50 million or more	605	87,548,158	37%	439,758

This asset category includes the value of includible life insurance, net of policy loans. Includible insurance is any insurance on the decedent's life that is payable to the estate at the decedent's death or is payable to another beneficiary if the decedent retained some ownership of the policy.

Source: IRS, Statistics of Income Division
Estate Tax Returns Filed in 2021 by Tax Status and Size of Gross Estate

McGuireWoods

Scouting Report: Estate Tax and Estate Inclusion

20. **IRS Data Book Statistics for Fiscal Year 2021 (October 2022)**

All Estate Tax Returns			Returns Reporting: Farm Assets	
Estate Tax Returns Filed in 2021	Number of Returns	Gross Estate ($000s)	% of Total Returns	Gross Estate ($000s)
All Returns	6,158	189,647,122	13%	4,898,593
Under $10 million	532	4,008,485	12%	130,733
$10 million < $20 million	3,284	47,162,709	13%	1,741,153
$20 million < $50 million	1,737	50,927,770	13%	1,357,779
$50 million or more	605	87,548,158	19%	1,668,928

This asset category includes farm land and assets used in conjunction with a farm or agricultural business, as well as incorporated farms, farm partnerships, and farm sole proprietorships.

Source: IRS, Statistics of Income Division
Estate Tax Returns Filed in 2021 by Tax Status and Size of Gross Estate

McGuireWoods

Scouting Report: Estate Tax and Estate Inclusion

20. IRS Data Book Statistics for Fiscal Year 2021 (October 2022)

	All Estate Tax Returns		Returns Reporting: Private Equity / Hedge Funds	
Estate Tax Returns Filed in 2021	Number of Returns	Gross Estate ($000s)	% of Total Returns	Gross Estate ($000s)
All Returns	6,158	189,647,122	19%	6,930,875
Under $10 million	532	4,008,485	12%	52,409
$10 million < $20 million	3,284	47,162,709	15%	408,232
$20 million < $50 million	1,737	50,927,770	21%	809,360
$50 million or more	605	87,548,158	37%	5,660,874

This asset category includes both private equity funds and hedge funds. Usually structured as limited partnerships, these private investment funds are typically open to a limited range of professional and wealthy investors and pay performance fees to their investment managers.

Source: IRS, Statistics of Income Division
Estate Tax Returns Filed in 2021 by Tax Status and Size of Gross Estate

McGuireWoods

Scouting Report: Estate Tax and Estate Inclusion

20. IRS Data Book Statistics for Fiscal Year 2021 (October 2022)

	All Estate Tax Returns		Returns Reporting: Retirement Assets	
Estate Tax Returns Filed in 2021	Number of Returns	Gross Estate ($000s)	% of Total Returns	Gross Estate ($000s)
All Returns	6,158	189,647,122	68%	8,737,658
Under $10 million	532	4,008,485	59%	372,087
$10 million < $20 million	3,284	47,162,709	70%	4,073,232
$20 million < $50 million	1,737	50,927,770	68%	2,640,923
$50 million or more	605	87,548,158	63%	1,651,416

This asset category includes annuities, assets held in defined contribution plans, such as Individual Retirement Accounts (IRAs) and 401(k)s, and the taxable portion of survivor benefits from defined benefit plans such as traditional employer pensions.

Source: IRS, Statistics of Income Division
Estate Tax Returns Filed in 2021 by Tax Status and Size of Gross Estate

McGuireWoods

Scouting Report: Estate Tax and Estate Inclusion

20. **IRS Data Book Statistics for Fiscal Year 2021 (October 2022)**

All Estate Tax Returns			Returns Reporting: Art	
Estate Tax Returns Filed in 2021	**Number of Returns**	**Gross Estate ($000s)**	**% of Total Returns**	**Gross Estate ($000s)**
All Returns	6,158	189,647,122	21%	3,535,363
Under $10 million	532	4,008,485	16%	21,224
$10 million < $20 million	3,284	47,162,709	16%	177,776
$20 million < $50 million	1,737	50,927,770	25%	508,496
$50 million or more	605	87,548,158	45%	2,827,866

This asset category includes items such as paintings, sculptures, busts, engravings, and etchings.

Source: IRS, Statistics of Income Division
Estate Tax Returns Filed in 2021 by Tax Status and Size of Gross Estate

McGuireWoods

Scouting Report: Estate Tax and Estate Inclusion

20. **IRS Data Book Statistics for Fiscal Year 2021 (October 2022)**

All Estate Tax Returns			Returns Reporting: Total Lifetime Transfers	
Estate Tax Returns Filed in 2021	**Number of Returns**	**Gross Estate ($000s)**	**% of Total Returns**	**Gross Estate ($000s)**
All Returns	6,158	189,647,122	59%	85,797,140
Under $10 million	532	4,008,485	52%	1,333,822
$10 million < $20 million	3,284	47,162,709	56%	17,803,080
$20 million < $50 million	1,737	50,927,770	64%	21,883,350
$50 million or more	605	87,548,158	71%	44,776,888

Total lifetime transfers equals the sum of all assets that were given by the decedent to others during life and were includible in his/her gross estate under sections 2035(a), 2036, 2037, or 2038 of the Internal Revenue Code.

Source: IRS, Statistics of Income Division
Estate Tax Returns Filed in 2021 by Tax Status and Size of Gross Estate

McGuireWoods

Scouting Report: Estate Tax and Estate Inclusion

21. *Estate of Machelhenny v. Commissioner* (March 15, 2023); *H. Yale Gutnick, et al., v. U.S.*, No. 2:23-cv-00139 (W.D. Pa); *Estate of Spizzirri v. Commissioner*, T.C. Memo 2023-25 (February 28, 2023

> **Recent cases address deductibility of certain debts and expenses in estate tax returns.**

McGuireWoods

37

Scouting Report: Other Items of Interest

46. *Bittner v. United States, No. 20-1195 (February 28, 2023)*

> **U.S. Supreme Court rules in favor of taxpayer on FBAR reporting case; penalties not assessed per account but per report.**

McGuireWoods

38

Scouting Report: Other Items of Interest

47. *United States v. Moshe Lax, et. al., No. 1:18-cv-04061 (EDNY) (December 29, 2022)*

> **Court rules that Executor waived attorney-client privilege through discovery disclosure, crime fraud exception applies.**

McGuireWoods

39

Questions or Comments?

Michael Barker

mbarker@mcguirewoods.com

Bill Sanderson

wsanderson@mcguirewoods.com

McGuireWoods

40

McGuireWoods

Trust and Estate Scouting Report

45th Annual UCLA-CEB Estate Planning Institute
April 21, 2023

PRESENTED BY:
Bill Sanderson

Uncovering Tax and Fiduciary Trends to Better Plan and Prepare

For at least the last two decades, the federal wealth transfer tax has been in a state of continued—sometimes gradual, sometimes fast-paced—evolution. This program will review the landscape of federal legislation dealing with the estate and gift tax, and it will address trends in recent cases, regulatory guidance, and administrative updates that have an impact on estate planning and estate administration.

Last updated April 14, 2023

Presenter Profile

Bill Sanderson, Partner

202.857.1703 | wsanderson@mcguirewoods.com | Washington D.C. | Charlottesville, Virginia

Bill Sanderson represents both high-net-worth individuals and families on a variety of sensitive and complex estate and business planning matters. His practice focuses on the areas of estate planning and estate and trust administration. He is a member of the firm's fiduciary advisory services practice.

A frequent speaker, Bill has also taught Federal Taxation Practice and Procedure at Virginia Commonwealth University School of Business.

Prior to completing his law degree at the University of Virginia School of Law, Bill completed coursework at the University of South Carolina School of Law. While attending the University of Virginia, Bill was a member of the Raven Society and the Jefferson Literary and Debating Society.

Bill is a Fellow in the American College of Trust and Estate Counsel. Since March 2022, he has served as chair of its Washington Affairs Committee.

Key Contributors

Michael H. Barker
Partner

mbarker@
mcguirewoods.com

Stephen W. Murphy
Partner

swmurphy@
mcguirewoods.com

Kristen Frances Hager
Partner

khager@
mcguirewoods.com

William I. Sanderson
Partner

wsanderson@
mcguirewoods.com

Meghan Gehr Hubbard
Partner

mghubbard@
mcguirewoods.com

Farhan N. Zarou
Associate

fzarou@
mcguirewoods.com

Special Acknowledgements

Charles D. Fox IV
Retired Partner

Sean F. Murphy
Retired Partner

Trust and Estate Scouting Report:
Uncovering Tax and Fiduciary Trends to Better Plan and Prepare

Trust and Estate Scouting Report:
Uncovering Tax and Fiduciary Trends to Better Plan and Prepare[1]

LEGISLATIVE AND REGULATORY DEVELOPMENTS

1. Legislation Affecting the Transfer of Assets During Life and at Death Introduced in the 118th Congress

> **Legislation to modify or repeal the estate, gift, and generation skipping tax and to introduce a capital gains tax on the transfer of assets during life or at death and forms of wealth tax introduced or discussed in Congress**

The 118th Congress convened on January 3, 2023, and ushered in a change in leadership in the Congress.

The Republican party gained the majority in the U.S. House of Representatives, bringing changes in the top leadership in that chamber and throughout the committee structure. The Republicans hold a 222 to 213 vote majority:

435[2]

Kevin McCarthy (R) (CA 20) serves as Speaker of the House of Representatives. Jason Smith (R) (MO 8) serves as Chair of the House Ways and Means Committee, the committee charged with tax writing responsibility in the House. As a member of that committee, Smith had authored several bills aimed at repealing the estate tax. Hakeem Jeffries (D) (NY 8) was elected Minority Leader for the Democrats, and Richard Neal (D) (MA 1) serves as the ranking member for the Democrats on the Ways and Means Committee.

---

[1] These materials are based on materials prepared by Michael Barker, Kristen Hager, Meghan Gehr Hubbard, Stephen W. Murphy, William I. Sanderson, and Farhan Zarou of McGuireWoods LLP. We would like to acknowledge former or retired partners Sean Murphy, Andrea Chomakos, Charles D. Fox IV, and Ron Aucutt for their contributions to previous versions of these materials.
[2] Image Source: https://en.wikipedia.org/wiki/118th_United_States_Congress

The Democratic party retained control of the U.S. Senate, with 48 Democrats and 3 Independents known to caucus with the party. Republicans control 49 seats:

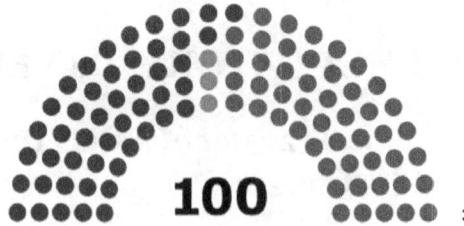

100 [3]

Chuck Schumer (D)(NY) serves as the majority leader in the Senate, with veteran tax-writer Ron Wyden (D)(OR) leading the Senate Finance Committee. Mitch McConnell (R)(KY) leads the Republican minority with Mike Crapo (R)(ID) serving as ranking member of the Senate Finance Committee.

In the early days of the Congress, three bills have been introduced in the Congress aimed at repealing the estate tax:

H.R. 338: Permanently Repeal the Estate Tax Act of 2023

Introduced by: Robert E. Latta (R)(OH 5) with 7 co-sponsors.

Summary: This bill aims to repeal the federal estate tax effective for estates of decedents dying after December 31, 2022.

H.R. 108: Small Business Prosperity Act of 2023

Introduced by: Andy Biggs (R)(AZ 5) with 7 co-sponsors.

Summary: The bill aims to repeals the estate tax for estates of decedents dying after 2022. In targeted relief for pass-through businesses, the bill proposes to (1) make the deduction for qualified business income (currently scheduled to expire on December 31, 2025) permanent, (2) limit to 21% the top tax rate on qualified business income, (3) repeal the limitation on the deduction based on amount of wages paid, and (4) revise the definition of *qualified trade or business* to mean any trade or business other than the trade of business of performing services as an employee. The bill would also provide that a change in the organizational structure of a corporation is not a taxable event if there is no change among the owners, their ownership interests, or the assets of the organization.

---

[3] Image Source: https://en.wikipedia.org/wiki/118th_United_States_Congress

H.R. 25: Fair Tax Act of 2023

Introduced by: Earl L. "Buddy" Carter (R)(GA 1) with 26 co-sponsors.

Summary: This bill seeks to impose a national sales tax on the use or consumption in the United States of taxable property or services in lieu of the current income taxes, payroll taxes, and estate and gift taxes.

2.   Revenue Ruling 2023-06 (March 15, 2023)

Climbing interest rates lead to higher AFRs, Section 7520 rate; Impact on Estate Planning Techniques Varied

Each month, the IRS provides various prescribed rates for federal income tax purposes. These rates, known as Applicable Federal Rates (AFRs), are regularly published as revenue rulings.

The following table provides the Short-, Mid-, and Long-Term AFR (for annual compounding) published in Revenue Ruling 2023-06.

Applicable Federal Rates – April 2023		
Short-Term AFR (Annual Compounding)	4.86%	⬆
Mid-Term AFR (Annual Compounding)	4.15%	⬆
Long-Term AFR (Annual Compounding)	4.02%	⬆
Section 7520 Rate (Annual Compounding)	5.0%	⬆

Many common estate planning techniques leverage the applicable federal rates in intra-family loan transactions, including direct loans to family members and loans made in connection with a sale of assets. For term loans with a duration of the of less than three years, the loan will not be deemed to be a gift if the interest rate is equal to or greater than the Short-Term AFR for the month the loan is made. For term loans with a duration of at least three years but less than nine years, the loan will not be deemed to be a gift if the interest rate is equal to or greater than the Mid-Term AFR for the month the loan is made. For term loans with a duration of nine years or more, the loan will not be deemed to be a gift if the interest rate is equal to or greater than the Long-Term AFR for the month the loan is made.

The following charts are drawn from the Internal Revenue Service Applicable Federal Rate Rulings[4] and shows the recent historical trajectory of the AFRs from 2006 through April 2023.

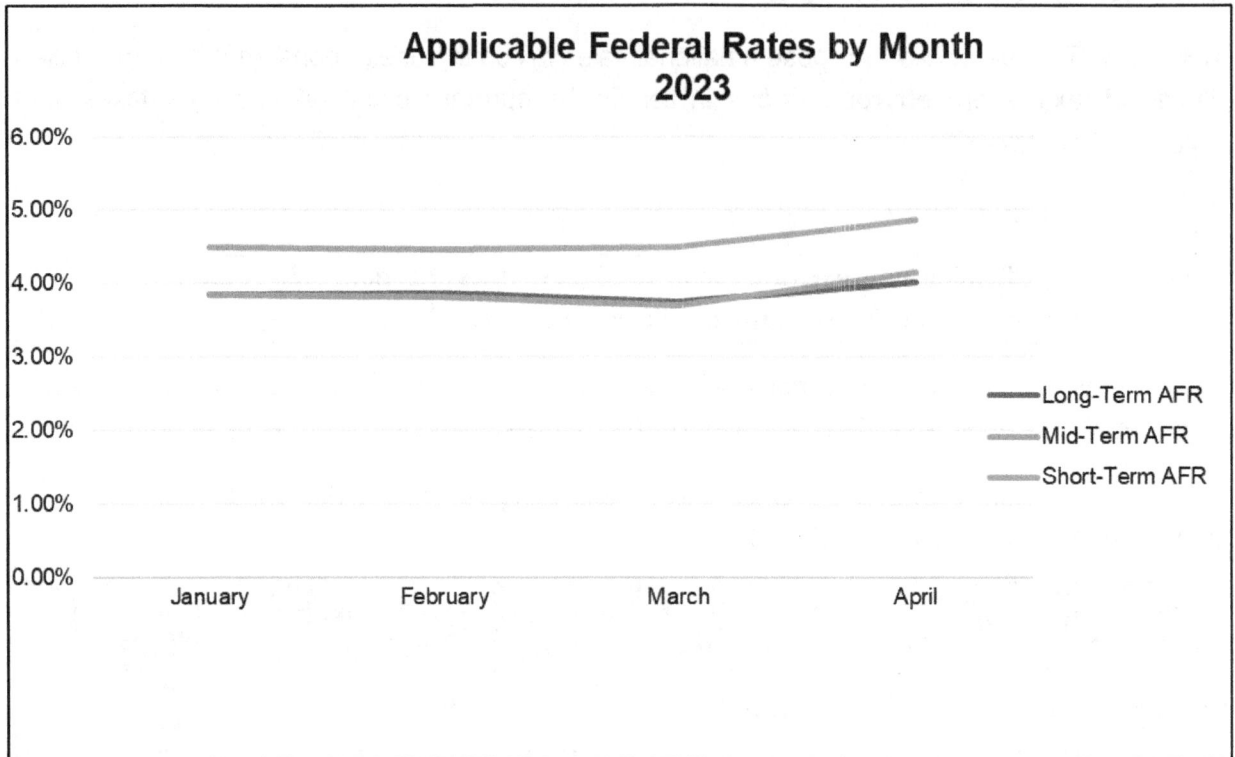

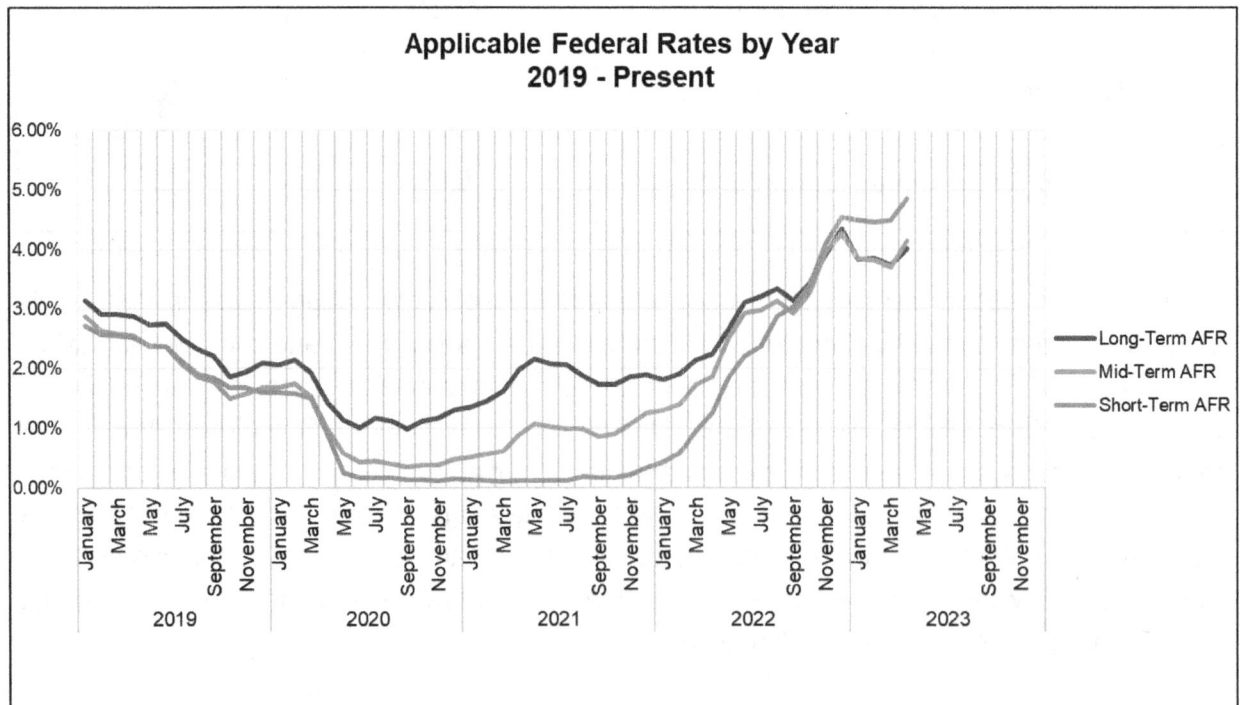

Applicable Federal Rates by Month
2023

Long-Term AFR
Mid-Term AFR
Short-Term AFR

Applicable Federal Rates by Year
2019 - Present

Long-Term AFR
Mid-Term AFR
Short-Term AFR

---

[4] https://www.irs.gov/applicable-federal-rates

Applicable Federal Rates by Year
January 2006 - April 2023

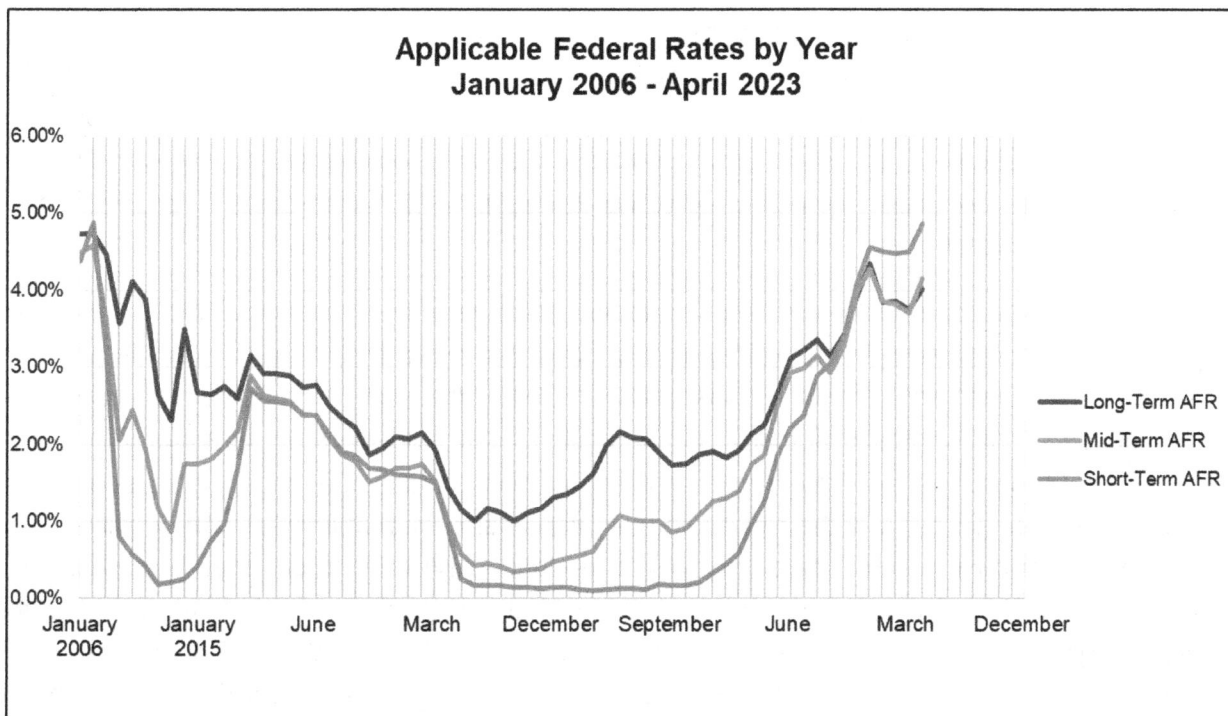

During a rising interest rate environment, consideration should be given both to establishing new loans and revisiting existing loans. With respect to new loans, estate planning professionals and clients will need to model the ability of borrowers – whether individuals or trusts – to repay the loans. And in the case of an installment sale, where the asset sold is expected to provide cash flow to the trust to service the loan, particular emphasis should be paid to the impact of increasing rates, generally speaking, on the performance of the underlying asset and the asset's ability to provide cash flow. Whether the underlying asset is an operating business, income producing real estate, or a blend of other investments, a rising interest rate environment may reduce or impair cash flow from the asset, from market conditions or because of debt at the asset level. If the cash flow is impaired, the ability of the purchaser in an installment sale to satisfy the loan terms may likewise be impaired.

With respect to existing loans, estate planning professionals should give consideration to the opportunity to prepay or refinance outstanding loans. If loans are set to mature, and rates are likely to be higher at maturity, clients may consider refinancing loans to lock in favorable – or at least certain – rates for a set time. Consideration has been given to the gift tax consequences of refinancing intra-family loans in the context of a changing rate environment. That consideration usually addresses refinancing a loan to capture a lower interest rate, for example when the AFR has dropped over time. In that analysis, and in the absence of guidance or case law on point, commentators have looked to market transactions for guidance. In an arm's length transaction, if there is no prohibition on prepayment, a borrower can repay a loan and refinance on more favorable terms. That often includes certain transaction costs, including at times prepayment penalties, but it remains the option of the borrower. The same can be aid of an intra-family loan, provided the loan does not prohibit prepayment. In a period of rising interest rates, the borrower may actually be choosing to pay more interest for a longer term than the current loan requires, in exchange for not refinancing at a later time when the costs could be even higher. Because this option may require a borrower paying more, thorough financial analysis should be undertaken to understand the risks – in higher costs – and rewards – avoiding even higher costs.

Consideration should also be given to the structure of the refinancing. While there is no guidance that prohibits refinancing intra-family loans, the more that the parties act in an arm's length fashion, the more likely the transaction – whether the loan or the entire installment sale transaction – can withstand scrutiny. In approaching this, parties to an intra-family loan may consider: (i) obtaining separate representation for both parties; (ii) engaging in substantive negotiations on the terms of the refinancing; (iii) addressing market interest rate conditions; (iv) having the borrower prepay some principal to the lender; (v) offering or renewing collateral as security for the loan; (vi) engaging in underwriting, similar to a arm's length lender, to assure the creditworthiness of the borrower; and (vii) requiring fixed payments, including payment of principal and interest where appropriate. In addition to these factors, proper documentation and record keeping is recommended.[5]

Other estate planning techniques require calculations of the value of certain interests based on the Section 7520 Rate. In general, HIGHER Section 7520 Rates are GOOD for QPRTs, CRATs, and CGAs and BAD for GRATs, CLATs, and private annuities and LOWER 7520 RATES are GOOD for GRATs, CLATs, and private annuities and BAD for QPRTs, CRATs, and CGAs

The following chart shows the recent trajectory of the Section 7520 Rate.

---

[5] For more on issues related to the estate and gift tax treatment of intra-family promissory notes, including a discussion of issues related to refinancing notes, see Akers, Stephen R. and Hayes, Philip J. (2012) "Estate Planning Issues With Intra-Family Loans and Notes," *ACTEC Law Journal*: Vol. 38: No. 2, Article 2.

Section 7520 Rate
January 2006 -
April 2023

IRS Applicable Federal Rate Rulings (https://www.irs.gov/applicable-federal-rates)

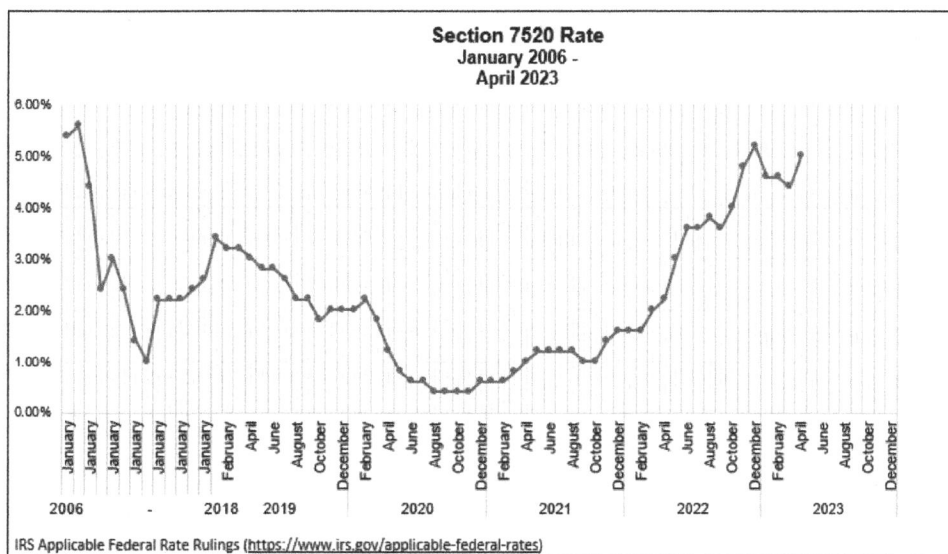

3. Revenue Procedure 2022-38 (October 18, 2022)

IRS announces inflation adjustments for 2023

The following are some of the inflation adjustments for 2023 relevant for estate and gift tax matters.

Basic Exclusion Amount

For an estate of any decedent dying in calendar year 2023, the basic exclusion amount is **$12,920,000** for determining the amount of the unified credit against estate tax under Section 2010.

Annual Exclusion for Gifts

(1) For calendar year 2023, the first **$17,000** of gifts to any person (other than gifts of future interests in property) are not included in the total amount of taxable gifts under Section 2503 made during that year.

(2) For calendar year 2023, the first $175,000 of gifts to a spouse who is not a citizen of the United States (other than gifts of future interests in property) are not included in the total amount of taxable gifts under Section 2503 and 2523(i)(2) made during that year.

Interest on a Certain Portion of the Estate Tax Payable in Installments

For an estate of a decedent dying in calendar year 2023, the dollar amount used to determine the "2-percent portion" (for purposes of calculating interest under Section 6601(j)) of the estate tax extended as provided in Section 6166 is $1,750,000.

Valuation of Qualified Real Property in Decedent's Gross Estate

For an estate of a decedent dying in calendar year 2023, if the executor elects to use the special use valuation method under § 2032A for qualified real property, the aggregate decrease in the value of qualified real property resulting from electing to use § 2032A for purposes of the estate tax cannot exceed $1,310,000.

Estate and Trust Income Tax Rate Schedule

For taxable years beginning in 2023, estates and trusts will pay income tax at the highest rate bracket where taxable income is more than **$14,450**. The tax rate tables under § 1 for estates and trusts are as follows:

If Taxable Income is:	The Tax is:
Not over $2,900	10% of the taxable income
Over $2,900 but not over $10,550	$290 plus 24% of the excess over $2,900
Over $10,550 but not over $14,450	$2,126 plus 35% of the excess over $10,550
Over $14,450	$3,491 plus 37% of the excess over $14,450

Qualified Business Income Under Section 199A

For taxable years beginning in 2023, the threshold amount under Section 199(e)(2) is:

- $364,200 for married filing joint returns

- $182,100 for married filing separate returns

- $182,100 for single and head of household returns

The phase-in range amount is:

- $464,200 for married filing joint returns

- $232,100 for married filing separate returns

- $232,100 for single and head of household returns

4.   Washington D.C. – Administrative Roundup

> This section provides headlines of interest to practitioners following IRS and Treasury administrative matters

- **September 15, 2022: Yellen outlines plan for increased IRS funding; targets taxpayer experience and fairness**. With passage of the Inflation Reduction Act of 2022, Congress agreed to a significant increase in funding for the Internal Revenue Service. It total, the budget for the IRS will increase by nearly $80 billion.

IRS Funding Increases by Function

Enforcement	+$45.6 billion
Operations Support	+$25.3 billion
Business System Modernization	+$4.8 billion
Taxpayer Services	+$3.2 billion
Other	+$0.7 billion
Total	**+$79.6 billion**

Source: https://taxfoundation.org/inflation-reduction-act-irs-funding/; Inflation Reduction Act of 2022, https://www.democrats.senate.gov/07/27/2022/inflation-reduction-act-of-2022.

The following table provides the Short-, Mid-, and Long-Term AFR (for annual compounding) published in Revenue Ruling 2022-17.

On September 15, 2022, in a visit to an IRS facility, Secretary of the Treasury Janet Yellen laid out priorities for allocation of the increased budget.

- Treasury will fully staff the IRS Tax Assistance Centers, where individual taxpayers can get help at an in-person location. By adding resources, it will triple the number of taxpayers that can be served. In the last filing season, 900,000 Americans were helped in these Tax Assistance Centers. With increased funding, Treasury estimates that up to 2.7 million Americans can be served. Yellen noted that one study suggests the average taxpayer spends 13 hours preparing and filing a return, compared to taxpayers in Sweden that can file returns by responding to a text message.

- The IRS will add 5,000 jobs at call centers. In earlier filing seasons, call centers averaged a 10%-15% "level of service," meaning 2 of every 10 calls were answered. The additional funding will greatly improve this, and Treasury has set a minimum expectation to reach the 85% level of service. Treasury estimates that 5 times the number of calls will be answered. *Yellen noted that on just one day, March 15, 2021, the IRS received 8.6 million phone calls.*

- The funds allocated for business modernization will largely be allocated to digitizing the current manual processes. In many cases, IRS employees manually transcribe paper returns. For the next filing season, the IRS will scan paper returns, leading to fewer errors, faster processing, and faster refunds. In addition, the IRS will increase capability for taxpayers to engage with the IRS online, including responding to notices.

- Treasury will engage "industry-leading customer service experts from the private sector" to advise on modernization efforts and best practices.

In addition to updating the systems and processes, the IRS will dedicate increased budget resources to enforcement. Yellen addressed the "tax gap," or the amount of tax that goes unpaid under current laws. Citing the Treasury Department studies, Yellen estimated taxes that will go uncollected over the next decade could be as high as $7 trillion. To address this, Treasury will focus enforcement priorities on taxpayers with income over $400,000. In addition to the increase of audits on high earners, the increased presence will address large, complicated corporate returns (averaging 6,000 pages/return) or partnerships (where one-third of the income is reported annually).

For more on the remarks delivered by Secretary Yellen and the statistics cited, see: https://home.treasury.gov/news/press-releases/jy0952#_ftnref10.

- **June 28, 2022: IRS, Treasury Issue Guidance Under Section 2053 Regarding Deduction for Interest Expense and Amounts Paid Under a Personal Guarantee, Certain Substantiation Requirements, and Applicability of Present Value Concepts (REG-130975-08).** The proposed regulations provide guidance on the proper use of present-value principles in determining the amount deductible by an estate for funeral expenses, administration expenses, and certain claims against the estate. In addition, the proposed regulations provide guidance on the deductibility of interest expense accruing on tax and penalties owed by an estate, and interest expense accruing on certain loan obligations incurred by an estate. The proposed regulations also amend and clarify the requirements for substantiating the value of a claim against an estate that is deductible in certain cases. Finally, the proposed regulations provide guidance on the deductibility of amounts paid under a decedent's personal guarantee. The proposed regulations will affect estates of decedents seeking to deduct funeral expenses, administration expenses, and/or certain claims against the estate under section 2053.

5.   Revenue Ruling 2023-2 (March 29, 2023)

> **IRS releases long-awaited guidance confirming that basis "step up" does not apply to assets in an irrevocable grantor trust not included in a decedent's estate.**

In Revenue Ruling 2023-2, the IRS addressed an oft-discussed topic regarding the use of grantor trusts: "Is there a basis adjustment under § 1014 of the Internal Revenue Code to the assets of a trust on the death of the individual who is the owner of the trust under chapter 1 of the Code if the trust assets are not includible in the owner's gross estate pursuant to chapter 11 of the Code." Some commentators have suggested that assets transferred to an irrevocable grantor trust *may* be eligible for a step up in basis under § 1014 at the death of the grantor; the IRS has closed that door.

Section 1014 of the Code generally provides that the basis of property in the hands of a person acquiring property from a decedent, or to whom the property passed from a decedent (if not sold, exchanged, or otherwise disposed of before the decedent's death by that person, is the fair market value of the property at the date of the decedent's death. Code § 1014(b) lists types of property that are considered to have been "acquired from or to have passed from the decedent," including most commonly property acquired by bequest, devise, or inheritance. Types of property passing in trust that are considered "acquired from" the decedent include property in trust where the decedent held a power to revoke or amend the trust or a general power of appointment over the assets held in trust.

In analyzing the application of § 1014(b) to a lifetime transfer to a grantor trust, the Revenue Ruling addresses the definition of "bequests," "devises," and "inheritances." In each case, the IRS concludes that courts and other sources of jurisprudence have construed those words to mean property passing by will or intestacy. And further, a court in <u>Bacciocco v. United States</u>, 286 F.2d 551, 554-55 (6th Cir. 1961) found that property transfer in trust before the decedent's death is not "bequeathed or inherited because it did not pass by will or intestacy" and "the decedent's death did not transfer the assets to the trust." The ruling cites further support in the Congressional committee report, explaining that the intent of the basis step up adjustment was to apply where property had been included in the gross estate of the decedent. In looking at the other types of property, including property in trust, that may be eligible for a basis step up under § 1014(b)(2),(3),(4),(6), (9), or (10), the IRS finds no match.

The ruling confirms that the assets transferred to an irrevocable grantor trust during an individual's lifetime do not meet the test under § 1014(b)(1) for bequests, devises, and inheritances, or any other type of property eligible for a basis adjustment. As such, the fair market value will not be adjusted to fair market value as a result of the decedent's death.

Irrevocable grantor trusts, structured to be excluded from the grantor's gross estate for estate tax purposes, have become a common gift planning vehicle, with clients transferring assets by gift and sale to the trusts during their lifetime. Many practitioners have assumed – and advised clients accordingly – that the assets would not receive a step up in basis at the death of the decedent because they are not included in the estate of the transferor at death. This ruling provides confirmation and legal support for that conclusion.

6. SEC Amendments to Forms 4 and 5 - 17 CFR Parts 229, 232, 240, and 249 (December 14, 2022)

> **SEC announces new rules regarding disclosure of gifts of publicly traded securities by "insiders"**

In December 2022, the Securities and Exchange Commission issued wide-ranging guidance, adopting new amendments to certain rules under the Securities and Exchange Act of 1934. A majority of the rules address the affirmative defenses to trading on the basis of material nonpublic information (sometimes referred to as 10b5 plans, in reference to the section authorizing insiders to sell securities according to choreographed and predetermined trading plans). Those 10b5 plans are familiar to public company compliance departments, public company executives, and many financial advisors. The SEC also adopted new rules targeted to increase disclosure of insider trading policies at public companies and for individual SEC filers.

For individual directors, executives, or others that may have access to material nonpublic information (sometimes referred to as "insiders"), the SEC requires certain forms to be filed to disclose individual trading activity. Before the proposed amendments were announced, any insider or "reporting person" was required to report a "bona fide gift" of registered securities on a Form 5, which is generally required to be filed within 45 days after the public company's fiscal year end in which the gift occurred. The rules defined a bona fide gift as "a gift that is not required or inspired by any legal duty or that is in any sense a payment to settle a debt or other obligation, and is not made with the thought of reward for past services or hope for future consideration." In effect, the rules allowed delayed reporting of gifts, such that a reporting person may have as much as one year to report the gift. The SEC expressed concern about the delayed reporting, referencing problematic practices, including making stock gifts to maximize tax benefits associated with the gifts. The announcement cited a Duke Law Journal article that found insiders' charitable gifts of securities were unusually well timed, suggesting that the results were likely due to the possession of material nonpublic information and from backdating of stock gifts. The allegation is that the insiders would make a gift (or backdate a gift) when the stock price was high, to claim the higher charitable deduction, knowing that the stock price would eventually fall. Under the proposal, reporting persons would have to disclose a gift of securities on Form 4, which is required to be filed with the SEC on the end of the second business day following the date of execution of the transaction. This change would allow investors and the SEC to better evaluate the actions of insiders in making gifts.

Many commenters to the proposed rule argued that the rule was overly broad or the compliance burden would have a chilling effect on estate planning transactions, and particularly gifts to charitable organizations. Those commenters argued to narrow the scope of the rule, to only apply to gifts to charitable entities affiliated with the reporting person or to lengthen the deadline for reporting for certain gifts. The SEC was not persuaded by these arguments and recognized the impact that this might have on estate planning and charitable gift transactions.

The rule acknowledges that gifts that are made pursuant to a plan adopted under Rule 10b5, where the gifts are predetermined based on an acceptable formula (involving sales price, volume, and dates) and executed by a third party, may still be acceptable, however that formula cannot be based on a tax objective, such as a gift of an amount of shares that would maximize the reporting person's income tax charitable deduction.

The new rules will increase the compliance burden on reporting persons and make charitable gifts of stock, especially year-end gifts, more complicated. Reporting persons and their advisors will need to carefully consider the reporting requirements under this new SEC guidance.

In addition, because the rules have required public companies, or "issuers," to disclose more details about insider trading policies, and in light of the changes adopted, many public company compliance departments are evaluating insider trading policies. And reporting persons will need to confirm that any planned gifts comport with both the SEC guidance and the insider trading policy of their organization. Depending on the view adopted by the compliance departments of the public companies, new insider trading policies may have far reaching effects for estate planning transactions, including annual gifts to individuals, gifts to GRATs, CRTs, CLTs, as well as the annual charitable gifts addressed above.

7. General Explanations of the Administration's Fiscal Year 2024 Revenue Proposals (March 9. 2023)

> **Treasury releases information regarding President Biden's budget proposals**

President Biden's Fiscal Year 2024 Budget proposes a number of reforms that would "enhance revenues, improve tax administration, and make the tax system more equitable and efficient." The General Explanations of the Administration's Fiscal Year 2024 Revenue Proposals, commonly referred to as the "Greenbook," provides detailed explanations of the various proposals, including a description of the current law, the policy reasons for the proposed change, and a description of the President's proposal.

The Greenbook breaks down the Administration's proposals into three categories: (i) reforms to the business and international tax system aimed at collecting additional revenue and reducing corporate tax incentives that encourage profit shifting and offshoring of jobs; (ii) reforms aimed at strengthening the taxation of high-income taxpayers; and (iii) proposals that would improve, modernize, and simplify tax administration.

The reforms aimed at strengthening the taxation of high-income taxpayers fell into three categories:

Strengthening Taxation of High-Income Taxpayers

- Apply the net investment income tax to pass-through business income of high income taxpayers
- Increase the net investment income tax rate and additional medicare tax rate for high income taxpayers
- Increase the Top Marginal Income Tax Rate for High Earners
- Reform the Taxation of Capital Income
- Impose a Minimum Income Tax on the Wealthiest Taxpayers

The first two proposals in this section are new and would apply an increased net investment income tax to pass through income. The other three proposals track similar proposals addressed in the 2023 Greenbook – returning the highest marginal rate to 39.6% and reforming capital income by taxing long-term capital gains at ordinary income rates for the highest earners and treating gifts and death as realization events for transfers of appreciated property. In addition, the Administration included a proposal that would propose a minimum 20% tax on total income (including unrealized capital gains) for all taxpayers with a net worth greater than $100 million. This proposal blends two tax proposals that were raised in 2021 – a wealth tax on the highest net worth families and a minimum tax on all income, which was initially proposed as a corporate minimum tax.

Modifying Estate and Gift Taxation

- Modify Income, Estate, and Gift Tax Rules for Certain Grantor Trusts
- Require Consistent Valuation of Promissory Notes
- Improve Tax Administration for Trusts and Decedents' Estates
- Limit Duration of Generation-Skipping Transfer Tax Exemption

The 2024 Greenbook carries forward the proposals from the 2023 Greenbook and tracks the proposals introduced by President Biden and Democratic lawmakers in legislation throughout 2021 and 2033.

Closing Loopholes

- Tax Carried (Profits) Interests as Ordinary Income
- Repeal Deferral of Gain from Like-Kind Exchanges
- Require 100 Percent Recapture of Depreciation Deductions as Ordinary Income for Certain Depreciable Real Property
- Limit Use of Donor Advised Funds to avoid Provide Foundation Payout Requirement
- Exclude Payments to Disqualified Persons from Counting Toward Private Foundation Payout Requirement
- Extend the Period for Assessment of Tax for Certain Qualified Opportunity Fund Investors

- Impose Ownership Diversification Requirement for Certain Small Insurance Companies
- Expand Pro Rata Interest Expense Disallowance for Business-Owned Life Insurance
- Modify Rules for Insurance Products that Fail the Statutory Definition of Life Insurance Contract
- Correct Drafting Errors in the Taxation of Insurance Companies under the Tax Cut and Jobs Act of 2017
- Define the Term "Ultimate Purchaser" for Purposes of Diesel Fuel Exportation

In this section, the Greenbook proposals continue to address provisions that the President and Treasury have identified as providing significant tax advantage to high income taxpayers by taking advantage of certain rules.

For detailed explanations of these and all proposals, see:

https://home.treasury.gov/system/files/131/General-Explanations-FY2024.pdf

8.   2022-2023 Priority Guidance Plan (November 4, 2022)

> **Treasury Department and Internal Revenue Service release their 2022-2023 Priority Guidance Plan**

On November 4, 2022, the Treasury Department and the Internal Revenue Service released their 2022-2023 Priority Guidance Plan, which lists those projects which will be the focus of the IRS's efforts during the twelve-month period from July 1, 2022 through June 30, 2023. The 2021-2022 Priority Guidance Plan contains 205 guidance projects. The following are the projects in the "Gifts and Estates and Trusts."

- Final regulations under §§1014(f) and 6035 regarding basis consistency between estate and person acquiring property from decedent. Proposed and temporary regulations were published on March 4, 2016.
- Guidance regarding availability of §1014 basis adjustment at the death of the owner of a grantor trust described in §671 when the trust assets are not included in the owner's gross estate for estate tax purposes. See Revenue Ruling 2023-2.
- Regulations under §2010 addressing whether gifts that are includible in the gross estate should be excepted from the special rule of § 20.2010-1(c). Proposed regulations were published on April 27, 2022.
- Guidance on portability regulatory elections under §2010(c)(5)(A). See Rev. Proc. 2022-32 (July 8, 2022).
- Regulations under §2032(a) regarding imposition of restrictions on estate assets during the six-month alternate valuation period. Proposed regulations were published on November 18, 2011.
- Final regulations under §2053 regarding the deductibility of certain interest expenses and amounts paid under a personal guarantee, certain substantiation requirements, and

the applicability of present value concepts in determining the amount deductible. Proposed regulations were published on June 28, 2022.

- Regulations under §20.2056A-2 for qualified domestic trust elections on estate tax returns, updating obsolete references.

- Regulations under §2632 providing guidance governing the allocation of generationskipping transfer (GST) exemption in the event the IRS grants relief under §2642(g), as well as addressing the definition of a GST trust under §2632(c), and providing ordering rules when GST exemption is allocated in excess of the transferor's remaining exemption.

- Final regulations under §2642(g) describing the circumstances and procedures under which an extension of time will be granted to allocate GST exemption. Proposed regulations were published on April 17, 2008.

- Final regulations under §2801 regarding the tax imposed on U.S. citizens and residents who receive gifts or bequests from certain expatriates. Proposed regulations were published on September 10, 2015.

- Regulations under §7520 regarding the use of actuarial tables in valuing annuities, interests for life or terms of years, and remainder or reversionary interests. Proposed regulations were published on May 5, 2022.

9.   REG-118913-21 – "Clawback" Proposed Regulations (April 27, 2022)

> **IRS, Treasury issue proposed regulations providing an exception to the anti-clawback rule for the estate and gift tax basic exclusions**

The Tax Cuts and Jobs Act became law in 2017, doubling the basic exclusion amount used in calculating estate and gift taxes only until December 31, 2025. Unless the law is extended or made permanent, the basic exclusion amount ("BEA") will drop by half again. In order to provide certainty for taxpayers, Congress included a new Code section 2001(g)(2), granting Treasury the "authority to prescribe such regulations as may be necessary or appropriate to carry out section 2001 with respect to any difference between the BEA applicable at the time of a decedent's death and the BEA applicable with respect to any gifts made by the decedent." The regulations issued in 2019 were commonly referred to as the "anti-clawback" regulations, as they confirmed that taxpayers that made gifts when the BEA was higher at the time of gift than at the time of death would enjoy the higher BEA in the final calculation of tax, and the benefit would not be clawed back (Regs. Sec. 20.2010-1(c)).

The special rule outlined in Regs. Sec. 20.2010-1(c) was a computational rule that did not distinguish between: (i) completed gifts that are treated as adjusted taxable gifts for estate tax purposes and that, by definition, are not included in the donor's gross estate; and (ii) completed gifts that are treated as testamentary transfers for estate tax purposes and are included in the donor's gross estate (what IRS/Treasury called, an "includible gift"). Certain includible gifts create no problem when the special rule/anti-clawback rule applies, such as an includible gift that was eligible for the charitable or marital deduction. However, "the application of the special rule to [a subset of] includible gifts results in securing the benefit of the increased BEA in circumstances where the donor continues to have the title, possession, use, benefit, control, or enjoyment of the transferred property during life." In order to prevent that outcome, IRS and Treasury are proposing an exception to the special rule (87 FR 24918), such that the following classes of gift will not be eligible for the special rule:

- Gifts subject to a retained life estate or subject to other powers or interests as described in Code sections 2035 through 2038 and 2042
- Gifts made by enforceable promise as described in Rev. Rul. 84-25
- Gifts subject to the special valuation rules of Code sections 2701 and 2702

This confirms what many practitioners expected: In the case of a gift to a trust, such as a GRAT or a QPRT, where a gift was made at the time of the creation of a trust, but the value of the trust assets are includible in the estate of the donor if the donor dies during the term under Code section 2701, the BEA at the donor's death, and not the BEA at the time of the gift, apply to the includible assets. The same would apply to a "gift of a promissory note," where a donor attempts to use up the donor's BEA (before reduction) without parting with assets. The fact that the "gift" was made during a year when the BEA was higher would not hold. The value of the assets used to satisfy the promise, included and valued as of the decedent's death, and the BEA at the donor's death would apply in calculating the tax under this proposed rule.

GIFT TAX

10.   ILM 202152018 (October 4, 2021, Released 12/30/2021)

In a legal memorandum, the IRS determined that a taxpayer could not ignore a possible merger that a willing buyer and willing seller would take into account when relying on an appraisal of shares contributed to a grantor retained annuity trust before the merger was completed.

The taxpayer founded a successful business and sought investment advice about possibly selling it. The taxpayer also had the company valued for section 409A purposes at the end of the year when the process started. About six months later, five companies presented initial bids to buy the taxpayer's business. Three days after the last bid came in, the taxpayer created a GRAT with a two-year term, funded the GRAT with an interest in the business, and used the now 7-month-old appraisal to value those shares. Four of the prospective buyers increased their bids over the next three months. Shortly after the increased offers were submitted, taxpayer funded a charitable remainder trust with an interest in the business. For purposes of establishing value for the charitable deduction attributable to the contribution, the taxpayer obtained a *new* qualified appraisal, which based the value of the interest on the tender offer that the taxpayer accepted, which valued the company at three times the value used in funding the GRAT, some three months earlier.

When pressed on why the taxpayer used the lower, 409A valuation in connection with the GRAT funding but obtained a new, qualified appraisal for the charitable deduction, the taxpayer argued that the 409A valuation was only 6 months old at the time the GRAT was funded and the charitable deduction requirements under Code section 8283 required the new, qualified appraisal.

After the GRAT closed, the purchaser paid four times the share price of the first appraisal for the rest of the business's stock.

The IRS determined that the 409A valuation did not represent the fair market value of the interests at the GRAT funding and said that "to ignore the facts and circumstances of the pending merger undermines the basic tenets of fair market value and yields a baseless valuation, and thereby casts more than just doubt upon the bona fides of the transfer to the GRAT." Beyond just revaluing the interest transferred to the GRAT, the IRS determined that "intentionally basing the fixed amount required by § 2702(b)(1) and § 25.2702-3(b)(1)(i) on an undervalued appraisal causes the retained interest to fail to function exclusively as a qualified interest from the creation of the trust." This meant that the taxpayer did not retain a qualified annuity interest, and the entire GRAT failed.

11.   *Smaldino v. Commissioner*, T.C. Memo 2021-127 (2021)

Louis Smaldino ("Louis") owned various rental properties in southern California, of a portfolio that was apparently valued at about $80 million. He placed 10 of these properties into Smaldino Properties, LLC (the "LLC").

Louis was married to Agustina Smaldino in 2006. Louis had 6 children and 10 grandchildren from a prior marriage.

In 2012, Louis began to work on some estate and tax planning. Louis and Agustina continued to keep their assets separate. It was apparently Louis' goal of transferring his real estate interests to his descendants. In 2012, Louis established the Smaldino 2012 Dynasty Trust (the "Dynasty Trust"), an irrevocable trust for the benefit of certain of his descendants, with his son Allen as Trustee. Agustina was not a beneficiary of the Dynasty Trust.

In 2013, Louis transferred 8% of the LLC interests to the Dynasty Trust. He then purported to transfer about 41% of the LLC interests to Agustina. Agustina then purported to transfer that interest to the Dynasty Trust.

Louis' 2013 gift tax return reported the 8% transfer of the LLC to the Dynasty Trust. Louis took the position that the gift of 41% to Agustina qualified for the marital deduction. Louis did not report the gift to his wife on his gift tax return.

Agustina's 2013 gift tax return reported the 41% transfer of the LLC to the Dynasty Trust. Because the 41% gift was sheltered by her gift tax exemption, she reported no gift tax due.

Louis and Agustina did not elect to split gifts.

On review of these transfers, the IRS argued that the substance of the 41% transaction was a transfer directly from Louis to the Dynasty Trust, and that the form of the transaction (that is, a transfer to Agustina, then a transfer by her to the Dynasty Trust) should not be respected. The IRS determined that Louis was the actual transferor of the 41% to the Dynasty Trust, in addition to the 8% he already gifted to the Dynasty Trust. And because Louis had no more gift tax exemption remaining (hence the need to ask Agustina to make an additional gift to the Dynasty Trust), the IRS determined that Louis had a $1,154,000 gift tax deficiency for 2013.

Various facts supported the IRS' argument that Agustina had never become an actual owner of an interest in the LLC. The LLC's operating agreement was never updated to reflect Agustina as a Member. Agustina was not listed as a member of the LLC on the LLC's partnership tax return for 2013.

The various transfer documents did not reflect a date that they were signed, suggesting that perhaps the transfer documents were signed at the same time, and were all executed in August 2013, which is when the purported transfer by Agustina to the LLC occurred. The Tax Court also noted that the assignment documents for the first round of transfers, which were purported to be effective in April, were based on calculations that would have only been known after the preparation of a valuation report in August, which led the Tax Court to conclude that those transfer documents were signed in August.

Meanwhile, other facts suggested that the transfers were part of a prearranged plan to transfer the LLC units to the Dynasty Trust. For example, Agustina testified that before the transfer, she had already made a "commitment, promise" to her husband that she would transfer the LLC units to the Dynasty Trust. And when asked whether she could have changed her mind and not transferred the units to the Dynasty Trust, she responded, "No, because I believe in fairness."

The Tax Court upheld the finding that Louis was the actual transferor of the additional 41% to the Dynasty Trust.

Various other provisions of the opinion are worthy of discussion, including a relatively brief discussion of certain "guaranteed payments" under the LLC and their relevant for valuation purposes under Section 2701.

This case is a cautionary tale for transfers to a spouse or other third party to allow that party to make additional gifts (if the party so chooses). There is risk of the IRS collapsing the transactions and considering the first party as the actual donor, which might result in additional tax liability. The client should be advised of those risks and the appropriate steps should be taken to address such risks, including properly documenting the transfers so that the spouse or third party actually is in control of those assets, and documenting that these transfers are not part of a prearranged plan for further gifting.

12.   Letter Ruling 202116001 (Issued July 9, 2020; Released April 23, 2021)

IRS rules on gift tax consequences of splitting QTIP Trust and then distributing one resulting trust to children

---

Decedent died survived by spouse and two daughters. A marital trust, designated as the "Qualified Trust," was created at decedent's death. The Qualified Trust was a QTIP Marital Deduction Trust. Subsequently, the trustee divided the Qualified Trust into two trusts, Qualified Trust-A and Continuing Qualified Trust. The terms and provisions of each of the new trusts were identical to the terms in the original trust. Qualified Trust-A was funded with a specific amount of cash and marketable securities. All other assets were held in the Continuing Qualified Trust.

Subsequently, the trustees, the spouse, and the two daughters petitioned a state court to change the provisions of Qualified Trust-A. Under the modification, Qualified Trust-A would terminate upon the death of the last surviving income beneficiary. However, at any time prior to the spouse's death, Qualified Trust-A could be terminated as to a beneficiary's interest and any part of the trust property representing that terminated beneficiary's interests would be distributed to that beneficiary if the trustee considered such distribution to be in the best interests of the beneficiary. The modification of the trust eliminated the surviving spouse as a beneficiary of Qualified Trust-A.

The IRS ruled first that the division of the Qualified Trust into Qualified Trust-A and the Qualified Continuing Trust did not cause the assets remaining in the Continuing Qualified Trust to be subject to gift tax under either Section 2512 or 2511.

However, the modification of the terms of Qualified Trust-A to change the beneficial interest to the spouse and the two daughters permitted the termination of spouse's income interest. As a result, the spouse was deemed to have made a transfer of all the property of the Qualified Trust-A, other than the value of her qualifying income interest under Section 2519, and the spouse was deemed to have made a transfer of her qualifying interest in Qualified Trust-A under Section 2511. The transfers occurred when the court entered the order by which the income interest of the spouse in Qualified Trust-A was terminated and distributions from Qualified Trust-A were permitted to be made prior to the death of the spouse. Section 2519 provides that any disposition of all or part of a qualifying income interest for wife is subject to gift tax other than the qualifying income interest. Section 2511 would then apply to the gift of the qualifying income interest.

13. *Cavallaro v. Commissioner*, T.C. Memo 2014-189; 842 F.3d 16 (1st Cir. 2016), aff'g in part, rev'g in part and remanding; and T.C. Memo 2019-144

Tax Court holds that husband and wife are liable for gift tax following company merger, but reduces amount of additional gift upon remand from First Circuit Court of Appeals

---

In 1979, Mr. and Mrs. Cavallaro started Knight Tool Company. Knight was a contract manufacturing company that made tools and machine parts. In 1982, Mr. Cavallaro and his eldest son developed an automated liquid dispensing machine they called CAM/ALOT. Subsequently, in 1987, Mr. and Mrs. Cavallaros' three sons incorporated Camelot Systems, Inc., which was a business dedicated to the selling of the CAM/ALOT machines made by Knight. The two companies operated out of the same building, shared payroll and accounting services, and collaborated in the further development of the CAM/ALOT product line. Knight funded the operations of both companies and paid the salaries and overhead costs for both.

In 1994, Mr. and Mrs. Cavallaro sought estate planning advice from a big four accounting firm and a large law firm. The professionals advised Mr. and Mrs. Cavallaro that the value of CAM/ALOT Technology resided in Camelot (the sons' company) and not in Knight and that they should adjust their estate planning. Mr. and Mrs. Cavallaro and their three sons merged Knight and Camelot in 1995 and Camelot was the surviving entity. Part of the reason for the merger was to qualify for Conformite Europeenne, which means European conformity, so that the CAM/ALOT machines could be sold in Europe. In the 1995 merger, Mrs. Cavallaro received 20 shares, Mr. Cavallaro received 18 shares, and 54 shares were distributed to the three sons. In valuing the company, the accounting firm assumed that the premerger Camelot had owned the CAM/ALOT technology. The Tax Court found that Camelot had not owned the CAM/ALOT technology, and as a result, the Tax Court found that the appraiser overstated the relative value of Camelot and understated the relative value of Knight at the time of the merger.

In 1996, Camelot was sold for $57 million in cash with a contingent additional amount of up to $43 million in potential deferred payments based on future profits. No further payments were made after the 1996 sale.

Three issues were under review by the tax court:

- Whether the 19 percent interest received by Mr. and Mrs. Cavallaro in Camelot Systems, Inc., in exchange for their shares of Knight Tool Company in a tax-free merger, was full and adequate consideration, or whether it was a gift.
- Whether Mr. and Mrs. Cavallaro were liable for additions to tax under Section 6651(a)(1) for failure to file gift tax returns for 1995, or whether the failure was due to reasonable cause.

- Whether there were underpayments of gift tax attributable to the gift tax valuation understatement for purposes of the accuracy related penalty, or whether any portions of the underpayment were attributable to reasonable cause.

With respect to the valuation issue, the Cavallaros offered two experts regarding the value of the combined entity. One expert valued the entity at between $70 million and $75 million and opined that only $13 million to $15 million of that value was attributable to Knight. A second appraiser valued the combined entity at $72.8 million.

The IRS retained its own appraiser, Marc Bello of Edelstein & Company. Bello assumed that Knight owned the CAM/ALOT technology. He valued the combined entities at approximately $64.5 million and found that 65 percent of that value, or $41.9 million, was Knight's portion.

In reaching its decision on the gift tax liability, the Tax Court noted that the 1995 merger transaction was notably lacking in arm's-length characteristics and Camelot may have been a sham company. It also discussed how the law firm in 1995 had tried to document the ownership of the CAM/ALOT technology by the sons but that such documentation was insufficient. The Court did not accept the testimony of the accounting firm. It noted that the IRS had conceded during the litigation that the value of the combined entities was not greater than $64.5 million and that the value of the gift made in the merger transaction was not greater than $29.6 million. As a result, the Tax Court concluded that Mr. and Mrs. Cavallaro made gifts totaling $29.6 million in 1995.

The Tax Court rejected the imposition of penalties for failure to file a gift tax return and accuracy-related penalties. It found that in both instances, Mr. and Mrs. Cavallaro had been advised by an accountant or lawyers and that there was reasonable cause for the failure to file a gift tax return and failure to pay the appropriate amount of tax. It noted that Mr. and Mrs. Cavallaro relied on the judgment and advice of the professional advisors and that the CAM/ALOT technology had been owned by the sons' company since 1987 (and thus was not being transferred in 1995). In documenting its finding of reasonable cause to avoid the penalties, the Tax Court went into great detail about Mr. and Mrs. Cavallaros lack of formal education beyond high school and that they had built the business themselves.

In their appeal, Mr. and Mrs. Cavallaros argued that the Tax Court erred in three respects:

- Its failure to shift the burden of proof to the IRS.
- Concluding that Knight owned the intangible assets (the CAM/ALOT technology).
- Misstating the Cavallaros' burden of proof and failing to consider flaws in the opinion offered by Marc Bello.

The First Circuit Court of Appeals in 2016 held that the Tax Court was correct in not shifting the burden of proof to the IRS and that Knight owned the intangibles including the CAM/ALOT technology. The First Circuit remanded the case to the Tax Court on the issue of the Tax

Court's failure to accept the Cavallaros' argument that the IRS's valuation was "arbitrary and excessive" by challenging Bello's methodology. The Tax Court had refused to hear that challenge on the grounds that, even if the Cavallaros were correct, they were unable to show the correct amount of their tax liability. The First Circuit held that the Tax Court should evaluate the Cavallaros' argument that Bello's appraisal contained methodological flaws that made arbitrary and excessive.

The Tax Court on remand rejected all but one of the Cavallaros' arguments with respect to Bello's appraisal. The Tax Court first found that Bello's failure to interview the principals of Knight and Camelot and his failure to do a site visit did not cause him to misunderstand the nature of the business of each of Knight and Camelot. The Tax Court also rejected the Cavallaros' challenges of Bello's profit reallocation calculation and discounted cash flow calculation. The Tax Court did find that Bello's placement of Camelot in the 90th percentile of similar businesses was based on a statistically unreliable method and was incorrect. Instead, Camelot should have been in the 88.3d percentile and this would make a significant difference in valuation. This reduced the rounded value of the gift by $6.9 million from $29.6 million to $22.8 million.

14. Revenue Procedure 2021-3, 2021-1 IRB 140 (January 4, 2021)

> **Service states that it will not issue rulings on consequences of incomplete non-grantor trusts**

In Item (17) of Section V of Revenue Procedure 2021-3, the Internal Revenue Service stated that it would no longer issue letter rulings with respect to incomplete gift non-grantor trusts which are sometimes referred to as "INGS," "DINGS" (if set up under Delaware law), or "NINGS" (if set up under Nevada law) when it added incomplete gift non-grantor trusts to the areas that under study. Letter rulings will only be issued when the Service resolves the issue through the publication of a revenue ruling, revenue procedure, regulation, or otherwise.

Previously, in Revenue Procedure, 2020-3, 2020-1 IRB 131 (January 2, 2020), the Service stated that it will not issue letter rulings with respect to beneficiary incomplete non-grantor trusts if the proposed trusts did not follow the provisions set forth in those trusts which the Service had approved in prior letter rulings.

An ING is structured to be a non-grantor trust for income tax purposes that is funded by transfers from the grantor that are incomplete gifts for gift tax purposes. Assuming the trust is established in a state that doesn't tax the income accumulated in the trust (such as Delaware or Nevada), the trust will avoid state income taxes as long as the state of residence of the grantor or beneficiaries doesn't subject the trust's income (or accumulated income) to tax. Moreover, if structured and administered properly, the trust property should be protected from the grantor's creditors.

The ING allows a grantor to achieve both of these benefits while still being able to receive discretionary distributions of trust property and without paying gift tax (or using any gift tax exemption) on the transfer of property to the trust. A gift from the grantor will be complete upon a subsequent distribution from the trust to a beneficiary other than the grantor, and whatever property remains in the trust will be subject to estate tax at the grantor's death.

An ING is particularly attractive for a highly appreciated asset in anticipation of sale of that asset. For example, the founder of a business that is going to be sold may face hundreds of thousands or even hundreds of millions of dollars of capital gain because he or she has so little basis. Avoiding state income tax on those gains can be a significant benefit.

Letter Ruling 202017018 (issued November 29, 2019; released April 24, 2020) is a recent example of many letter rulings with similar facts on the tax consequences of an incomplete non-grantor trust. Previous rulings on this subject include Letter Ruling 201836006 (issued May 30, 2018; released September 2018) and Letter Ruling 202014001 (issued August 26, 2019; released April 3, 2020).

In Letter Ruling 202017018, grantor created an irrevocable trust. The beneficiaries were grantor, grantor's spouse, grantor's issue, grantor's parents, and other issue or grantor's parents. A corporate trustee was the sole trustee of the trust.

The trust created a distribution committee. The distribution committee was initially composed of the grantor, grantor's spouse, grantors parents, and grantor's sister. Until the death of the grantor, the distribution committee was to have at least two members, other than grantor or grantor's spouse.

Under the terms of trust, the trustee was to distribute income and principal of the trust as directed by the distribution committee, grantor, or both as follows:

- Grantor's Consent Power. Income or principal to any beneficiary other than the grantor's spouse as determined by a majority of the distribution committee, other than grantor or grantor's spouse, acting in a non-fiduciary capacity with the written consent of grantor.
- Unanimous Committee Power. Income or principal to any beneficiary as determined by the unanimous decision of the distribution committee, other than grantor or grantor's spouse, acting in a non-fiduciary capacity.
- Grantor' Sole Power. Principal to any beneficiary other than grantor or grantor's spouse as determined by grantor acting in a non-fiduciary capacity for the support, health, or education of a beneficiary.
- Grantor held a testamentary power of appointment to the issue of grantor's parents (other than the grantor, his estate, or the creditors of either); grantor's spouse, or one or more charitable organizations. The balance not effectively appointed by grantor upon his death would be distributed to a designated trust.

The taxpayer sought the following rulings:

- During the period that the distribution committee was serving, there would be no income tax consequences to the grantor or any member of the distribution committee under the grantor trust rules.
- The grantor's contribution of property of the trust was not a completed gift subject to federal gift tax.
- Any distribution of property from the trust by the distribution committee to the grantor was not a completed gift for gift tax purposes by a member of the distribution committee to the grantor.
- Any distribution of property by the distribution committee from the trust to any beneficiary of the trust other than the grantor was not a completed gift for gift tax purposes by any member of the distribution committee to that beneficiary.
- No member of the distribution committee would be deemed to have a taxable general power of appointment pursuant to Section 2041 or Section 2514 upon his or her death.

The Service first ruled that none of the provisions of the trust would cause the grantor to be treated as the owner of the trust for income tax purposes under any of Sections 673, 674, 676, 677, 678, or 679 as long as the distribution committee remained in existence and was serving, and the trust was a domestic trust.

The Service stated that examination of the trust revealed none of the circumstances that would cause administrative controls to be considered exercisable primarily for the benefit of the grantor under Section 675. A determination of whether Section 675 would cause the grantor to be treated as the owner of any portion of the trust for income tax purposes was deferred until the federal income tax returns of the trust were examined.

The Service next ruled that a contribution of property to the trust was not a completed gift by the grantor for gift tax purposes. Any distribution from the trust to the grantor was merely a return of grantor's property. Upon grantor's death, the fair market value of the property in the trust was subject to estate tax in the grantor's gross estate.

The Service lastly ruled that any distribution of property by the distribution committee to a beneficiary of the trust, other than the grantor, would not be a gift subject to gift tax by any member of the distribution committee. Instead, any such distribution would be a completed gift by the grantor. In addition, the powers held by the distribution committee were not general powers of appointment under Section 2041 and, accordingly, no property held in the trust would be included in the gross estate of any member of the distribution committee upon his or her death under Section 2041.

CHARITABLE GIFTS

15.   *Hoensheid v. Commissioner*, No. 18606-19, T.C. Memo 2023-34 (March 15, 2023)

Tax Court rules against taxpay in assignment of income case; declines to uphold accuracy related penalty

On March 15, 2023, the Tax Court issued an opinion concluding that donating stock two days before closing on a third-party sale transaction was clearly too late to avoid tax. The Tax Court declined to specify a "bright line" deadline for making a donation and instead focused on the substance of the underlying transactions. All in all, these taxpayers paid income taxes on the recognized gain on the shares they no longer owned *and* didn't get the charitable tax deduction for failure to meet the strict substantiation rules.

In the *Estate of Scott M. Hoensheid, et al. v. Commissioner* (T.C. Memo 2023-34), the taxpayers were clear at the outset that they wanted to "wait as long as possible to pull the trigger" on donating shares valued at more than $3 million to charity because they wanted to make sure the sale of the company was going to occur. They were also clear that the purpose for donating was to avoid paying income taxes on any gain associated with the donated shares. To reach these stated goals, the taxpayers worked closely with their tax/estate planning attorney and a financial adviser to structure the stock sale transaction hoping for an $80 million target price and to find a charity that was willing to accept the stock and then participate in the third-party sale transaction without much hassle.

In early 2015, the taxpayers' financial adviser started soliciting bids for the company and received significant interest from private equity firms. In mid-April 2015, the taxpayers' tax attorney advised them that "the transfer [to the charity] would have to take place before there is a definitive agreement in place." Concurrently, the taxpayers began working with Fidelity Investments Charitable Gift Fund, a large tax-exempt organization that serves as a sponsoring organization with regard to establishing donor-advised funds, to accept the donation of company stock. Fidelity Charitable provided a similar warning to the taxpayers that the gift must take place before any purchase agreement is executed to avoid the Internal Revenue Service raising the anticipatory assignment of income doctrine.

Anticipatory Assignment of Income Doctrine

The anticipatory assignment of income doctrine has been around since at least the 1930s. See *Lucas v. Earl*, 281 U.S. 111 (1930). Under this doctrine, income is taxed "to those who earn or otherwise create the right to receive it." See *Helvering v. Horst*, 311 U.S. 112, 119 (1940). The courts have been clear that taxpayers cannot avoid tax by entering into anticipatory arrangements and contracts where a person with a fixed right to receive income from property arranges for another person to gratuitously take title before the income is actually received.

The person who gratuitously takes title usually has a lower effective income tax rate or does not pay tax at all on recognized gains (i.e., many charitable organizations). If the doctrine is triggered, the donor is deemed to have effectively realized the income and then assigned that income to another. This results in the donor paying tax on the income that he or she did not actually receive. For charitable donations, the donor likely is unable to force the charity to rescind the transaction, causing the taxpayer to use personal funds to pay the taxes on the income received by the charity.

Unfortunately, the Tax Court's ruling in *Estate of Hoensheid* did not specify a bright line deadline for making a donation to give donors assurance that the anticipatory assignment of income doctrine would not apply. Instead, to determine who has a fixed right to the income, the Tax Court stated that it looks at the realities and substance of the underlying transactions rather than formalities or hypothetical possibilities. Factors considered include (i) the donee's obligation to sell the shares, (ii) the acts of the parties to effect the sale transactions, (iii) unresolved sale contingencies as of the date of the donation and (iv) corporate formalities necessary to effect the transaction.

In reviewing the substance of the underlying transactions in the *Estate of Hoensheid* case, the Tax Court found that Fidelity Charitable did not have any obligation to sell the shares, which was a factor in favor of the taxpayers. However, the court was not persuaded by the taxpayers' arguments that the donation occurred over a month before the transaction closed. Importantly, nine days before the transaction closed, the taxpayers' attorney indicated that the amount of shares being transferred was unclear and that the stock assignment had not been executed.

In the end, the court concluded that Fidelity Charitable accepted the gift only two days before the stock sale transaction closed when one of the taxpayers' advisers emailed a copy of the company stock certificate issued in the name of Fidelity Charitable.

As of the date of contribution, the Tax Court opined that there were no unresolved sale contingencies and noted that the shareholders had emptied the company's working capital by distributing cash to the owners (not including Fidelity Charitable).

Finally, the Tax Court looked at the corporate formalities. While the taxpayers argued that negotiations were ongoing all the way through the closing date of July 15, 2015, the Tax Court said the signing of the definitive purchase agreement on that date was purely ministerial and any decision not to sell as of the date of donation was remote and hypothetical. These facts led to the conclusion that the transaction was "too far down the road to enable [the taxpayers] to escape taxation on the gain attributable to the donated shares."

When considering the enumerated factors, donors should be very careful to avoid creating an informal, prearranged understanding with the charity that would constitute an obligation for the charity to agree to sell. Additionally, the donor must bear some risk at the time of the contribution that the sale will not close. In the *Estate of Hoensheid*, the taxpayers sought to eliminate any risk that the sale would not go through, and as a result, the Tax Court agreed with the Internal Revenue Service imposing the anticipatory assignment of income doctrine to force the taxpayers to recognize gain on the contributed shares as a result of the later sale to the private equity firm.

The key takeaways from this case are: (i) waiting until shortly before a purchase agreement is executed significantly increases the risk that the Internal Revenue Service will assert the anticipatory assignment of income doctrine; and (ii) the Internal Revenue Service and the courts will look closely at the transaction documents, intent of the donor, correspondence between the donor and his or her advisers, and the records of the charity to determine the date of the gift and the application of this doctrine. This does not mean that donors must make such gifts before a transaction is contemplated, or even before a nonbinding letter of intent is executed. This case is simply a cautionary tale to remind taxpayers that the Internal Revenue Service will closely scrutinize donations of stock in advance of a stock sale transaction. Maybe one day the Internal Revenue Service or the courts will provide a "bright line," but for now caution is key.

Loss of Charitable Deduction

After reaching its conclusion related to the anticipatory assignment of income doctrine, the Tax Court turned to the Internal Revenue Service's argument that the taxpayers should not be permitted a charitable deduction for the donated shares for failing to comply with the rigid substantiation requirements. For a more complete discussion of these requirements, see McGuireWoods' Nov. 10, 2022, alert. As a reminder, when the Internal Revenue Service challenges a charitable deduction on procedural grounds, it is not disputing the fact that a charitable contribution was made. In fact, the Internal Revenue Service admits that the contribution was made but nonetheless challenges the taxpayers' ability to claim a tax deduction.

Here, the Internal Revenue Service argued that the taxpayers failed to engage a qualified appraiser and the appraisal did not satisfy the basic requirements for a qualified appraisal.

A qualified appraiser is someone who has obtained an appraisal designation from a recognized professional organization or otherwise has sufficient education and experience, and who regularly performs appraisals for compensation. The qualified appraisal must include all of the following:

1. A description of the contributed property in sufficient detail, including the physical condition of any real or tangible property.

2. The valuation effective date. For qualified appraisals prepared before the date of contribution, the valuation effective date must be no earlier than 60 days before the date of contribution and no later than the actual date of contribution. For qualified appraisals

prepared after the contribution, the valuation effective date must be the date of contribution.

3. The fair market value of the contributed property on the valuation effective date.

4. The date or expected date of contribution.

5. The terms of any agreement relating to the use, sale or other disposition of the contributed property. This includes any restrictions on the donee's ability to dispose of the property, any rights to income from the property or rights to vote any contributed securities.

6. The name, address and taxpayer identification number of the qualified appraiser or the partnership or employer who employs the qualified appraiser.

7. The qualifications of the appraiser, including education and experience.

8. A statement that the appraisal was prepared for income tax purposes.

9. The method of valuation used (e.g., income approach, market-data approach, replacement-cost-less-depreciation approach) and the specific basis for the valuation (e.g., specific comparable sales, statistical sampling).

10. A description of the fee arrangement between the donor and qualified appraiser.

11. This declaration: "I understand that my appraisal will be used in connection with a return or claim for refund. I also understand that, if there is a substantial or gross valuation misstatement of the value of the property claimed on the return or claim for refund that is based on my appraisal, I may be subject to a penalty under Section 6695A of the Internal Revenue Code, as well as other applicable penalties. I affirm that I have not been at any time in the three-year period ending on the date of the appraisal barred from presenting evidence or testimony before the Department of Treasury of the Internal Revenue Service pursuant to 31 U.S.C. 330(c)."

12. The signature of the qualified appraiser and the appraisal report date. The qualified appraisal must be signed and dated no earlier than 60 days before the date of contribution and no later than the due date for the tax return (including extensions) on which the deduction is claimed.

In *Estate of Hoensheid*, the taxpayers decided to use the services of their financial adviser that worked on the sales transaction to save the costs of having an outside expert prepare the appraisal. This cost-saving move ended up actually costing the taxpayers their entire $3.3 million claim of a charitable deduction for the donated stock. Because the taxpayers' financial adviser did not have any appraisal certifications, did not hold himself out as an appraiser, and prepares valuations only once or twice a year in order to solicit business for his financial advisory firm, the Tax Court agreed with the Internal Revenue Service that the taxpayer failed to engage a qualified appraiser.

The Tax Court reviewed the Internal Revenue Service's arguments that the contents of the appraisal attached to the tax return were deficient. The Tax Court agreed and indicated that the appraisal (i) included the incorrect date of contribution, (ii) did not include the statement that it was prepared for federal income tax purposes, (iii) included a premature date of appraisal, (iv) did not sufficiently describe the method for the valuation, (v) was not signed by the appraiser, (vi) did not include the appraiser's qualifications as an appraiser, (vii) did not describe the donated property in sufficient detail and (viii) did not include an explanation of the specific basis for the valuation.

While the taxpayers did not dispute that the appraisal had defects, they sought to rely on the "substantial compliance" doctrine to excuse these stringent substantiation requirements. The Tax Court analyzed the substantial compliance argument but rejected it, stating that the appraisal failed with regard to multiple substantive requirements of the applicable regulations. As a result, no deduction for the contribution of shares to Fidelity Charitable was allowed.

16.   *PLR 202305017* (February 3, 2023) and *PLR 202306011* (February 10, 2023)

IRS denies exemption application of proposed organizations

In two unrelated rulings, the IRS denied the exemption application of two organizations.

In PLR 202306011, an organization sought tax exempt status under Code § 501(c)(4) as a social welfare organization. The organization was a non-profit corporation under state law, but the charter was silent on charitable purpose and the governance provided for distribution of the assets on termination to another exempt organization. The organization was a home provider agency formed exclusively for the care of the daughter of the CEO of the organization. State law where the organization is located allows families to set up home provider agencies to serve a single individual. The IRS looked at the purpose of social welfare organizations, including their focus on the common good and general welfare of the community. In denying exempt status, the IRS held that to qualify for exemption under IRC Section 501(c)(4), an organization must primarily benefit the community as a whole, rather than select individuals or group.

In PLR 202305017, a self-described "Hunting Organization" sought exempt status as a charitable organization under Code §501(c)(3). The organization filed a Form 1023-EZ, providing details of their organization, including the primary focus on conducting hunting and shooting activities on leased land by members who pay dues to participate. In short, the form described a traditional "hunt club." An organization must be both organized and operated exclusively for purposes described in IRC Section 501(c)(3), which are charitable purposes. The

IRS held that this organization failed the operational test, in that it was not operated for public purposes but for the private interests of its members. Exempt status was denied.

17. *Calvin A. Lim and Helen K. Chu v. Commissioner*, T.C. Memo 2023-11 (January 23, 2023)

Tax Court hears case of the "Ultimate Tax Plan" involving charitable gift of LLC Units

---

In this opinion, Judge Lauber of the Tax Court responded to a partial motion for summary judgment filed by the IRS, seeking a ruling as a matter of law that the petitioners, Calvin Lim and Helen Chu, were not entitled to certain charitable deductions for tax year 2016 because (1) petitioners did not in fact donate assets to charity in the tax year, and (2) petitioners failed to satisfy the substantiation requirements of Code § 170(f).

Lim and Chu were the sole shareholders of Integra Capital Group, Inc., a S corporation doing business in California. At the end of December in 2016, Lim and Chu met Michael Meyer, an attorney promoting a scheme he called "The Ultimate Plan: the Ultimate Tax, Estate and Charitable Plan." Petitioners executed an engagement agreement with Mr. Meyer, who agreed to form a "Charitable Limited Liability Company" (CLLC) as a charitable giving vehicle. He agreed to create documents that would transfer assets to the CLLC, to create documents that would transfer CLLC units to a charity, and to supply an appraisal supporting the valuation claimed for the gift. He also agreed to represent petitioners before the IRS and this Court if the tax return on which petitioners reported the gift was selected by the IRS for examination. The engagement letter specified that Mr. Meyer's fee would be the greater of $25,000 or an amount calculated by reference to the assets transferred to the CLLC. The engagement letter contemplated that the assets transferred to the CLLC would be five promissory notes with an aggregate face amount of $2,008,500. Copies of the promissory notes were attached to the engagement letter.

That same day Mr. Meyer created ABC Foundation Legacy, LLC (ABC), as the CLLC for the "Ultimate Tax Plan." ABC was a single member LLC incorporated in Indiana. Mr. Meyer listed himself as ABC's registered agent.

On December 30, 2016, petitioners and Integra executed with respect to ABC an agreement prepared by Mr. Meyer (ABC agreement). The ABC agreement named petitioners as ABC's managers, Integra as ABC's single member, and Mr. Meyer as its registered agent. Attached to the ABC agreement were the five promissory notes referenced in the engagement letter. Each note is dated December 31, 2016. By these notes Chu, as payor, promised to pay ABC a total of $2,008,500 in seven years. Chu signed each note as payor, and both petitioners signed each note (on behalf of ABC) as payees.

The charitable recipient under the "Ultimate Tax Plan" was to be the Indiana Endowment Foundation, Inc. (Foundation). The Foundation was an Indiana corporation incorporated on June 2, 2016. Mr. Meyer's name does not appear on the certificate of incorporation. However, he is listed as the Foundation's "registered agent" in a Business Entity Report filed in April 2017 with the Indiana secretary of state.

Petitioners assert that Integra, ABC's single member, donated "units" of ABC to the Foundation on December 31, 2016. But petitioners have supplied no evidence to establish that any property was actually transferred to the Foundation during that year. The only evidence of the transfer offered by Lim and Chu was a letter, dated January 1, 2017, that purports to be a "contemporaneous written acknowledgement of the contribution" within the meaning of section 170(f)(8)(A). The letter reads as follows:

> We received your non-cash donation of one thousand (1,000) units in C&H FAMILY LLC in 2016. Indiana Endowment Foundation, Inc., provided no goods or services to you in exchange for your contribution. Please allow this letter to serve as official receipt of your unrestricted gift of 1000 units received in 2016. Your support is greatly appreciated.

This document appears to be a form letter into which were input the taxpayer-specific items shown in bold. The letter is odd in several respects.

On January 4, 2017, Mr. Meyer issued an invoice to petitioners calculating his fee as $84,000, as stated in the engagement letter. The premise for this calculation was that the "deductible amount" of assets to which the engagement letter referred was roughly $1.6 million. That "deductible amount" was based on a purported appraisal prepared by Mr. Meyer and dated January 31, 2017.

The January 31, 2017, document is captioned "Appraisal of the Fair Market Value of [the] LLC Interests of ABC" that were allegedly transferred to the Foundation on December 31, 2016. At that time, the only assets allegedly possessed by ABC were the five promissory notes executed by petitioner wife, showing ABC as the payee. Thus, the fair market value (FMV) of the LLC interests of ABC could be expected to approximate the value of the notes.

The IRS selected petitioners' 2016 and 2017 returns for examination. On September 9, 2020, the IRS issued petitioners a timely notice of deficiency, disallowing the deductions at issue for lack of substantiation. Petitioners timely petitioned this Court for redetermination.

Section 170(a)(1) allows as a deduction any charitable contribution made within the taxable year. If the taxpayer makes a charitable contribution of property other than money, the amount of the contribution is generally equal to the FMV of the property at the time of contribution. *See* Treas. Reg. § 1.170A-1(c)(1). "A charitable contribution shall be allowable as a deduction only if verified under regulations prescribed by the Secretary." § 170(a)(1).

The Secretary has prescribed extensive regulations governing the verification of noncash charitable contributions. *See* Treas. Reg. § 1.170A-13. In the case of a contribution of property (other than publicly traded securities) valued in excess of $5,000, the taxpayer must obtain a "qualified appraisal" of the property. § 170(f)(11)(C). The taxpayer must also attach to his return "such information regarding such property and such appraisal as the Secretary may require," which includes a fully completed appraisal summary on Form 8283.

Section 170(a) allows a deduction for a charitable contribution "payment of which is made within the taxable year." The amount of the contribution must be "actually paid during the taxable year." Treas. Reg. § 1.170A-1(a). To show that "payment" of the claimed contribution was made during the taxable year, a taxpayer must establish that he or she surrendered dominion and control over the property allegedly contributed.

Petitioners have conceded that they have no evidence to establish a physical transfer of property to the Foundation during 2016. The court ruled that the pPtitioners would face a decidedly uphill task in attempting to prove that Integra actually transferred ABC units to the Foundation during 2016. However, viewing all facts in the light most favorable to petitioners, declined to rule on the IRS's motion for summary judgement and concluded that Petitioners could present evidence at trial of the transfer.

In ruling on the veracity of the appraisal and the substantiation requirement for the appraisal, the Court ruled that the engagement letter from Meyer constituted an impermissible fee agreement with respect to qualified appraisals, and his report was not a "qualified appraisal" within the meaning of section 170(f)(11)(D).

18.   *Estate of Warne v. Commissioner*, T.C. Memo 2021-17

> **Court determines valuation of LLC interests for gift tax, estate tax inclusion, and estate tax charitable deduction purposes and upholds penalties for late filing of gift tax return**

Thomas and Miriam Warne, who were residents of California, created the Warne Family Trust, a revocable joint trust for their benefit, in 1981. Over the subsequent years, the Family Trust became the majority interest holder of five limited liability companies:

- WRW Properties LLC
- Warne Ranch, LLC
- VJK Properties, LLC
- Warne Investments LLC
- Royal Gardens LLC

Each of the LLCs held ground leases in various properties in California. The operating agreement of each of the LLCs provided the majority interest holder with considerable rights, including the ability with the manager to dissolve the LLC. Each operating agreement also put restrictions on the ability of a member to withdraw from the LLC. Thomas Warne died in 1999. Miriam Warne, as the trustee of the Family Trust, served as the managing member of each LLC.

On December 27, 2012, Miriam Warne gave fractional interests in three of the five LLCs to her two sons and three granddaughters. Miriam Warne subsequently died on February 20, 2014. Upon her death, the Family Trust, the assets of which were includable in Miriam Warne's estate, owned the following percentage of each of the five LLCs:

- WRW   78%
- Warne Ranch   72.5%
- VJK   86.3%
- Warne Investments 87.432%
- Royal Gardens   100%

Under the terms of the Family Trust, Miriam Warne left 75 percent of Royal Gardens to the Warne Family Charitable Foundation and the remaining 25 percent to St. John's Lutheran Church. The balance of the Family Trust assets appears to have passed to or for the benefit of family members.

On May 19, 2015, the estate filed the gift tax return for the 2012 gifts that Miriam Warne made to each of her two sons and three granddaughters. The estate tax return was timely filed, also on May 19, 2015. Discounts were taken for lack of marketability and lack of control in valuing the interests of the Family Trust in the LLCs. With respect to the gift of the interest in Royal Farms, the estate used the same value for the gross estate and for the combined fractional interests passing to the two charities.

The IRS challenged both the gift tax and estate tax valuations. On the gift tax return, the IRS increased the values of the interests in the three LLCs given in 2012. The IRS also imposed a penalty for the late filing of the gift tax return. On the estate tax return, the IRS determined a $8,351,970 deficiency. This was due to increases in the value of the LLCs and a reduction of the charitable deduction for the Royal Gardens gifts to the fractional value of each gift rather than the pro rata share of the value at which Royal Gardens was reported for purposes of determining the gross estate.

During the proceedings, the estate's expert, Philip Schwab, concluded that there should be a 10 percent total discount for lack of control and lack of marketability while the IRS's expert determined that there should be a 4 percent total discount for lack of control and lack of marketability with respect to the LLCs other than Royal Gardens.

With the respect to Royal Gardens, the estate and the IRS stipulated that the value was $25,600,000 for inclusion in the estate. The parties conditionally stipulated that with respect to the estate tax charitable deduction, if the court decided that a discount was appropriate for the 25 percent contribution of Royal Gardens to the church, the discount would be 27.385 percent for a total value of $4,650,000. The parties also conditionally stipulated that the 75 percent interest of Royal Gardens donated to the foundation should have a discount of 4 percent and a total value of $18,443,000 if the court decided that a discount was appropriate.

The court indicated the following issues were to be decided:

- The fair market values of the leased fee interest as of the date of the gift
- The fair market values of the leased fee interest as of the date of Miriam Warne's death
- The appropriate discounts for lack of control and marketability for the majority interest that the Family Trust held in the LLCs
- Whether to apply a discount to the separate fractional interests in Royal Gardens donated to the two charities
- Whether the penalty for late filing of the gift tax return would apply

With respect to the different valuation issues, the court found flaws in the analysis of each of the estate's experts and the IRS's experts and took a middle ground. In a lengthy discussion, it concluded that discounts for lack of control of 4 percent and lack of marketability of 5 percent for the LLCs were appropriate.

On the calculation of the estate tax charitable deduction, the court found, based on its reading of *Ahmanson Foundation v. United States*, 674 F.2d 761 (9th Cir. 1981), that Royal Farms should be included in the estate at its full value. This is because nothing in the statutes or case law suggests that the valuation of the gross estate should take into account the fact that the assets will come to rest in several hands rather than one. The value of an asset as part of an estate is determined without regard to the later disposition of that asset.

However, when property is split as part of charitable contribution, a different principle applies for purposes of determining the estate tax charitable deduction. An estate may only take an estate tax charitable deduction for what the charity actually receives. Another way of putting this was that for purposes of the estate tax charitable deduction one does not value what the estate contributed, one values what each of the charities received. As a result, the estate had to include 100 percent of Royal Gardens in the value of the gross estate. Because the discount applied to the charitable contribution deduction, the court accepted the 27.385 percent discount for the 25 percent interest given to the church and the 4 percent discount for the interest given to the family foundation to which the parties conditionally stipulated.

The court upheld the penalty for the late filing of the gift tax return. It noted that the gift tax return for the 2012 gift was due by April 15, 2013. The estate filed the gift tax return on May 19, 2015, without requesting an extension. As a result, the filing was late. Although the estate claimed that Miriam Warne had reasonable cause for the late filing, it produced no evidence in support of this. This caused an addition to tax to apply under Section 6651(a)(1).

19. *Hoffman Properties II, LP v. Commissioner*, No. 19-1831, 2020 WL 3839687 (6th Cir. 2020)

> **Ability of donor to make changes to donated charitable easement whenever the donee fails to act within 45 days of notice of the proposed change violates the requirement that donation be perpetual**

This was an appeal from the decision of the Tax Court.

Hoffman Properties owned a historic building in Cleveland, Ohio. Over ten years ago, Hoffman donated an easement in the façade of the building and certain airspace restrictions to the American Association of Historic Preservation "AAHP"). Under the conservation easement, Hoffman agreed not to alter the historic character of the façade or to build in the airspace above or next to the building. Hoffman then sought a $15 million income tax charitable deduction.

The IRS concluded that Hoffman was not entitled to an income tax charitable deduction because the donation was not "exclusively for conservation purposes" and did not meet the requirements for a "qualified conservation contribution" under Section 170(f)(3)(B)(iii). In later proceedings, the Tax Court agreed and granted summary judgment to the IRS. The Tax Court found that Hoffman's donation failed multiple requirements for a donation to be considered "exclusively for conservation purposes" under Section 170(h)(4)(B). The Sixth Circuit considered only one, which is that the conservation purposes must be protected in perpetuity under Section 170(h)(5)(A).

Hoffman reserved the right to make certain changes so long as the AAHP approved. AAHP's failure to act within 45 days of a receipt of a proposed change would be deemed to constitute approval and to permit Hoffman to undertake the proposed actions. In other words, Hoffman gave AAHP a 45-day window in which to prevent changes in the façade or airspace. The court then stated that "it almost goes without saying that this provision violated the perpetuities requirement."

Hoffman made several arguments, which the Sixth Circuit declined to accept. For example, Hoffman argued that the case fell within the narrow exception of the perpetuity requirement for remote future events. To fall within this exception, the possibility that the conservation purpose may be defeated must be "so remote as to be negligible." However, the Sixth Circuit interpreted the donation agreement as containing multiple terms that specifically addressed the possibility that the conservation purpose would be defeated. As a result, the decision of the Tax Court was upheld.

ESTATE TAX AND ESTATE INCLUSION

20. IRS Data Book Statistics for Fiscal Year 2021 (October 2022)

IRS issues estate tax filing statistics for fiscal year 2021

Each year, the Internal Revenue Service – Statistics of Income Division publishes data regarding the number of estate tax returns filed and the assets and deductions claimed on those returns. Generally, an estate files a federal estate tax return (Form 706) in the year after a decedent's death. So, in 2021, **most returns were filed for deaths that occurred in 2020**, for which the filing threshold was $11.58 million of gross estate. Because of filing extensions, however, some returns were filed in 2021 for deaths that occurred prior to 2020, for which filing thresholds were lower. There are also a small number of returns filed for deaths that occurred in 2021, for which the filing threshold was $11.70 million.

The following are select statistics pulled from the filing data tables:

Estate Tax Returns Filed in 2021	All Estate Tax Returns		Returns Reporting: Personal Residence	
	Number of Returns	Gross Estate ($000s)	% of Total Returns	Gross Estate ($000s)
All Returns	6,158	189,647,122	69%	7,005,971
Under $10 million	532	4,008,485	54%	253,453
$10 million < $20 million	3,284	47,162,709	70%	2,763,776
$20 million < $50 million	1,737	50,927,770	73%	2,304,832
$50 million or more	605	87,548,158	72%	1,683,910

This asset category includes the home identified as the decedent's residence. At most, one item of residential real estate per return is included in this asset category.

Source: IRS, Statistics of Income Division
Estate Tax Returns Filed in 2021 by Tax Status and Size of Gross Estate

All Estate Tax Returns			Returns Reporting: Other Real Estate	
Estate Tax Returns Filed in 2021	Number of Returns	Gross Estate ($000s)	% of Total Returns	Gross Estate ($000s)
All Returns	6,158	189,647,122	79%	14,265,395
Under $10 million	532	4,008,485	67%	360,921
$10 million < $20 million	3,284	47,162,709	77%	5,141,619
$20 million < $50 million	1,737	50,927,770	82%	4,388,866
$50 million or more	605	87,548,158	87%	4,373,989

This asset category includes commercial property, undeveloped land, real estate mutual funds (REITs), and residential property other than the personal residence.

Source: IRS, Statistics of Income Division
Estate Tax Returns Filed in 2021 by Tax Status and Size of Gross Estate

All Estate Tax Returns			Returns Reporting: Closely Held Stock	
Estate Tax Returns Filed in 2021	Number of Returns	Gross Estate ($000s)	% of Total Returns	Gross Estate ($000s)
All Returns	6,158	189,647,122	33%	15,830,487
Under $10 million	532	4,008,485	21%	153,494
$10 million < $20 million	3,284	47,162,709	28%	2,816,274
$20 million < $50 million	1,737	50,927,770	37%	3,926,063
$50 million or more	605	87,548,158	53%	8,934,655

This asset category includes the total value of stock held in closely held corporations. Closely held corporations are those whose ownership is concentrated among a relatively small number of owners, and whose stock is not traded publicly.

Source: IRS, Statistics of Income Division
Estate Tax Returns Filed in 2021 by Tax Status and Size of Gross Estate

All Estate Tax Returns			Returns Reporting: Cash	
Estate Tax Returns Filed in 2021	Number of Returns	Gross Estate ($000s)	% of Total Returns	Gross Estate ($000s)
All Returns	6,158	189,647,122	99%	17,251,450
Under $10 million	532	4,008,485	99%	373,154
$10 million < $20 million	3,284	47,162,709	98%	3,924,340
$20 million < $50 million	1,737	50,927,770	99%	4,199,326
$50 million or more	605	87,548,158	99%	8,754,630

This asset category includes all liquid assets, such as actual cash, bank accounts, certificates of deposit (CDs), money market accounts, such as Money Market Deposit Accounts (MMDAs) and Money Market Mutual Funds (MMMFs), and call and sweep accounts held in a brokerage.

Source: IRS, Statistics of Income Division
Estate Tax Returns Filed in 2021 by Tax Status and Size of Gross Estate

All Estate Tax Returns			Returns Reporting: Retirement Assets	
Estate Tax Returns Filed in 2021	Number of Returns	Gross Estate ($000s)	% of Total Returns	Gross Estate ($000s)
All Returns	6,158	189,647,122	68%	8,737,658
Under $10 million	532	4,008,485	59%	372,087
$10 million < $20 million	3,284	47,162,709	70%	4,073,232
$20 million < $50 million	1,737	50,927,770	68%	2,640,923
$50 million or more	605	87,548,158	63%	1,651,416

This asset category includes annuities, assets held in defined contribution plans, such as Individual Retirement Accounts (IRAs) and 401(k)s, and the taxable portion of survivor benefits from defined benefit plans such as traditional employer pensions.

Source: IRS, Statistics of Income Division
Estate Tax Returns Filed in 2021 by Tax Status and Size of Gross Estate

All Estate Tax Returns			Returns Reporting: Private Equity / Hedge Funds	
Estate Tax Returns Filed in 2021	Number of Returns	Gross Estate ($000s)	% of Total Returns	Gross Estate ($000s)
All Returns	6,158	189,647,122	19%	6,930,875
Under $10 million	532	4,008,485	12%	52,409
$10 million < $20 million	3,284	47,162,709	15%	408,232
$20 million < $50 million	1,737	50,927,770	21%	809,360
$50 million or more	605	87,548,158	37%	5,660,874

This asset category includes both private equity funds and hedge funds. Usually structured as limited partnerships, these private investment funds are typically open to a limited range of professional and wealthy investors and pay performance fees to their investment managers.

Source: IRS, Statistics of Income Division
Estate Tax Returns Filed in 2021 by Tax Status and Size of Gross Estate

All Estate Tax Returns			Returns Reporting: Net Life Insurance	
Estate Tax Returns Filed in 2021	Number of Returns	Gross Estate ($000s)	% of Total Returns	Gross Estate ($000s)
All Returns	6,158	189,647,122	37%	1,765,186
Under $10 million	532	4,008,485	31%	48,569
$10 million < $20 million	3,284	47,162,709	38%	835,029
$20 million < $50 million	1,737	50,927,770	37%	441,830
$50 million or more	605	87,548,158	37%	439,758

This asset category includes the value of includible life insurance, net of policy loans. Includible insurance is any insurance on the decedent's life that is payable to the estate at the decedent's death or is payable to another beneficiary if the decedent retained some ownership of the policy.

Source: IRS, Statistics of Income Division
Estate Tax Returns Filed in 2021 by Tax Status and Size of Gross Estate

All Estate Tax Returns			Returns Reporting: Art	
Estate Tax Returns Filed in 2021	Number of Returns	Gross Estate ($000s)	% of Total Returns	Gross Estate ($000s)
All Returns	6,158	189,647,122	21%	3,535,363
Under $10 million	532	4,008,485	16%	21,224
$10 million < $20 million	3,284	47,162,709	16%	177,776
$20 million < $50 million	1,737	50,927,770	25%	508,496
$50 million or more	605	87,548,158	45%	2,827,866

This asset category includes items such as paintings, sculptures, busts, engravings, and etchings.

Source: IRS, Statistics of Income Division
Estate Tax Returns Filed in 2021 by Tax Status and Size of Gross Estate

All Estate Tax Returns			Returns Reporting: Farm Assets	
Estate Tax Returns Filed in 2021	Number of Returns	Gross Estate ($000s)	% of Total Returns	Gross Estate ($000s)
All Returns	6,158	189,647,122	13%	4,898,593
Under $10 million	532	4,008,485	12%	130,733
$10 million < $20 million	3,284	47,162,709	13%	1,741,153
$20 million < $50 million	1,737	50,927,770	13%	1,357,779
$50 million or more	605	87,548,158	19%	1,668,928

This asset category includes farm land and assets used in conjunction with a farm or agricultural business, as well as incorporated farms, farm partnerships, and farm sole proprietorships.

Source: IRS, Statistics of Income Division
Estate Tax Returns Filed in 2021 by Tax Status and Size of Gross Estate

All Estate Tax Returns			Returns Reporting: Total Lifetime Transfers	
Estate Tax Returns Filed in 2021	**Number of Returns**	**Gross Estate ($000s)**	**% of Total Returns**	**Gross Estate ($000s)**
All Returns	6,158	189,647,122	59%	85,797,140
Under $10 million	532	4,008,485	52%	1,333,822
$10 million < $20 million	3,284	47,162,709	56%	17,803,080
$20 million < $50 million	1,737	50,927,770	64%	21,883,350
$50 million or more	605	87,548,158	71%	44,776,888

Total lifetime transfers equals the sum of all assets that were given by the decedent to others during life and were includible in his/her gross estate under sections 2035(a), 2036, 2037, or 2038 of the Internal Revenue Code.

Source: IRS, Statistics of Income Division
Estate Tax Returns Filed in 2021 by Tax Status and Size of Gross Estate

The following table charts the total number of estate tax returns filed since the year 2000 and the total value of the gross estate reported on those returns:

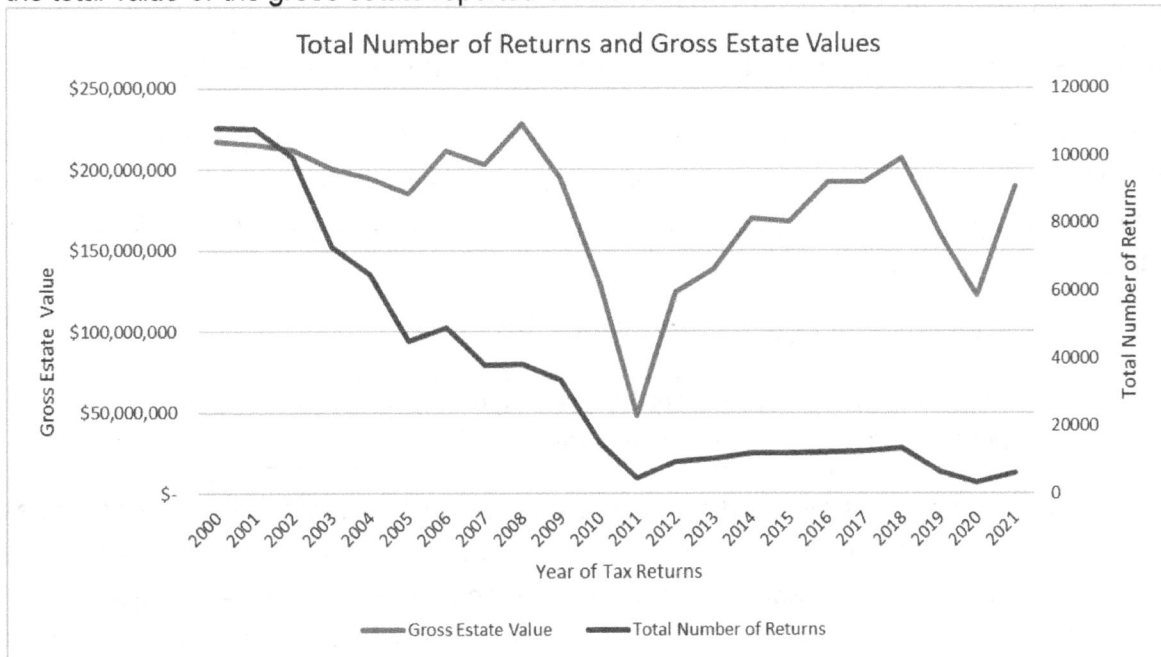

Total Number of Returns and Gross Estate Values

21. *Estate of Machelhenny v. Commissioner (March 15, 2023); H. Yale Gutnick, et al., v. U.S., No. 2:23-cv-00139 (W.D. Pa); Estate of Spizzirri v. Commissioner, T.C. Memo 2023-25 (February 28, 2023)*

> **Recent cases address deductibility of certain debts and expenses in estate tax returns.**

Estate of Machelhenny v. Commissioner (March 15, 2023)

The Tax Court held that an estate could not deduct the value of two consent judgments against the decedent from the value of the gross estate because the debts were not the decedent's personal obligations at the time of his death and held that the decedent's children received taxable gifts when they purchased property at a discount.

H. Yale Gutnick, et al., v. U.S., No. 2:23-cv-00139 (W.D. Pa)

The Co-executors of an estate filed a complaint in U.S. district court seeking a nearly $69 million estate tax refund stemming from the estate's obligation to indemnify trustees of an inter vivos trust, which reduced the taxable estate. The Co-executors filed protective claims for refund with the timely filed estate tax return.

Estate of Spizzirri v. Commissioner, T.C. Memo 2023-25 (February 28, 2023)

The Tax Court ruled that the estate cannot claim deductions for payments to a surviving spouse and children of the surviving spouse (by another marriage), where the payments were made in satisfaction of the terms of a premarital agreement but not included in the testamentary documents of the decedent.

22. *Wildenstein v. Commissioner (April 20, 2022)*

> **Tax Court Enters Stipulated Decision Related to Estate Tax inclusion of Valuable Art Collection**

In a case involving an extensive and valuable art collection with stops in the United States, France, and Switzerland, the United States Tax Court entered a stipulated decision, finding that the estate was not liable for an estate tax deficiency or accuracy related penalty and is liable for some addition to tax. Suit was brought by the estate of the late billionaire art dealer Daniel Wildenstein over whether his art collection was located in the United States and thus subject to U.S. estate tax (*Estate of Wildenstein v. Commissioner*, No. 3423-18 (Feb. 3, 2020). The family's New York gallery had managed the collection, which was held by the Delta Trust, a Bahamas discretionary trust that Wildenstein set up in 1998. Certain pieces of art were shipped from the United States to a duty-free warehouse in Switzerland before Wildenstein's death and later returned to the United States. These pieces weren't included in Wildenstein's estate. The Internal Revenue Service found a tax deficiency based on its view that property was still sited in the United States even if it's temporarily located outside the country. Assuming that Wildenstein was residing in France at the time of his death, the United States/France Tax Treaty applies. That provides that "tangible movable property which is in transit shall be considered situated at the place of destination." So, the IRS argued that the artwork that made a round trip from the United States to Switzerland before and after Wildenstein's death should be regarded as in transit at the date of death. The estate countered that because the art was physically located outside the United States at the time of Wildenstein's death, it wasn't subject to estate tax.

23. *Estate of Stanley E. Fulton v. Commissioner (April 4, 2022)*

Estate Petitions Tax Court for Redetermination of Estate Tax Deficiency, Accuracy-Related Penalties Related to Debts Claimed from Decedent's Failure to Abide by Divorce Arrangement

Stanley E. Fulton ("Fulton") died on January 4, 2018, in Nevada. Michael B. Fulton and Elizabeth Fulton Jones qualified as the Co-Executors of Fulton's estate and timely filed a Form 706 reporting a gross estate for federal estate tax purposes of $857,695,568. The IRS examined the estate tax return, denied certain deductions for debts related to creditors' claims, and issued a notice of deficiency and assessing accuracy-related penalties. The Co-Executors filed a petition in the United States Tax Court challenging the denial of deductions and penalties.

As a young man, Fulton married Elizabeth McFerren ("Betty"), and together they had six children (the "Fulton Children"). After a 24-year marriage, during which Fulton had enjoyed considerable business success and his family had enjoyed a high standard of living, Fulton and Betty decided to divorce. Fulton and Betty negotiated a property settlement agreement. Betty agreed to relinquish claims to Fulton's property or the marital estate in exchange for (i) alimony, (ii) a lump-sum payment upon divorce, (iii) a promissory note, whereby Betty would be paid interest monthly and principal upon the sale of Fulton's business interests, and (iv) certain other tangible property. Fulton retained all of his business interests and certain other property. As part of the property settlement agreement, both Fulton and Betty agreed that "two-thirds of each of their respective net estates (after payment of expenses and taxes)" would pass to the Fulton Children.

Betty died on March 5, 2017 and complied with her obligation to leave at least two-thirds of her net estate to Fulton Children.

After Betty's death, Fulton modified his estate plan (a Will and the Fulton Family Trust) to provide for a gift of voting interests in one business – the Sunland Park Racetrack & Casino – to be divided equally into separate shares for the Fulton Children. After certain other gifts of tangible property and specific gifts, the balance of his estate would pass to the Stanley E. Fulton Family Foundation (a to-be-established qualified, tax-exempt foundation). After Fulton's will was admitted to probate, each of the Fulton Children filed creditor claims in the Nevada probate case and identical claims against the trustees of the Fulton Family Trust. The nearly identical creditor claims sought to enforce the Fulton Children's rights as third-party beneficiaries to receive at least two-thirds of the net value of Fulton's estate as provided for in the property settlement agreement with Betty. The creditor claims valued the interest of each Fulton Child at $82,333,333.

The Co-Executors of Fulton's estate, the trustees of the Fulton Family Trust, the executor and trustee of Betty's will and trust, The Fulton Children, and the newly created foundation entered into a comprehensive settlement agreement, whereby the Fulton Children would receive, in total, two-thirds of the "Final Settlement Value" less $18,925,000.

After the Nevada court approved the settlement agreement providing for this amount to be paid from Fulton's estate and the Fulton Family Trust to the Fulton Children, the Co-Executors of Fulton's estate filed a federal estate tax return a claimed total Debts, Expenses, and Taxes of $480,312,886, of which $472,530,178 was attributable to the comprehensive settlement agreement to setline the claims of the Fulton Children as third-party beneficiaries of the property settlement between Fulton and Betty.

After an examination of the estate tax return, which included interviews with five of the six Fulton Children, the IRS issued a Notice of Deficiency and accuracy-related penalties. In the Notice of Deficiency, the IRS completely disallowed the deduction of $472,530,178 as debt of the decedent under I.R.C. section 2053, reducing the total of that deduction to $0 and increasing the federal estate tax due by $214,622,063. In addition, the IRS assessed a $42 million accuracy-related penalty under I.R.C. section 6662.

The petition of the Co-Executors filed in the Tax Court challenges the denial of the deduction and the imposition of the accuracy-related penalty. The government answered on June 1, 2022. Updates on the posture of the case or settlement will be reported as available.

24. *Estate of Marion Levine v. Commissioner (U.S. Tax Court, February 28, 2022)*

> **Tax Court addresses split-dollar life insurance arrangement and valuation of note receivable**

Marion Levine was a real estate investor who owned mobile home parks and renaissance fairs (described by the court as "a bit like state fairs, if the state were a small principality in fifteenth century Europe populated entirely by modern people who enjoy costumed role-playing and adding extra "e's" to works like "old" and "fair"). Mrs. Levine engaged in thoughtful and careful estate planning, including proper business governance and structuring, creation of a revocable trust for carrying out her estate plan, and creating and funding GRATs and QPRTs.

In an effort to continue the estate planning, Mrs. Levine entered into split-dollar life insurance arrangements requiring her revocable trust to pay premiums on life insurance policies on the lives of her daughter and son-in-law. It was a carefully researched, crafted, and executed intergenerational split dollar arrangement. A life insurance trust agreed to buy insurance policies on the lives of her daughter and son-in-law. Levine's revocable trust agreed to pay the premiums on the insurance policies, and the insurance trust assigned the policies to her revocable trust as collateral. Levine's revocable trust retained the right to be paid the greater of the total amount of the premiums paid for these policies ($6.5 million) and (ii) either (a) the current cash-surrender values of the policies upon the death of the last surviving insured or (b) or the cash-surrender values of the policies on the date that they were terminated, if they were terminated before both insureds died.

During her lifetime, Mrs. Levine had made gifts, through her revocable trust, to the insurance trust and its beneficiaries because the money her revocable trust would get in later years was not equal to the $6.5 million it had given to the insurance trust to buy the policies. In 2008 and 2009, Levine's gift tax returns reported the value of the gift as the economic benefit transferred from her revocable trust to the insurance trust. Under the valuation rules of Treas. Reg. §25.2512-1, the value of the gift was reported as $2,644.

In addition, the promise of the insurance trust to pay the revocable trust an amount in the future was an asset to reported on Levine's estate tax return. Mrs. Levine's estate reported the split-dollar receivable on her estate tax return at $2 million (at her death the cash surrender value was $6.5 million). IRS issued a notice of deficiency to the estate for more than $3 million and determined that the Estate was liable for a 40% gross-misvaluation penalty under section 6662(h) because the value reported for the split-dollar receivable was too low.

The Court held that the split dollar arrangement met with the requirements under Morrisette I, and the only issue before the court would be the value of the asset included in Levine's estate. In an opinion delivered by Judge Holmes, the Court addressed the question of what would be included in Mrs. Levine's estate: (i) the value of her revocable trust's right to be repaid in the future at the death of her son and daughter-in-law or (ii) the cash-surrender values of the life-insurance policies at Mrs. Levine's date of death.

The IRS argued that the combined cash-surrender values of the life insurance policies should be included in Levine's estate under section 2036(a)(2) or section 2038, arguing that Levine's attorneys-in-fact (her daughter, son-in-law, and trusted advisor) were also the trustees of her revocable trust, and as such could have exercised control over the policies and unlocked the cash value at any time. The Court, however, looked closely at the role of the insurance trust, with an independent South Dakota trustee. Levine's trusted advisor, Larson, was the investment director of the insurance, with a power over the policies. But he owed fiduciary obligations to the beneficiaries of the insurance trust, which included Levine's more remote descendants and not just her daughter and son-in-law. In light of the careful planning and drafting the Court concluded that neither 2036 nor 2038 applied, and the cash surrender value would not be included in the estate under those theories. The IRS also tried to bootstrap an argument under Code section 2703, suggesting that the restriction on Levine's access the funds transferred to the insurance companies for the benefit of the insurance trust should be disregarded in determining the value of property includable in Levine's estate, and if that restriction is disregarded, she would be deemed to have access to the full value of the insurance policies. The Court rejected this argument, agreeing with the Estate's response that section 2703 only applies to property owned by Levine at her death and not property she disposed of or property that she did not own, like the life insurance policies.

Ultimately, the Court ruled that the receivable was worth approximately $2 million. The Court declined to address the valuation of the gift between Levine and the insurance trust, as reported on her gift tax returns. Judge Holmes identifies it as a "weakness," though one driven by the valuation rules in the regulations and not an argument brought before the Court in this case.

25. *Estate of Michael J. Jackson v. Commissioner*, T.C. Memo 2021-48

Tax court rules on estate tax values of Michael Jackson's likeness and image, 50 percent stake in Sony/ATV Music Publishing, and compositions written or co-written by Jackson

In an extraordinarily detailed and lengthy opinion, Judge Holmes of the Tax Court decided three issues related to the valuation of assets in the estate of legendary musician, Michael Jackson, who died on June 25, 2009. The three assets on which the estate and the IRS disagreed on the value were:

- Jackson's image and likeness
- Jackson's interest in New Horizon Trust II ("NHT II"), through which he held a 50 percent interest in Sony/ATV Music Publishing, LLC (which owned the John Lennon-Paul McCartney music catalogue)
- Jackson's interest in New Horizon Trust III ("NHT III") which contained MiJack Music, a music publishing catalog that owned the copyrights to compositions that Jackson wrote or co-wrote as well as compositions by other songwriters

The opinion first discusses Michael Jackson's life and career in length. At the time of his death, each of the three disputed assets were distressed. His image and likeness were producing no noticeable income and Jackson had not even been able to contract for the sale of tour merchandise containing his image and likeness because of the damage done by various allegations, lawsuits, and court trials related to Jackson's personal life. Jackson's interest in Sony/ATV secured $303,000,000 in loans with maturity dates less than 18 months away. Jackson's interests in MiJack secured over $72,000,000 in debt. The "This Is It" tour, which was viewed as the way to turn around the decline in Jackson's career, was in rehearsal when he died.

After his death, John Branca, an entertainment lawyer and longtime advisor, who had recently returned after a falling out with Jackson several years prior, was one of the co-executors. He and other advisors went to work to shore up the estate's troubled finances. As the court noted:

> "What Jackson had created during his lifetime was now fixed and it was to the considerable benefit of the estate that he was no longer able to get in the way of the rational profit maximizers who were now in control. And nearly everyone involved in these early days after Jackson's death turned out to be accomplished in the business side of the entertainment business. As crass as it might have seen to Jackson's more sentimental fans, the business began almost immediately."

One of the efforts of the executors was the creation of the documentary "Michael Jackson's This Is It," derived from videos of Jackson's rehearsals for the This Is It tour. The success of that film was unprecedented and as of July 2011, the movie generated cumulative gross receipts of over $240,000,000. There were subsequent deals with Cirque du Soleil as well as various other ventures and deals. For example, Sony acquired the estate's 50 percent interest in Sony/ATV and became the 100 percent owner for a price of $750,000,000.

In preparing the federal estate tax return, the estate retained Moss Adams, a large accounting consulting firm, to value Jackson's image and likeness and his interest in MiJack. Relying entirely on the income approach to valuation, Moss Adams valued Jackson's image and likeness at $2,105 and MiJack at $70,860,000. The estate used the Salter Group, an independent financial and strategic advisory firm to value the 50 percent ownership interest in Sony/ATV. The Salter Group used only the income method by which it valued Jackson's ownership interest in Sony/ATV at $0. Based on these appraisals, the estate reported the value of Jackson's image and likeness at $2,105, NHT II, which held his 50 percent interest in Sony/ATV at $0 and NHT III, which held MiJack, at $2,207,351.

The IRS on audit greatly increased the estate's reported values when it issued a notice of deficiency in May 2013. The IRS's values were:

Image and Likeness	$434,261,895
NHT II	$469,005,086
NHT III	$58,478,593

The adjusted valuation led the IRS to conclude that the estate underpaid Jackson's estate tax by more than $500 million. The IRS also tacked on undervaluation penalties of nearly $200 million.

After lengthy negotiations the estate and the IRS were unable to agree on the valuation of the image and likeness, ATV/Sony (held in NHT II), and MiJack (held in NHT III).

The estate used four experts at trial. Mark Roesler, the founder and CEO of CMG Worldwide Inc., an international licensing and rights management company, and Jay Fishman, a professional business valuation appraiser, valued Jackson's image and likeness. Fishman came up with a value of about $3 million instead of $2,105 for the value of the image and likeness.

Alan Wallis, who led the Media and Entertainment Group in Ernst & Young's UK valuation practice, was engaged to value Jackson's interest in Sony/ATV. Wallis valued the Sony/ATV interest, using both the market approach and the income approach. Both approaches led Wallis to conclude, after taking account of debt secured by Jackson's interest in Sony/ATV, that NHT II had no value.

Owen Dahl, who had a great deal of experience in valuing high-profile music catalogs, valued Jackson's interest in MiJack Music. Dahl concluded that the fair market value of NHT III was about $2.7 million.

Each of the estate's experts and their valuations reduced the cash flows produced by the assets using tax affecting to take account of the tax implications to a hypothetical buyer.

The IRS used Weston Ansen, the Chairman of Consor Intellectual Asset Management, to value all three assets. To value Jackson's image and likeness, Ansen considered five "opportunities" that he believed a hypothetical buyer could reasonably foresee at Jackson's death (themed attractions and products, branded merchandise, a Cirque du Soleil show, a film, and a Broadway musical). Using the income approach, Ansen valued Jackson's image and likeness at $161 million. Ansen valued Jackson's interest in Sony/ATV using both the income and market approaches and valued NHT II at $206 million. Ansen valued Jackson's interest in MiJack using only the income approach and valued NHT III at $114 million.

Ansen's credibility suffered greatly at trial. During trial, he indicated that he had never worked for the IRS before. Ansen had to correct that misstatement because he had prepared a valuation report on the fair market value of Whitney Houston's intangible property rights for the IRS. He also testified that neither he nor his firm ever advertised to promote his business, which was also a misstatement because, in the midst of the trial, Ansen's firm touted his testimony in an email blast to clients and others.

In a lengthy evaluation of all the appraisals, the court reached the following determination as to the value of the three interests. Jackson's image and likeness was worth $4,153,912, NHT II (Sony/ATV) was worth $0, and NHT III (MiJack Music) was worth $107,313,561.

Although the estate had undervalued the assets by approximately $111,000,000, the court declined to impose any undervaluation penalties.

26. Changes in State Death Tax Exemptions from 2020 to 2023

> **Numerous changes occur in state death tax exemptions because of legislation or inflation adjustments**

As in past years, there have been numerous changes in the exemptions allowed from the separate estate taxes that twelve states and District of Columbia apply in addition to the federal estate tax. An additional five states have separate inheritance taxes. The full state death tax chart which shows the death taxes applicable in the different states is found in the Appendix to these materials.

Legislative Activity. Connecticut, Vermont, and the District of Columbia each saw increases in their state exemptions pursuant to legislation. Connecticut increased its state death tax exemption from $5,100,000 in 2020 to $7,100,000 in 2021 and Vermont increased its exemption from $4,250,000 in 2020 to $5,000,000 in 2021. The District of Columbia reduced its exemption from $5,762,000 in 2020 to $4,000,000 in 2021. The District of Columbia's exemption will be indexed for cost of living beginning in 2022. Iowa passed a phase-out of its inheritance tax on others than ascendants and descendants in which the tax rate is reduced 20 percent each year beginning in 2021 so that the inheritance tax is phased out completely as of January 1, 2025.

Indexing Exemptions for Inflation. One development to which estate planning professionals need to pay attention is the increases in the exemptions as a result of inflation adjustments provided in some, but not all, of the states with separate state estate taxes. This area is increasingly complex. The federal estate death exemption was increased to $10,000,000 (adjusted for inflation) in 2018 as part of the 2017 Tax Act. The 2021 federal exemption is $11,700,000. No state with a state death tax has yet increased its separate state death tax exemption to match the federal exemption although Connecticut is currently scheduled to increase its exemption to match the federal exemption starting in 2023.

Maine, New York, and Rhode Island each adjusted their state death tax exemption for inflation in 2021. In addition, Hawaii, although it appears that its exemption is supposed to be adjusted for inflation, has failed to do so since 2018.

Finally, the State of Washington has not adjusted its exemption for inflation since 2018. In 2018, the Washington State Department of Revenue sent a notice stating that pursuant to Revised Code of Washington § 83.100, the department must adjust the Washington applicable estate tax exclusion map annually using the Seattle-Tacoma-Bremerton Metropolitan Area October Consumer Price Index (Seattle CPI). As of January 1, 2018, the U.S. Bureau of Labor and Statistics no longer calculated Seattle CPI. Instead, the Bureau of Labor and Statistics is calculating CPI for the Seattle-Tacoma-Bellevue core base statistical area. As a result of these changes, the term Consumer "Price Index" as defined in the statute did not match the current CPI measure calculated by the United States Bureau of Labor Statistics. Consequently, there has been no increase in the exemption in Washington State since 2018.

All of these different changes in recent years mean that only two states have the same exemption from state death tax. These are Massachusetts and Oregon, which each have the lowest state death tax exemption of any of the states, at $1,000,000.

The changes in the exemptions for those states with a state estate tax and the District of Columbia from 2020 to 2022 are summarized in the chart below:

Changes in Exemptions in State Death Taxes — 2020-2022

States Currently Imposing a Death Tax

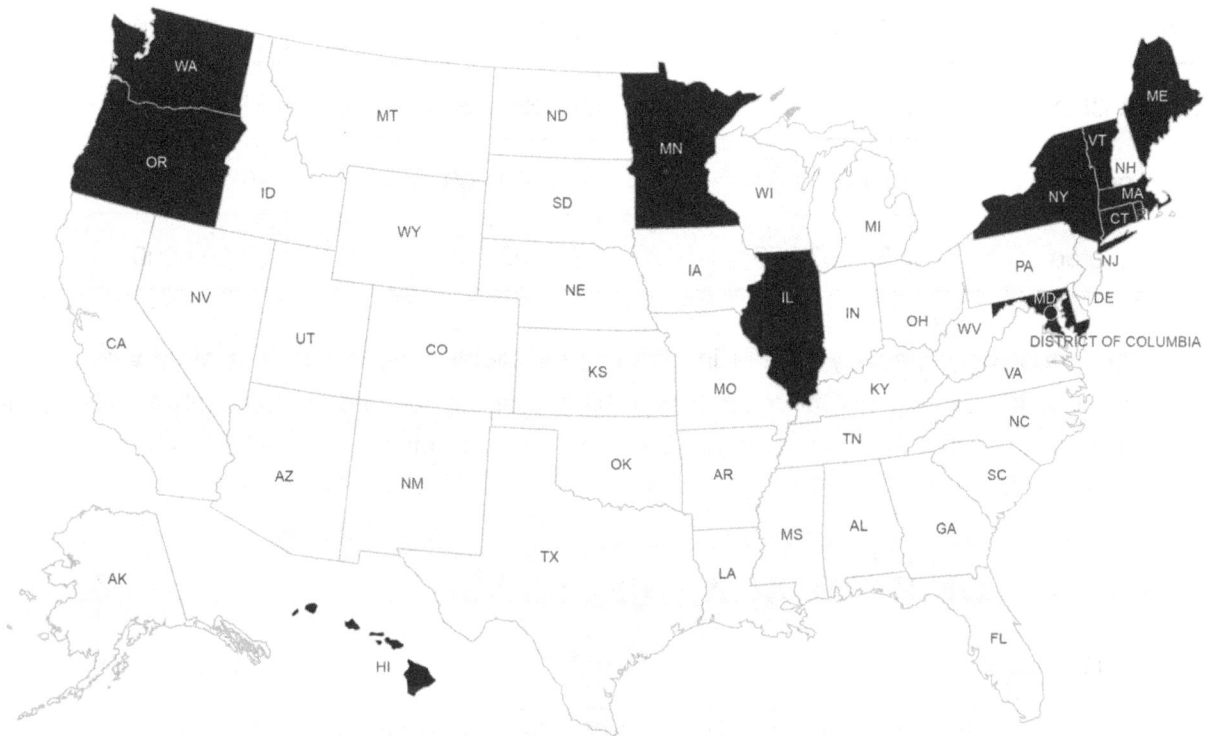

State	2020 State Death Tax Exemption	2021 State Death Tax Exemption	2022 State Death Tax Exemption
Connecticut	$5,100,000	$7,100,000	$9,100,000
District of Columbia	$5,762,400	$4,000,000	$4,254,800
Hawaii	$5,490,000	$5,490,000	$5,490,000
Illinois	$4,000,000	$4,000,000	$4,000,000
Maine	$5,800,000	$5,870,000	$6,010,000

State	2020 State Death Tax Exemption	2021 State Death Tax Exemption	2022 State Death Tax Exemption
Maryland	$5,000,000	$5,000,000	$5,000,000
Massachusetts	$1,000,000	$1,000,000	$1,000,000
Minnesota	$3,000,000	$3,000,000	$3,000,000
New York	$5,850,000	$5,930,000	$6,110,000
Oregon	$1,000,000	$1,000,000	$1,000,000
Rhode Island	$1,579,922	$1,595,156	$1,648,611
Vermont	$4,250,000	$5,000,000	$5,000,000
Washington	$2,193,000	$2,193,000	$2,193,000

Planners must be especially careful in planning for clients who reside in a state with a state estate tax or the District of Columbia or who have property located in state with a state estate tax and subject to that state's estate tax. The different exemptions can make this planning quite complicated.

MARITAL DEDUCTION AND PORTABILITY

27. Revenue Procedure 2022-32 (July 8, 2022)

Guidance Extends Time, Simplifies Method for Making Portability Election

---

The estate of a decedent dying after December 31, 2010, who was survived by a spouse, is eligible to file a federal estate tax return under I.R.C. section 2010(c)(5)(A) for the sole purpose of passing on the decedent spouse's Deceased Spouse Unused Exemption (DSUE) to the surviving spouse. In Rev. Proc. 2017-34, the IRS provided a simplified method for obtaining an extension of time to make a portability election under I.R.C. section 2010(c)(5)(A) if that estate was not required by I.R.C. section 6018(a) to file an estate tax return. Under Rev. Proc. 2017-34, this simplified method (which is used in lieu of the letter ruling process) was available for two years after the decedent's date of death.

Even after Rev. Proc. 2017-34 extended the time, the IRS continued to grant relief under Reg. § 301.9100-3, extending the time for an estate to make the portability election. The IRS observed that a significant percentage of the ruling requests for a further extension of time came from estates of decedents who died within **five** years of the request for a relief. To react to and respond to the fact that many estates of decedents are attempting to make the late portability election within five years, instead of two, the IRS issues Rev. Proc 2022-32 extending the period within which the estate of a decedent may make the portability election under that simplified method to on or before the fifth anniversary of the decedent's date of death.

The simplified method of making the late portability election pursuant to Rev. Proc. 2022-32 is available if:

- The decedent: (i) was survived by a spouse; (ii) died after December 31, 2010; and (iii) was a citizen or resident of the United States on the date of death.
- The executor is not required to file an estate tax return under I.R.C. section 6018(a) as determined based on the value of the gross estate and adjusted taxable gifts and without regard to the need to file for portability purposes.
- The executor did not otherwise timely file a federal estate tax return.
- The executor: (i) files a complete and properly prepared federal estate tax return (Form 706) on or before the fifth annual anniversary of the decedent's date of death and (ii) Form 706 includes a statement at the top of the return stating that the return is "FILED PURSUANT TO REV. PROC. 2022-32 TO ELECT PORTABILITY UNDER § 2010(c)(5)(A)."

The IRS further stated that the simplified method would be the exclusive method for obtaining relief for making a late portability election on or before the fifth anniversary of a decedent's date of death, and letter rulings would not be issues on matters in that time frame. Relief may be available under appropriate circumstances through a private letter ruling if the relief is being requested because the election is being made with the respect to the estate of decedent dying more than five years ago.

28. *Kucerak v. United States*, No. 5:22-cv-00007 (W.D. Tex) (January 7, 2022)

> **Estate of a decedent who was in a same-sex relationship as of her date of death files for a refund of estate tax, seeking to have her relationship recognized as a common-law marriage under applicable law and to qualify for the marital deduction under Obergefell**

Susan M. Wood ("Susan") and Gerry L. Saum ("Gerry"), both women, had a "continuing loving relationship" of about 45 years. They were residents of Texas. Susan passed away on May 4, 2012, at the age of 66. At the time of Susan's death, Texas law did not recognize same-sex marriages, and Susan and Gerry were never formally wed in Texas or any other jurisdiction. Upon Susan's death, certain assets passed to Gerry; but because at the time they were not considered married under federal law, the gift did not qualify for the marital deduction from estate tax, and Susan's Estate paid about $1,153,123 in estate tax.

After Susan's death, the United States Supreme Court handed down the opinion in Obergefell v. Hodges, 135 S. Ct. 1732 (2015), which held that federal and state governments must recognize marriages between same-sex partners, under the Due Process Clause and the Equal Protection Clause of the Fourteenth Amendment to the United States Constitution. The Supreme Court had earlier handed down the opinion in United States v. Windsor, 570 U.S. 744 (2013), which held that it was unconstitutional for the Defense of Marriage Act to deny federal recognition of a same-sex marriage that was recognized under state law. That is, Windsor held that the federal government must recognize a valid same-sex marriage under state law; and Obergefell held that state governments must recognize same-sex marriage under state law and must give same-sex partners the ability to be married and to have that marriage recognized under that state's laws.

In the Complaint filed in this matter, Susan's Estate conceded that Susan and Gerry had not been formally married during their lifetimes. But the Estate argued that Texas law should recognize their relationship as a common-law marriage, and that Windsor and Obergefell should apply retroactively with respect to treatment of their marriage under federal law.

Susan's Estate filed for a refund of the estate tax paid, and the IRS denied their claim, asserting that Susan and Gerry were not married under Texas law.

Under Texas law, the elements of a common-law marriage are (1) an agreement to be married, (2) sufficient co-habitation, and (3) holding out to others that the couple is married.

In this case, Susan's Estate also conceded that Susan and Gerry had not held themselves out as married, nor had they used terms like spouse, wife, and married. The Complaint alleges that evidence would show that the two referred to each other as "life partners" and a "committed couple".

But the Complaint asserted that it would be unreasonable to require Susan and Gerry to have used such terms under Texas law at the time, in order for them to receive the status of married under Obergefell. The Complaint argues that if Susan and Gerry had used such terms, at a time when Texas law did not recognize such same-sex marriages, they would have appeared "foolish, uninformed or delusional". That is, the Complaint argues,

> [R]equiring a same-sex couple to say that they were 'married' invidiously discriminates against them because opposite-sex couples can access the Texas common law marriage statute by saying something that—at the time—the community knows to be legally correct, whereas non-traditional couples must publicly state

something that the community—at the time—knows to be legally incorrect.

The Complaint therefore argues that the Texas common-law marriage laws were unconstitutional as applied to Susan and Gerry, and that (1) Texas law must recognize their same-sex relationship as a marriage under state law, and (2) therefore, federal law must recognize that marriage as valid for purposes of federal law.

This case remains pending.

This case is a reminder of the development of the legal landscape of same-sex relationships, although the more time that passes since Obergefell, the less likely it will be that clients face a similar fact pattern as Susan and Gerry. Clients who feel that they were denied the marital deduction or other benefits should consider whether to bring a claim for relief.

This case is also a reminder of the fact that Windsor and Obergefell only require the government to recognize a same-sex marriage that is valid under state law. These cases do not automatically transform unmarried same-sex partners into married same-sex spouses. Practitioners should continue to advise clients of the need to become lawfully married under applicable law in order to be considered married for purposes of the Obergefell analysis. Practitioners should also continue to advise their clients of the duties and obligations of married couples under the law, such as the elective share and similar rights of spouses, as they advise their clients of whether to become married or not.

29. Letter Ruling 202133010 (Issued April 8, 2021; Released August 20, 2021)

IRS grants extension of time to make QTIP election

A married couple lived in a community property state. The first spouse's estate plan used both a will and revocable trust. Upon the first spouse's death, a marital deduction trust was created which was to be funded with some of the first spouse's separate property and the first spouse's one-half interest in the community property. The first spouse's intention, as stated in the terms of his will and revocable trust, was for the trustee or the executor to make the QTIP election for the marital trust.

The surviving spouse served as the sole trustee of the trust and sole executor of the estate. Nine months later, child became the sole trustee of the trust and sole executor of the estate. The spouse and the child retained an accountant to prepare the Form 706. The accountant prepared both a Form 706 and supplemental Form 706. Although the due date for filing the Form 706 was extended by six months, neither the Form 706 nor the supplemental Form 706 was timely filed and no QTIP election was made for the marital trust.

An attorney whom the surviving spouse subsequently retained for estate planning advice discovered the failure to make the QTIP election. An extension of time under Treas. Reg. § 301.9100-3 to make a QTIP election for the marital trust was requested.

The Service granted the request. Under Treas. Reg. § 301.9100-3, a request will be granted when the taxpayer shows that the taxpayer acted reasonably and in good faith and that granting relief will not prejudice the interests of the government. A taxpayer is deemed to have acted reasonably and in good faith if the taxpayer reasonably relied on a qualified tax professional and the tax professional failed to make or advise the taxpayer to make the election. The IRS concluded that these requirements were satisfied.

30. *Estate of Grossman v. Commissioner*, T.C. Memo 2021-65 (May 27, 2021)

> **Tax Court recognizes religious divorce and Israeli marriage and allows estate tax marital deduction for property passing to surviving spouse**

This matter came before the court on cross motions for partial summary judgment. The issue was whether Ziona Grossman was the surviving spouse of Semone Grossman for purposes of the estate tax marital deduction. Semone and Ziona, both Jewish and residents of New York, celebrated their marriage in Israel in 1987 pursuant to Israeli laws after Semone obtained a religious divorce from his first wife Hilda, who was also Jewish and a New York resident. After their marriage, Semone and Ziona returned to New York, had two daughters, and lived together as husband and wife for twenty-seven years until Semone's death in 2014.

Semone and Hilda were married in 1955. In 1967, Semone began a new relationship with Katia, who was not Jewish, and obtained a divorce in Mexico in which Hilda neither appeared nor participated. In 1974, after Semone's and Katia's relationship had ended, Hilda challenged the validity of the Mexican divorce in New York state court. The New York court declared that Hilda's marriage to Semone was not legally dissolved, and that the marriage of Semone with Katia was null and void.

Later, Semone met Ziona. In 1986, before Semone married Ziona, Hilda agreed with Semone to him giving her a get which is a religious divorce under rabbinical law and which was granted. In 1987, Semone and Ziona were married in Israel in an Orthodox Jewish religious ceremony and issued a marriage certificate by the Israeli Ministry of Religious Services.

After their marriage, Semone and Ziona filed joint income returns. When he died in 2014, Semone was buried in Israel alongside Ziona's parents. Semone in his will directed that any reference to "my wife" meant Ziona.

Hilda lived in New York until her death in 2014. Hilda on her federal income tax returns listed herself as single. Hilda never challenged Semone's marriage to Ziona. Upon Semone's death in New York in 2014, Hilda made no statutory claim against his estate as a surviving spouse.

Semone had a large estate which was valued at approximately $87 million on a gross basis. The bulk of the estate ($79 million) was left to Ziona.

The Internal Revenue Service, in the audit of Semone's federal estate tax return, determined that Semone and Ziona were not married to each other for federal estate tax purposes and that the amounts left to Ziona failed to qualify for the estate tax marital deduction. The IRS asserted that Semone's estate owed an additional $35,497,032 in federal estate tax and imposed an accuracy related penalty under Section 6662 of $7,099,406.

The court ruled that Semone and Ziona were properly married. The court focused on Semone's and Ziona's marriage and said that New York law would recognize Semone's and Ziona's marriage if it was lawful under the laws of the place in which marriage was celebrated which in this case was Israel. Israel had recognized the marriage as lawful.

The court quoted the oft-expressed concern that "Congress did not intend that the Commissioner in making tax determinations around marital status, or the courts in passing upon them, should set themselves up as domestic relations tribunals." *Estate of Borax v. Commissioner*, 349 F.2d 666, 676 (2d Cir. 1965) (Friendly, J. dissenting). It noted that the parties most interested in the status of Semone and Ziona's marriage, Semone, Ziona, and Hilda, did not challenge the marriage. No New York court (or any other court) found the marriage invalid. As a result, the court was not going to assume, based on the facts presented, that Semone and Ziona were not husband and wife under New York law. As a result, the court granted the estate's motion for partial summary judgment and denied the IRS's motion for partial summary judgment.

31.   Letter Ruling 202120004 (Issued September 10, 2020; Released May 21, 2021)

> **IRS grants extension of time to file the necessary form to notify IRS that the beneficiary of qualified domestic trust had become a United States citizen**

The surviving spouse was not a U.S. citizen at the time of the first spouse's death and the surviving spouse received an outright distribution. After the decedent's death, the spouse established and funded a qualified domestic trust (QDOT) to hold the assets that she received outright from the decedent. After the funding of the QDOT, the spouse became a U.S. citizen.

The original co-trustees of the QDOT were the son and an individual U.S. citizen. The QDOT named Bank 1 as a successor co-trustee in the event of a death of an original co-trustee. Two events occurred prior to the spouse becoming a U.S. citizen. Son died and Bank 2, as the successor to Bank 1, took possession of the QDOT assets. The individual U.S. trustee believed that Bank 2 as successor co-trustee was handling all administrative matters for the QDOT, including tax matters. However, Bank 2 did not accept appointment as co-trustee of the QDOT and the individual U.S. trustee was the sole trustee of the qualified domestic trust after the son's death.

The individual U.S. trustee lacked experience in U.S. estate tax matters and was unaware of the need to provide notification and certification of the spouse's U.S. citizenship. Consequently, neither the required Form 706 (QDT) to terminate the QDOT nor an extension of time for filing the Form 706 (QDT) was ever filed.

Upon discovering the failure to file the necessary form, the individual U.S. trustee submitted a request for an extension of time to file the return.

Treas. Reg. § 9100-3 provides that the IRS should grant relief if the taxpayer acted reasonably and in good faith and that the granting of relief will not prejudice the interests of the government. A taxpayer is deemed to have acted reasonably and in good faith if the taxpayer failed to make an election because, after exercising reasonable diligence (taking to account the taxpayer's experience and the complexity of the return or issue), the taxpayer was unaware of the need of the election. The IRS determined that this standard was met and an extension of time to file the required notice and certification that the spouse had become a United States citizen was allowed.

32.   Letter Ruling 202115002 (April 16, 2021)

Estate granted extension of time to make QTIP election

The first spouse died leaving the residue of her estate in a marital trust for the benefit of the surviving spouse. The trust document provided that the marital trust property was to be treated as QTIP property for federal and state death tax purposes if the executor made the necessary election to do so.

The surviving spouse, as the personal representative, retained an accountant to prepare the Form 706 (Estate Tax Return). A CPA firm prepared the Form 706. The Form 706 reported the marital trust assets as "all other property" on Schedule M and reported no QTIP property. A marital deduction was claimed for all property After the filing of the Form 706, the CPA firm discovered the mistake. As a result, the spouse requested an extension of time to make a QTIP election for the marital trust.

Treas. Reg. § 301.9100-1(c) gives IRS the discretion to grant a reasonable extension of time for a regulatory election. Under Treas. Reg. § 301.9100-3, a request for an extension of time will be granted when the taxpayer shows that the taxpayer acted reasonably and in good faith and that granting the relief will not prejudice the interests of the government. A taxpayer is deemed to have acted reasonably and in good faith if the taxpayer reasonably relied on a qualified tax professional and the tax professional failed to make or advise the taxpayer to make an election.

The IRS found that the requirements of Treas. Reg. § 301.9100-3 had been satisfied and granted an extension of time for the estate to make the QTIP election for the marital trust.

33. Letter Rulings 2021027003 (February 19, 2021); 202115001 (April 16, 2021); 202116005 (April 23, 2021); 202120002 (May 21, 2021); 202120007 (May 21, 2021); 202134015 (August 27, 2021)

Decedent's estate granted extension to make portability election

---

These letter rulings are some of the most recent numerous letter rulings with similar fact patterns in which the IRS has granted the estate of the first spouse to die an extension of time to make the portability election.

The facts of these letter rulings following this general pattern. Decedent died survived by spouse. Decedent's estate was not required to file an estate tax return. Decedent had unused applicable exclusion and a portability election was necessary to allow the surviving spouse to take into account that unused applicable exclusion (DSUE amount). Since the availability of portability in 2011, the portability election is to be made on a timely filed complete and properly prepared estate tax return. Spouse's tax advisor did not advise her about the portability election. Consequently, an estate tax return was not timely filed, and the portability election was not made.

After the discovery of the missed portability election, decedent's estate requested an extension of time under Treas. Reg. § 301.9100-3 to make the portability election. Treas. Reg. § 301.9100-3 provides that an extension of time to make an election when the due date is prescribed by a regulation (and not expressly provided by statute) will be granted when the taxpayer provides evidence to establish that the taxpayer acted reasonably and in good faith and that granting the relief will not prejudice the interests of the government. Because the time for filing the portability election is fixed by the regulations, the Internal Revenue Service had the discretionary authority under Treas. Reg. § 301.9100-3 to grant an extension of time.

Based on the information, affidavits, and representations submitted on behalf of the decedent's estate, the Service granted the request for an extension of time. The Service did note that if it was later determined that decedent's estate was large enough to require the filing of an estate tax return, the Service lacked the authority under Treas. Reg. § 301.9100-3 to grant an extension of time to elect portability. In that situation, the extension of time to elect portability would be deemed null and void.

GENERATION-SKIPPING TRANSFER ("GST") TAX

34. Letter Ruling 202239003 (September 30, 2022)

> **Proposed trust modification to account for beneficiary with disability will not cause distribution from the trust or termination of any interest in trust to be subject to GST tax.**

Grandmother created a trust for the benefit of her descendants on September 25, 1985. The trust was exempt from generation-skipping transfer tax. Pursuant to the terms of the trust, the trustees divided the trust property into equal parts, with one part for each child of the grantor at the time of creation. The separate trusts were held undivided, and when a grandchild was born, the trustees created a share of the child's trust for the benefit of such grandchild.

The grandchild's separate trust provided for discretionary distributions of income and principal until the grandchild reached age 25. Upon reaching age 25, the grandchild would have the right to withdrawal up to one-half of the principal of the separate trust held for them, and the trustees held the balance for the benefit of the grandchild. At age 35, or sooner if the grandchild dies, the trustee would terminate the trust and pay over the trust property to the grandchild or as the grandchild directed the trust property to be paid in a power of appointment. If the grandchild died without exercising the power of appointment, the property would pass to the closest living relatives of the grandchild who were descendants of the grandmother.

After the grandmother created the trust, a grandchild was born with cognitive deficits and other disabilities that required the grandchild's parents to be appointed as permanent conservatives. Pursuant to a state statute, the court was authorized to modify "the administrative or dispositive terms of a trust or terminate the trust if, because of circumstances not anticipated by the settlor, modification or termination will further the purposes of the trust" in accordance with the settlor's probably intendent or if continuation of the trust on its existing terms would be impracticable or wasteful or impair the trust's administration."

The trustees of the grandchild's trust petitioned the court to modify the grandchild's trust. If the grandchild is less than 25 years of age at the time of her death, the remaining trust property of her share is to be paid over to her issue, *per stirpes*; or, if she has no issue then living, to the then living issue of her parent, who is the grandmother's child, *per stirpes*; or, if there is no such issue then living, to said parent; otherwise *per stirpes* to the grandmother's then living issue; or, if there is no issue of the grandmother then living, to a charitable organization. If the grandchild is at least 25 years of age but less than 35 years of age at the time of her death, one-half of the remaining property of said share is to be paid over to the personal representatives of her estate to be disposed of as part of her estate. The balance of the property is to be paid over to her issue, *per stirpes*; or, if she has no issue then living, to the then living issue of her parent, who is the grandmother's child, *per stirpes*; or, if there is no such issue then living, to said parent; otherwise *per stirpes* to the grandmother's then living issue; or, if there is no issue of the grandmother then living, to a charitable organization. If the grandchild is at least 35 years of age at the time of her death, the remaining property of said share is to be paid over to the personal representatives of her estate to be disposed of as part of her estate.

In evaluating the proposed modification, the Service noted that the resulting trust (i) will not result in a shift of any beneficial interest in the trust to any beneficiary who occupies a generation lower than the persons holding the beneficial interests and (ii) will not extend the time for vesting of any beneficial interest in the modified trust beyond the period provided for in the original trust. In light of the limited and tailored modification, the IRS found that after the proposed modification of the trust, the trust will remain exempt from the application of the GST tax and that no distribution from or termination of any interest in the trust will be subject to the GST tax.

35. Private Letter Ruling 202206008 (November 3, 2021, Released February 11, 2022).

In this Private Letter Ruling, the Trustee of a GST-exempt trust sought to modify the trust (perhaps through a decanting) to grant a child a general power of appointment over certain assets of the trust. According to the Trustee, such a change was needed "due to family dynamics, including separation and divorce, as well as changing tax laws".

The granting of the general power of appointment to the child would include those trust assets in the child's gross estate for estate tax purposes. This would have various other benefits, including allowing those assets to receive a step-up in basis for income tax purposes. Meanwhile, if the child had sufficient estate tax exemption to shelter those assets, then no additional estate tax would be due upon the child's death.

But two beneficiaries opposed the purported modification. Following negotiations, the parties reached a court-approved settlement, which granted the child a general power of appointment based on a formula of the trust assets. Based on this formula, a share would be created over which the child has a general power of appointment, based on the amount that the child could pass free of transfer taxes at the child's death (the "GPOA Share"), and the child would not have a general power of appointment over the remainder of the trust (the "Non-GPOA Share").

The IRS ruled that the modification would not subject the trust to GST tax at the child's death, because the granting of a general power of appointment to the child would not shift any interest to a generation lower than the current beneficiaries, and because certain other tests were met under Treas. Reg. §26.2601-1(b)(4)(i)(D).

The IRS also ruled that the modification would only cause the GPOA Share to be included in the child's estate for estate tax purposes, and the modification would not cause the Non-GPOA Share to be included in the child's estate for estate tax purposes.

This ruling reflects a strategy that is often advisable for clients in order to grant beneficiaries flexibility over an irrevocable trust at death, and to enable those assets to receive a step-up in basis, given the high estate tax exemption and the fact that inclusion in the beneficiary's estate might not trigger estate tax. But this ruling also notes the potential risks of this approach, and the possibility that these steps might undo the GST-exempt status of a trust or have other adverse tax implications.

36. Letter Rulings 202116002, 202116003, and 202116004, (Issued July 13, 2020; Released April 23, 2021)

> **Amendment of trust pursuant to state court order will not cause grandfathered trust to lose GST tax exempt status or otherwise be subject to GST tax**

Donor created a trust prior to September 25, 1985, that consequently was grandfathered from the GST tax. The trust was for the benefit of spouse and issue. Upon the death of spouse, the trustees were to divide the trust on a per stirpital basis into separate trusts for then living children and the issue of deceased children. The trustees were authorized to pay the net income from each trust to each child and the issue of the deceased child at least quarterly. The trustees could distribute principal for the education for the beneficiary and for any medical, surgical, hospital or other institutional care. Upon the death of a child, the property in the child's trust would be divided into separate trusts for that child's issue on a per stirpital basis. Each trust would terminate when a great grandchild's share terminated.

The beneficiaries requested a court order, contingent on obtaining a favorable private letter ruling, to amend the trust to create separate trusts for each grandchild (descended from the deceased child) or the issue of a deceased grandchild at each child's death. The amended trust would also provide that the termination date for each trust would be the later of the death of the grandchild for whom the trust was set apart and the date on which no living beneficiary of such trust was a great grandchild of the donor or was under a set age as long as the rule against perpetuities was not violated. The following rulings were requested:

- The amendment to the trust would not cause a loss of the GST exempt status.
- The amendment to the trust would not cause any beneficiary to be treated as having made a gift of any portion of the trust.
- The amendment to the trust would not cause any portion of the original trust to be included in the gross estate of any beneficiary.
- The amendment to the trust would not give rise to any taxable income or cause a beneficiary to recognize gain or loss from a sale or other disposition of property.

The IRS noted that an examination of the relevant trust instruments, affidavits, and representations indicated that the donor intended for the trust property be held in trust for future generations, to be divided into separate trusts for each grandchild upon a child's death, and to benefit a child's family line as long as there were descendants living in that family line. This intent was not carried out in the trust instrument due to a scrivener's error. The proposed court action would correct this error.

Moreover, the proposed court action was consistent with applicable state law that would be applied by the highest court of the state. As a result, the proposed amendment through the order of a state court would not cause the trust to lose its exempt status. Treas. Reg. § 26.2601-1(b)(4)(i)(C) provides that the judicial construction of a governing instrument to resolve an ambiguity in the terms of the instrument or to correct a scrivener's error will not cause an exempt trust to be subject to GST tax if the judicial action involves a bona fide issue and the construction is consistent with applicable tax law that would be applied by the highest court of the state under the test in *Commissioner v. Estate of Bosch*, 387 U.S. 456 (1967). These requirements were met.

The IRS then ruled that the proposed amendment to the trust would not cause any beneficiary to be treated as making a taxable gift of any portion of the original trust upon the modification, the proposed amendment would not cause any portion of the original trust to be includable in the gross estate of any beneficiary prior to termination; and that there would be no adverse income tax consequences as a result of the amendment.

37. Letter Ruling 202120003 (Issued October 22, 2020; Released May 21, 2021)

> **IRS rules that beneficiary's exercise of limited power of appointment over grandfathered GST trust will have no adverse estate or generation-skipping tax consequences**

Son was the beneficiary of a grandfathered generation-skipping trust created prior to September 25, 1985. The son proposed to exercise a limited testamentary power of appointment over the trust assets to divide the property, per stirpes, into separate trusts for his three children. The son also proposed to provide a lifetime limited power of appointment to charity and a testamentary broad limited power to anyone other than the estate, the creditors of the estate, and the creditors of the holder of the power for each child or grandchild for whom a trust was created at the son's death. Any exercise of a special power of appointment would be subject to the existing perpetuities provisions for the trust. The trust was subject to a set perpetuities period. The trust terms required a corporate trustee.

The son requested two rulings.

The son's proposed exercise of the testamentary limited power of appointment would not cause the property in the grandfathered trust to be included in the son's estate for estate tax purposes. The son's proposed exercise of the testamentary limited power of appointment would not subject the trust or the property transferred to generation-skipping tax.

With respect to the first request, the son had a broad limited testamentary power of appointment to and among such persons and/or charitable organizations as he shall see fit. The trust expressly provided, however, that the son could not exercise the testamentary power of appointment in favor of himself, his creditors, his estate, the creditors of the estate. As a result, the son's testamentary power of appointment was not a general power of appointment under Section 2041(a)(2). The possession of this power would not cause inclusion of the trust of the son's estate for estate tax purposes.

The son also had a power to remove the current or successor trustee, which had to be a national bank, but he did not have the power to appoint a successor bank trustee of the trust. Thus, the son lacked any control over a bank trustee. This power of removal was not within the definition of a general power of appointment.

On the second request, the two requirements of Treas. Reg. § 26.2601-1(b)(1)(v)(B) to avoid adverse generation-skipping tax consequences were met (the limited power was created in an irrevocable trust and the exercise could not extend the existing perpetuities period). The power was not a general power of appointment, and the power of appointment would not be exercised in a manner that might postpone or suspend the vesting of the trust or the successor trusts for a period beyond the existing perpetuities period. The ruling noted that son's proposed exercise of the power of appointment would create powers of appointment over the property in the successor trusts. However, those powers would not postpone or suspend the vesting of any interest in the successor trust beyond the existing perpetuities period.

38. Letter Rulings 202107001 and 202107002 (Issued June 30, 2020; Released February 19, 2021)

> **Service grants taxpayer and spouse extensions of time to opt out of automatic allocation rules for GST exemption**

In each of these letter rulings, Taxpayer and spouse created an irrevocable family trust with GST Tax potential for the benefit of their issue. Apparently, at the time of the creation of the family trust, Taxpayer and Spouse had no children. Taxpayer also established a grantor retained annuity trust ("GRAT") in the same year and funded the GRAT with limited partnership interests in one entity. The terms of the GRAT provided that upon termination of the taxpayer's retained annuity interest, the assets remaining in the GRAT passed to the family trust. The taxpayer survived the annuity term and the assets in the GRAT passed to the family trust. For purposes of the GST Tax, the estate tax inclusion period ("ETIP") ended upon the termination of taxpayer's retained interest and part of the taxpayer's GST exemption was automatically allocated to the family trust pursuant to Section 2632(c)(1).

Taxpayer and spouse, having created the family trust primarily for the benefit of their children, did not intend to for the trust to provide benefits for any potential grandchildren. Spouse also created a GRAT that paid out the remainder interest to the family trust upon the termination of the Spouse's annuity interest.

The lawyer who advised the taxpayer and the spouse on the creation and funding of the family trust and the two GRATs failed to advise the taxpayer and the spouse about the automatic allocation rules of Section 2632(c) and the ability to opt out of the automatic allocation rules by making that election on a gift tax return. Neither the taxpayer nor the spouse made the opt-out election on a gift tax return.

The taxpayer requested an extension of time to opt out of the automatic allocation rules pursuant to Sections 2642(g) and Treas. Reg. § 301.9100-3. Under Treas. Reg. § 301-9100-3, a request for relief will be granted when the taxpayer shows that the taxpayer acted reasonably and in good faith and the grant of relief will not prejudice the interests of the government. A taxpayer is deemed to have acted reasonably and in good faith when the taxpayer reasonably relied on a tax professional and the tax professional failed to make or advise the taxpayer to make an election. The Service found that this standard had been met in the fact situation in each of these rulings and provided an extension of time for the making of the election to opt out of the automatic allocation rules.

39. Letter Rulings 202117002 and 202117003 (Issued July 14, 2020; Released April 30, 2021)

IRS grants extension of time to opt out of automatic allocation rules for GST exemption

---

These two letter rulings involve a situation in which the taxpayer and spouse establish separate irrevocable trusts, one for their daughter and one for their son. Funds were transferred to each of the two irrevocable trusts and each trust had GST potential.

In addition, each taxpayer established three irrevocable Grantor Retained Annuity Trusts (GRATs). Each GRAT had either a two- or three-year annuity term. At the end of the annuity term, the property in each GRAT passed to the separate irrevocable trusts for the daughter and the son which had GST potential. The ETIP period for each GRAT would end upon the conclusion of the annuity term.

The taxpayers retained an attorney and an accountant to provide tax advice. Neither the attorney nor the accountant advised the taxpayer of the rules under Section 2632(c) regarding the automatic allocation of GST exemption to trusts with GST tax potential and the ability to elect out of the automatic allocation rules. Because the taxpayer failed to opt out of the automatic allocation rules, GST exemption was automatically allocated to the two irrevocable trusts and the GRATs.

The taxpayer requested an extension of time to opt out of the automatic allocation rules.

The IRS granted the request for an extension of time to opt out of the automatic allocation rules Section 2642(g) permits the granting of an extension of time if all relevant circumstances are taken into account. Under Treas. Reg. § 301-9100-3, an extension of time to opt out of the automatic allocation rules may be granted when the taxpayer proves to the IRS that the taxpayer acted reasonably and in good faith and that the grant of the relief will not prejudice the interests of the government. A taxpayer is deemed to have acted reasonably and in good faith if the taxpayer relied on a tax professional and the tax professional failed to make or advise the taxpayer to make the election. Those requirements had been met in this case and the IRS granted an extension of time to opt out of the automatic allocations of GST exemption.

40. Letter Ruling 202133008 (Issued April 16, 2021; Released August 20, 2021)

IRS grants request for extension of time to opt out of the automatic allocation rules for GST exemption

Grantor established an irrevocable grantor retained annuity trust ("GRAT") for the primary benefit of spouse and two children. The trust had GST tax potential after the annuity term. The grantor retained an accountant to provide tax advice and to prepare any necessary tax returns for the GRAT. The accountant failed to advise the grantor of the automatic allocation rules for the GST exemption and the ability to opt out of the automatic allocation rules. While grantor timely filed the Form 709, the grantor failed to opt out of the automatic allocation of GST exemption.

Grantor requested an extension of time to elect out of the application of the automatic allocation of GST exemption to the GRAT. Treas. Reg. § 9100-3 permits extensions of time when the taxpayer shows that the taxpayer acted reasonably and in good faith and that grant of relief will not prejudice the interests of the government. A taxpayer is deemed to have acted reasonably and in good faith if the taxpayer reasonably relied on a qualified tax professional and the tax professional failed to advise the taxpayer to make an election.

The IRS determined that these requirements were satisfied and granted the extension of time to opt out of the automatic allocation rules.

41. Letter Ruling 202133007 (Issued April 2, 2021; Released August 20, 2021)

IRS grants extension of time to opt out of the automatic allocation rules for GST exemption

Husband created four different grantor retained annuity trusts (GRATs). The gifts to each of the four GRATs were treated as made by both husband and wife. Each of the GRATs had GST tax potential period. Although an accountant and a lawyer worked with husband and wife on the GRATs, both the accountant and the lawyer failed to advise the taxpayers of the automatic allocation rules for the GST exemption and the ability to elect out of the automatic allocation rules. After discovering the failure to opt out of the automatic allocation rules, the husband and wife requested an extension of time to opt out.

Treas. Reg. § 301.9100-3 permits an extension of time when a taxpayer shows that the taxpayer acted reasonably and in good faith and that the grant of the relief will not prejudice the interests of the government. A taxpayer is deemed to have acted reasonably and in good faith if the taxpayer reasonably relied on a qualified tax professional and the tax professional failed to make or advise the taxpayer to make the election.

The IRS determined that these requirements were satisfied and granted the extension of time to opt out of the automatic allocation rules.

42. Letter Ruling 202116006 (Issued August 26, 2020; Released April 23, 2021)

> **Estate granted extension of time to allocate GST exemption to irrevocable exempt trusts for children**

Wife was survived by three children and three grandchildren. The value of the property in the Marital Trust and the Survivor's Trust created at husband's prior death exceeded the amount of the available GST exemption at wife's death. As a result, separate exempt and non-exempt trusts were created to benefit each child and that child's issue.

The trustees instructed an accounting firm to prepare the federal estate tax return for the wife's estate, which was timely filed on extension. The accounting firm failed to prepare and include the Schedule R (Generation-Skipping Transfer Tax) with the federal estate tax return and the wife's GST exemption was not affirmatively allocated to each child's exempt trust. This error was discovered when the attorney for the estate requested a copy of and reviewed the federal estate tax return for the estate.

Wife's estate requested an extension of time to allocate wife's remaining GST exemption to the exempt trusts for the children.

Under Treas. Reg. § 301.9100-1(c), the IRS has the discretion to grant a reasonable extension of time. Treas. Reg. § 301.9100-3 provides that relief will be granted when the taxpayer acted reasonably and in good faith and that the grant of relief will not prejudice the interests of the government. A taxpayer is deemed to have acted reasonably and in good faith if the taxpayer reasonably relied on a qualified tax professional to make the election. The IRS concluded that the requirements of Treas. Reg. § 301.9100-3 had been satisfied and granted the request for an extension of time to allocate wife's GST exemption.

43. Letter Ruling 202117001 (Issued July 14, 2020; Released April 30, 2021)

> **IRS grants extension of time to allocate GST exemption to family trust and exempt marital trust**

Decedent had an A/B Estate Plan which created a family trust and marital trust at his death. The marital trust was further divided into an exempt marital trust and non-exempt marital trust for GST tax purposes. The spouse of the decedent, in her capacity as executor, hired an attorney and accountant to help with the administration of the estate and to prepare and provide advice on all necessary tax returns. The executor was advised of the ability to allocate the decedent's available GST exemption to the family trust and the exempt marital trust and intended to do so. However, the accountant inadvertently failed to file an application for the extension of time to file the federal estate tax return. The accountant discovered the error in preparing the decedent's federal estate tax return and filed the return on a date prior to what would have been its extended due date had an extension been obtained.

The executor requested an extension of time to allocate decedent's GST exemption to the family trust and the exempt marital trust.

The IRS granted the request for an extension pursuant to Section 2642(g) and Treas. Reg. § 301.9100-3. Section 2642(g) provides that in determining whether to grant relief, the IRS will take into account all relevant circumstances, including evidence of intent contained in the governing instrument and such other relevant factors.

Treas. Reg. § 9100-3 provides that relief will be granted when the taxpayer provides evidence to establish that the taxpayer acted reasonably and in good faith and that granting the relief will not prejudice the interests of the government. The taxpayer is deemed to have acted reasonably and in good faith if the taxpayer reasonably relied on a qualified tax professional and the tax professional failed to make or failed to advise the taxpayer to make an election.

The Service determined that the requirements of Treas. Reg. § 9100-3 had been met and granted an extension of time.

44. Letter Ruling 202133006 (Issued March 3, 2021; Released August 20, 2021)

> **IRS grants extension of time to allocate generation-skipping tax exemption to charitable remainder unitrust**

Prior to the enactment of the automatic allocation of GST exemption rules for indirect skips, Donor funded a charitable remainder unitrust (CRUT) which paid a unitrust amount for life to grandchild with the remainder to charity at grandchild's death. Donor and spouse elected to split gifts and relied on an accounting firm to prepare separate Form 709s for the transfer to the CRUT. The accounting firm reported the value of the transfer to CRUT but did not allocate any part of either donor or spouse's GST exemptions to the transfer to the CRUT. Donor subsequently died. The executor of donor's estate and the spouse learned of the GST tax consequences when the Form 706 was prepared for the donor's estate.

The executor and the spouse both requested an extension of time to allocate GST exemption to the transfer to the CRUT.

Treas. Reg. § 301.9100-3 permits an extension of time when a taxpayer shows that the taxpayer acted reasonably and in good faith and that the grant of the relief will not prejudice the interests of the government. A taxpayer is deemed to have acted reasonably and in good faith if the taxpayer reasonably relied on a qualified tax professional and the tax professional failed to make or advise the taxpayer to make the election. The IRS determined that these requirements were satisfied and granted the extension of time to allocate GST exemption to the CRUT.

FIDUCIARY INCOME TAX

45. T.D. 9918 (September 21, 2020)

IRS issues final regulations on effect of Section 67(g) on certain deductions for estates and nongrantor trusts under Section 67(e)

In Notice 2018-61, 2018-31 IRB 278 (July 13, 2018), the Treasury Department and the IRS announced that they intended to issue regulations on the impact of new Section 67(g) of the Internal Revenue Code on certain deductions for estates and nongrantor trusts. Section 67(g) was added to the Code by the 2017 Tax Act and suspended temporarily miscellaneous itemized deductions for tax years beginning on or after January 1, 2018 through December 31, 2025. Proposed regulations on Section 67(g) were issued almost two years after the issuance of Notice 2018-61 on May 7, 2020. The final regulations adopted the proposed regulation with few changes.

The final regulations make clear that certain deductions for irrevocable nongrantor trusts and estate are still available. Administrative expenses such as trustee's fees and appraisal fees can be deducted. Also, certain expenses giving rise to excess deductions can be passed on to beneficiaries upon the termination of a trust or estate. While separating the deductions will require more work, this will allow beneficiaries to use some excess deductions on their income tax returns to reduce their adjusted gross income.

Under Section 67(e) of the Code, the adjusted gross income of an estate or nongrantor trust is computed in the same manner as that of an individual, with two exceptions. Section 67(e)(1) permits an estate or nongrantor trust to deduct in computing adjusted gross income the costs incurred in connection with the administration of the estate or trust that would not have been incurred if the property were not held in the estate or trust. Such expenses generally include, for example, fiduciary compensation and court accounting costs. Section 67(e)(2) provides an exception for deductions allowable under Section 642(b) (relating to the personal exemption of an estate or nongrantor trust), Section 651 (relating to distributions of income to beneficiaries of simple trusts), and Section 661 (relating to distributions of income and principal to beneficiaries of complex trusts).

Tax practitioners expressed concern that Section 67(g) might inadvertently eliminate the deduction for costs of estate and trust administration. Practitioners also requested guidance on whether the suspension of miscellaneous itemized deductions prohibits trust and estate beneficiaries from deducting on their individual returns the excess deductions of the trust or estate incurred during the trust's or estate's final taxable year. The final regulations clarify that the costs of trust or estate administration are not miscellaneous itemized deductions suspended by Section 67(g).

The final regulations also address the impact of Section 67(g) on the ability of beneficiaries to deduct the excess deductions of an estate or trust upon the termination of the estate or trust. On the termination of a nongrantor trust or estate, Section 642(h) of the Code allows the beneficiaries succeeding to the property of the nongrantor trust or estate to deduct the trust's or estate's unused net operating loss carryovers under Section 172 of the Code and unused capital loss carryovers under Section 1212 of the Code. If an estate or nongrantor trust has deductions (other than deductions for personal exemptions or charitable contributions) in excess of gross income in its final taxable year, then Section 642(h) allows the beneficiaries succeeding to the property of the estate or trust to deduct such excess on their individual returns. Capital loss carryovers and net operating loss carryovers are taken into account in calculating adjusted gross income and are not miscellaneous itemized deductions. Section 67(g) therefore does not affect the ability of a beneficiary to make use of a capital loss carryover or net operating loss carryover received from an estate or non-grantor trust.

The excess deductions of an estate or non-grantor trust, however, are allowable only in computing taxable income and are not covered by an exception from miscellaneous itemized deductions in Section 67(b).

The final regulations preserve the tax character of the three categories of expenses rather that grouping all non-Section 67(e) expenses together, to allow for such expenses to be separately stated and to facilitate reporting it to beneficiaries. Each deduction comprising the Section 642(h)(2) excess deduction retains its separate character, specifically: as an amount allowed in arriving at adjusted gross income; a non-miscellaneous itemized deduction; or a miscellaneous itemized deduction. The final regulations also require fiduciaries to identify deductions that may be limited when claimed by a beneficiary.

The final regulations state that the principles under Treas. Reg. § 1.652(b)-3 will be used to allocate each deductible item among the classes of income in the year of termination in order to determine the character and amount of the excess deductions under Section 642(h)(2). Any remaining deductions that are not directly attributable to a specific class of income and any deductions that exceed the amount of directly attributable income, may be allocated to any item of income, but a portion must be allocated to tax-exempt income.

Existing regulations under Treas. Reg. § 1.642(h)-4 provide that carryovers and excess deductions to which Section 642(h) applies are allocated among the beneficiaries succeeding to the property of an estate or trust proportionately according to the share of each in the burden of the loss or deduction. A person who qualifies as a beneficiary succeeding to the property of an estate or trust with respect to one amount and who does not qualify with respect to another amount is a beneficiary succeeding to the property of the estate of the trust as to the amount with respect to which the beneficiary qualifies.

OTHER ITEMS OF INTEREST

46. *Bittner v. United States*, No. 20-1195 (February 28, 2023)

> **U.S. Supreme Court rules in favor of taxpayer on FBAR reporting case; penalties not assessed per account but per report.**

The United States Supreme Court, in a 5-4 decision, ruled that the provisions of the Bank Secrecy Act penalty for the nonwillful failure to file a compliant report accrues on a per-report, not a per-account, basis.

The Bank Secrecy Act (BSA) requires U. S. persons with certain financial interests in foreign accounts to file an annual report known as an "FBAR"—the Report of Foreign Bank and Financial Accounts. The BSA imposes a maximum $10,000 penalty for nonwillful violations of the reporting requirement. The FBAR reports are designed to help the government trace funds that may be used for illicit purposes and identify unreported income that may be subject to taxation.

Alexandru Bittner, a dual citizen of both Romania and the United States, first learned of the BSA and FBAR reporting requirements when he returned to the United States in 2011. Bittner filed FBAR reports that were deemed inaccurate or incomplete. He prepared and filed corrected reports showing a total of 272 foreign accounts that he had control over from 2007 – 2011. The government accepted the corrected reports as accurate and did not assess that the earlier, mis-filed reports were a willful violation of the BSA.

The government assessed the $10,000 penalty per account and not per report and issued a notice of penalty to Bittner totalling $2,720,000. Bittner challenged the penalty, arguing that the penalty for nonwillful violations should apply per report and not per account. The Fifth Circuit upheld the government's penalty assessment. The Supreme Court reversed, holding that the correct statutory interpretation of the violation the penalty is assessed against is the filing of the report, and the penalty should be based on that violation and not the number of accounts detailed in the report. In addition to the statutory interpretation, the majority, led by Justice Gorsuch, found contextual support for the holding, recognizing that Congress has the ability to levy account-specific penalties and has done so in other contexts, and that the government's own literature on the subject indicates that the "violation" covered by the penalty is the filing of the report.

Bittner's penalty was reduced to $50,000, $10,000 per report for each of the 5 reports filed.

47. *United States v. Moshe Lax, et. al.*, No. 1:18-cv-04061 (EDNY) (December 29, 2022)

Court rules that Executor waived attorney-client privilege through discovery disclosure, crime fraud exception applies

---

This case arises out of an action brought by the United States of America against Moshe Lax and others to collect unpaid federal income and estate tax liabilities owed by the Estate of Chaim Lax and to obtain money judgments related to alleged schemes undertaken to shield businesses and property held by Lax and others from creditors of the Estate, including the IRS.

The government alleged that Lax and other defendants engaged in a series of schemes to evade the collection of the liabilities of the estate of Chaim Lax. The schemes involved "a series of fraudulent transfers and other artificial transactions designed to hide the Lax family assets from the IRS and other creditors and make it appear as though the Estate was insolvent.

During the discovery phase, the government sought information from Lax's emails. As part of the process, certain emails were turned over to the government subject to certain stipulations. Lax had the opportunity to claim privilege over certain attorney-client communications and produce those communications only through a privilege log. Certain emails were disclosed that contained communications between Lax and his counsel, and Lax did not assert privilege over those communications. Those communications became subject of deposition testimony, where Lax learned that the emails were disclosed to the government and not part of the privilege log. When questioned about the emails in a deposition, Lax's attorney claimed attorney-client privilege.

The government sought a ruling from the court declaring that Lax had waived the attorney-client privilege by disclosing the emails in discovery and asserted that crime fraud exception applied, given the nature of the communications. In response to the government motion, Lax sought to claw back the privileged emails pursuant to the discovery stipulations, but he was neither thorough nor responsive in his clawback requests.

Lax argued that his disclosure of the emails was inadvertent and should not waive privilege. The government contended that even if disclosure was inadvertent, Lax failed to make reasonable efforts to prevent and rectify the disclosure.

In reviewing the facts, the court was not persuaded by Lax's claim that he "reviewed carefully on his own thousands of electronically personal and attorneys e-mails, worked very closely with Interactive documents co. and Ms. Larson to have it done right and deliver in set time frames." Lax failed to describe how he conducted that review or what efforts he made to prevent the inadvertent disclosure of privileged documents. And Lax did not state that he implemented any specific measures to safeguard against inadvertent disclosure.

The Court found that a party asserting privilege has the burden to show that he acted reasonably to prevent inadvertent disclosure and that Lax's actions evince a degree of indifference and carelessness that weighs in favor of finding that the privilege was waived. Moreover, the Court found that Lax failed to adequately explain why he delayed four months before requesting the return of the emails. His inordinate delay in making that request weights in favor of a waiver of the privilege. Citing these reasons, and the unfairness to the government for having relied on the documents, the Court ruled that Lax waived attorney-client privilege with regard to the emails in question.

The Court also allowed the government limited discovery beyond the emails, based on the crime fraud exception, to conduct a deposition of the law firm into the advice concerning the structuring of the transaction that allowed Lax to avoid payments to creditors.

48.   *Sander v. Comm'r of Internal Revenue*, T.C. Memo 2022-103 (October 6, 2022)

Tax Court rules on proper party to challenge deficiency after taxpayer dies, looks to state law

---

Sandra Sander, a resident of Florida, created The Sandra E. Sander Lifetime Trust (the "Trust") and served as co-trustee of the Trust with her daughter, Sandra transferred all her assets, including her tangible personal property, to the Trust.   Under the terms of the trust, upon Sandra's death, Leda would serve as the sole trustee, and the assets would be divided into separate, equal trusts for Sandra's children (including Leda).

Sandra died on July 4, 2016. Leda was also nominated as the personal representative of Sandra's estate under the terms of Sandra's will. On advice of a lawyer, Leda did not probate the will or qualify as personal representative because "there [were] no assets to probate."

Two weeks after her death, the IRS issued a notice of deficiency to Sandra determining income tax deficiencies of $28,123 for 2013 and $25,544 for 2014 as well as a section 6662(a) penalty of 20% of the determined amount of the deficiency for each year. On October 17, 2016. Leda filed a Petition for redetermination of the deficiencies in Sandra's name. It advised the Court that Sandra had died. The Petition was signed by Leda, a resident of Missouri when the Petition was filed. Later, Leda moved to substitute parties and change the caption such that, as trustee of the Sandra E. Sander Lifetime Trust, Leda would be substituted as the petitioner in the case. The IRS moved to dismiss the case, arguing that Leda, as trustee of the Trust, was not the proper party and only the personal representative of Sandra's estate could stand in for Sandra in the action.

In determining the proper party to bring a petition on behalf of a taxpayer, the Tax Court looked to Rule 60 of the Tax Court's Rules of Practice and Procedure. Rule 60 makes clear that a "case shall be brought by and in the name of the person against whom the Commissioner [i.e., the IRS] determined the deficiency (in the case of a notice of deficiency) or liability (in the case of a notice of liability), or by and with the full descriptive name of the fiduciary entitled to institute a case on behalf of such person." And further, the determination of when a fiduciary has the capacity to engage in litigation turns on the state law of the domicile of the taxpayer."

Leda argued that because no personal representative had been appointed, as sole trustee of the Trust, authorized under the trust instrument to pay expenses, including taxes, and compromise claims and debts, she was authorized to petition the Tax Court, in the place of Sandra, to contest the deficiency.

The Tax Court looked to the Florida Probate Code, and found there that the personal representative – duly appointed by the circuit court – has the authority to "[p] rosecute or defend claims or proceedings in any jurisdiction for the protection of the estate, of the decedent's property, and of the personal representative." No provisions are made in the Florida Probate Code for someone other than the personal representative to act in this capacity.

The Tax Court distinguished this case from the holding in *Estate of Galloway v. Commissioner*, 103 T.C. 700 (1994). In *Estate of Galloway*, the Tax Court ruled that the daughter of a decedent-taxpayer, nominated but never qualified as the personal representative, had standing to serve as the decedent's successor in interest before the Tax Court. Looking to California, the law of the domicile of the taxpayer, the Tax Court found support. Specifically, California Civil Procedure Code § 377.33 provides that the "court in which an action is commenced or continued under this article may make any order concerning parties that is appropriate to ensure proper administration of justice in the case, including appointment of the decedent's successor in interest as a special administrator or guardian ad litem." In effect, the California Probate Code gave *any* court the authority to appoint a special administrator when the interests of justice were best served in that way, and so the Tax Court allowed the daughter to serve.

The Florida Probate Code has no corresponding statute. Rather, the Florida Probate Code clearly reserves to the Florida circuit court, acting in its probate capacity, as the sole court with the capacity to appoint a personal representative or any special administrator for the Tax Court action. The Tax Court found support for this in other rulings in Florida courts.

The Tax Court ultimately ruled that Leda, as trustee of the Trust, was not a proper party to appear to contest the deficiency and deferred ruling on the Motion to Dismiss for six months in order to allow an opportunity for a probate action to be commenced for Sandra's estate and a personal representative appointed.

49. *Busch v. Commissioner (U.S. Tax Court, No. 14085-20S)*

Tax Court requires careful review before filing

In an opinion delivered from the bench, Judge Lewis R. Carluzzo held that the taxpayer's failure to carefully review a tax return undermined the argument that the taxpayer acted with reasonable cause and in good faith in substantially underpaying tax and would be liable for an accuracy related penalty.

Taxpayers Candice and Randall Busch prepared their individual income tax return using a "popular version of return preparation software." In doing so, the taxpayers failed to realize that the software did not accept the input of a decimal point in data entry, so the couple's mortgage interest deduction, entered as $21,201.25 resulted in a deduction taken totaling $2,120,125.

The overstated deduction zeroed out the taxpayers' taxable income and federal income tax, resulting in a refund of all tax withheld from their wages. The IRS adjusted the mortgage interest deduction to reflect to correct amount, issuing a notice of deficiency and an accuracy-related penalty.

The taxpayers represented themselves before the court and argued that the penalty should not apply where they acted with reasonable cause and in good faith. The Court agreed with the taxpayers, "…that not every mistake made on a Federal income tax return should result in an accuracy-related penalty." Such "honest" mistakes should not require a taxpayer to pay a heavy burden. The Court found that the mistake the taxpayers made was not in data entry but in failing to review the final return, and act reasonably and in good faith, when the final return resulted in no taxable income.

The Court upheld the imposition of the accuracy related penalty.

50. *CCA 202202011 (January 14, 2022)*

Office of Chief Counsel advises on statute of limitations for estate tax returns filed in the wrong service center

The Office of Chief Counsel was asked to advise on when the statute of limitation for a delinquent Form 706, *United States Estate (and Generation-Skipping Transfer) Tax Return*, begins to run. The Chief Counsel's Office noted that, under the holding in *Winnett*, 96 T.C. 802 (1991), the assessment statute would not begin until the delinquent Form 706 has been received by the Kansas City Service Center consistent with the instructions on IRS.gov; but the Chief Counsel's Office also noted that it is possible a court could find the running of the assessment statute to have begun when the return is filed in accordance with the Form 706 instructions.

Appendix

Alabama

Type of Tax: None

Current Law: Tax is tied to federal state death tax credit. AL ST § 40-15-2.

Alaska

Type of Tax: None

Current Law: Tax is tied to federal state death tax credit. AK ST § 43.31.011.

Arizona

Type of Tax: None

Current Law: Tax was tied to federal state death tax credit. AZ ST §§ 42-4051; 42-4001(2), (12).

On May 8, 2006, Governor Napolitano signed SB 1170 which permanently repealed Arizona's state estate tax.

Arkansas

Type of Tax: None

Current Law: Tax is tied to federal state death tax credit. AR ST § 26-59-103; 26-59-106; 26-59-109, as amended March 2003.

California

Type of Tax: None

Current Law: Tax is tied to federal state death tax credit. CA REV & TAX §§ 13302; 13411.

Colorado

Type of Tax: None

Current Law: Tax is tied to federal state death tax credit. CO ST §§ 39-23.5-103; 39-23.5-102.

Connecticut

Type of Tax: Separate Estate Tax

Current Law: On October 31, 2017, the Connecticut Governor signed the 2018-2019 budget which increased the exemption for the Connecticut state estate and gift tax to

$2,600,000 in 2018, to $3,600,000 in 2019, and to the federal estate and gift tax exemption in 2020.

On May 31, 2018, Connecticut changed its estate tax law to extend the phase-in of the exemption to 2023 to reflect the increase in the federal exemption to $10 million indexed for inflation in the 2017 Tax Act. The exemption will be phased in as follows:

2019: $3.6 million

2020: $5.1 million

2021: $7.1 million

2022: $9.1 million:

2023: federal exemption for deaths on or after January 1, 2023.

Beginning in 2019, the cap on the Connecticut state estate and gift tax is reduced from $20 million to $15 million (which represents the tax due on a Connecticut estate of approximately $129 million).

Delaware

Type of Tax: None

Current Law: On July 2, 2017, the Governor signed HB 16 which sunset the Delaware Estate Tax on December 31, 2017.

District of Columbia

Type of Tax: Pick-up Only

Current Law: DC Bill B22-0685 was introduced in the DC City Council on February 8, 2018. This proposal cut the DC threshold to $5.6 million adjusted for inflation retroactive to January 1, 2018. This change was enacted by the DC City Council on September 5, 2018, as part of the Budget Support Act.

In August 2020, the DC City Council enacted the "Estate Tax Adjustment Amendment Act of 2020," which reduces the DC threshold to $4 million in 2021 and which will be adjusted for inflation beginning in 2022.

No separate QTIP election.

Florida

Type of Tax: None

Current Law: Tax is tied to federal state death tax credit. FL ST § 198.02; FL CONST. Art. VII, Sec. 5.

Georgia

Type of Tax: None

Current Law: Effective July 1, 2014, the Georgia estate tax was repealed. See § 48-12-1.

Hawaii

Type of Tax: Modified Pick-up Tax

Current Law: On May 2, 2012, the Hawaii legislature passed HB 2328 which conforms the Hawaii estate tax exemption to the federal estate tax exemption for decedents dying after January 25, 2012.

On June 7, 2018, the governor signed SB 2821, which amended HI ST § 236E-6 to reduce the Hawaiian exemption, effective January 1, 2018, to $5,000,000 indexed for inflation.

The Hawaii Department of Taxation released Announcement 2018-13 on September 4, 2018, in which it announced that the exemption will remain at the amount available to decedents dying during 2017.

In response to calls from practitioners, the Hawaii Department of Taxation indicated that was not going to adjust the exemption for inflation in 2019.

Effective January 1, 2020, Hawaii increased the rate of its state estate tax on estates valued at over $10,000,000 to 20 percent. See Act No. 3 (April 4, 2019).

Idaho

Type of Tax: None

Current Law: Tax is tied to federal state death tax credit. ID ST §§ 14-403; 14-402; 63-3004 (as amended Mar. 2002).

Illinois

Type of Tax: Modified Pick-up Only

Current Law: On January 13, 2011, Governor Quinn signed Public Act 096-1496 which increased Illinois' individual and corporate income tax rates. Included in the Act was the reinstatement of Illinois' estate tax as of January 1, 2011, with a $2 million exemption.

Senate Bill 397 passed both the Illinois House and Senate as part of the tax package for Sears and CME on December 13, 2011. It increased the exemption to $3.5 million for 2012 and $4 million for 2013 and beyond. Governor Quinn signed the legislation on December 16, 2011.

Illinois permits a separate state QTIP election, effective September 8, 2009. 35 ILCS 405/2(b-1).

Indiana

Type of Tax: None

Current Law: Pick-up tax is tied to federal state death tax credit. IN ST §§ 6-4.1-11-2; 6-4.1-1-4.

On May 11, 2013, Governor Pence signed HB 1001 which repealed Indiana's inheritance tax retroactively to January 1, 2013. This replaced Indiana's prior law enacted in 2012 which phased out Indiana's inheritance tax over nine years beginning in 2013 and ending on December 31, 2021 and increased the inheritance tax exemption amounts retroactive to January 1, 2012.

Iowa

Type of Tax: Inheritance Tax

Current Law: Pick-up tax is tied to federal state death tax credit. IA ST § 451.2; 451.13.

Effective July 1, 2010, Iowa specifically reenacted its pick-up estate tax for decedents dying after December 31, 2010. Iowa Senate File 2380, reenacting IA ST § 451.2.

Iowa has a separate inheritance tax on transfers to others than lineal ascendants and descendants.

On June 16, 2021, the governor signed SF 619 which, among other tax law changes, reduces the inheritance tax rates by twenty percent each year beginning January 1, 2021 through December 31, 2024 and results in the repeal of the inheritance tax as of January 1, 2025.

Kansas

Type of Tax: None

Current Law: For decedents dying on or after January 1, 2007 through December 31, 2009, Kansas had enacted a separate stand-alone estate tax. KS ST § 79-15, 203

Kentucky

Type of Tax: Inheritance Tax

Current Law: Pick-up tax is tied to federal state death tax credit. KY ST § 140.130.

Kentucky has not decoupled but has a separate inheritance tax and recognizes by administrative pronouncement a separate state QTIP election.

Louisiana

Type of Tax: None

Current Law: Pick-up tax is tied to federal state death tax credit. LA R.S. §§ 47:2431; 47:2432; 47:2434.

Maine

Type of Tax: Pick-up Only

Current Law: For decedents dying after December 31, 2002, pick-up tax was frozen at pre-EGTRRA federal state death tax credit and imposed on estates exceeding applicable exclusion amount in effect on December 31, 2000 (including scheduled increases under pre-EGTRRA law) (L.D. 1319; March 27, 2003).

On June 20, 2011, Maine's governor signed Public Law Chapter 380 into law, which increased the Maine estate tax exemption to $2 million in 2013 and beyond. The rates were also changed, effective January 1, 2013, to 0% for Maine estates up to $2 million, 8% for Maine estates between $2 million and $5 million, 10 % between $ 5 million and $8 million and 12% for the excess over $8 million.

On June 30, 2015, the Maine legislature overrode the Governor's veto of LD 1019, the budget bill for fiscal years 2016 and 2017. As part of the law, the Maine Exemption was tagged to the federal exemption for decedents dying on or after January 1, 2016.

The tax rates are:

- 8% on the first $3 million above the Maine Exemption

- 10% on the next $3 million above the Maine Exemption

- 2% on all amounts above $6 million above the Maine Exemption

The new legislation did not include portability as part of the Maine Estate Tax.

On September 12, 2018, LP1655 became law without the Governor's signature. The new law amends M.R.S. Title 36, Section 4102 and Section 4119 to make the Maine exemption $5,600,000 adjusted for inflation for decedents dying on and after January 1, 2018.

For estates of decedents dying after December 31, 2002, Sec. 2058 deduction is ignored in computing Maine tax and a separate state QTIP election is permitted. M.R.S. Title 36, Sec. 4062.

Maine also subjects real or tangible property located in Maine that is transferred to a trust, limited liability company or other pass-through entity to tax in a non-resident's estate. M.R.S. Title 36, Sec. 4064.

Maryland

Type of Tax: Pick-up Tax

Inheritance Tax

Current Law: On May 15, 2014, Governor O'Malley signed HB 739 which repealed and reenacted MD TAX GENERAL §§ 7-305, 7-309(a), and 7-309(b) to do the following:

1. Increased the threshold for the Maryland estate tax to $1.5 million in 2015, $2 million in 2016, $3 million in 2017, and $4 million in 2018. For 2019 and beyond, the Maryland threshold will equal the federal applicable exclusion amount.

2. Continued to limit the amount of the federal credit used to calculate the Maryland estate tax to 16% of the amount by which the decedent's taxable estate exceeds the Maryland threshold unless the Section 2011 federal state death tax credit is then in effect.

3. Continued to ignore the federal deduction for state death taxes under Sec. 2058 in computing Maryland estate tax, thus eliminating a circular computation.

4. Permitted a state QTIP election.

On April 5, 2018, HB 0308 became law. The new law provides that for 2019 and thereafter, the Maryland threshold will be capped at the fixed amount of $5 million rather than being equal to the inflation-adjusted federal exemption as provided under prior law.

The new law also provides for the portability of the unused predeceased spouse's Maryland exemption amount to the surviving spouse beginning in 2019.

Massachusetts

Type of Tax: Pick-up Only

Current Law: For decedents dying in 2002, pick-up tax is tied to federal state death tax credit. MA ST 65C §§ 2A.

For decedents dying on or after January 1, 2003, pick-up tax is frozen at federal state death tax credit in effect on December 31, 2000. MA ST 65C §§ 2A(a), as amended July 2002.

Tax imposed on estates exceeding applicable exclusion amount in effect on December 31, 2000 (including scheduled increases under pre-EGTRRA law), even if that amount is below EGTRRA applicable exclusion amount.

See, Taxpayer Advisory Bulletin (Dec. 2002), DOR Directive 03-02, Mass. Guide to Estate Taxes (2003) and TIR 02-18 published by Mass. Dept. of Rev.

Massachusetts Department of Revenue has issued directive, pursuant to which separate Massachusetts QTIP election can be made when applying state's new estate tax based upon pre-EGTRRA federal state death tax credit.

Michigan

Type of Tax: None

Current Law: Tax is tied to federal state death tax credit. MI ST §§ 205.232; 205.256.

Minnesota

Type of Tax: Pick-up Only

Current Law: Tax frozen at federal state death tax credit in effect on December 31, 2000, clarifying statute passed May 2002. MN ST §§ 291.005; 291.03; MN Revenue Notice 02-16.

Tax imposed on estates exceeding federal applicable exclusion amount in effect on December 31, 2000 (including scheduled increases under pre-EGTRRA law), even if that amount is below EGTRRA applicable exclusion amount.

Separate state QTIP election permitted.

On May 30, 2017, the governor signed the budget bill, H.F. No. 1 which increased the Minnesota estate tax exemption for 2017 from $1,800,000 to $2,100,000 retroactively, and increases the exemption to $2,400,000 in 2018, $2,700,000 in 2019, and $3,000,000 for 2020 and thereafter.

A provision enacted in 2013 to impose an estate tax on non-residents who own an interest in a pass-through entity which in turn owned real or personal property in Minnesota was amended in 2014 to exclude certain publicly traded entities. It still applies to entities taxed as partnerships or S Corporations that own closely held businesses, farms, and cabins.

Mississippi

Type of Tax: None

Current Law: Tax is tied to federal state death tax credit. MS ST § 27-9-5.

Missouri

Type of Tax: None

Current Law: Tax is tied to federal state death tax credit. MO ST §§ 145.011; 145.091.

Montana

Type of Tax: None

Current Law: Tax is tied to federal state death tax credit. MT ST § 72-16-904; 72-16-905.

Nebraska

Type of Tax: County Inheritance Tax

Current Law: Nebraska through 2006 imposed a pick-up tax at the state level. Counties impose and collect a separate inheritance tax. NEB REV ST § 77-2101.01(1).

Nevada

Type of Tax: None

Current Law: Tax is tied to federal state death tax credit. NV ST Title 32 §§ 375A.025; 375A.100.

New Hampshire

Type of Tax: None

Current Law: Tax is tied to federal state death tax credit. NH ST §§ 87:1; 87:7.

New Jersey

Type of Tax: Inheritance Tax

Current Law: On October 14, Governor Christie signed Assembly Bill A-12 which was the tax bill accompanying Assembly Bill A-10 which revised the funding for the state's Transportation Fund. Under this law, the Pick-Up Tax had a $2 million exemption in 2017 and was eliminated as of January 1, 2018. The new law also eliminated the tax on New Jersey real and tangible property of a non-resident decedent.

The repeal of the pick-up tax did not apply to the separate New Jersey inheritance tax.

New Mexico

Type of Tax: None

Current Law: Tax is tied to federal state death tax credit. NM ST §§ 7-7-2; 7-7-3.

New York

Type of Tax: Pick-up Only

Current Law: The Executive Budget of 2014-2015 which was signed by Governor Cuomo on March 31, 2014, made substantial changes to New York's estate tax.

The New York estate tax exemption, which was $1,000,000 through March 31, 2014, was increased as follows:

April 1, 2014 to March 31, 2015 -- $2,062,500

April 1, 2015 to March 31, 2016 -- $3,125,000

April 1, 2016 to March 31, 2017 -- $4,187,500

April 1, 2017 to December 31, 2018 -- $5,250,000

As of January 1, 2019, the New York estate tax exemption amount will be the same as the federal estate tax applicable exclusion amount prior to the 2017 Tax Act which is $5,000,000 adjusted for inflation.

The maximum rate of tax will continue to be 16%.

Taxable gifts within three years of death between April 1, 2014 and December 31, 2018 will be added back to a decedent's estate for purposes of calculating the New York tax.

The New York estate tax is a cliff tax. If the value of the estate is more than 105% of the then current exemption, the exemption will not be available.

On April 1, 2015, as part of 2015-2016 Executive Budget, New York enacted changes to the New York Estate Tax. New York first clarified that the new rate schedule enacted in 2014 applies to all decedents dying after April 1, 2014. Previously, the rate schedule only applied through March 31, 2015. New York then modified the three-year gift add-back provision to make it clear that the gift add-back does not apply to any individuals dying on or after January 1, 2019. Previously, the gift add-back provision did not apply to gifts made on or after January 1, 2019.

New York continues not to permit portability for New York estates and no separate state QTIP election is allowed when portability is elected on a federal return.

North Carolina

Type of Tax: None

Current Law: On July 23, 2013, the Governor signed HB 998 which repealed the North Carolina estate tax retroactively to January 1, 2013.

North Dakota

Type of Tax: None

Current Law: Tax is tied to federal state death tax credit. ND ST § 57-37.1-04.

Ohio

Type of Tax: None

Current Law: Governor Taft signed the budget bill, 2005 HB 66, repealing the Ohio estate (sponge) tax prospectively and granting credit for it retroactively. This was effective June 30, 2005 and killed the sponge tax.

On June 30, 2011, Governor Kasich signed HB 153, the biannual budget bill, which contained a repeal of the Ohio state estate tax effective January 1, 2013.

Oklahoma

Type of Tax: None

Current Law: Tax is tied to federal state death tax credit. OK ST Title 68 § 804.

The separate estate tax was phased out as of January 1, 2010.

Oregon

Type of Tax: Separate Estate Tax

Current Law: On June 28, 2011, Oregon's governor signed HB 2541 which replaced Oregon's pick-up tax with a stand-alone estate tax effective January 1, 2012.

The new tax has a $1 million threshold with rates increasing from ten percent to sixteen percent between $1 million and $9.5 million.

Determination of the estate for Oregon estate tax purposes is based upon the federal taxable estate with adjustments.

Pennsylvania

Type of Tax: Inheritance Tax

Current Law: Tax is tied to the federal state death tax credit to the extent that the available federal state death tax credit exceeds the state inheritance tax. PA ST T. 72 P.S. § 9117 amended December 23, 2003.

Pennsylvania had decoupled its pick-up tax in 2002 but has now recoupled retroactively. The recoupling does not affect the Pennsylvania inheritance tax which is independent of the federal state death tax credit.

Pennsylvania recognizes a state QTIP election.

Rhode Island

Type of Tax: Pick-up Only

Current Law: Tax frozen at federal state death tax credit in effect on January 1, 2001, with certain adjustments (see below). RI ST § 44-22-1.1.

Rhode Island recognized a separate state QTIP election in the State's Tax Division Ruling Request No. 2003-03.

Rhode Island's Governor signed into law HB 5983 on June 30, 2009, effective for deaths occurring on or after January 1, 2010, an increase in the amount exempted from Rhode Island estate tax from $675,000, to $850,000, with annual adjustments beginning for deaths occurring on or after January 1, 2011, based on "the percentage of increase in the Consumer Price Index for all Urban Consumers (CPI-U). rounded up to the nearest five-dollar ($5.00) increment." RI ST § 44-22-1.1.

On June 19, 2014, the Rhode Island Governor approved changes to the Rhode Island Estate Tax by increasing the exemption to $1,500,000 indexed for inflation in 2015 and eliminating the cliff tax.

South Carolina

Type of Tax: None

Current Law: Tax is tied to federal state death tax credit. SC ST §§ 12-16-510; 12-16-20 and 12-6-40, amended in 2002.

South Dakota

Type of Tax: None

Current Law: Tax was permanently repealed in 2014 with repeal of all of SDCL § 10-40A, effective July 1, 2014.

Tennessee

Type of Tax: None

Current Law: Pick-up tax is tied to federal state death tax credit. TN ST §§ 67-8-202; 67-8-203.

Tennessee had a separate inheritance tax which was phased out as of January 1, 2016.

Texas

Type of Tax: None

Current Law: Tax was permanently repealed effective as of September 15, 2015, when Chapter 211 of the Texas Tax Code was repealed. Prior to September 15, 2015, the tax was tied to the federal state death tax credit.

Utah

Type of Tax: None

Current Law: Tax is tied to federal state death tax credit. UT ST § 59-11-102; 59-11-103.

Vermont

Type of Tax: Modified Pick-up

Current Law: In 2010, Vermont increased the estate tax exemption threshold from $2,000,000 to $2,750,000 for decedents dying on or after January 1, 2011. As of January 1, 2012, the exclusion equaled the federal estate tax applicable exclusion amount, so long as the FET exclusion was not less than $2,000,000 and not more than $3,500,000.

On June 18, 2019, Vermont enacted H. 541 which increased the Vermont estate tax exemption to $4,250,000 in 2020 and $5,000,000 in 2021 and thereafter. VT ST T. 32 § 7442a.

No separate state QTIP election permitted.

Vermont does not permit portability of its estate tax exemption.

Virginia

Type of Tax: None

Current Law: Tax is tied to federal state death tax credit. VA ST §§ 58.1-901; 58.1-902.

The Virginia tax was repealed effective July 1, 2007. Previously, the tax was frozen at federal state death tax credit in effect on January 1, 1978. Tax was imposed only on estates exceeding EGTRRA federal applicable exclusion amount.

Washington

Type of Tax: Separate Estate Tax

Current Law: LEGISLATIVE FRAMEWORK. On February 3, 2005, the Washington State Supreme Court unanimously held that Washington's state death tax was unconstitutional. The tax was tied to the current federal state death tax credit, thus reducing the tax for the years 2002 - 2004 and eliminating it for the years 2005 - 2010. *Hemphill v. State Department of Revenue* 2005 WL 240940 (Wash. 2005).

In response to *Hemphill*, the Washington State Senate on April 19 and the Washington House on April 22, 2005, by narrow majorities, passed a stand-alone state estate tax with rates ranging from 10% to 19%, a $1.5 million exemption in 2005 and $2 million thereafter, and a deduction for farms for which a Sec. 2032A election could have been taken (regardless of whether the election is made). The Governor signed the legislation.

Washington voters defeated a referendum to repeal the Washington estate tax in the November 2006 elections.

On June 14, 2013, Governor Inslee signed HB 2075 which closed an exemption for marital trusts retroactively immediately prior to when the Department of Revenue was about to start issuing refund checks, created a deduction for up to $2.5 million for certain family-owned businesses and indexes the $2 million Washington state death tax threshold for inflation. WA ST §§ 83.100.040; 83.100.020.

SEPARATE QTIP ELECTION. Washington permits a separate state QTIP election. WA ST §83.100.047.

NO INDEXING FOR INLFATION IN 2019. Washington State was supposed to index the exemption annually for inflation. However, this was not done for 2019.

On December 18, 2018, the Department of Revenue sent an email stating that pursuant to Revised Code of Washington (RCW) 83.100, the Department must adjust the Washington applicable estate tax exclusion amount annually using the Seattle-Tacoma-Bremerton metropolitan area October consumer price index (Seattle CPI). As of January 1, 2018, the U.S. Bureau of Labor and Statistics (USBLS) no longer calculates the consumer price index for the Seattle-Tacoma-Bremerton metropolitan area. Instead, the USBLS will calculate the consumer price index for the Seattle-Tacoma-Bellevue Core Based Statistical Area for the Puget Sound region.

As a result of these changes, the definition of "consumer price index" in RCW 83.100.020(1)(b) does not match with the current CPI measure calculated by the USBLS. The Department is using the last CPI figure for the Seattle CPI. This resulted in no increase in the applicable exclusion amount for 2019 and subsequent years.

West Virginia

Type of Tax: None

Current Law: Tax is tied to federal state death tax credit. WV § 11-11-3.

Wisconsin

Type of Tax: None

Current Law: Tax is tied to federal state death tax credit. WI ST § 72.01(11m).

WI ST §§ 72.01; 72.02, amended in 2001.

For deaths occurring after September 30, 2002, and before January 1, 2008, tax was frozen at federal state death tax credit in effect on December 31, 2000 and was imposed on estates exceeding federal applicable exclusion amount in effect on December 31, 2000 ($675,000), not including scheduled increases under pre-EGTRRA law, even though that amount is below the lowest EGTRRA applicable exclusion amount. Thereafter, tax imposed only on estates exceeding EGTRRA federal applicable exclusion amount.

On April 15, 2004, the Wisconsin governor signed 2003 Wis. Act 258, which provided that Wisconsin will not impose an estate tax with respect to the intangible personal property of a non-resident decedent that has a taxable situs in Wisconsin even if the non-resident's state of domicile does not impose a death tax. Previously, Wisconsin would impose an estate tax with respect to the intangible personal property of a non-resident decedent that had a taxable situs in Wisconsin if the state of domicile of the non-resident had no state death tax.

Wyoming

Type of Tax: None

Current Law: Tax is tied to federal state death tax credit. WY ST §§ 39-19-103; 39-19-104.

160477780_7

7

Multistate Estate Planning Techniques

Dr. Gerry W. Beyer
Laurelle M. Gutierrez

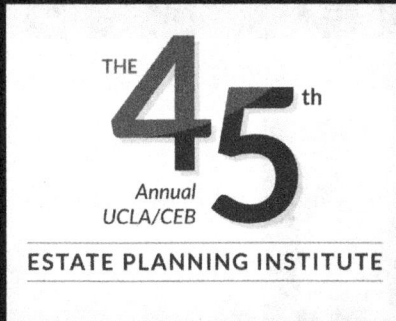

MULTISTATE ESTATE PLANNING TECHNIQUES

THE 45th Annual UCLA/CEB ESTATE PLANNING INSTITUTE

Dr. Gerry W. Beyer
Governor Preston E. Smith Regents Professor of Law
Texas Tech University School of Law

Talking with deceased family members

Unexpected problem results from long life

Betty Ashley

Making funerals friendlier

Overview of Presentation

1. Importance of planning for state law differences
2. Ascertaining governing law
3. Will execution issues
4. Change in circumstances – Property
5. Change in circumstances – People
6. Interpretation and construction
7. Estate administration

5

Importance

- **Clients move**
  - **Almost 8,000,000 people move to a different state each year.**

- **Clients own land in other states**

6

Ascertaining Governing Law

- A. **Personal vs. Real Property**
  - Personal = domicile at death
  - Real = situs of property

  - Thus, will may be interpreted under the law of several states even if client does not move.

7

Ascertaining Governing Law

- B. **Property ownership (marital rights)**
  - Ownership of property (assuming it can be traced) is governed by law of domicile at the time the property was acquired.
  - Absent agreement, marital title does not change as the couple moves between community and common law property states.

8

Ascertaining Governing Law

- C. Will validity
  - A savings statute may protect will from being invalid for failure to satisfy local requirements.

9

Ascertaining Governing Law

- D. Interpretation and construction
  - Generally, governed by law of jurisdiction under which the property passes.
    - Personal property = domicile at death
    - Real property = situs of property

  - A few cases allow court to look at rules of state where will executed.

  - Advice = include choice of law provision in the will.

10

Will Execution

- **The formal requirements for a valid will vary among the states.**

- **Although a savings or substantial compliance statute may "save the day" when a client moves states, prudent practice is to have a will execution ceremony which is likely to satisfy the requirements of as many states as possible.**

11

Will Execution

- **A. Location of testator signature**

  - Anywhere?
  - At end?

  - Advice = at end

12

Will Execution

- B. Proxy testator signature

  - Proxy signs testator's name?
  - Proxy signs both testator's name and proxy's name?

  - Advice = Proxy signs both names

13

Will Execution

- C. Witnessing

  - If allowed, should notarization be used to substitute for witnesses?

  - Advice = No, too risky that state in which will needs to probated lacks savings statute.

14

Will Execution

- D. Publication

  - Witnesses must know they are witnessing a will?
  - Witnesses do not need to know they are witnessing a will?

  - Advice = Tell witnesses they are witnessing a will.

15

Will Execution

- E. Presence requirements
  - Testator signs or acknowledges a prior signature in witnesses' presence.
  - Witnesses attest in testator's presence.
  - Witnesses attest in each other's presence.

  - States vary as to which presences are required.

  - Advice = Satisfy all three.

16

Will Execution

- F. Interested witness

  - Voids gift?
  - Irrelevant?

  - Advice = Do not use beneficiaries as witnesses.

17

Will Execution

- G. Improperly completed self-proving affidavit

  - Some states have savings statutes so if SPA valid in state where will executed, it is effective.

I, _____ the testator, sign my name to this instrument this _____ day of _____ and being first duly sworn, do declare to the undersigned authority that I sign and execute this instrument as my will and that I sign it willingly, or willingly direct another to sign for me, that I execute it as my free and voluntary act for the purposes expressed in that document and that I am eighteen years of age or older, of sound mind and under no constraint or undue influence.

_____

Testator

We, _____ the witnesses, sign our names to this instrument being first duly sworn and do declare to the undersigned authority that the testator signs and executes this instrument as his/her will and that he/she signs it willingly, or willingly directs another to sign for him/her, and that each of us, in the presence and hearing of the testator, signs this will as witness to the testator's signing and that to the best of our knowledge the testator is eighteen years of age or older, of sound mind and under no constraint or undue influence.

_____

Witness

_____

Witness

The State of _____

County of _____

Subscribed, sworn to and acknowledged before me by _____ the testator, and subscribed and sworn to before me by _____ and _____ witnesses, this _____ day of _____

(Seal)

(Signed)_____

_____

(Official capacity of officer)

18

Changed Circumstances -- Property

- **A. Ademption by extinction**

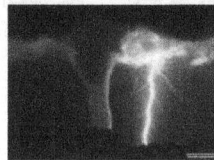

19

Changed Circumstances -- Property

- **A. Ademption by extinction**
  - Gift fails?
  - Tracing into proceeds?
  - Value of adeemed gift?
  - Substantial equivalent gift if in estate?

  - Advice = For every specific gift, expressly indicate what happens if the property is not in the estate.

20

Changed Circumstances -- Property

- B. Ademption by Satisfaction
  - Arises if testator makes cash gift to legatee while alive.
  - How do other beneficiaries prove the gift was in satisfaction?
    - Presumption?
    - Extrinsic evidence?
    - Writing?

  - Advice = Include express language in will.

21

Changed Circumstances -- Property

- C. Change in value to corporate securities
  - Who gets stock splits, stock dividends, cash dividends, etc.
    - Depends on whether specific or general (words of possession or identification)?
    - Depends on whether the testator owned gifted securities at time of will execution?
  - States vary in making this determination.

  - Advice = Explain in will.

22

Changed Circumstances -- Property

- D. Interest on legacies
  - One year after death?
  - One year after executor appointed?
  - Rate?

  - Advice = Explain in the will.

23

Changed Circumstances -- Property

- E. Exoneration
  - Presumed?
  - Not presumed?

  - Advice = Indicate the testator's intent in the will.

24

Changed Circumstances -- Property

- **F. Abatement**

  - Common law or statutory order may not be what testator wants.

  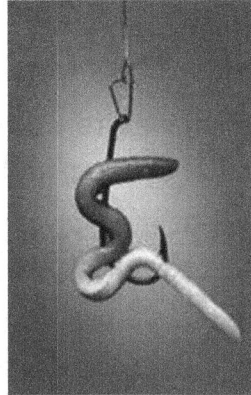

  - Advice = provide express directions

25

Changed Circumstances -- People

- **A. Marriage**
  - No effect on will?
  - Will automatically revoked?
  - Forced share possibility?
  - Creation of community property?

  - Advice: Have client return to office to prepare new will or enter into marital agreement.

26

Changed Circumstances -- People

- **B. Divorce**
  - Provisions for ex-spouse normally void.
  - Other ex-relatives, such as step-children?
  - What if divorce pending at time of death?
  - Advice = Include will provisions addressing these issues.

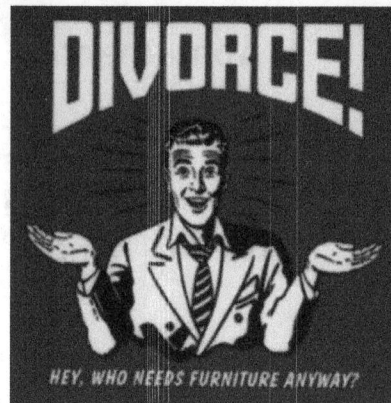

DIVORCE!

HEY, WHO NEEDS FURNITURE ANYWAY?

27

Changed Circumstances -- People

- **C. Pretermitted children**
  - After born/adopted?
  - Prior born/adopted but not provided for?
  - Methods to prevent a forced share?
  - Advice = Explain in will and hope that jurisdiction allows will to trump statute.

I'm the Pretermitted Child Of an Unborn Widow Who was married to a Fertile Octogenarian

28

Changed Circumstances -- People

- ■ D. Lapse

  - ■ Anti-lapse statute?
  - ■ Closeness of relationship needed between testator and predeceased beneficiary?

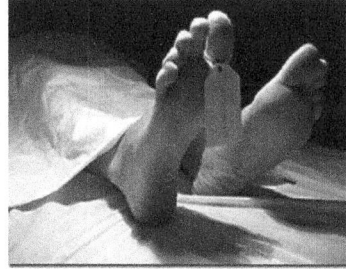

  - ■ Advice = Include express language on what happens if a beneficiary predeceases.

29

Changed Circumstances -- People

- ■ E. Survival period

  - ■ Time required?

  - ■ Advice = include a survival period in the will.

30

Interpretation & Construction

- **A. No apparent ambiguity**

  - Plain meaning rule?
  - Intent rule?

  - Advice = Draft clearly!

31

Interpretation & Construction

- **B. Class gift membership**
  - Afterborn, adopted, non-marital, and ART children/grandchildren
    - Included?
    - Excluded?

  - Advice = Include express statement of testator's intent.

32

Interpretation & Construction

- C. Incorporation by reference

  - Doctrine recognized?
  - Doctrine not recognized?

  - Advice = Avoid this technique if at all possible.

33

Interpretation & Construction

- D. Tangible personal property document

  - Authorized?
  - Not authorized?

  - Advice = Avoid unless client warned that it may not be effective if the client changes state of domicile.

Memorandum for Distribution of Tangible Personal Property of WILLIAM SAMPLE

Pursuant to Article Seven of the WILLIAM SAMPLE LIVING TRUST dated May 24, 2004, and any amendments thereto, I hereby request my Trustee to distribute the following items of nonbusiness tangible personal property as follows:

Description of Tangible Personal Property	Recipient of Tangible Personal Property
_____	_____
_____	_____
_____	_____
_____	_____
_____	_____
_____	_____
_____	_____
_____	_____

If a recipient of a particular item of nonbusiness personal property does not survive me, such item shall be disposed of as though it had not been listed in this memorandum. In the event there is a conflict between this memorandum and the WILLIAM SAMPLE LIVING TRUST dated May 24, 2004, and any amendments thereto, the terms of my trust shall control. It is my desire and intent that for purposes of distribution of the tangible personal property listed above, THIS MEMORANDUM BE DEEMED AN AMENDMENT TO MY LIVING TRUST, even though it may not be signed with the same formality as my trust agreement, and that this memorandum, even if signed prior to a subsequent restatement of my trust, remain in force and effect so long as none of the tangible personal property listed above is specifically directed to be distributed to some other party under such later restatement.

Dated: _____

_____
WILLIAM SAMPLE

34

Interpretation & Construction

- E. Election may be triggered if attempt to gift an entire community asset to non-spouse and spouse is also a beneficiary.

  - Advice = Include provision stating no gift is meant to put spouse to an election unless that is actually the testator's intent.

35

Estate Administration

- A. Authorizing state-specific methods

  - State may require certain language for preferred administration method.

  - Hard to anticipate as state requirements are different.

  - Warn client to have will checked upon moving states.

36

Estate Administration

- **B. Bond**

  - **Default required?**
  - **Default not required?**

  - **Advice = Include express language.**

37

Estate Administration

- **C. Compensation**

  - **Reasonable?**
  - **Formula?**
  - **Schedule?**
  - **No fee?**

  - **Advice = Include express compensation provision.**

38

Estate Administration

- D. Pay "just debts" provision

  - Advice = do not include as could revive debts barred by statute of limitations or bankruptcy.

39

Other Estate Planning Documents

- Other estate planning documents may need to be in a form mandated by state statute:
  - Durable power of attorney for property
  - Medical power of attorney
  - Directive to physicians
  - Mental health treatment declaration
  - Pre-designation of guardian
  - Anatomical gifts
  - Body disposition

40

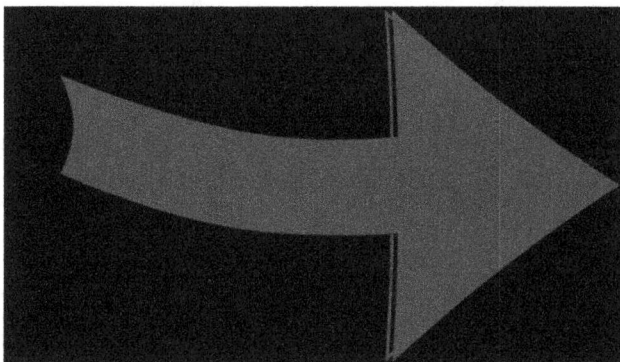

41

MULTI-STATE ESTATE PLANNING TECHNIQUES

Laurelle M. Gutierrez

McDermott Will & Emery LLP

415 Mission Street, Suite 5600
San Francisco, CA 94105-2616

lgutierrez@mwe.com

April 2023
mwe.com

THE **45**th
Annual
UCLA/CEB
ESTATE PLANNING INSTITUTE

McDermott Will & Emery

AGENDA

The Mobile Client

Benefits of Non-California Trust Situs

State Income Taxation of Trusts

Planning Considerations

THE MOBILE CLIENT

3   mwe.com

THE MOBILE CLIENT

- Residency
- Marriage
- Community Property/Separate Property

4   mwe.com

THE MOBILE CLIENT
Standards for Determining Residency

- Where is the individual resident?
  - Domicile
  - Residence

THE MOBILE CLIENT
Basics of Residence

- Residence and domicile are not the same
  - Domicile: "Home"
  - Residence: More than a temporary place of abode
  - Days present in a state can establish or provide the evidence for residence
  - *Appeals of Stephen D. Bragg,* 2003-SBE-002, 2003 Cal. Tax Lexis 175 (May 28, 2003), and the *Bragg* factors

THE MOBILE CLIENT

Breaking the Ties that Bind

The departing state will claim that domicile and residence have not changed

Actions and words must be clear as to intent to change domicile

Proving non-residency is not the same as changing domicile without intent to make a permanent change of place of abode

Establishing a new permanent abode

Usually easy to establish residency

Do not rely solely on the rules to establish residency to prove residency has changed

Embrace (not just state) the intent to permanently reside

7   mwe.com   Breaking and Establishing Domicile

THE MOBILE CLIENT
Marriage

- Defense of Marriage Act defined marriage for federal purposes as a union between one man and one woman
- *Obergefell v. Hodges,* 576 U.S. 644 (2015) - constitutional right to same sex marriage under the Due Process Clause and Equal Protection Clause of the Fourteenth Amendment
- *Dobbs v. Jackson, 597* U.S. ___ (2022) – in addition to eliminating abortion protection, challenge to protection of same sex and interracial marriage under the Fourteenth Amendment
- Respect for Marriage Act (December 2022)

8   mwe.com

THE MOBILE CLIENT
Marriage

- Common law marriage, if valid under law of state of residence, then acknowledged by other states under full faith and credit clause
  - Colorado, District of Columbia, Iowa, Kansas, Montana, New Hampshire (only for inheritance purposes), Oklahoma, *Rhode Island*, Texas and Utah (only if judicially recognized)
  - Generally requires intention to be married together with couple holding themselves out as married; no definite time requirement
- Domestic Partnership/Civil Union
- Cohabitation rights

9   mwe.com

THE MOBILE CLIENT
Community Property/Separate Property

- Community Property
  - Community Property States: Arizona, California, Idaho, Louisiana, Nevada, New Mexico, Texas, Washington, Wisconsin
  - Community Property Election States: Alaska, South Dakota, Tennessee, Florida (for trusts)
- Quasi-Community Property
  - Some states acknowledge quasi-community property for inheritance purposes only (e.g. Washington), others acknowledge quasi-community property for divorce or legal separation purposes only, some acknowledge it in both situations (e.g., California and Arizona)
- Separate Property
  - Note that income from separate property earned during marriage can be community property (e.g., in Texas)

10   mwe.com

NON-CALIFORNIA TRUST SITUS

11   mwe.com

NON-CALIFORNIA TRUST SITUS

- What Laws Will Apply to Your Trust?
  - Modern and Flexible Trust Laws
  - Privacy/Secrecy and Notice Requirements
  - Self-Settled Asset Protection Trusts
  - Decanting of Trusts

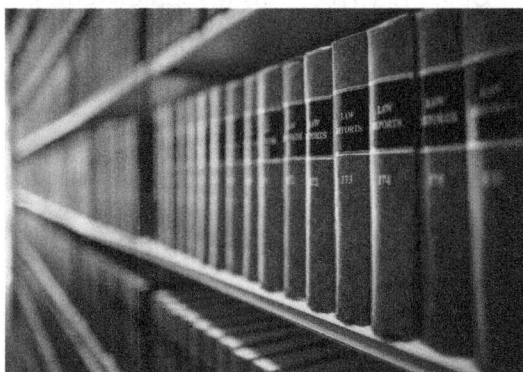

12   mwe.com

NON-CALIFORNIA TRUST SITUS
What State Laws Will Apply to Your Trust

- Governing Law Determination
  - Governing law is complicated
    - Governing law provision in a trust typically addresses three issues: validity, construction/interpretation, and administration
    - Validity may not be entirely within the choice of the grantor and seems fixed at the creation of the trust
    - Construction rules could be hard wired into the instrument, at least in theory
  - Law of state in which trustee resides usually governs administration
  - Both the law of the state governing the construction and validity of the trust and the law of the state governing the administration of the trust must be understood

13   mwe.com

NON-CALIFORNIA TRUST SITUS
Modern Trust Laws

- Many states have adopted the Uniform Trust Code, which was patterned after the California Trust Law (Probate Code § 15000 *et seq.*)
- Other Uniform acts that provide greater flexibility in trust administration include:
  - The Uniform Principal and Income Act
  - The Uniform Decanting Act
  - The Uniform Directed Trust Act
  - The Uniform Prudent Investor Act

14   mwe.com

NON-CALIFORNIA TRUST SITUS
Flexible Trust Laws

- Trust Flexibility
  - Importance of Trustor's Intent
    - Is the Trustor still alive
    - Is it set forth in the trust?
    - Is it stated in writing?

15   mwe.com

NON-CALIFORNIA TRUST SITUS
Flexible Trust Laws

- Trust Flexibility
  - Power to Adjust:
    - Does state law allow for a power to adjust between income and principal?
    - Does the state have a unitrust conversion statute, or a statute that allows for a conversion to a "total return trust"?
  - Power to Modify:
    - Are nonjudicial modifications allowed?
    - Are nonjudicial settlements allowed?
    - Can a trust be merged or divided?

16   mwe.com

NON-CALIFORNIA TRUST SITUS
Perpetual Trust Laws

- Will the Move to a New State Affect the Perpetuities Period of the Trust?
  - Common-law Rule Against Perpetuities
    - No [nonvested property] interest is good unless it must vest, if at all, not later than 21 years after some life in being at the creation of the interest
  - Uniform Statutory Rule Against Perpetuities (1986/1990)
    - Adopts "wait and see" approach; no violation until 90 years passes
    - A nonvested property interest is invalid unless one of the following conditions is satisfied:

      (a) When the interest is created, it is certain to vest or terminate no later than 21 years after the death of an individual then alive

      (b) The interest either vests or terminates within 90 years after its creation

17   mwe.com

NON-CALIFORNIA TRUST SITUS
Purpose Trusts

- Will a Purpose Trust be Valid?
  - Pet Trusts
  - Trusts for maintenance of property (art collection, jewelry, digital assets)
  - Trusts for maintenance of real property (family homes and vacation properties)
  - Trusts for maintenance of gravesites
  - Trusts for maintenance of businesses
  - Maintenance of Private Family Trust Companies
  - Maintenance of special purpose entities
  - Charitable Trusts

18   mwe.com

NON-CALIFORNIA TRUST SITUS
Directed Trust Laws

- Directed Trust: Division or Delegation of Powers Over a Trust
  - One or more persons can have the power to direct an action by, or to veto or consent to any actual or proposed action by
    - a trustee,
    - trust advisor, or
    - trust protector
  - Relates to the investment of trust assets, distributions, or any other aspects of the trust's administration

19   mwe.com

NON-CALIFORNIA TRUST SITUS
Privacy/Secrecy and Notice Requirements

- Privacy Trusts: used to protect the identity of the settlors and beneficiaries
- Quiet Trusts: used to protect the beneficiaries from themselves
  - Terms of trust may expand, restrict, eliminate or otherwise vary any laws applicable to the trust, including the duty to inform beneficiaries of trust's existence
  - Designated Representative can represent the interests of beneficiaries until
    - a certain age, or
    - a term of years, or
    - during the lifetime of the trustor and/or the trustor's spouse

20   mwe.com

NON-CALIFORNIA TRUST SITUS
Self-Settled Asset Protection Trusts

- Domestic Asset Protection Trusts (DAPT)
  - Currently 20 DAPT States: Alabama, Alaska, Connecticut, Delaware, Hawaii, Indiana, Michigan, Mississippi, Missouri, Nevada, New Hampshire, Ohio, Oklahoma, Rhode Island, South Dakota, Tennessee, Utah, Virginia, West Virginia, and Wyoming
  - Creditors of the settlor cannot attach the assets of the trust with a spendthrift provision except in limited situations, which include:
    - A "fraudulent transfer", if proved by clear and convincing evidence that the transfer was made to defraud creditors;
    - Claims arising from torts caused by the settlor that occurred prior to the transfer;
    - Alimony, child support, and other payments required to a former spouse under a divorce decree or marital settlement agreement
  - Powers or interests the settlor can retain include:
    - To veto a trust distribution;
    - To retain and exercise a lifetime or testamentary nongeneral power of appointment over the trust assets;
    - Potential or actual receipt of income or principal from the trust, including for the purpose of paying income taxes due on income of the trust, if allowed under the trust instrument; and
    - To remove a trustee/adviser and to appoint a new or additional trustee/adviser

21   mwe.com

NON-CALIFORNIA TRUST SITUS
Trust Decanting

- Decanting allows for trust modernization, corrections, and tax planning
  - Statutory decanting in 29 states
  - Common law decanting
  - Examples of Trust Decanting Laws:
    - No notice requirements to beneficiaries
    - Trusts with an ascertainable standard can be decanted to change administrative provisions
    - Trusts with an ascertainable standard can be decanted into fully discretionary trusts
    - No copies of the existing or proposed new trusts must be provided to the beneficiaries
    - A mandatory income interest can be reduced or eliminated
    - The interests of a remainder beneficiary can be accelerated
    - New trust cannot add beneficiaries but can increase the beneficiaries' interests; appointee under a power of appointment is not considered a new beneficiary
    - Trust can be decanted by modifying or amending trust instrument

22   mwe.com

STATE INCOME TAXATION OF TRUSTS

23   mwe.com

STATE INCOME TAXATION OF TRUSTS
Where Does a Trust Reside?

- Where does a trust reside for state tax purposes?
  - Can be difficult to determine because a trust (unlike an individual or a corporation) is neither a physical being nor a juridical entity
  - A trust is a "fiduciary relationship with respect to property"
  - A trust's beneficiaries have a beneficial interest in the assets of a trust, but there are many different kinds of beneficiaries
  - There often are other officeholders with fiduciary or quasi-fiduciary duties

24   mwe.com

STATE INCOME TAXATION OF TRUSTS
How Does a State Determine a Trust's Tax Residency?

- State taxation statutes generally consider the following factors:
  - Residence of grantor (at time of death or time when trust became irrevocable)
  - Place of administration
  - Residence or place of business of trustee (or *fiduciary* in California)
  - Residence of beneficiary
  - Other

- Source of income
- Factors vary state-to-state which presents planning opportunities for practitioners

25   mwe.com

STATE INCOME TAXATION OF TRUSTS
How Does a State Determine a Trust's Tax Residency?

- Administration of a trust is complicated: different functions may be carried out in several states, but often would be where the trustee resides
- Settlor's domicile at the time of death (in the case of a testamentary trust) or at the creation or funding of an irrevocable lifetime trust
- Multiple beneficiaries residing in a number of different states, the taxpayer/trustee has no control over where a beneficiary resides, and may not have all of the facts that would be necessary to assess the residence of the beneficiaries

26   mwe.com

STATE INCOME TAXATION OF TRUSTS
State Authority For Taxation

- Residence of grantor alone is not sufficient contact with a state to impose a tax on all of the trust's income under the Due Process Clause or the Commerce Clause
  - Planning consideration:
    - Many state laws tax a trust *permanently* based on residence of grantor when trust created. Residency changes, and ongoing taxation may be unconstitutional
  - Due Process Clause: "No State shall make or enforce any law which shall…deprive any person of life, liberty, or property, without due process of law…"
    - Does the state have a "minimal connection" to the trust to make it fair to impose tax?
  - Commerce Clause: "Congress shall have power to lay and collect taxes" and to "regulate Commerce…among the several States"
    - Does a state law interfere with interstate commerce?
    - There must be a "sufficient nexus" with the state

LET THE PLANNING BEGIN
THINGS TO CONSIDER

PLANNING CONSIDERATIONS
What to Do with New Planning?

- What to do if your client moves out of California?
  - Make sure they are OUT of California
  - Revise estate planning documents
    - Pay attention to family definitions
  - Consider how to treat community property
  - Consider creating separate property revocable trusts
  - Creating new irrevocable trusts?
    - What state will tax the new irrevocable trust?
    - Self-settled trust in a DAPT state?

29   mwe.com

PLANNING CONSIDERATIONS
What to Do with an Existing Irrevocable Trust?

- What to do if your client moves out of California?
  - Look at irrevocable trusts in which client is the trustee
    - State tax based on place of administration?
    - State tax based on residence of trustee?
    - What is the governing law or law of administration?
    - Notice rules?
    - Decanting or nonjudicial modifications allowed in new state?
  - Look at irrevocable trusts in which client is the beneficiary?
    - State tax based on residence of noncontingent beneficiary?
    - Notice rules?

30   mwe.com

THANK YOU!
QUESTIONS?

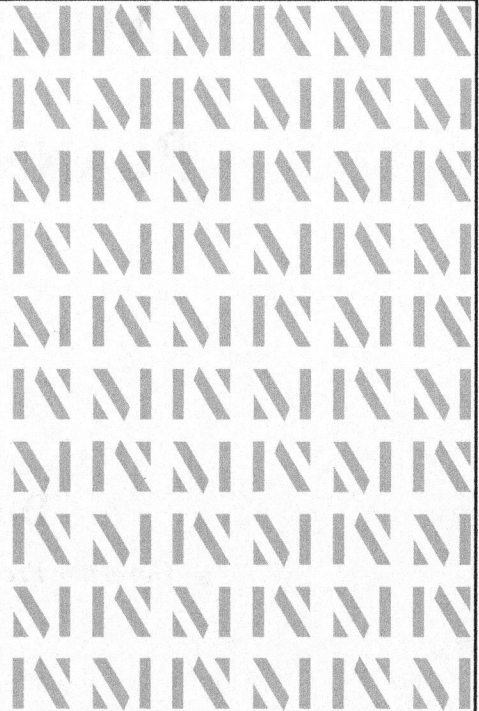

MULTISTATE ESTATE PLANNING TECHNIQUES

DR. GERRY W. BEYER

Governor Preston E. Smith Regents Professor of Law
Texas Tech University School of Law
3311 18th Street
Lubbock, TX 79409-0004

(806) 834-4270
gwb@ProfessorBeyer.com
www.ProfessorBeyer.com
www.BeyerBlog.com

45TH ANNUAL UCLA-CEB ESTATE PLANNING INSTITUTE

April 21, 2023

Virtual

GERRY W. BEYER

Governor Preston E. Smith Regents Professor of Law
Texas Tech University School of Law
Lubbock, TX 79409-0004
(806) 834-4270
gwb@ProfessorBeyer.com – www.ProfessorBeyer.com

EDUCATION

B.A., Summa Cum Laude, Eastern Michigan University (1976)
J.D., Summa Cum Laude, Ohio State University (1979)
LL.M., University of Illinois (1983)
J.S.D., University of Illinois (1990)

SELECTED PROFESSIONAL ACTIVITIES

Bar memberships: United States Supreme Court, Texas, Ohio (inactive status), Illinois (inactive status)
Member: American Law Institute; American College of Trust and Estate Counsel (Regent and Academic
    Fellow); American Bar Foundation; Texas Bar Foundation; Texas State Bar Association
Editor-in-Chief, REPTL Reporter, State Bar of Texas (2013-present)
Keeping Current Probate Editor, *Probate and Property* magazine (1992-present)

CAREER HISTORY

Private Practice, Columbus, Ohio (1980)
Instructor of Law, University of Illinois (1980-81)
Professor, St. Mary's University School of Law (1981-2005)
Governor Preston E. Smith Regents Professor of Law, Texas Tech University School of Law (2005 – present)
Visiting Professor, Boston College Law School (1992-93)
Visiting Professor, University of New Mexico School of Law (1995)
Visiting Professor, Southern Methodist University School of Law (1997)
Visiting Professor, Santa Clara University School of Law (1999-2000)
Visiting Professor, La Trobe University School of Law (Melbourne, Australia) (2008 & 2010)
Visiting Professor, The Ohio State University Moritz College of Law (2012)
Visiting Professor (virtual), Boston University School of Law (2014 & 2016)

SELECTED HONORS

Order of the Coif
Distinguished Probate Attorney Lifetime Achievement Award, REPTL Section, State Bar of Texas (2022)
Estate Planning Hall of Fame, National Association of Estate Planners & Councils (2015)
ABA Journal Blawg 100 Hall of Fame (2015)
Outstanding Professor Award – Phi Alpha Delta (Texas Tech Univ.) (2016) (2015) (2013) (2010) (2009) (2007) (2006)
Excellence in Writing Awards, American Bar Association, Probate & Property (2012, 2001, & 1993)
President's Academic Achievement Award, Texas Tech University (2015)
Outstanding Researcher from the School of Law, Texas Tech University (2017 & 2013)
Chancellor's Council Distinguished Teaching Award (Texas Tech University) (2010)
President's Excellence in Teaching Award (Texas Tech University) (2007)
Professor of the Year – Phi Delta Phi (St. Mary's University chapter) (1988) (2005)
Student Bar Association Professor of the Year Award – St. Mary's University (2001-2002) (2002-2003)
Russell W. Galloway Professor of the Year Award – Santa Clara University (2000)
Distinguished Faculty Award – St. Mary's University Alumni Association (1988)
Most Outstanding Third Year Class Professor – St. Mary's University (1982)
State Bar College – Member since 1986

SELECTED PUBLICATIONS

WILLS, TRUSTS, AND ESTATES: EXAMPLES AND EXPLANATIONS (7th ed. 2019); FAT CATS AND LUCKY DOGS – HOW TO LEAVE (SOME OF) YOUR ESTATE TO YOUR PET (2010); TEACHING MATERIALS ON ESTATE PLANNING (4th ed. 2013); 9 & 10 TEXAS LAW OF WILLS (Texas Practice 2022); TEXAS WILLS, TRUSTS, AND ESTATES (2018); 12, 12A, & 12B WEST'S TEXAS FORMS — ADMINISTRATION OF DECEDENTS' ESTATES AND GUARDIAN-SHIPS (4th ed. 2019); *When You Pass on, Don't Leave the Passwords Behind: Planning for Digital Assets*, PROB. & PROP., Jan./Feb. 2012, at 40; *Wills Contests – Prediction and Prevention*, 4 EST. PLAN. & COMM. PROP. L.J. 1 (2011); *Digital Wills: Has the Time Come for Wills to Join the Digital Revolution?*, 33 OHIO N.U.L. REV. 865 (2007); *Pet Animals: What Happens When Their Humans Die?*, 40 SANTA CLARA L. REV. 617 (2000); *Ante-Mortem Probate: A Viable Alternative*, 43 ARK. L. REV. 131 (1990).

TABLE OF CONTENTS

MULTISTATE ESTATE PLANNING TECHNIQUES[*]

I. INTRODUCTION

"This thorn in my side is from the tree I've planted."[1]

All it takes is one carelessly drafted will provision to place you in the hot seat for months or years where you might watch your personal, professional, and financial life crumble around you.

One type of drafting error is the failure to anticipate that your client's estate plan will be in whole or in part governed by the laws of another state. This can happen for two main reasons.

First, your client may die domiciled in another state. Statistical studies show that approximately 7,628,000 people move to a different state each year.[2] Second, your client may own real property in another state.

This article focuses on some of the major state law differences in substantive and procedural law.[3] Once you recognize these differences, you may then take proper steps to plan for them as you draft your clients' wills and trusts. [4]

---

[*] Portions of this article are adapted from GERRY W. BEYER, WILLS, TRUSTS, AND ESTATES: EXAMPLES & EXPLANATIONS (8th ed. 2022).

[1] Metallica, *Bleeding Me* (track 7, Load) (1996).

[2] *See* David Bancroft Avrick, *How Many People Move Each Year – and Who Are They?*, MelissaData.com available at https://www.melissadata.com/enews/articles/0705b/1.htm (last visited on Feb. 17, 2018).

[3] Note that this article is not designed to be a comprehensive review of all state law differences that you may need to consider. Instead, I am attempting to highlight those that arise with greater frequency or are of greater importance.

[4] You may also need to do planning for clients who move to another country. Each year, approximately 1,269,000 people move to a different country. Planning for clients who change their country of residence or citizenship is beyond the scope of this seminar.

II. ASCERTAINING GOVERNING LAW

A. Personal vs. Real Property

Issues regarding the transfer of real property at death are governed by the law of the state in which the land is located. On the other hand, the law of the decedent's domicile at the time of death governs personal property matters. Thus, you may need to apply the probate laws of several states to determine the proper distribution of a decedent's estate.

B. Property Ownership (Marital Rights)

If the decedent was married at the time of death, it is crucial to determine which property the decedent owned at death and which property actually belongs to the surviving spouse. Only the deceased spouse's property will pass through intestacy or be controlled by the deceased spouse's will.

You must determine what type of marital property system governs the parties and their property. Two types of marital property systems are used in the United States: *common law* and *community property.* Under a common law system, each spouse owns his or her entire income as well as any property brought into the marriage or acquired during the marriage by gift. Under a community property system, each spouse owns any property brought into the marriage or acquired during the marriage by gift, but only one-half of his or her income; the other half of the income vests in the other spouse as soon as it is earned. Although only nine states use the community property system (Arizona, California, Idaho, Louisiana, Nevada, New Mexico, Texas, and Washington along with Wisconsin due to its adoption of the Uniform Marital Property Act), these states account for over 25 percent of the population of the United States. One state, Alaska, permits married couples to hold their property as community property if they so desire.

If the spouses have lived in more than one type of marital property jurisdiction during the marriage, you must determine whether a spouse's earnings (and, consequently, any property purchased with those earnings) belong solely to the spouse who earned the money or whether the earnings are co-owned.

The general rule is that the ownership of the earnings is governed by the law of the spouse's domicile at the time the property was acquired. Marital title does not change as the couple moves from one type of marital property state to another.

For example, assume Wife earned $100,000 while domiciled in a common law marital property state and placed it into a certificate of deposit (CD-1). Husband and Wife then moved to a community property marital property state. Wife earned an additional $100,000 and placed it into another certificate of deposit (CD-2). What property may Wife dispose of by her will?

CD-1: The $100,000 Wife earned and placed in CD-1 is her separate property under the law of the common law marital property state in which she earned the money. The key issue is what happens to the characterization of CD-1 when the couple moves into the community property state. Under the law of many community property states, CD-1 would remain Wife's separate property, and she could leave it to whomever she desires. However, some community property states would characterize CD-1 as *quasi-community property*, that is, property that was acquired in a common law marital property state but that would have been community property if acquired in the community property state. Under the law of these community property states, Husband would become the owner of one-half of CD-1 upon Wife's death and Wife would only be able to control the disposition of the other half. Another important issue is the characterization of the interest that CD-1 has earned. Pre-move interest will either be Wife's separate property (allowing her to dispose of all the pre-move interest) or quasi-community property (allowing her to dispose of one-half of the pre-move interest). Depending on the particular law of the community property state, post-move interest may either remain Wife's separate property (allowing her to dispose of all of the post-move interest) or become community property (allowing her to dispose of one-half of the post-move interest).

CD-2: CD-2 is community property because Wife earned the money placed in CD-2 while domiciled in a community property state, which treats income as if earned equally by each spouse. Thus, Wife may dispose of one-half of CD-2, both principal and interest, by her will.

C. Will Validity

The only way for a person to avoid having the probate estate pass to heirs under the law of intestate succession is to execute a valid will. A person has, however, no right to make a will. The United States Supreme Court confirmed that "[r]ights of succession to the property of a deceased … are of statutory creation, and the dead hand rules succession only by sufferance. Nothing in the Federal Constitution forbids the legislature of a state to limit, condition, or even abolish the power of testamentary disposition over property within its jurisdiction."[5]

Although not required to do so, all state legislatures have granted their citizens the privilege of designating the recipients of their property upon death. A state legislature could take away this privilege at any time. Of course, any legislator who voted to curtail the ability of a person to execute a will would be highly unlikely to be reelected!

Because the ability to execute a will is a privilege, a will typically has no effect unless the testator has precisely followed all the requirements. Most states demand strict compliance with the requirements discussed in this chapter; one trivial deviation may cause the entire will to fail. A few states, however, have adopted the *substantial compliance* standard of U.P.C. § 2-503, which grants the court a *dispensing power* to excuse a harmless error if there is clear and convincing evidence that the testator intended the document to be a will.

---

[5] Irving Trust Co. v. Day, 314 U.S. 556, 562 (1942).

Most states have a *savings statute* permitting a will that does not meet the requirements of a valid will under local law nonetheless to be effective under certain circumstances. For example, U.P.C. § 2-506 provides that a testator's written will is valid, even though it does not satisfy the normal requirements, if it "complies with the law at the time of execution of the place where the will is executed, or of the law of the place where at the time of execution or at the time of death the testator is domiciled, has a place of abode, or is a national."

D. Will Construction and Interpretation

Issues of will construction and interpretation are generally governed by the law of the jurisdiction under which the property at issue passes. Thus, for personal property, the law of the testator's domicile at time of death normally controls. For real property, the law of the situs of the real property controls. There are some cases, however, that hold that if the testator lived the majority of the testator's life in one state and was domiciled in a different state at the time of death, the law of the first state controls.

The default rules regarding many construction and interpretation issues vary greatly among the states. It is difficult to anticipate all the possibilities when drafting a will. One technique that might work is for the testator to specify the state law which the testator desires to be used to interpret and construe the will.

III. WILL EXECUTION

The formal requirements for a valid will vary among the states. Although a savings or substantial compliance statute may "save the day" when a client moves states, prudent practice is to have a will execution ceremony which is likely to satisfy the requirements of as many states as possible. This section discusses some of the main differences among the states.

A. Location of Testator's Signature

The original Statute of Frauds and the law of most states today do not mandate the location in which the testator's signature must appear. See U.P.C. § 2-502. Thus, the testator's signature may appear at the top, in the body, in the margin, or at the end of the will. However, some states follow the lead of the 1837 Wills Act and require that wills be subscribed or signed at the end or *foot* of the instrument.

B. Proxy Testator Signature

Most states permit the testator's signature to be affixed to the will by another person. A proxy signature, also called a signature per alium, must meet statutory requirements, which typically include two main components. First, the proxy must sign in the testator's presence; second, the proxy must sign at the testator's direction. See U.P.C. § 2-502(a)(2). Some states require the proxy's own signature to appear on the will as well. Even if the proxy's signature is not required, it is good practice to obtain it.

C. Witnessing

Originally, the Statute of Frauds required an attested will to have three or four witnesses. The Wills Act of 1837 reduced the number of witnesses to two. All states now require two witnesses. Note that until July 1, 2006, Vermont required three witnesses. Some extra-cautious practitioners routinely have extra witnesses just in case additional testimony is needed to prove what occurred during the will execution ceremony.

In a break from tradition, U.P.C. § 2-502(a)(3) dispenses with the witnessing requirement if the testator acknowledges the will in front of a notary public or other individual authorized to take acknowledgments. A few states have already enacted this new provision.

D. Publication

In most states and under U.P.C. § 2-502(a), there is no requirement that a testator *publish* the will to the witnesses, that is, tell the witnesses that the document they are witnessing is a will.

There are, however, a significant number of states that require publication either for the will itself or for the self-proving affidavit. In these states, the witnesses must know that they are witnessing a will. The testator should tell the witnesses, "This is my will," show them the top of the first page of the document, or take some other step to make certain the witnesses are aware of the nature of the document. Even in the states that require publication, the witnesses do not need to know the contents of the will.

E. Presences

States vary considerably regarding which one or ones of the three presences are required for a valid will. Good practice is to assure that all three presences are satisfied during every will execution ceremony.

1. Testator Signs in Witnesses' Presence

Good practice mandates that the testator sign the will in the presence of the witnesses. However, many states do not impose this requirement. The testator may simply acknowledge the testator's signature to the witnesses. See U.P.C. § 2-502(a)(3). This acknowledgment can be by express words such as, "This is my signature" or "I signed this already," or by some gesture that carries the appropriate message, for example, pointing to the signature, nodding, and giving a thumbs-up sign.

2. Witnesses Attest in Testator's Presence

Consistent with the Statute of Frauds requirement dating from 1676, the vast majority of states require the witnesses to attest in the presence of the testator. This requirement helps ensure that the witnesses attest the testator's actual will and not some other instrument that was either accidentally or intentionally substituted. A few jurisdictions, however, have followed the lead of U.P.C. § 2-502(a) by eliminating this requirement. In these states, it is possible for the witnesses to attest even after the testator has died as long as the attestation occurs within a reasonable time after the testator signed the will or acknowledged the will or the signature to the witnesses.

The testator does not actually need to see the witnesses attest. Compliance with such a requirement would be extremely difficult to prove and would prevent visually impaired individuals from executing wills. The most widely accepted approach is *conscious presence*. Under this rule, an attestation is proper if the testator was able to see it from the testator's actual position or from a slightly altered position if the testator has the power to make the alteration without assistance. A few states adopt a relatively tough *line of sight* rule meaning that the testator needs to have been in a position where the testator could have seen the attestation if the testator were looking.

3. Witnesses Attesting in Each Other's Presence

The 1837 Wills Act required the witnesses to be present at the same time when the testator signed or acknowledged the will. Although some states have retained this requirement, most states do not require the witnesses to be together either (1) when the testator signs or acknowledges the will, or (2) when the witnesses attest to the will.

F. Interested Witnesses

An interested witness is a witness who stands to benefit if the testator's will is valid. The most common type of interest is being a beneficiary under the will. The testimony of an interested witness about the attestation is suspect because the witness has a motive to lie. The potential ramifications of having an interested person serve as a necessary witness to the will vary significantly among the states.

- The entire will is void. This was the original common law rule unless there was a supernumerary (extra) witness to validate the will. The witness/beneficiary was deemed totally incompetent to testify about the will because the witness lacked competency at the time of the witnessing.

- The gift to the witness is void. The witness forfeits any benefit under the will and is thus made disinterested and capable of giving testimony about the will. A statutory provision providing this result is often called a *purging* statute.

- The gift to the witness is void unless the witness is also an heir, in which case the witness can receive the gift provided it does not exceed the share of the testator's estate the witness would take under intestate succession. With regard to the smaller of the gift under the will or the intestate share, the witness has no motive to lie because the witness will receive that amount regardless of the validity of the will.

- The gift to the witness is void unless a disinterested person (either another witness or a third party who was present) can corroborate the testimony of the witness.

- The gift to the witness is presumed to be the result of fraud or undue influence. However, the witness may bring forth evidence to rebut this presumption and, if successful, take under the will.

- No effect, and thus the beneficiary takes the property exactly as the testator specified in the will. This is the approach adopted by U.P.C. § 2-505(b).

G. Self-Proving Affidavit

The requirements for a self-proving affidavit vary among the states. Some states have savings statutes, similar to those for the will itself, so that an out-of-compliance affidavit will be effective if it was valid under the law of the testator's domicile at the time of will execution or where the testator executed the will.

IV. CHANGED CIRCUMSTANCES AFTER WILL EXECUTION -- PROPERTY

The property of a testator is not frozen when the testator executes a will. The composition and value of the estate are in constant flux. Likewise, the identity of the individuals whom the testator wishes to benefit may change due to births, adoptions, deaths, marriages, and divorces. All these changes in circumstance can have a profound effect on the testator's intent, an existing will, and the distribution of property upon death both under the will and due to the application of legal rules.

States have developed a sophisticated set of rules to deal with changed circumstances. The general approach is for the legislature or the courts to create relatively rigid presumptions based on what they believe testators, in general, would have wanted had the testators thought about these issues. Courts then apply the presumptions to determine the appropriate distribution of property. Some of these rules are relatively uniform among the states while others are 180 degrees apart.

To avoid the application of these presumptions, a testator should include express provisions in the will dealing with each of these issues. A testator who provides specific instructions for how to handle circumstance changes empowers the court to carry out the testator's actual intention, rather than a presumed intent as determined by statutory or case law.

In this section, changes that occur to the testator's property are discussed and the next section focuses on changes that happen to beneficiaries and family members.

A. Ademption by Extinction

Ademption refers to the failure of a specific gift because the property is not in the testator's estate when the testator dies. The asset could have been sold, given away, consumed, stolen, or destroyed.

Most jurisdictions apply a very rigid rule, often called the *identity theory* or *Lord Thurlow's Rule.* If the exact item the testator attempted to give away in the will is not in the testator's estate, the gift adeems and the beneficiary receives nothing. No evidence that the testator intended ademption to occur is required. Likewise, the beneficiary does not receive the value of the attempted gift, may not demand that the executor obtain the item for the beneficiary, and cannot trace into the proceeds of the asset.

A minority of states have departed from the traditional rule to avoid the harsh results that sometimes occur under the identity rule. These jurisdictions have adopted rules that attempt to preserve specific gifts under a variety of circumstances. *Intent view* jurisdictions may allow tracing and may even permit the beneficiary to receive the value of the missing property. See U.P.C. § 2-606, which imposes a presumption that the testator did not want the gift to adeem and provides alternate gifts under a wide variety of circumstances.

To avoid ademption problems and to make certain the courts follow the testator's wishes, each specific gift should contain an express statement of the testator's intent should the gifted property not be in the estate. The testator should either (1) provide a substitute gift (e.g., another specific gift or a sum of money), or (2) state that the beneficiary receives nothing if the exact item is not part of the estate.

B. Adaption by Satisfaction

Satisfaction is the failure of a testamentary gift because the testator has already transferred the property to the beneficiary between the time of will execution and time of death. At common law, the doctrine applied only to gifts of personal property while the modern trend is to permit gifts of real property to be satisfied as well. Common law courts applied the doctrine of *ejusdem generis*. Under this doctrine, the character of the testamentary gift and the inter vivos gift had to be the same before satisfaction took place (e.g., the same item). However, some modern statutes reject this doctrine and testamentary gifts may be satisfied by a wide variety of inter vivos transfers even if the gifts are of very different types of property.

Courts must determine whether the testator intended an inter vivos transfer to cause the satisfaction of a testamentary gift. Common law courts applied a rebuttable presumption in this endeavor. Satisfaction had to be proven unless the beneficiary was the testator's child, or someone over whom the testator was in the position of a parent, in which case satisfaction was presumed. Most states no longer follow this presumption and instead require that extrinsic evidence proves that the testator intended for the inter vivos gift to be a satisfaction in all cases.

The modern trend is to restrict the types of evidence that may be used to prove a satisfaction. For example, U.P.C. § 2-609 requires either (a) a writing signed by the testator or the beneficiary declaring the gift to be a satisfaction, or (b) express directions in the will providing for the deduction of inter vivos gifts from testamentary ones.

To avoid confusion, wills should contain express language addressing satisfaction issues.

C. Changes in Value to Corporate Securities

Gifts of corporate securities are commonly the subject of dispute because of the tremendous variety of changes that may occur to them between will execution and death. If the change is merely one of form, the beneficiary stands a good chance of taking the securities resulting from the change (e.g., a stock split, stock dividend, or shares resulting from a merger or reorganization). However, if the change is one of substance (e.g., a cash dividend or shares acquired via a dividend reinvestment plan), the beneficiary will usually not benefit from the newly-acquired securities. Many states codify the applicable rules. See U.P.C. § 2-605.

To avoid uncertainty, these issues should be covered in wills that make gifts of corporate securities.

D. Interest on Legacies

Interest, if any, earned by a legacy prior to the testator's death does not pass to the legatee as it is not part of the money that the testator is actually giving. At common law, unpaid legacies began to earn interest starting one year after the testator's death. Many modern statutes, such as U.P.C. § 3-904, change this rule and delay the running of interest by providing that interest does not begin to accrue until one year after the appointment of a personal representative. The rate of this interest is typically the judgment or legal rate in effect in that jurisdiction.

Accordingly, wills containing legacies should state when and if interest begins accruing and at what rate.

E. Exoneration

Specifically devised or bequeathed property is often subject to encumbrances. Real property may be burdened by a mortgage or deed of trust, and the testator may have used personal property as collateral under a security agreement governed by Article 9 of the Uniform Commercial Code. Does the beneficiary of encumbered specific gifts take them free from the liens or does the beneficiary take subject to the liens receiving only the testator's equity in the property?

At common law, exoneration was presumed. A testator presumably would not have wanted to burden the recipient of a gift with a debt and thus there was, in effect, an implied gift of sufficient money to pay off the debt. Because of the potential of exoneration causing tremendous disruption of the testator's intent, many states and U.P.C. § 2-607 reverse the common law presumption by providing that exoneration occurs only if there is express language requiring it in the will.

Prudent practice is for the testator to address the potential for exoneration each time a gift of encumbered (or potentially encumbered) property is made.

F. Abatement

A testator may attempt to give away more property in the testator's will than the testator is actually able to give. This could occur because the testator misjudged the value of the testator's estate. Just because a testator leaves a $500,000 legacy in the testator's will does not mean the testator actually has that money to give. The testator may also not have accounted for all of the testator's debts, including funeral and burial costs and expenses of last illness. In most situations, the claims of creditors have priority over assertions to property by beneficiaries.

Abatement is the reduction or elimination of a testamentary gift to pay an obligation of the estate or a testamentary gift of a higher priority. Most states, either by judicial decision or through legislation, have established an abatement order. The usual abatement order is set forth below:

1. Property passing via intestate succession (that is, the testator died partially intestate).
2. Residuary gifts.
3. General gifts.
4. Demonstrative gifts.
5. Specific gifts.

Consequently, a beneficiary of a specific gift stands a much greater chance of actually receiving the gift than a residuary beneficiary. Some jurisdictions retain the common law rule of

requiring personal property in each category to be exhausted before real property from that category may be used. Other states no longer make a distinction between real and personal property. See U.P.C. § 3-902. Within a category, abatement is pro rata so that each gift is reduced by the same percentage. A few jurisdictions give certain types of gifts top priority; that is, they are the last to abate, regardless of the classification of the gift. The most common gift given this super-priority is a gift to a spouse.

A testator may wish to provide an express abatement order to make certain the testator's true intent is followed.

V. CHANGED CIRCUMSTANCES AFTER WILL EXECUTION – PEOPLE

A. Marriage

At common law, the mere fact that a male testator got married after executing his will had no effect on the disposition of property under his premarriage will unless a child was born to the marriage. However, the marriage did give rise to the wife's dower rights, that is, a life estate in one-third of all real property that her husband owned at any time during the marriage.

On the other hand, the valid will of a single woman was revoked upon her marriage at common law. This automatic revocation was based on the common law view that marriage removed a woman's legal capacity to execute a will or revoke a previously existing will. Because the wife could not revise her will to take her new family into account, the courts thought it inappropriate to force the wife to stick with the terms of the premarriage will and thus deemed her will revoked upon her marriage.

1. Common Law Marital Property Jurisdictions

Under modern law, the effect of marriage on a will written before marriage no longer depends on the gender of the testator. While the laws of a few states deem a premarriage will totally ineffective upon marriage causing the deceased spouse's entire probate estate to pass under intestacy, most states revoke only a portion of the will, and then only if the will does not provide the surviving spouse with a sufficient amount of property. To protect a surviving spouse from being disinherited or receiving a relatively small share of the deceased spouse's estate, the surviving spouse is given the right to a *forced* or *elective* share of the deceased spouse's estate. This share is in lieu of the benefits, if any, provided to the surviving spouse in the deceased spouse's will. The surviving spouse is entitled to this statutory amount regardless of the deceased spouse's intent as documented in the will.

The method used to compute the surviving spouse's forced share varies tremendously among the states and thus must be considered when drafting a will. Below are some commonly used schemes.

1. A fixed percentage of the net probate estate, e.g., one-third.

2. Fixed percentages of the net probate estate depending on the number of children, with the surviving spouse receiving a smaller percentage if the deceased spouse had children, e.g., one-half if no children, one-third if children.

3. A minimum dollar amount plus a fixed percentage of any additional property in the net probate estate, e.g., the first $100,000 plus one-third of any excess.

4. Variable percentages depending on the length of the marriage, e.g., U.P.C. § 2-202, which begins at 3 percent for a marriage lasting one to two years and increases to 50 percent for marriages of fifteen or more years.

Many statutes apply the elective share formula on an *augmented estate,* rather than the net probate estate. See U.P.C. §§ 2-201 through 2-214. The augmented estate may contain the value of nonprobate assets such as the deceased spouse's share of jointly held property passing because of rights of survivorship and life insurance proceeds that are not payable to the surviving spouse. Under the law of a few states, even some property the deceased spouse gave away while alive is treated as part of the augmented estate when computing the forced share. The augmented estate concept prevents the deceased spouse from reducing the surviving spouse's elective share by using probate avoidance techniques to dispose of the property. If the surviving spouse received the benefit of a nonprobate transfer, however, some statutes require these amounts to offset the forced share.

2. Community Property Marital Property Jurisdictions

Under the law of community property states such as Arizona, California, Idaho, Louisiana, Nevada, New Mexico, Texas, Washington, and Wisconsin, spouses own undivided interests in the property they acquire from earnings during marriage. Thus, the marriage of a testator typically has no impact on the property disposition provided for in a premarriage will. The surviving spouse does not need a forced share to be protected from disinheritance because the surviving spouse already owns one-half of the community property; the deceased spouse's will may not dispose of the surviving spouse's share of the community without the survivor's consent.

3. Change in Domicile

The general rule in the United States is that the ownership of earnings between spouses is governed by the law of the spouse's domicile at the time the property was acquired. Marital rights in property do not change as the couple moves from one type of marital property state to another.

B. Divorce

Divorce was not a common occurrence in the early history of England or the United States. Thus, there is little common law addressing the ramifications of a divorce on a will executed during marriage that made a gift to a person who is now an ex-spouse. Early decisions usually held that the divorce had no effect on the will. The courts realized that a testator probably did not intend for the property to pass to an ex-spouse but felt that they had no legal basis for voiding the gift.

Most states now have statutes providing that upon divorce, all provisions of a will executed during marriage in favor of an ex-spouse are void. The balance of the will remains effective as written. See U.P.C. § 2-804. Thus, the ex-spouse would not be able to take as a beneficiary or serve in a fiduciary capacity such as the executor of the will, the guardian of any minor children, or the trustee of a testamentary trust. If the spouses remarry each other and remain married until the first spouse dies, the will typically remains effective as originally written. Some states also permit a will to include a provision validating a gift in favor of a spouse regardless of whether the spouses are married or divorced at the time of the testator's death.

States vary regarding whether gifts to other ex-relatives like a former step-child are also automatically voided upon divorce. In addition, the voiding provisions typically apply only upon a final divorce.

Accordingly, the will should directly address what happens if a divorce action is pending at the time of death and the result if the divorce is final.

C. Pretermitted Heirs

Parents normally have no obligation to provide testamentary gifts for their children, even if they are minors, under the law of common law jurisdictions. Thus, a parent may intentionally disinherit one or more of the parent's children. To protect a child from an accidental or inadvertent disinheritance, state legislatures have enacted statutes that may provide a forced share of the parent's estate for a pretermitted (omitted) child under certain circumstances.

Under the law of most states, a child must be born or adopted after the testator executed the will to receive a forced share as a pretermitted child. See U.P.C. § 2-302. In a few states, however, even an omitted child who was born before the parent executed the will can claim a forced share.

Jurisdictions use a variety of methods to determine the share of a pretermitted child. Traditionally, the pretermitted child receives the share the child would have received if the testator had died intestate. Some states still follow the common law view that if a testator executes a will and then marries and has a child, the entire will is revoked so that the testator's entire estate passes by intestacy. Modern statutes are not so

extreme and often do not base the pretermitted child's share on the size of the testator's probate estate. For example, some states give the pretermitted child an intestate share only of the property that does not pass to the child's other parent. If the testator's will leaves property to some of the testator's children, some states limit the pretermitted child to an intestate share based solely on gifts made to these children. This restriction prevents the pretermitted child from receiving a larger share of the estate than the children, as a class, who were actually provided for in the will.

Accordingly, a testator should expressly indicate how all children, born, unborn, and to be adopted, are to be handled.

D. Lapse

Lapse occurs when a gift fails because the beneficiary predeceases the testator, either biologically or legally such as properly disclaiming or dying within the survival period. Unless the anti-lapse statute applies, the subject matter of the gift will then pass under the will's residuary clause, or, if the lapsed gift was the residuary, via intestacy.

Anti-lapse statutes prevent lapse by providing substitute beneficiaries for the lapsed gift. The goal of these statutes is to provide a distribution that the testator would have preferred over the property passing under the residuary clause or via intestacy. These statutes operate on the presumption that if the testator had anticipated that the beneficiary would die first, the testator would have supplied an alternate gift to the descendants of the predeceased beneficiary who survive the testator. The manner of distribution among these descendants may be per stirpes, per capita with representation, or per capita at each generation depending on the jurisdiction.

Anti-lapse statutes vary among the states. Some statutes are narrow and save gifts made to only a limited number of the testator's predeceased relatives such as descendants (children, grandchildren, etc.) or descendants of the testator's parents (brothers, sisters, nieces, nephews, etc.). Other anti-lapse statutes are broader. For example, U.P.C. § 2-603 saves gifts made to grandparents or descendants of grandparents (aunts, uncles, cousins, siblings, nieces, nephews, etc.). A few states have wide-sweeping anti-lapse statutes that save lapsed gifts in all cases where the predeceased beneficiary left descendants who survived the testator, even if there is no familial relationship between the testator and the beneficiary.

Most states apply anti-lapse statutes to class gifts, as well as to gifts to individuals. Thus, if a will provides, "I leave all my property to my children," the children of any predeceased child will take the predeceased child's share. However, if the predeceased child died before the testator executed the will, many states would not permit this predeceased child's descendants to take because the class never included the predeceased child.

To prevent the result of lapse from being governed by rules that may not comport with the testator's intent, each gift should expressly indicate who receives the property in the event of lapse. For example, the testator could make an express gift over to a contingent beneficiary, indicate that the gift passes to the descendants of a deceased beneficiary, or merely state that the gift passes via the residuary clause.

E. Survival

At common law and under the 1953 version of the Uniform Simultaneous Death Act, a beneficiary needed to outlive the testator for only a mere instant to take under the will. This rule often caused litigation over who survived whom when the deaths of the testator and beneficiary occurred close together in an automobile accident, airplane crash, tornado, or other unfortunate event.

Most jurisdictions now impose a survival period by statute. Thus, a beneficiary must not only outlive the testator, but must also outlive by the statutorily specified period of time. Under the 1991 version of the Uniform Simultaneous Death Act and U.P.C. § 2-702, the beneficiary must survive by at least 120 hours (five days). If the beneficiary survives the testator but dies prior to the expiration of the survival period, the gift passes as if the beneficiary had actually died prior to the testator.

Testators may lengthen or shorten the survival period by express provision in the will. States vary regarding whether the use of the phrase "if she survives me" reduces the survival period to a mere instant or functions only as a restatement of the statutory rule. Some statutes provide that any mention of survival trumps the survival statute while others require the testator to provide an express survival period to supplant the statutory period.

Most testators will want to increase the survival time period as the property could never reach the hands of a beneficiary within a mere five days. Thus, the will should contain an express statement of a longer time period.

VI. INTERPRETATON AND CONSTRUCTION

A. No Apparent Ambiguity

A no apparent ambiguity situation arises when the will provision is neither latently nor patently ambiguous but yet someone wants to introduce extrinsic evidence that the testator did not mean for the will to say what it appears to say. Jurisdictions are sharply divided on this issue.

Traditionally, courts follow the *plain meaning rule,* also called the *single plain meaning rule.* Under this approach, extrinsic evidence cannot be used to disturb the clear meaning of the will. This rule enhances predictability for both the testator and the testator's attorney. A testator can rest assured that the words chosen will take effect as written. Otherwise, the testator could make a gift of "$10,000 to Mother" and then have Mother claim that the gift should be of some higher amount such as $100,000 and Father claim that the legacy was actually meant for him.

Other jurisdictions adopt a more liberal rule that permits the use of extrinsic evidence. These courts hold that the evidence is significant and assists the court to carry out the testator's intent. Although this approach makes it more difficult for the testator to be certain that the will is not tampered with or misconstrued after the testator's death, it operates to carry out the testator's intent when it is clear the will does not say what the testator meant it to say. Courts do keep a tight rein on these situations and generally allow the extrinsic evidence to alter the will's clear meaning only when the will was not professionally prepared and the evidence is very strong (e.g., clear and convincing rather than a preponderance) that carrying out the exact terms of the will would frustrate the testator's intent.

In 2008, § 2-805 was added to the Uniform Probate Code which allows for reformation to correct mistakes even if the will is unambiguous. This section allows the court to reform the terms of an instrument, if it can be shown by clear and convincing evidence that transferor's intent and the terms of the instrument were affected by a mistake of fact or law either in expression or in inducement.

The will drafter must appreciate how the difference in the applicable rules could impact how people may attempt to "alter" the gifts the testator makes in the will.

B. Class Gift Membership

The types of individuals entitled to qualify as class members is an often litigated issue. Assume that a gift is made to your "children." Does this gift include individuals you adopt while they are minors, individuals you adopt after they become adults, or children born outside of a marriage? What if the gift was made instead to your "issue" or to your "bodily heirs"?

Historically, courts presumed that a testator intended to include adopted individuals in a class gift to the testator's own children. However, if the class gift was to someone else's children, courts typically followed the *stranger-to-the-adoption rule,* which created a presumption that the testator did not intend to include the adopted individuals. These presumptions could be rebutted by evidence of the testator's intent to the contrary. For example, the testator may have known that the other person could not have biological children and the testator may have had a close relationship with that person's adopted children.

Modern courts and statutes have been very inclusive in determining class membership. For example, U.P.C. § 2-705(b) provides that adopted individuals, persons born outside of the marriage,

children born by assisted reproduction, and gestational children are generally included in a class gift. However, under U.P.C. § 2-705(e) and (f), adopted individuals and persons born outside of the marriage usually need to have been treated as a child before the child reached eighteen years of age for the child to be included in the class gift.

States vary significantly on how to handle children born as the result of alternative reproductive techniques. Some do not address the issue, some provide that the person must be born within a fixed time period after death such as two or three years, while others require that the child be in utero at the time of death.

To resolve class gift issues, the testator should carefully explain the categories of individuals the testator wishes to encompass within a class gift. For example, a class gift to children should address adopted-in minors, adopted-in adults, adopted-out individuals, children born out of wedlock, and children born via alternative reproduction techniques. Courts are extremely willing to follow the testator's intent as expressed in the will even if that intent is contrary to normal construction rules.

C. Incorporation by Reference

Incorporation by reference is a method for treating a document as testamentary in character even though that document is not physically part of the testator's will. If the testator successfully incorporates a document by reference into the will, the will is treated as if the terms of the incorporated document are actually contained in the will. Although the incorporated document is not really part of the will, this doctrine creates the legal fiction that the will contains an exact copy of the incorporated document. Although practically all states and U.P.C. § 2-510 recognize the doctrine of incorporation by reference, some do not and thus prudent practice may be to avoid using this technique.

D. Tangible Personal Property Document

A limited number of states and U.P.C. § 2-513 authorize a testator to use a separate writing to dispose of tangible personal property even though that writing (a) does not meet the requirements of a will and thus could not be probated as a testamentary instrument, (b) was not in existence at the date of will execution and thus could not be incorporated by reference, and (c) exists for no reason other than to dispose of property at death and thus could not be a fact of independent significance.

The testator must comply with some relatively easy requirements to use this technique. Generally, the will must expressly refer to the list, the testator must sign the list, and the list must describe the items and the recipients with reasonable certainty. The type of property the testator can dispose of with this instrument is usually limited to tangible personal property that is not already specifically gifted in the will. Thus, the list could not be used to make cash legacies, bequests of corporate securities, or devises of real property. The list may be prepared before or after the testator executes the will and the testator may alter the list at any time.

Proponents of this technique recognize that it is a tremendous departure from established law. However, they believe that the risks of fraud and misuse are counterbalanced by the potential of enhancing the law's ability to assist the testator in accomplishing the testator's desires. This technique permits the testator to control the disposition of a portion of the testator's estate without having to endure the expense and inconvenience of (1) initially providing a lengthy list of specific gifts to the drafting attorney, and (2) later needing to execute a codicil or new will to make changes to that list. In addition, these gifts are usually not of great monetary value. Instead, the gifts are of jewelry, photograph albums, videorecordings, books, furniture, and other items the testator wants to transfer primarily for sentimental or emotional reasons.

If the testator moves from a state recognizing this technique to one that does not, it is possible that the tangible personal property document will have no effect. Thus, this technique must be used with great care.

E. Election Wills in Community Property Jurisdictions

"The principal of election is, that he who accepts a benefit under a will, must adopt the whole contents of the instrument, so far as it concerns him; conforming to its provisions, and renouncing every right inconsistent with it."[6] Election provisions are occasionally placed in wills where one spouse wants to dispose of the entire interest in some or all of the community property. The surviving spouse may consent to the disposition of the surviving spouse's share of the community assets because the will gives the spouse a significant interest in the deceased spouse's community or separate property.

Attorneys must be careful, however, not to inadvertently create an election situation. Although there is a normally a presumption that an election will be imposed only if the will is open to no other construction, an attorney could create an election scenario without having this intention.[7] Thus, the will should include a provision expressly stating the testator's intent regarding election.

VII. ESTATE ADMINISTRATION

A. Authorizing State-Specific Methods

Many states have specialized types of administration which the testator must authorize in the will. It is difficult to anticipate what language is needed without knowing the exact state in which the administration will occur.

B. Bond

The personal representative may need to post bond conditioned on the faithful performance of the representative's duties. The court sets the amount of the bond based on the value of the decedent's estate. The personal representative may deliver that amount in cash to the court; however, the personal representative typically obtains the bond from a surety company. In exchange for the payment of premiums, the surety company agrees to pay the amount of the bond to the creditors and beneficiaries if the personal representative breaches the applicable fiduciary duties. Of course, if the surety is

---

[6] Philleo v. Holliday, 24 Tex. 38, 45 (1859).

[7] Wright v. Wright, 154 Tex. 138, 143; 274 S.W.2d 670, 674 (1955).

required to pay, the surety will seek reimbursement from the personal representative.

States are divided on the bonding requirement. Some state statutes require a bond unless the will expressly waives the bond. On the other hand, some statutes do not require a bond unless the testator expressly requires it in the will or the court deems it necessary. See U.P.C. § 3-603. In addition, some states exempt corporate fiduciaries from the bonding requirement.

To be certain the testator's intent is effectuated, the will should expressly state whether the executor must post bond.

C. Compensation

The default method of executor compensation varies significantly among the states. Some provide the executor with reasonable compensation while others have formulas ranging from the simple to the complex.

To avoid compensation issues, the testator should expressly explain how the executor's compensation should be computed.

D. Payment of "Just Debts" Provision

The traditional, but inappropriate, direction to the executor to pay "just debts" should not be included in a will. A specific will clause requiring that the executor pay all of the testator's "just debts" raises the question whether the executor is required to pay debts barred by limitations, and whether the executor is required to pay installments on long-term indebtedness that are not yet due.[8]

---

[8] Bernard E. Jones, *10 Drafting Mistakes You Don't Want to Make in Wills and Trusts (and How to Avoid Them)*, in UNIVERSITY OF TEXAS SCHOOL OF LAW CLE, 8TH ANNUAL ESTATE PLANNING, GUARDIANSHIP, AND ELDER LAW CONFERENCE, Tab B, at 5 (2006).

8

Trust Revocation & Modification: What Is the Law These Days & Does Location Matter?

Patrick A. Kohlmann
Vivian Lee Thoreen

Trust Revocation & Modification: What Is The Law These Days And Does Location Matter?

45th Annual CEB/UCLA Estate Planning Institute
Patrick A. Kohlmann
Vivian L. Thoreen

Friday, April 21, 2023
12:30 p.m. – 1:30 p.m.

A. Probate Code Sections

1. Prob. Code, § 15401: Revocable trusts; methods; multiple settlors; granting power to revoke; modification or revocation by attorney in fact

(a) A trust that is revocable by the settlor or any other person may be revoked in whole or in part by any of the following methods:

(1) By compliance with any method of revocation provided in the trust instrument.

(2) By a writing, other than a will, signed by the settlor or any other person holding the power of revocation and delivered to the trustee during the lifetime of the settlor or the person holding the power of revocation. If the trust instrument explicitly makes the method of revocation provided in the trust instrument the exclusive method of revocation, the trust may not be revoked pursuant to this paragraph.

(b)(1) Unless otherwise provided in the instrument, if a trust is created by more than one settlor, each settlor may revoke the trust as to the portion of the trust contributed by that settlor, except as provided in Section 761 of the Family Code.

(2) Notwithstanding paragraph (1), a settlor may grant to another person, including, but not limited to, his or her spouse, a power to revoke all or part of that portion of the trust contributed by that settlor, regardless of whether that portion was separate property or community property of that settlor, and regardless of whether that power to revoke is exercisable during the lifetime of that settlor or continues after the death of that settlor, or both.

(c) A trust may not be modified or revoked by an attorney in fact under a power of attorney unless it is expressly permitted by the trust instrument.

(d) This section shall not limit the authority to modify or terminate a trust pursuant to Section 15403 or 15404 in an appropriate case.

2. Prob. Code, § 15402: Modification of trust

Unless the trust instrument provides otherwise, if a trust is revocable by the settlor, the settlor may modify the trust by the procedure for revocation.

3. Prob. Code, § 15403: Modification or termination of irrevocable trust by all beneficiaries

(a) Except as provided in subdivision (b), if all beneficiaries of an irrevocable trust consent, they may petition the court for modification or termination of the trust.

(b) If the continuance of the trust is necessary to carry out a material purpose of the trust, the trust cannot be modified or terminated unless the court, in its discretion, determines that the reason for doing so under the circumstances outweighs the interest in accomplishing a material purpose of the trust. If the trust is subject to a valid restrain on the transfer of a beneficiary's interest. . . the trust may not be terminated unless the court determines there is good cause to do so.

4. Prob. Code, § 15404: Modification or termination by settlor and all beneficiaries

(a) A Trust may be modified or terminated by the written consent of the settlor and all beneficiaries without court approval of the modification or termination.

(b) If any beneficiary does not consent to the modification or termination of the trust, the court may modify or partially terminate the trust upon petition to the court by the other beneficiaries, with the consent of the settlor, if the interests of the beneficiaries who do not consent are not substantially impaired.

5. Prob. Code, § 15409: Modification or termination in changed circumstances

(a) On petition by a trustee or beneficiary, the court may modify the administrative or dispositive provisions of the trust or terminate the trust if, owing to circumstances not known to the settlor and not anticipated by the settlor, the continuation of the trust under its terms would defeat or substantially impair the accomplishment of the purposes of the trust. In this case, if necessary to carry out the purposes of the trust, the court may order the trustee to do acts that are not authorized or are forbidden by the trust instrument.

(b) The court shall consider a trust provision restraining transfer of the beneficiary's interest as a factor in making its decision whether to modify or terminate the trust, but the court is not precluded from exercising its discretion to modify or terminate the trust solely because of a restraint on transfer.

3

B. Case Illustrations

Case	*Huscher v. Wells Fargo Bank* (2004) 121 Cal.App.4th 956
District	Second
Facts	<ul><li>In 1983, Settlor executed a Trust, naming his four step-grandchildren as beneficiaries.</li><li>During his lifetime, Settlor made eight amendments to the Trust, one of which removed one of his step-grandchildren as beneficiary. Settlor, but not the Trustee, signed each of these amendments.</li><li>After Settlor died, the step-grandchild removed from the Trust as a beneficiary petitioned the court to find the amendment invalid.</li></ul>
Trust Language	Trustor "may at any time amend any of the terms of the trust by an instrument in writing signed by [Trustor] and the Trustee."
Applicable Code Section(s)	Prob. Code, § 15401, subd. (a)(1); former Civ. Code., § 2280, repealed by statute
Issue	Whether the law prior to Probate Code section 15401 permitted a revocation method not mentioned in the Trust
Holding	Because the method for revocation in the Trust was not exclusive, the Settlor's amendment was **valid**.
Reasoning	<ul><li>Under the law prior to Probate Code section 15401, a trust can be modified unless the trust implicitly or explicitly specifies an exclusive modification procedure.</li><li>The terms of the Trust did not indicate that the method for revocation was exclusive or that there were restrictions on methods for revocation.</li></ul>

Case	*Masry v. Masry* (2008) 166 Cal.App.4th 738
District	Second
Facts	• Husband and wife as joint Settlor-Trustees executed a family Trust. • Shortly before his death, husband executed a "Notice of Revocation of Interest in Trust and Resignation as Trustee" to transfer his assets to a new trust, the beneficiaries of which were his children from a prior marriage. Wife did not receive notice of the revocation until after the husband's death. • Wife filed a petition to ascertain beneficiaries, arguing that husband's revocation was invalid.
Trust Language	"Each of the Trustors hereby reserves the right and power to revoke this Trust, in whole or in part, from time to time during their joint lifetimes, by written direction delivered to the other Trustor and to the Trustee."
Applicable Code Section(s)	Prob. Code, § 15401, subd. (a)(2)
Issue	Whether the Trust explicitly provided that its stated method of revocation is exclusive
Holding	The Trust's language does not state that the method of revocation it provides is explicitly exclusive, and therefore the revocation was **valid**.
Reasoning	• Husband complied with Section 15401, subdivision (a)(2), by giving notice to himself as Trustee. • If the language in the trust was sufficient to qualify as the explicitly exclusive method, then the language in Section 15401, subdivision (a)(2) would be unnecessary.

Case	*King v. Lynch* (2012) 204 Cal.App.4th 1186
District	Fifth
Facts	• Joint Settlor-Trustees created a revocable trust that provided for the Joint Settlors during their lifetimes and for the Settlors' children thereafter. • After one of the Settlors suffered a severe brain injury, the other Settlor executed an amendment that named himself as Sole Trustee and altered the amount of money each child would receive under the Trust. • After both Settlors died, the children filed a petition to invalidate the amendments.
Trust Language	The trust "may be amended, in whole or in part, with respect to jointly owned property by an instrument in writing signed by both Settlors and delivered to the Trustee. . . ." The trust may "be revoked, in whole or in part, with respect to jointly owned property by an instrument signed by either Settlor and delivered to the Trustee and the other Settlor. . . ."
Applicable Code Section(s)	Prob. Code, §§ 15401 & 15402
Issue	Whether Section 15402 provides that the settlor must comply with the amendment procedure in the instrument
Holding	The Settlor's amendment naming himself Sole Trustee and altering the bequests to the beneficiaries was **invalid** because the instrument stated a procedure for amendment and the Settlor failed to follow that procedure.
Reasoning	• The meaning of "unless the trust instrument provides otherwise" under Section 15402 indicates that if any modification method is specified in the trust, that method must be used to amend the trust. • If a trust could be modified by the revocation procedures set forth in Section 15401 unless the trust explicitly provides that the stated modification method is exclusive, "[S]ection 15402 would become surplusage."

6

Case	*Pena v. Dey* (2019) 39 Cal.App.5th 546
District	Third
Facts	<ul><li>After being diagnosed with abdominal and brain cancer, Settlor-Trustee reached out to an attorney to make changes to his estate plan.</li><li>Settlor-Trustee sent interlineations to the attorney regarding his Trust and previous amendments. The interlineations reflected changes to the amount beneficiaries of the Trust would receive. Also attached was a Post-it note.</li><li>The attorney drafted an Amendment to the Trust based on the interlineations, but Settlor-Trustee died before signing or finalizing the Amendment.</li><li>Successor Trustee petitioned the court for instructions as to the validity of the interlineations.</li></ul>
Trust Language	"Any amendment, revocation, or termination of this trust shall be made by written instrument signed by the settlor and delivered to the trustee."
Applicable Code Section(s)	Prob. Code, §§ 15401 & 15402
Issue	Whether Settlor-Trustee's unsigned interlineations were a proper amendment to the Trust
Holding	Settlor-Trustee's interlineations **invalidly** attempted to amend the Trust because the Trust specifically required that amendments be made by a written instrument signed by the Settlor and delivered to the Trustee.
Reasoning	<ul><li>Although interlineations can constitute a written instrument separate from a trust, and the interlineations here were clearly delivered to the Trustee, they were never signed, which was required by the Settlor's Trust.</li><li>Under Probate Code section 15401, the specified method of modification is the method that must be used.</li></ul>

Case	*Cundall v. Mitchell-Clyde* (2020) 51 Cal.App.5th 571
District	Second
Facts	• Settlor-Trustee had his revocable Trust drafted by his neighbor, who was also named as the Successor Trustee of the Trust. Settlor-Trustee named his other neighbor as sole beneficiary. • After he began to suspect that the neighbors stole from him, Settlor-Trustee sought to revoke Trust with the assistance of a new estate planning attorney. Settlor-Trustee executed the revocation, but he was the only one who signed it. • After Settlor-Trustee died, the neighbor named as Successor Trustee in the original Trust filed a petition for instructions to determine whether the Trust was validly revoked.
Trust Language	"During the Grantor's lifetime, the Grantor may revoke at any time, and/or the Grantor may amend, this Agreement by delivering to the Trustee and the Successor Trustee an appropriate written revocation or amendment, signed by the Grantor and his attorney. . . ."
Applicable Code Section(s)	Prob. Code, § 15401, subd. (a)(1)
Issue	Whether the revocation procedure in Section 15401 is available when the trust document does not explicitly state that it establishes an exclusive revocation method
Holding	Settlor-Trustee's revocation was a proper and valid use of the statutory method of revocation under Probate Code section 15401 because the method provided for in the Trust was not exclusive.
Reasoning	• Under Section 15401, unless a trust document contains an explicit statement that the trust's revocation method is exclusive, the statutory revocation is available, regardless of whether the trust document requires that a particular person approve the revocation. • Simply establishing a particular method of revocation does not *explicitly* make that method exclusive.

Case	*Haggerty v. Thornton* (2021) 68 Cal.App.5th 1003, review granted Dec. 12, 2021, S271483
District	Fourth
Facts	<ul><li>Sole Settlor-Trustee amended her revocable trust such that her niece would become Trustee in the event of the Settlor's death and receive a residual distribution as a beneficiary.</li><li>Settlor signed the amendment, and the document was witnessed by a notary public. Above the notary's signature, the documented stated, "This instrument was acknowledged before me on 10-25-16, by [settlor]." The document failed to include a notarial seal or stamp.</li><li>Settlor subsequently drafted a beneficiary list and another amendment, neither of which mentioned the niece and only the amendment was signed. Neither was witnessed nor notarized.</li><li>The niece and the Trustee named in the subsequent amendment filed competing petitions to determine the validity of the respective amendments.</li></ul>
Trust Language	Settlor "reserves the following rights, each of which may be exercised whenever and as often as [she] may wish: [¶] A. Amend or Revoke. The right by an acknowledged instrument in writing to revoke or amend this Agreement or any trust hereunder."
Applicable Code Section(s)	Prob. Code, §§ 15401 & 15402
Issue	Whether the subsequent amendment leaving out the niece was valid under Sections 15401 and 15402
Holding	The subsequent amendment was valid because the Settlor-Trustee signed it and delivered it to herself in compliance with Section 15401.
Reasoning	<ul><li>Section 15402 does not establish an independent rule regarding modification and thus an available method of revocation is also an available method of modification unless the trust instrument provides otherwise.</li><li>The Trust did not distinguish between revocation and modification and thus did not "provide otherwise" within the meaning of Section 15402.</li><li>Therefore, the statutory method of revocation under Section 15401 (requiring only signing and delivery to the trustee) was available to the Settlor-Trustee.</li></ul>

Case	*Balistreri v. Balistreri* (2022) 75 Cal.App.5th 511, review granted May 11, 2022, S273909
District	First
Facts	<ul><li>Husband and Wife as co-settlor-trustees sought to amend a revocable trust, specifically by striking a provision that would have distributed the property in the trust to the co-settlor-trustees' children and stepchildren.</li><li>Instead, the co-settlor-trustees opted for the property to "remain in trust" and proceeded to sign, accept and adopt the amendment as co-trustees but failed to notarize it.</li><li>The day after the attempted amendment, Husband died.</li><li>Wife petitioned to construe the Trust and for an order confirming the validity of the amendment.</li></ul>
Trust Language	"During our joint lifetimes, this Trust may be modified and amended by either of us acting alone as to any separate property of that trustor, and by both of us acting jointly as to any of our community property." . . . "Any amendment, revocation, or termination . . . shall be made by written instrument signed, with signature acknowledged by a notary public, by the trustor(s) making the revocation, amendment, or termination, and delivered to the trustee."
Applicable Code Section(s)	Prob. Code, § 15402
Issue	Whether the Husband's method of amendment was proper under Section 15402
Holding	Trust amendment, which was accepted and adopted by Co-Trustees but not notarized, was invalid under the Trust provision requiring notarization.
Reasoning	<ul><li>Under Section 15402, when a trust specifies a method of amendment – regardless of whether the method is exclusive or permissive, and regardless of whether the trust provides for identical or different methods of amendment and revocation, Section 15402 provides no basis for validating an amendment that was not executed in compliance with that method.</li></ul>

B.   Case Summaries

1.   *Huscher v. Wells Fargo Bank* (2004) 121 Cal.App.4th 956

Factual Background: George Marx executed the George Marx Trust in June 1983, naming his four step-grandchildren as beneficiaries. Subsequently, George made eight amendments to the Trust by way of handwritten instructions that were always signed by him and never signed by the Trustee. In one of those amendments, George removed one of his step-grandchildren, Scott Huscher, as a beneficiary because George had established a separate fund for Scott that made the bequest unnecessary.

Trust Language: The Trust provided that as Trustor, George "may at any time amend any of the terms of the trust by an instrument signed by [Trustor] and the Trustee (who was not the Trustor)."

Trial Court Opinion: After George died, Scott petitioned the probate court to determine that he was still a beneficiary of the Trust on the grounds that the amendment removing Scott as beneficiary was invalid. Scott argued that the Trust required that any amendments be signed by both George and the Trustee. The court denied Scott's petition, finding that the Trust's provision for obtaining the Trustee's signature was merely permissive, not mandatory.

Holding and Reasoning of Court of Appeal: The court applied now-former Civil Code section 2280, the predecessor statute to Probate Code section 15401, because the Trust was executed before July 1, 1987. The court stated that Section 2280 allows a trust to be modified in the manner provided by Section 2280 unless the trust instructions either implicitly or explicitly specify an exclusive method of modification.

Here, the language in the Trust was neither explicitly or implicitly inclusive because it did not contain detailed language that prohibited other methods of revocation in an attempt to protect the Trustor. Additionally, the Trust provided that the powers to revoke and modify were personal to George. As such, invalidating the amendments because the Trustee failed to sign them would violate that provision by effectively granting the Trustee a form of veto power over George's otherwise valid modifications.

2.   *Masry v. Masry* (2008) 166 Cal.App.4th 738

Factual Background: Edward and Joette Masry, a married couple, executed the Edward and Joette Masry Family Trust as joint Settlor-Trustees. A year after the Trust was created, Edward revoked his interest in the Trust in an attempt to transfer his assets from the Trust to a new trust for the benefit of his children from a previous marriage. Joette did not find out about the revocation until two weeks after Edward's death, which happened shortly after the revocation.

Trust Language: The Trust states in pertinent part, "Each of the Trustors hereby reserves the right and power to revoke this Trust, in whole or in part, from time to time during their joint lifetimes, by written direction delivered to the other Trustor and to the Trustee."

11

Trial Court Opinion: After discovering her deceased husband's revocation, Joette filed a petition to ascertain beneficiaries, arguing that Edward's revocation was invalid because she was not given notice during his lifetime, which was required under the Trust. The court disagreed with Joette and held that the Trust did not explicitly make delivery of the revocation to the other Trustor the exclusive method of revocation under Probate Code section 15401, subdivision (b).

Holding and Reasoning of Court of Appeal: The court adopted the holding in *Huscher v. Wells Fargo Bank*, that a modification is explicitly exclusive when the trust instrument directly and unambiguously states that the procedure is the exclusive one. In this case, the Trust did not state that the method of revocation provided was explicitly exclusive. Instead, the method provided was simply one method of revocation in addition to that provided in Section 15401, subdivision (a)(2), which permits revocation if notice is given to the Trustee. Since Edward gave notice of the revocation to himself as Trustee, he complied with Section 15401, subdivision (a)(2).

The court reasoned that if the language in the trust were sufficient to qualify as the explicitly exclusive method, then the language in Section 15401, subdivision (a)(2) permitting revocation by other means would be unnecessary.

3. *King v. Lynch* (2012) 204 Cal.App.4th 1186

Factual Background: In 2004, Zoel Night Lynch and Edna Mae Lynch, a married couple, created a revocable Trust designating themselves as the initial Trustees.

The original Trust provided that after the death of the Settlors, their surviving children – Nancy, Mary, Judith and David – would receive distributions of $100,000 each and their two grandchildren (daughters of a predeceased child of the Settlors) would receive $50,000 each. David was named the remainder beneficiary and Successor Trustee on the death of the last Settlor.

In 2006, after Edna suffered a severe brain injury, Zoel executed three Amendments that reduced the monetary bequests ultimately to $10,000 to each child and $5,000 to each grandchild, named himself as sole Trustee and left intact the designation of David as the remainder beneficiary. Only Zoel signed these Amendments. Zoel died on January 18, 2010 and Edna died on August 10, 2010.

Trust Language: Article "FOURTH" of the trust concerned modification and revocation. That article provided in pertinent part:

> During the joint lifetimes of the Settlors, this Trust may be amended, in whole or in part, with respect to jointly owned property by an instrument in writing signed by both Settlors and delivered to the Trustee, and with respect to separately owned property by an instrument in writing signed by

the Settlor who contributed that property to the Trust, delivered to the Trustee.

During the joint lifetimes of the Settlors, this Trust may be revoked, in whole or in part, with respect to jointly owned property by an instrument in writing signed by either Settlor and delivered to the Trustee and the other Settlor, and with respect to separately owned property by an instrument in writing signed by the Settlor who contributed that property to the Trust, delivered to the Trustee. . . .

Trial Court Opinion: After Zoel and Edna's deaths, Nancy, Mary and Judith, as well as the Settlors' grandchildren filed a petition to invalidate the Amendments that modified their bequests. The trial court granted the petition on the grounds that the Amendments were signed by only one of the Settlors in contravention of the express terms of the Trust. David appealed.

Holding and Reasoning of the Court of Appeal: On appeal, David argued that the provision requiring that an amendment be signed by both Settlors and delivered to the Trustee was not expressly or impliedly exclusive and therefore Zoel alone could amend the Trust by the revocation procedures set forth in Section 15401.

The Court of Appeal disagreed with David's argument, reasoning that David's analysis would require concluding that no distinction exists between trust amendment provisions and trust revocation provisions under Sections 15401 and 15402. To the contrary, the language of these sections is distinct. Because the sections are worded differently, the court was concerned that David's view of Section 15401 and 15402 would make Section 15402 "mere surplusage."

The Court of Appeal held that the method for amendment designed in the Trust was the exclusive method, reasoning that the language "unless the trust instrument provides otherwise" under Section 15402 indicates that if any modification method is specified in the trust, that method must be used to amend the trust. Accordingly, since Zoel failed to follow that procedure, the Amendments were invalid. The Court of Appeal affirmed the trial court's ruling.

4.   *Pena v. Dey* (2019) 39 Cal.App.5th 546

Factual Background: In 2004, James Robert Anderson signed his eponymous Trust and named himself Settlor and Trustee. In 2008, Rob executed the First Amendment to The trust in compliance with the method of amendment. The Amendment added a paragraph 5.5, dividing the remainder of the trust estate into shares of various percentages for 15 named beneficiaries.

In February 2014, Rob called an attorney to make changes to his estate plan. The attorney was not the attorney who drafted the 2004 trust or 2008 amendment, so he asked Rob to send him copies and "'put in writing the proposed changes he was considering.'"

Rob interlineated the First Amendment: He crossed out 11 of the 15 shares. The 4 remaining shares' percentage was reduced from 49% to 7% each. In the margin, Rob listed 3 other individuals, of which Grey Dey was one, as also receiving "7% of 49%." Also in the margin, Rob wrote, "' 51% to 3 organizations ~ See beneficiary list.'"

The attorney received the trust instrument and interlineated First Amendment in March 2014. Attached to these documents was a Post-it® note, on which Anderson wrote: "Hi Scott, Here they are. First one is 2004. Second is 2008. Enjoy! Best, Rob." The attorney's staff prepared an initial draft of a second amendment to the Trust. The attorney's review of the draft caused him to call Rob in April for clarification as to some of the requested changes. Rob was out of town and said he would get back to the attorney the following week. That same day as the call, Rob was admitted to the hospital. He died May 24, 2014. Rob never finalized or signed a second amendment to his Trust.

Trust Language:

> Paragraph 3.1 of the Trust provides:
>
> > <u>Power of Revocation and Amendment</u>. This trust may be amended, revoked, or terminated by the settlor, in whole or in part, at any time during his lifetime. After the settlor's death, this trust shall be irrevocable and not subject to amendment.
>
> Paragraph 3.2 provides:
>
> > <u>Method of Revocation or Amendment</u>. Any amendment, revocation, or termination of this trust shall be made by written instrument signed by the settlor and delivered to the trustee. An exercise of the power of amendment substantially affecting the duties, rights, and liabilities of the trustee shall be effective only if agreed to by the trustee in writing.

Trial Court Opinion: Margaret Pena, the Successor Trustee, petitioned for instructions regarding the validity of the Settlor's handwritten interlineations on the Trust. Margaret subsequently filed a motion for summary judgment, claiming the interlineations did not constitute a valid amendment to the Trust as a matter of law. The trial court granted the Successor Trustee's motion for summary judgment, and concluded that Rob's interlineations did not validly amend the Trust.

Holding and Reasoning of Court of Appeal: Dey appealed. He argued the interlineations manifested an unambiguous intent to amend and, either standing alone or in conjunction with the Post-it® note attached to the trust documents Rob sent to his attorney, effectively amended the Trust as a matter of law. When the trust instrument expressly requires that an amendment be made by a signed writing, handwritten interlineations on a trust instrument by the settlor did not constitute a valid amendment because they were not signed by the settlor. In this case, although it was clear that the Settlor intended to amend his Trust, it was also clear he never actually signed a writing in compliance with the Trust's terms to effectuate his intent. The Trust required that amendments "be made by written instrument signed by the settlor and delivered to the trustee."

The interlineations did constitute a writing separate and apart from the printed trust instrument itself, as required. And because the Settlor was also the Trustee, he also effected delivery. However, the interlineations were not signed by the Settlor. Instead, he sent them to his attorney to have them formalized into a second amendment to the Trust and prepared for his signature, evidencing his intent to sign the changes to his Trust at a later date. The interlineations therefore did not comply with the Trust's express requirement that amendments be signed. Nor did the Court of Appeal consider the Post-it® note that the Settlor attached to the documents he sent his attorney be deemed a part of the written instrument such that the Settlor's signature on the note effectively signed the interlineations. That Post-it® note was a separate writing that simply identified the enclosed documents. The Court of Appeal affirmed the trial court's ruling.

5.   *Cundall v. Mitchell-Clyde* (2020) 51 Cal.App.5th 571

Factual Background: Decedent John Martin established a Trust in February 2009 ("February Trust") which specified a revocation method. Months later, Decedent then revoked the February Trust per the revocation method outlined in Prob. Code § 15401(a)(2) – not the one outlined in the February Trust – and established a new Trust in May 2009 ("May Trust"). Section 15401(a)(2) requires that the settlor of a trust sign a revocation and deliver it to the trustee (who, in this case, was the Decedent himself).

Trust Language: The February Trust's provision regarding revocation and amendment stated in full:

> During the Grantor's lifetime, the Grantor may revoke at any time, and/or the Grantor may amend, this Agreement by delivering to the Trustee and the Successor Trustee an appropriate written revocation or amendment, signed by the Grantor and his attorney, Frances L. Diaz. The powers of amendment may be exercised by a duly appointed and acting attorney-in-fact for the Grantor for the purpose of withdrawing and/or distributing assets from the Trust.

Trial Court Opinion: The sole beneficiary of the February Trust, Robert Cundall filed a petition for instructions seeking determination that the February Trust was not properly revoked because the method outlined in the February Trust was not utilized. The beneficiaries of the May Trust objected to Cundall's petition and filed a competing petition for an order that the February Trust was properly revoked and the May Trust was valid. The trial court held that the February Trust did not provide an exclusive method for revocation and concluded that Decedent's revocation of the February Trust was proper. Cundall appealed.

Holding and Reasoning of Court of Appeal: The Court of Appeal interpreted Section 15401 and applied it to the February Trust. The Court of Appeal also looked to *Masry v. Masry* (2008) 166 Cal.App.4th 738. In that case, the court held that a trust revocation procedure is not exclusive unless the trust document explicitly says that it is. The court agreed with this holding, which is consistent with both the language and the history of Section 15401. The February Trust did not state that its revocation procedure was exclusive, so the alternative revocation procedure under Section 15401 was therefore available to the Settlor.

The Court of Appeal affirmed, holding that a revocable trust can be revoked pursuant to the statutory method set forth in Probate Code section 15401, unless the trust document explicitly states that the revocation method provided in the document is the exclusive method for revocation.

6. *Haggerty v. Thornton* (2021) 68 Cal.App.5th 1003 [September 16, 2021; Review granted December 22, 2021]

Factual Background: In 2015, Aunt Jeane created a Trust. In 2016, Aunt Jeane herself wrote a first Trust Amendment, which was acknowledged before a notary public, and which named her niece as Successor Trustee and as a beneficiary. In 2017, Aunt Jeane again wrote, but did not sign, a beneficiary list, which did not include her niece.

In 2018, Aunt Jeane herself again wrote a Trust Amendment, the beneficiaries under which also did not include her niece. Above her signature, Aunt Jeane wrote, "I herewith instruct Patricia Galligan to place this document with her copy of the Trust. She can verify my handwriting." Galligan was her former estate attorney.

Trust Language: The Trust included the following reservation of rights:

> Settlor "reserves the following rights, each of which may be exercised whenever and as often as [she] may wish: [¶] A. Amend or Revoke. The right by an acknowledged instrument in writing to revoke or amend this Agreement or any trust hereunder."

Trial Court Opinion: After Aunt Jeane died, Thornton, a private professional fiduciary, filed a petition to confirm herself as Trustee, alleging (for unclear reasons) that the 2016 amendment had been revoked, and confirming the 2017 and 2018 amendments as valid. The niece objected, and sought to confirm herself as Trustee, based on her position that the 2016 amendment had been validly acknowledged, but the 2017 beneficiary list and 2018 amendment had not, and therefore each did not comply with the Trust clause requiring an "acknowledged instrument."

The niece's argument relied primarily on *King v. Lynch* (2012) 204 Cal.App.4th 1186. She alleged this case reasoned that the Trust provided for a method of amendment, so that method must be followed in order to validly amend the Trust. The trial court ruled against the niece, who appealed.

Holding and Reasoning of Court of Appeal: The appellate court confirmed that the niece's interpretation of the holding of *King* was not exactly accurate. In *King*, a married couple created a revocable trust. For jointly owned property, the trust instrument described separate modification procedures and revocation procedures. The trust could be modified "by an instrument in writing signed by both Settlors and delivered to the Trustee," whereas revocation required "an instrument in writing signed by either Settlor and delivered to the Trustee and the other Settlor." The language in Aunt Jeane's Trust differed significantly from the language in *King*, as it did not differentiate procedures for amendment and revocation.

The proper analysis is Probate Code section 15401(a), which provides that a revocable trust may be revoked either (1) by compliance with any method of revocation provided in the trust instrument or (2) by a writing, other than a will, signed by the settlor or any other person holding the power of revocation and delivered to the trustee during the lifetime of the settlor or the person holding the power of revocation. However, if the trust instrument explicitly makes the method of revocation provided in the trust instrument the exclusive method of revocation, the method in the trust instrument must be used. (See *Masry v. Masry* (2008) 166 Cal.App.4th 738.)

Aunt Jeane did not state an intent to bind herself to the specific method described in the trust agreement, to the exclusion of other permissible methods. Because the method of revocation and modification described in the trust agreement was not explicitly exclusive, the statutory method of revocation was available under Section 15401 for the procedure which could be followed to modify the trust, in addition to an acknowledged instrument. The niece's argument therefore failed.

Comment: The appellate court stated that it did "not need to comment on *King*'s interpretation of its trust instrument." Nor did it need to "consider whether *King* was ultimately correctly decided on its facts." But, as a general matter, the court felt it necessary to nevertheless go on to say the *King* dissent more accurately captures the meaning of Section 15402 than the majority opinion. By its disagreeing with another district, this appellate court perhaps solidified the California Supreme Court's decision to take a look.

Cases such as *Huscher v. Wells Fargo Bank* (2004) 121 Cal.App.4th 956, *Masry v. Masry* (2008) 166 Cal.App.4th 738, and *Cundall v. Mitchell-Clyde* (2020) 51 Cal.App.5th 571, emphasize the court's openness to finding in favor of settlor's intent unless the revocation provisions are expressly stated to be exclusive. What about structuring amendment provisions? What are best practices when drafting for married couples? For elderly or vulnerable clients?

7. *Balistreri v. Balistreri* (2022) 75 Cal.App.5th 511 [February 24, 2022; Review granted May 11, 2022]

Factual Background: Wife, the surviving spouse, filed a petition in probate court alleging that, the day before her husband died, the two had amended their revocable Trust.

Trust Language:

The revocation provision of the Trust provided as follows:

> The Trust "may be revoked or terminated, in whole or in part, by either of us as to any separate property of that trustor and as to any of our community property."

The amendment provisions of the trust provided as follows:

> "During our joint lifetimes, this Trust may be modified and amended by
> either of us acting alone as to any separate property of that trustor, and by
> both of us acting jointly as to any of our community property."

> . . .

> "Any amendment, revocation, or termination . . . shall be made by written
> instrument signed, with signature acknowledged by a notary public, by the
> trustor(s) making the revocation, amendment, or termination, and
> delivered to the trustee."

Trial Court Opinion: The probate court deemed the alleged amendment "null and void" and denied the petition. The court concluded the claimed amendment was invalid under Probate Code section 15402 because the Trust mandated that any amendment "shall be made by written instrument signed, with signature acknowledged by a notary public," and the amendment was not so acknowledged.

Holding and Reasoning of Court of Appeal: The appellate court affirmed.

Probate Code section 15401(a) sets out two alternative methods for the revocation of a trust. Under the first method, a trust may be revoked by "compliance with any method of revocation provided in the trust instrument." Under the second method, a trust may be revoked in "a writing, other than a will, signed by the settlor . . . and delivered to the trustee during the lifetime of the settlor." But, if "the trust instrument explicitly makes the method of revocation provided in the trust instrument the exclusive method of revocation," that method must be used. (*Brown v. Labow* (2007) 157 Cal.App.4th 795, 812; see *Pena v. Dey* (2019) 39 Cal.App.5th 546, 551 552.) To do so, the trust must contain "an explicit statement that the trust's revocation method is exclusive." (*Cundall v. Mitchell-Clyde* (2020) 51 Cal.App.5th 571, 581, 584.) Thus, "section 15401, subdivision (a)(2) 'provides a default method of revocation where the trust is silent on revocation *or does not explicitly provide the exclusive method.*'" (*Id.* at p. 587, italics in original.)

Probate Code section 15402, by contrast, governs modification of a trust. It states: "[u]nless the trust instrument provides otherwise, if a trust is revocable by the settlor, the settlor may modify the trust by the procedure for revocation." Under Section 15402, when "the trust instrument is silent on modification, the trust may be modified in the same manner in which it could be revoked, either statutorily or as provided in the trust instrument." (*King v. Lynch* (2012) 204 Cal.App.4th 1186, 1192.) When the trust instrument "specifies how the trust is to be modified," however, that "method must be used to amend the trust." (*Id.* at pp. 1192-1193.) Section 15402 "'recognizes a trustor may bind himself or herself to a specific method of . . . amendment of a trust by including that specific method in the trust agreement.'" (*Id.* at p. 1193.)

Thus, when a trust specifies an amendment procedure, a purported amendment made in contravention of that procedure is invalid.

The court acknowledged that *Haggerty v. Thornton* (2021) 68 Cal.App.5th 1003 reached a different result. There, a requirement that the amendment be acknowledged was not held to cause an unacknowledged amendment to be invalid as the trust agreement did not explicitly state that method was exclusive, and therefore the statutory method of revocation was available under Section 15401. But as a matter of legislative interpretation, a court cannot rewrite a statute, either by inserting or omitting language, to make it conform to a presumed intent that is not expressed.

Comment: We may finally reach the end of this issue once the California Supreme Court rules on this case and *Haggerty v. Thornton*. It is hard to disagree with the technical analysis of *Balistreri v. Balistreri*, although it effectively mitigates the court's ability to find in favor of settlor intent where an amendment does not exactly follow the trust's terms. Drafting attorneys should review their documents, and administration and litigation attorneys should add this to their checklist, as less than careful drafting may cause an amendment to be invalid, with limited recourse available to a trustee in such a situation. Then, there is the other issue of revocation, where much more flexibility exists unless the revocation provision is expressly stated to be exclusive. Again, what are best practices when drafting for married couples? For elderly or vulnerable clients?

C.   Appellate Review Status

Case	Status	Notable Facts
Haggerty v. Thornton (2021) 68 Cal.App.5th 1003, review granted Dec. 12, 2021, S271483	• Dec. 22, 2021: Petition for review to the California Supreme Court GRANTED. • March 9, 2022: AOB filed. • May 20, 2022: Respondent's Brief filed. • July 20, 2022: Reply Brief filed. • Oral argument has yet to be scheduled.	The Court has permitted citing the underlying Court of Appeal opinion, "not only for its persuasive value, but also for the limited purpose of establishing the existence of a conflict in authority that would in turn allow trial courts . . . to choose between sides of any such conflict."
Balistreri v. Balistreri (2022) 75 Cal.App.5th 511, review granted May 11, 2022, S273909	• May 11, 2022: Petition for review to the California Supreme Court GRANTED.	"Further action in this matter is deferred pending consideration and disposition of a related issue in *Haggerty v. Thornton.* . . ."
Cundall v. Mitchell-Clyde (2020) 51 Cal.App.5th 571	• After the Court of Appeal affirmed the trial court's order, the case was closed as of Sept. 14, 2020. • No appeal to the California Supreme Court.	
Pena v. Dey (2019) 39 Cal.App.5th 546	• After the Court of Appeal affirmed the trial court's order, the case was closed as of Oct. 30, 2019. • No appeal to the California Supreme Court.	
King v. Lynch (2012) 204 Cal.App.4th 1186	• After the Court of Appeal affirmed the trial court's order, Appellant filed a	

	petition for review to the California Supreme Court on May 22, 2012. • Review DENIED June 27, 2012.	
Masry v. Masry (2008) 166 Cal.App.4th 738	• Opinion modified on denial of rehearing Oct. 3, 2008. • Review DENIED Nov. 19, 2008	
Huscher v. Wells Fargo Bank (2004) 121 Cal.App.4th 956	• After the Court of Appeal affirmed the trial court's order, the case was closed as of Oct. 19, 2004. • No appeal to the California Supreme Court.	

D. The Current State of the Law by Appellate District

District	First	Second	Third	Fourth	Fifth
Case	*Balistreri v. Balistreri* (2022) 75 Cal.App.5th 511, review granted May 11, 2022	*Cundall v. Mitchell-Clyde* (2020) 51 Cal.App.5th 571	*Pena v. Dey* (2019) 39 Cal.App.5th 546	*Haggerty v. Thornton* (2021) 68 Cal.App.5th 1003, review granted Dec. 12, 2021	*King v. Lynch* (2012) 204 Cal.App.4th 1186
Trust Language	"Any amendment, revocation, or termination . . . shall be made by written instrument signed, with signature acknowledged by a notary public, by the trustor(s) making the revocation, amendment, or termination, and delivered to the trustee."	"During the Grantor's lifetime, the Grantor may revoke at any time, and/or the Grantor may amend, this Agreement by delivering to the Trustee and the Successor Trustee an appropriate written revocation or amendment, signed by the Grantor and his attorney. . . ."	"Any amendment, revocation, or termination of this trust shall be made by written instrument signed by the settlor and delivered to the trustee."	Trustor "reserves the following rights, each of which may be exercised whenever and as often as [she] may wish: [¶] A. Amend or Revoke. The right by an acknowledged instrument in writing to revoke or amend this Agreement or any trust hereunder."	The trust "may be amended, in whole or in part, with respect to jointly owned property by an instrument in writing signed by both Settlors and delivered to the Trustee. . . ." The trust may "be revoked, in whole or in part, with respect to jointly owned property by an instrument signed by either Settlor and delivered to the Trustee and the other Settlor. . . ."
Holding	Trust amendment, which was accepted and adopted by Co-Trustees but not notarized, was **INVALID** under the Trust provision requiring notarization.	Settlor-Trustee's revocation was a **VALID** and proper use of the statutory method of revocation under Probate Code section 15401 because the method provided for in the Trust was not exclusive.	Settlor-Trustee's interlineations **INVALIDLY** attempted to amend the Trust because the Trust specifically required that amendments be made by a written instrument signed by the settlor and delivered to the Trustee.	Trust amendment was **VALID** because the Settlor-Trustee signed the amendment and delivered it to herself in compliance with Section 15401 notwithstanding the notarization requirement in the instrument.	Settlor's amendment naming himself Sole Trustee and altering the bequests to the beneficiaries was **INVALID** because the instrument stated a procedure for amendment and the Settlor failed to follow that procedure.

9

Ten Pitfalls to Avoid With International Trusts

Cynthia D. Brittain

TEN PITFALLS TO AVOID WITH INTERNATIONAL TRUSTS

Cross-Border Succession Planning
The 45th UCLA/CEB ESTATE PLANNING INSTITUTE
APRIL 21, 2023

Cynthia D. Brittain
Karlin & Peebles, LLP
5900 Wilshire Blvd., Suite 500
Los Angeles, CA 90036

(805) 570 7652

KARLIN & PEEBLES, LLP
ATTORNEYS AT LAW

| GLOBALIZATION OF PEOPLE....

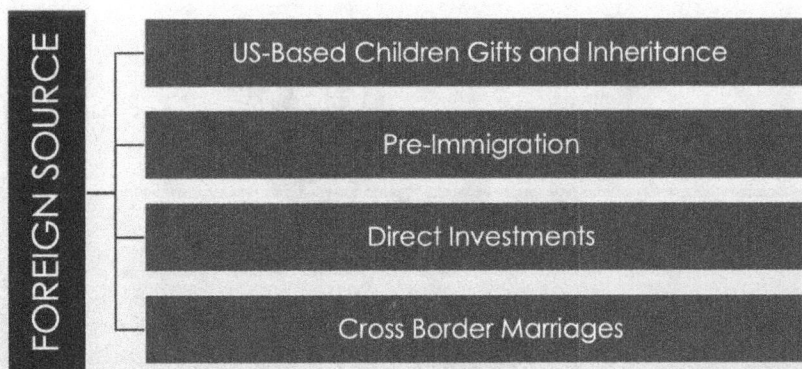

FOREIGN SOURCE
- US-Based Children Gifts and Inheritance
- Pre-Immigration
- Direct Investments
- Cross Border Marriages

KARLIN & PEEBLES, LLP
ATTORNEYS AT LAW

THE MAJORITY OF RECENT ARRIVALS FROM ASIA

The vast majority of California's immigrants were born in Latin America (50%) or Asia (39%). California has sizable populations of immigrants from dozens of countries; the leading countries of origin are Mexico (3.9 million), the Philippines (859,000), China (796,000), Vietnam (539,000), and India (513,000).

However, among immigrants who arrived between 2010 and 2019, more than half (53%) were born in Asia, while 31% were born in Latin America.

SOURCE: 2019 Census Bureau, decennial censuses, and the American Community

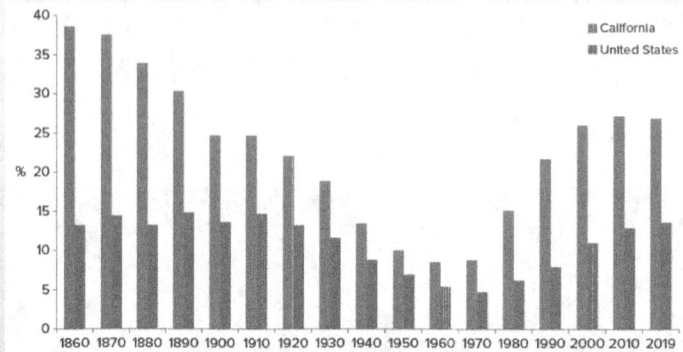

KARLIN & PEEBLES, LLP
ATTORNEYS AT LAW

WHERE ARE INVESTORS PUTTING THEIR MONEY IN THE US?

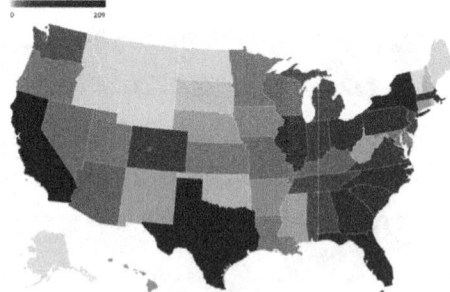

KARLIN & PEEBLES, LLP
ATTORNEYS AT LAW

| NRAS HAVE UNIQUE NEEDS

Stability:	POLITICAL UNCERTAINTY IN THE CLIENT'S HOME COUNTRY MAY BE CAUSING CURRENCY INSTABILITY.
Safety:	INSTITUTIONS IN THE HOME COUNTRY MAY LACK SUFFICIENT FINANCIAL STRENGTH.
Privacy:	HOME COUNTRY CONDITIONS MAY INCREASE CLIENT DESIRE FOR PRIVACY.
Diversification:	HOME COUNTRY MARKET MAY NOT OFFER SUFFICIENT ASSET DIVERSIFICATION.
Access:	DESIRE ACCESS TO U.S. MARKETS DIRECTLY.

KARLIN & PEEBLES, LLP
ATTORNEYS AT LAW

No. 1:
You Shouldn't Assume that Trusts are portable without consequence.

KARLIN & PEEBLES, LLP
ATTORNEYS AT LAW

CONCEPTS IN CONFLICT

KARLIN & PEEBLES, LLP
ATTORNEYS AT LAW

| IMPACT OF COMPETING AND CONFLICTING RULES

- My story...moving as trustee

- The Vacation Home in Santa Barbara

- Inadvertently ratting out your client (the attorney-client privilege)

- Planning for the child living in the U.K. or France

KARLIN & PEEBLES, LLP
ATTORNEYS AT LAW

No. 2:
You Shouldn't Assume Community Property Acts the Same Everywhere!

KARLIN & PEEBLES, LLP
ATTORNEYS AT LAW

U.S. – CHINA: CROSS BORDER PLANNING

KARLIN & PEEBLES, LLP
ATTORNEYS AT LAW

| China's Community Property

- Gifts Received By a Spouse can become part of the Community Property assets

- Inheritance Received By a Spouse can become part of the Community Property

- What may sever Community Property in California may not Sever Community Property in China

- While China is a Community Property Regime, it does not act the same as California's Community Property Regime.

KARLIN & PEEBLES, LLP
ATTORNEYS AT LAW

| IMPACT DISCUSSION:

When Chinese Citizen Wife moves from China to the U.S. what are Wife's U.S. tax obligations?
- Wife must report her worldwide income…but what constitutes her reportable income?
- China is a community property jurisdiction. So, do we report Wife's 50% Community Property interest in what her Husband in China is earning?

Generally:
- A U.S. person must reports worldwide income; offset by foreign tax credits
- In California: H & W files usually file a joint return for income;
- For U.S. resident Wife with non-resident Husband, they can file jointly;
- For U.S. resident Wife: Usually, U.S. spouse files "married, separate";

What do we do with Husband's Earnings which are Community Property?
- Look at IRC Sec 879: "Earned income (within the meaning of section 911(d)(2))…shall be treated as the income of the spouse who rendered the personal service. **(Careful: This exception does not include trade or business income or partner's distribute share of partnership income.)**
- **Impact:** U.S. Wife does not have to pick up her community property share of non-resident Husband's personal service earnings performed in other country, but she includes up all her community property earnings.
- **Important:** Community property income, however, means income under applicable community property laws…which in the above example means the community property laws of China.

KARLIN & PEEBLES, LLP
ATTORNEYS AT LAW

| IMPACT DISCUSSION:

When Chinese Citizen Wife moves from China to the U.S. what are U.S. Wife's U.S. tax obligations?

(A) A Form 5471 for certain ownership interest in a foreign corporation
(B) A Form 8938 for certain ownership in foreign financial assets
(C) A Form 114 (Foreign Bank Account Reporting ("FBAR") on all foreign bank accounts, foreign credit cards, and other accounts that are includible under the definition of foreign accounts for FBAR purposes.

- Recently debated this with my partner: U.S. beneficiary has Investment Advisor authority or Distribution Advisor authority...."direct community to the bank"
- **Signature Authority** – is the authority of an individual (alone or in conjunction with another individual) to "control" the disposition of assets held in a foreign financial account by **direct communication** (whether in writing or otherwise) to the bank or other financial institution.
- **Bittner v. United States** (February 28, 2023) – Failure to file carries maximum penalty of $10,000 per report, regardless of how many bank accounts are at issue;
- **Fahry v. Commissioner**, the taxpayer failed to file Forms 5471 reporting interest in a foreign corporation. The Tax Court held that the IRS lacks authority to assess penalties imposed by IRC Sec 6038(b)(1) or (2)
- **Wrzesinski refund case** – The IRS conceded penalties assessed against the taxpayer for failure to file Form 3520, receipt of a foreign gift.   Great facts...for taxpayer...

KARLIN & PEEBLES, LLP
ATTORNEYS AT LAW

Who Must File?	STATEMENT OF SPECIFIED FOREIGN FINANCIAL ASSETS FORM 8938	FOREIGN BANK ACCOUNTS AND FINANCIAL ACCOUNTS FORM 114 ("FBAR")
	Specified individuals and specified domestic entities that have an interest in specified foreign financial assets and meet the reporting threshold • Specified individuals include U.S citizens, resident aliens, and certain non-resident aliens • Specified domestic entities include certain domestic corporations, partnerships, and trusts	U.S. persons, which include U.S. citizens, resident aliens, trusts, estates, and domestic entities that have an interest in foreign financial accounts and meet the reporting threshold
Does the United States include U.S. territories?	No	Yes, resident aliens of U.S territories and U.S. territory entities are subject to FBAR reporting
Reporting Threshold (Total Value of Assets)	Specified individuals living in the US: • Unmarried individual (or married filing separately): Total value of assets was more than $50,000 on the last day of the tax year, or more than $75,000 at any time during the year. • Married individual filing jointly: Total value of assets was more than $100,000 on the last day of the tax year, or more than $150,000 at any time during the year. • Specified individuals living outside the US: • Unmarried individual (or married filing separately): Total value of assets was more than $200,000 on the last day of the tax year, or more than $300,000 at any time during the year. • Married individual filing jointly: Total value of assets was more than $400,000 on the last day of the tax year, or more than $600,000 at any time during the year. Specified domestic entities: Total value of assets was more than $50,000 on the last day of the tax year, or more than $75,000 at any time during the tax year.	Aggregate value of financial accounts exceeds $10,000 at any time during the calendar year. This is a cumulative balance, meaning if you have 2 accounts with a combined account balance greater than $10,000 at any one time, both accounts would have to be reported.

KARLIN & PEEBLES, LLP
ATTORNEYS AT LAW

When do you have an interest in an account or asset?	If any income, gains, losses, deductions, credits, gross proceeds, or distributions from holding or disposing of the account or asset are or would be required to be reported, included, or otherwise reflected on your income tax return	Financial interest: you are the owner of record or holder of legal title; the owner of record or holder of legal title is your agent or representative; you have a sufficient interest in the entity that is the owner of record or holder of legal title. Signature authority: you have authority to control the disposition of the assets in the account by direct communication with the financial institution maintaining the account. See instructions for further details.
What is Reported?	Maximum value of specified foreign financial assets, which include financial accounts with foreign financial institutions and certain other foreign non-account investment assets	Maximum value of financial accounts maintained by a financial institution physically located in a foreign country
How are maximum account or asset values determined and reported?	Fair market value in U.S. dollars in accord with the Form 8938 instructions for each account and asset reported. Convert to U.S. dollars using the end of the taxable year exchange rate and report in U.S. dollars.	Use periodic account statements to determine the maximum value in the currency of the account. Convert to U.S. dollars using the end of the calendar year exchange rate and report in U.S. dollars.
When Due?	Form is attached to your annual return and due on the date of that return, including any applicable extensions	Received by April 15 (6-month automatic extension to Oct 15)
Where to File?	File with income tax return pursuant to instructions for filing the return.	File electronically through FinCENs BSA E-Filing System. The FBAR is not filed with a federal tax return.
Penalties	Up to $10,000 for failure to disclose and an additional $10,000 for each 30 days of non-filing after IRS notice of a failure to disclose, for a potential maximum penalty of $60,000; criminal penalties may also apply	Civil monetary penalties are adjusted annually for inflation. For civil penalty assessment prior to Aug 1, 2016, if non-willful, up to $10,000; if willful, up to the greater of $100,000 or 50 percent of account balances; criminal penalties may also apply

KARLIN & PEEBLES, LLP
ATTORNEYS AT LAW

Types of Foreign Assets	Form 8938, Statement of Specified Foreign Financial Assets	FinCEN Form 114, Report of Foreign Bank and Financial Accounts (FBAR)
Financial (deposit and custodial) accounts held at foreign financial institutions	Yes	Yes
Financial account held at a foreign branch of a U.S. financial institution	No	Yes
Financial account held at a U.S. branch of a foreign financial institution	No	No
Foreign financial account for which you have signature authority	No, unless you otherwise have an interest in the account as described above	Yes, subject to exceptions
Foreign stock or securities held in a financial account at a foreign financial institution	The account itself is subject to reporting, but the contents of the account do not have to be separately reported	The account itself is subject to reporting, but the contents of the account do not have to be separately reported
Foreign stock or securities not held in a financial account	Yes	No
Foreign partnership interests	Yes	No
Indirect interests in foreign financial assets through an entity	No	Yes, if sufficient ownership or beneficial interest (i.e., a greater than 50 percent interest) in the entity. See instructions for further detail.
Foreign mutual funds	Yes	Yes
Domestic mutual fund investing in foreign stocks and securities	No	No
Foreign accounts and foreign non-account investment assets held by foreign or domestic grantor trust for which you are the grantor	Yes, as to both foreign accounts and foreign non-account investment assets	Yes, as to foreign accounts
Foreign-issued life insurance or annuity contract with a cash-value	Yes	Yes
Foreign hedge funds and foreign private equity funds	Yes	No
Foreign real estate held directly	No	No
Foreign real estate held through a foreign entity	No, but the foreign entity itself is a specified foreign financial asset and its maximum value includes the value of the real estate	No
Foreign currency held directly	No	No
Precious Metals held directly	No	No
Personal property, held directly, such as art, antiques, jewelry, cars and other collectibles	No	No
'Social Security'-type program benefits provided by a foreign government	No	No

KARLIN & PEEBLES, LLP
ATTORNEYS AT LAW

No. 3:

You Shouldn't Ignore Treaties; Structure Trusts and Underlying Companies for Effective Treaty Application – Without Treaty Shopping

(Investments and Jurisdiction)

A Treaty Rate Can Significantly Affect the U.S. Taxpayer's Tax Obligation

KARLIN & PEEBLES, LLP
ATTORNEYS AT LAW

Tax Treatment of Fixed, Determinable, Annual, or Periodical (FDAP) income --

FDAP income is taxed at a 30% withholding rate (or lower treaty rate).

For example, a <u>dividend</u> paid to someone in Hong Kong will be taxed in the U.S. at a 30% rate (withheld at source) on a payment of that dividend to its Hong Kong Shareholder.

Generally, a 30% rate applies to the gross amount of U.S. source fixed or determinable, annual, or periodical gains, profits, or income.

A Deductions and netting are not allowed against FDAP income.

The following items are examples of FDAP income:

- Compensation for personal services (such as commissions and gross proceeds from performances)
- Dividends
- Interest
- Original issue discount
- Pensions and annuities
- Real property income, such as rents, other than gains from the sale of real property
  (TO TAKE A DEDUCTION, MAKE AN ELECTION TO BE TREATED AS TRADE OR BUSINESS INCOME.)
- Royalties
- Scholarships and fellowship grants
- Other grants, prizes and awards
- A sales commission paid or credited monthly
- A commission paid for a single transaction

KARLIN & PEEBLES, LLP
ATTORNEYS AT LAW

U.S.-China Income Tax Treaty (U.S. treatment)

The U.S. China Income Tax Treaty provides very favorable rates for Chinese tax residents who invest in U.S. assets

- For example, 10% on FDAP income (as opposed to 30% general rate and 15% with other country tax treaties)

KARLIN & PEEBLES, LLP
ATTORNEYS AT LAW

No. 4:

You Shouldn't assume that a Green Card Holder can't engage in effective U.S. estate planning! It may not be too late!

(Domiciled versus non-domiciled)

KARLIN & PEEBLES, LLP
ATTORNEYS AT LAW

If someone with a green card didn't plan before moving to the U.S., what can that person do to remedy the U.S. income tax and U.S. estate tax issues?

Planning depends on the person's status as a domiciled or non-domiciled individual:

1. **Green card holder's intention regarding remaining in the U.S. indefinitely? (Example, after children graduate from high school?)**

    a) What is the difference between being U.S. domiciled versus being U.S. tax resident

        i.   **Domicile** – Subjective: Facts and circumstances to demonstrate **intent to remain in the U.S. Indefinitely**

            • If U.S. domiciled, then subject to U.S. gift and estate tax on worldwide assets

        i.   **Income Tax Resident** – Objective: Taxation is on worldwide income and gains under general international tax principles or applicable tax treaty rates

            • Tests
(A)	Citizen
(B)	Green Card
(C)	Substantial Presence Test
(D)	Tax Treaty Determination of Income Tax Resident
(E)	Elect to be a U.S. Tax Resident

KARLIN & PEEBLES, LLP
ATTORNEYS AT LAW

---

2. **With a U.S. Green Card, does U.S. gift tax apply if green card holder wants to gift U.S. or other worldwide assets to an effective trust (for U.S. estate planning purposes)?**

Depends...can you support non-U.S. domiciled status? Are you gifting intangible assets?

    Gifting assets – (Tangible – U.S. cash, real estate, art, jewelry) <u>versus</u> (Intangible – equities, certain partnership interest, T-bills)

    i. **Non-domiciled:**

        a) If the green card holder can be considered non-U.S. domiciled, then he can give away U.S. intangible assets, U.S. gift tax free.   He can gift all foreign assets U.S. gift tax free.   (Example, stock in U.S. investment account will not be subject to U.S. gift tax, but U.S. real estate would be subject to U.S. gift tax)

        b) Is there anything we can do with U.S. real estate owned by a non-domiciled person?
            i)   Consider contributing to a foreign partnership
            ii)   We will discuss U.S. real estate in a separate point.

        c) We need to understand exactly what the non-domiciled person owns to determine what gifting strategies can be used.

    i. **U.S. domiciled:**

        a) If the green card person is considered U.S. domiciled, then that person can gift only up to his applicable U.S. gift tax exemption amount ($12,920,000) of his worldwide assets, both tangible and intangible.

        b) We'd like to be able to gift as much out of her U.S. estate to mitigate U.S. estate tax on her worldwide assets, if she's considered U.S. domiciled.

KARLIN & PEEBLES, LLP
ATTORNEYS AT LAW

| THE NON-U.S. DOMICILED TAXABLE ESTATE

EXCLUDED: The "gross estate" shall not include certain property, even though physically in the U.S.

Examples:

- U.S. bank accounts, as defined
- Works of art on loan in the U.S.
- Life insurance – Owned by insured on his or her own life, issued by U.S. carriers
- Qualified debt obligations
- By treaty, sometimes shares of domestic companies (See, U.S. – U.K. estate tax treaty)
- Beware of U.S. real estate with no foreign blocker!

KARLIN & PEEBLES, LLP
ATTORNEYS AT LAW

---

3. Does U.S. estate tax apply to her worldwide assets if she is not U.S. "domiciled"?

No, only on her U.S. assets…but she may have a hard time saying she is not U.S. domiciled. It may become harder once she triggers long-term permanent residence status with her green card.

4. Should Wife give up her green card?

We don't know.

The Long-Term Permanent Resident Test is: Has she been in the U.S. for 8 out of the last 15 years. We don't know if IRC Section 877A applies to her, this applies to her, because 1 day equals a year. We'd have to look at her actual entry into the U.S. to determine if she can exit now. (Consider gifting to spouse or consider becoming non-U.S. domiciled and then gifting.)

KARLIN & PEEBLES, LLP
ATTORNEYS AT LAW

No. 5:
You Shouldn't Buy Your House Without Planning First...IRC Section 2104(b)

Section 2104(b) taint can cause U.S. estate tax planning to fail....

KARLIN & PEEBLES, LLP
ATTORNEYS AT LAW

| IRC Sec 2104(b)

Foreign Person

↓

U.S. Real Estate

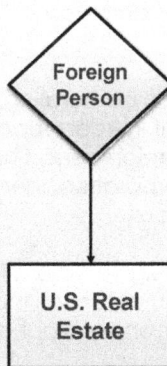

There are two threshold requirements for a trust interest to be includible in a nonresident decedent's gross estate for U.S. estate tax purposes.

- the trust must be a valid trust on the nonresident's date of death; and
- His interest in the trust must be indefeasibly vested in such manner as would cause estate tax inclusion if he were a U.S. citizen or domiciliary pursuant to IRC section 2033 through 2046.

If the above are met, then we must look at Sections 2104 and 2105 of the Code which sections classify the property as having a situs within and without the U.S.

2104: A nonresident alien decedent will be subject to U.S. estate tax inclusion where the nonresident settles a trust whereby he transferred U.S. situs property either at the time that the property is transferred to the trust, or at the time of his death, and retained strings so as to cause inclusion under sections 2035-2038.

KARLIN & PEEBLES, LLP
ATTORNEYS AT LAW

IRC Sec 2104(b)

```
    ┌─────────┐
    │ Foreign │
    │ Person  │
    └─────────┘
         │
         ▼
   ┌──────────┐
   │ U.S. Real│
   │  Estate  │
   └──────────┘
```

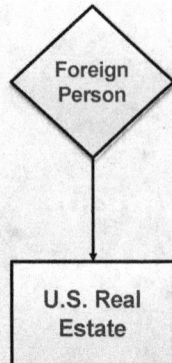

Estate Tax Consequences When Property is Transferred with Strings

Under IRC Sec 2104(b), if a nonresident alien owns U.S. property and gratuitously transfers that U.S. property to a foreign trust, or to a foreign corporation/partnership and then to a trust, and IRC sections 2035 through 2038 apply, then the property will be subject to U.S. estate tax.

IRC Sec 2036(a) provides, in part, for the inclusion in the gross estate of all property transferred by a decedent during life, by trust or otherwise, in which he has retained for life or for any period not ascertainable without reference to his death...the possession or enjoyment or, or the right to income from, the property, or the right to designate the persons who shall possess or enjoy the property or its income.

IRC Sec 2038(a)(1) provides, in part, that the value of the gross estate shall include the value of all property to the extent of any interest therein of which the decedent has at the time made a transfer, by trust or otherwise, where the enjoyment thereof was subject at the date of death to any change through the exercise of a power by the decedent alone or in conjunction with any other person to alter, amend, revoke, or terminate, or where any such power is relinquished during the 3-year period.

Thus, if at the time of transfer to a (foreign corporation) or trust, the decedent retained certain IRC Sec 2036 strings, then the nonresident should pay fair market value rent.

KARLIN & PEEBLES, LLP
ATTORNEYS AT LAW

REAL LIFE EXAMPLE

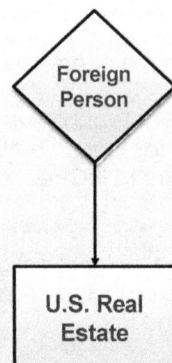

```
    ┌─────────┐
    │ Foreign │
    │ Person  │
    └─────────┘
         │
         ▼
   ┌──────────┐
   │ U.S. Real│
   │  Estate  │
   └──────────┘
```

Foreign Person buys U.S. real estate and discovers that he's subject to U.S. estate tax, with only a $60k exemption. He needs a U.S. estate tax blocker! It's a personal residence located in Beverly Hills, CA.

Transfer U.S. real estate to a foreign corporation;
- That triggers Foreign Investment in Real Property Tax Act and Section 2104(b) taint so foreign person has to pay rent.

Transfer U.S. real estate to U.S. Corporation, then transfer U.S. Corporation to Foreign Corporation;
- that triggers the inversion rules.

Transfers to U.S. LLC, then to a Foreign Corporation;
- that triggers FIRPTA, but also subject rental income to branch profits tax if Foreign Person rents out or sells U.S. real estate.

Transfers U.S. real estate to a foreign partnership;
- that triggers a FIRPTA Notice but it's not taxable. (May be the best option.)

Transfers through an entity to a foreign trust
- That triggers IRC Sec 2104(b), unless FMV rent is paid.

KARLIN & PEEBLES, LLP
ATTORNEYS AT LAW

U.S. Real Estate

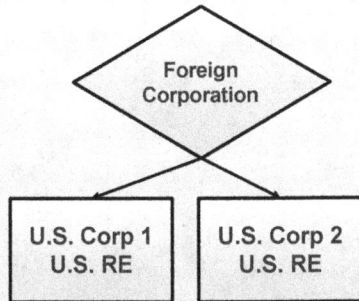

Foreign Person Needs to Set Up Foreign Entity First or foreign trust first, then the foreign entity or trust, sets up a U.S. entity that buys the U.S. real estate. (This could be a foreign partnership and underlying disregarded entities, like U.S. LLCs, with certain different results.)

1. The Foreign Corporation provides the effective U.S. estate tax blocker.
2. The underlying U.S. corporations hold the separate, individual U.S. real estate.
3. When U.S. Corp 1 sells its U.S. RE, a later (complete) distribution in complete liquidation of U.S. Corp 1 into Foreign Corporate Parent, (as long as no E & P), then the transfer up to Fparent is U.S. income tax (withholding tax) free.
4. If the two properties were in the same entity, then the distribution would not be U.S. income tax free and a U.S. dividend would apply.

KARLIN & PEEBLES, LLP
ATTORNEYS AT LAW

No. 6:

You Shouldn't Be Afraid of Foreign Non-grantor trusts...they can be effectively managed.

KARLIN & PEEBLES, LLP
ATTORNEYS AT LAW

FOREIGN NON-GRANTOR TRUST

KARLIN & PEEBLES, LLP
ATTORNEYS AT LAW

ANTI-DEFERRAL TAX REGIME: U.S. INCOME TAX ON DISTRIBUTIONS FROM FOREIGN NON-GRANTOR TRUSTS

- **Key concepts: DNI and UNI**

- Distributable net income (DNI) is the income of the trust computed for the calendar year from all sources under U.S. income tax principles.
  - DNI includes all capital gains.
  - DNI includes income exempt under treaty.
  - All deductions allowed, including deductions disallowed by section 265 (expenses relating to tax-exempt income).

- Undistributed net income (UNI) is DNI from prior taxable years that was not required to be distributed and was not actually distributed in the year the DNI was earned.

KARLIN & PEEBLES, LLP
ATTORNEYS AT LAW

| U.S. INCOME TAXATION OF DISTRIBUTIONS FROM FOREIGN NON-GRANTOR TRUSTS

- Throwback rule is designed to impose approximately the same tax on the accumulation distribution had the trust distributed the income in the year it was earned but with added interest charge and loss of capital gain tax treatment

- Accumulation distributions –
  - Ordinary income – capital gains included in the UNI will not preserve their character in the hands of the U.S. beneficiary.
  - Tax subject to interest charge calculated using underpayment rate.
  - Can carry credits for U.S. and foreign taxes paid by the trust.

- Exceptions:
  - Distributions in satisfaction of a gift of a specific sum of money or property as required by the trust instrument, paid at once or in no more than 3 installments.
  - Distributions that do no exceed trust accounting income in the year made.
  - Distributions limited to DNI in the Trust...

KARLIN & PEEBLES, LLP
ATTORNEYS AT LAW

| EMBRACE THE FOREIGN NON-GRANTOR TRUST

When a Foreign Nongrantor Trust has substantial UNI, the question is how to access the trust assets without throwback tax applying.

Option 1: Make distribution not in excess of its DNI for the current year. (The trust's DNI comes out and is taxable to the U.S. beneficiaries.)

Option 2: Keep the distribution less than trust accounting income. (There is never a tax to U.S. beneficiaries.)

Option 3: As allowed under IRC Section 663(a)(1), draft the Trust to require a specific sum of money or specific property which is to be paid or credited all at once or in not more than 3 installments. Such amounts are not included within IRC Section 662(a).

Option 4: Keeping Option 3 in mind, have the three installments pay to U.S. trusts to shield the amounts from U.S. estate tax.

Option 5: Make distributions within the Default Method. (Manage the assets to increase the DNI for several year under the default rule of income reporting. The default rule will assist with depleting the trust using solely DNI.)

KARLIN & PEEBLES, LLP
ATTORNEYS AT LAW

| EMBRACE THE FOREIGN NON-GRANTOR TRUST

LOOK AT DEFAULT METHOD TO WASH OUT UNI: WORK WITH INVESTMENT ADVISOR TO INCREASE DNI FOR SEVERAL YEARS

The "default" method of calculating the tax on distributions from a foreign non-grantor trust can enable distribution of UNI to be distributed to U.S. beneficiaries without triggering the onerous throwback tax.

Part III, Schedule A of Form 3520 provides the steps for determining the amount of allowable non-accumulation distribution in a given year.

1. *The U.S. beneficiaries enters the total distributions received from the foreign trust in the precedent 3 years...it is important for the investment advisor to increase DNI payments – selling more stock since capital gains are includible in FT DNI;*
2. *Then, the Default Method allows the U.S. beneficiary to multipy that total by 1.25;*
3. *The U.S. beneficiary has to divide the total in 2 by 3 (or by the number of years the trust has been a FNT, if fewer than 3).*

KARLIN & PEEBLES, LLP
ATTORNEYS AT LAW

| EMBRACE THE FOREIGN NON-GRANTOR TRUST

LOOK AT DEFAULT METHOD TO WASH OUT UNI: WORK WITH INVESTMENT ADVISOR TO INCREASE DNI FOR SEVERAL YEARS

(See, The Throwback Tax by Ellen K. Harrison, Carlyn S. McCaffrey, Amy E. Heller, and Elyse G. Kirshner for comprehensive discussion on how to manage and eliminate the Throwback Tax.)

J is the U.S. beneficiary that has been in existence since 2002. At the end of 2010, the FNT had assets worth $20,000,000. In each of the years 2002 through 2010, the FNT earned $1,000,000. Assume FNT has no income in 2011, 2012, 2013 and 2014 and that FNT distributes $2,000,000 to J in each such year. The amount of J's accumulation distribution in each year would be $2,000,000 under IRC Code 665(b). His situation would be improved considerably using the default method.

In 2011, the accumulation distribution under the default method would be the full $2,000,000 because there were no distribution to measure in any of the prior three years.

In 2012, the amount of the accumulation distribution is reduced to $1,166,667 ($2,000,000 – ($2,000,000 x 1.25/3)

In 2013, the amount of accumulation distribution is reduced further to $333,333 ($2,000,000 x 1.25/3)

In 2014, the amount of the accumulation distribution is reduced to 0 ($2,000,000 – ($6,000,000 x 1.25/3)

KARLIN & PEEBLES, LLP
ATTORNEYS AT LAW

|THROWBACK TAX MITIGATION SUMMARY

1. Use a U.S. non-grantor trust from inception – Taxed Currently

2. Embrace the Foreign non-grantor trust from inception – Not Taxed Currently
   a. Keep Distributions Below Trust Accounting Income
   b. Because above is usually smaller distributions – provide for three specific installments

3. Private placement life insurance – Consider for your CEOs who must get U.S. green card

4. Alternate distributions of income to foreign beneficiaries, then principal to U.S. beneficiaries

5. Distribution of current year income annually – to domestic follow-on trust
   • 20 years – 60% can move into the U.S.; 40 years – 90% can move into the U.S.*

6. Default Method distributions to U.S. beneficiaries (for faster cleanse, but less wealth transferred)

7. Hedge for currency risk

KARLIN & PEEBLES, LLP
ATTORNEYS AT LAW

No. 7:

Don't Forget Business Reasons for Cross Border Planning Transactions

Certain Effective U.S. Tax Planning Can Trigger
Ethical or Criminal Violations in Other Countries

KARLIN & PEEBLES, LLP
ATTORNEYS AT LAW

FOREIGN GRANTOR TRUST STRUCTURE WITH UNDERLYING CORPORATION(S) TO BLOCK U.S. TRANSFER TAX

STRUCTURE ESTABLISHED BY FOREIGN PERSON FOR U.S.- BENEFICIARIES (CAREFUL ATTENTION IF FOREIGN GRANTOR IS MOVING TO THE U.S.)

KARLIN & PEEBLES, LLP
ATTORNEYS AT LAW

| CORE PLANNING FOR U.S. BASED BENEFICIARIES - Foreign Grantor Trust Solution...

Foreign Mom and Dad

Foreign Grantor Trust:
Irrevocable – Lifetime to Parents; or
Revocable – Children can be beneficiaries

ForeignCo
US Assets

ForeignCo
For Assets

- NO U.S. ESTATE TAX (Dynasty Trust)
- NO U.S. GIFT TAX (Funding attention with T-Bill Option)
- BEST INCOME TAX OPTION – NO TAX DURING MOM AND DAD'S LIFETIME
- BASIS STEP-UP
- KEEP CONTROL Child could participate as the Investment Advisor.
- Provision for Section 1014(b)

KARLIN & PEEBLES, LLP
ATTORNEYS AT LAW

FOREIGN PARENT – FOREIGN GRANTOR

Corporate Trustee, U.S. TRUSTEE

Foreign Revocable Trust
(Shareholder of Underlying
Foreign Corporation

U.S. Beneficiaries
(Possible Foreign
Beneficiaries)

(Parents Assets:
Contributed to
Foreign companies
To avoid any argument
Beneficiary Grantor;
(§ 2104(b) taint)

Distributions to Beneficiaries made only
From Trust accounts;
Do Not Distribute From Corporate Accounts

ABC, USVI*
Estate Blocker
To Hold U.S.
Assets

ABC USVI*
Estate Blocker
To Hold
Foreign Assets

BVI
Company

Refresh Basis

Refresh Basis/CRS

Check the box

Check the Box

CFC of PFIC Issue?

KARLIN & PEEBLES, LLP
ATTORNEYS AT LAW

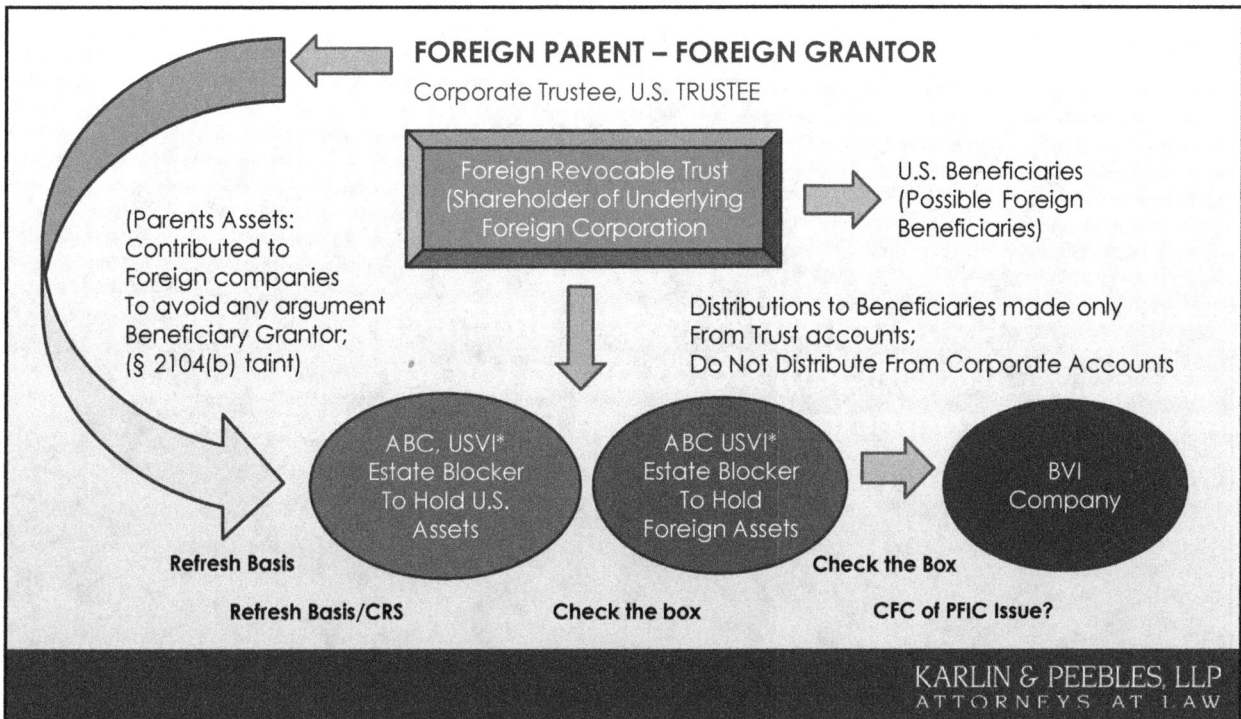

| BENEFITS OF THE FOREIGN REVOCABLE GRANTOR TRUST

Benefits:

1. Parents' transfer of wealth to U.S.-based children U.S. estate tax free
2. Parents funding of foreign grantor trust is not subject to U.S. gift tax as long as not U.S. situs assets (*i.e.*, intangible ok)
3. With proper investing, U.S. income tax minimized
4. Trust established for efficient tax planning for future generations
5. Some asset protection
6. Basis Step Up.....

Issues to Consider:

1. There may be more than one foreign corporation for U.S. tax efficiency
2. The proposed structure needs a corporate trustee
3. Investment management important to maintain U.S. tax efficiency
4. Draft for a pot trust or separate trusts
5. U.S. – Care if Assets are U.S. CFC and PFIC
6. China – Controlled Foreign Corporation issues

KARLIN & PEEBLES, LLP
ATTORNEYS AT LAW

No. 8:
Consider Ways to Sustain Effective U.S. tax efficient status of the foreign grantor trust: Foreign Estate Election

KARLIN & PEEBLES, LLP
ATTORNEYS AT LAW

| QUALIFIED REVOCABLE TRUST (QRT)

CONSIDERATIONS: When a foreign corporation is an asset of the trust....

- Should the trust be a foreign grantor trust designed under §§ 672(f)(2)(a)(i) or (ii)?
  - Revocable, or
  - Irrevocable with Husband and/or Wife as Sole Beneficiary during Grantor's lifetime.

- The Foreign Estate Election can buy U.S. beneficiaries two further years of U.S. tax efficiency.

- If the Trust holds a foreign company, the estate will need the time to restructure assets especially

- The foreign company can be restructured to optimal efficiency if the company is restructured to be held no more than 50% by U.S. Shareholders, for IRC Sec 245A deduction.

- PFICs can also be restructured so that PFIC status is no longer satisfied; simple as making a check the box election in most cases

- CFC can be restructured or check the box election should be considered

KARLIN & PEEBLES, LLP
ATTORNEYS AT LAW

U.S. Beneficiaries of Foreign Trusts with CFC, PFICs

CONSIDERATIONS: After the death of a foreign decedent, a FGT will toggle to FNGT status

- U.S. beneficiaries are generally considered to be the current shareholders or percentage owners of CFCs and PFICs.

- The above issue should be a consideration in drafting.

❑ Are there foreign beneficiaries as well? Consider a pot trust with discretionary distributions.
❑ Separate trusts may further support deemed (Subpart F and GILTI) distributions to U.S. beneficiaries even when no distribution has been made; same for PFIC income when actually distributed, even if made to another beneficiary!

KARLIN & PEEBLES, LLP
ATTORNEYS AT LAW

No. 9:
Generally, a portfolio should be managed in the currency of the beneficiary.

KARLIN & PEEBLES, LLP
ATTORNEYS AT LAW

CRITICAL CONSIDERATION IN CROSS BORDER WEALTH MANAGEMENT – CURRENCY RISK

- The appropriate base currency for each client must be considered. The added issue for international trusts is that the trust's home country currency may be different from the currency that the beneficiaries.

- In fact, if the trustees and beneficiaries are situated around the globe, the appropriate reference currency may be quite difficult to determine.

- "…[f]rom the dollar-based perspective of the US beneficiaries, hedging foreign currency exposure against the euro instead of the dollar will make the trust's investment performance significantly more volatile. Indeed, the chance of the trust suffering a 20% peak-to-trough loss during the 30-year period more than quadruples, and a 30% peak-to-trough loss becomes as likely as a coin toss. The reason for the greater volatility is simple: By hedging to the euro, the trustee exposes the US beneficiary not only to the underlying volatility of the trust's stocks and bonds, but also to the US dollar versus euro exchange rate." **[Research AllianceBernstein; THANK YOU JEAN HUANG!]**

- A Trust Generally Should Be Managed in the Currency of the Beneficiary.

KARLIN & PEEBLES, LLP
ATTORNEYS AT LAW

No. 10:
Consider U.S. Domestic Structures, but don't forget to file informational returns.

KARLIN & PEEBLES, LLP
ATTORNEYS AT LAW

DOMESTIC NON-GRANTOR TRUST

(This Structure Can Be Used between Foreign Spouses With Community or Separate Property, as long as equal for divorce purposes.)

KARLIN & PEEBLES, LLP
ATTORNEYS AT LAW

| CORE PLANNING FOR U.S.-BASED BENEFICIARIES – DOMESTIC SOLUTION PLANNING:

Foreign Spouses or Parent

U.S. Based Beneficiary
Domestic Dynasty Trust
(In United States)

- NO U.S. ESTATE TAX
- NO U.S. GIFT TAX (Funding Attention: T-Bill Option)
- SHIELDS U.S. ESTATE TAX GOING FORWARD – Dynasty Trust jurisdiction
- U.S. BENEFICIARY CAN CONTROL

- **Subject to U.S. Income tax**
- **No Basis Step-Up generally.**
- **Often used for the purchase of U.S. real estate to avoid Foreign Investment in Real Property Tax Act ("FIRPTA")**
- **Must File Form 3520!   Harsh Penalties if Not.**

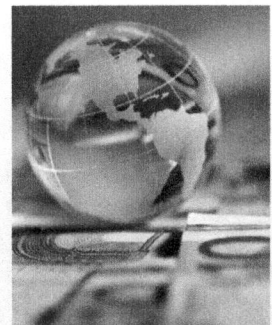

KARLIN & PEEBLES, LLP
ATTORNEYS AT LAW

CYNTHIA D. BRITTAIN

Cindy Brittain focuses her practice on high net worth, multinational families and individuals who themselves and their global companies require expertise in sophisticated cross-border income and estate tax planning strategies. Working closely with family members, Cindy obtains a comprehensive understanding of their values and dynamics, ensuring that unique personal and business goals are achieved. Cindy's extensive experience includes advising families on the complex issues relevant to pre-immigration planning, international corporate tax, and both international and domestic wealth and asset transfer strategies. Cindy also has extensive experience with cross-border regulatory laws that affect U.S. domestic planning as well as with U.S. tax compliance under the several voluntary disclosure regimes.

Cindy previously worked at a major accounting firm within its international mergers and acquisitions group, and has continued to advise clients on the effective integration of their global business operations into the U.S. tax regime. Over the course of her career, she has worked with clients in Brazil, Saudi Arabia, Dubai, London, Hong Kong, Mainland China, India, and the United States to develop overall income and estate planning strategies on behalf of large global families.

Practice focus

• Advanced domestic and international estate and tax planning; Transactional tax and corporate cross-border design

• Pre-immigration strategies for corporate assets; Multi-generational succession and entity planning

• Trust and legacy design; Multi-state trust strategies to mitigate California state income tax

• Charitable planning for effective tax and philanthropic goals; Family governance and family retreats for NextGen Education

KARLIN & PEEBLES, LLP
ATTORNEYS AT LAW

Make sure you are using the latest update

For your convenience, the following list identifies the most recent publication date of each CEB update (as of August 2023).

Update Title	Product Number	Publication Date
Advising California Common Interest Communities, 2d Edition	RE-30539	2/23
Advising California Employers and Employees	BU-33688	3/23
Advising California Nonprofit Corporations, 3d Edition	BU-33945	7/23
Advising California Partnerships, 3d Edition	BU-32886	2/23
Appeals and Writs in Criminal Cases, 3d Edition	CR-33667	6/23
Business Buy-Sell Agreements	BU-31495	6/23
California Administrative Hearing Practice, 2d Edition	CP-32678	10/22
California Administrative Mandamus, 3d Edition	CP-32892	5/23
California Attorney Fee Awards, 3d Edition	CP-34014	3/23
California Attorney's Guide to Damages, 2d Edition	CP-33551	12/22
California Automobile Insurance Law Guide, 2d Edition	TO-30209	11/22
California Basic Practice Handbook	MI-34277	11/22
California Business Litigation	BU-33572	7/23
California Child Custody Litigation and Practice	FA-31888	4/23
California Child and Spousal Support: Establishing, Modifying, and Enforcing	FA-33844	8/23
California Civil Appellate Practice, 3d Edition	CP-32439	5/23
California Civil Discovery Practice, 4th Edition	CP-32298	4/23
California Civil Litigation Forms Manual	CP-34476	10/22
California Civil Procedure Before Trial, 4th Edition	CP-31701	6/23
California Civil Writ Practice, 4th Edition	CP-33886	12/22
California Client Communications Manual: Sample Letters and Forms	MI-34267	3/23
California Conservatorship Practice	ES-33529	5/23
California Construction Contracts, Defects, and Litigation	RE-33796	11/22
California Criminal Law Forms Manual, 2d Edition	CR-33209	8/23
California Criminal Law Procedure and Practice, 2023	CR-32116	5/23
California Criminal Sentencing Enhancements 2023	CR-34163	4/23
California Decedent Estate Practice, 2d Ed V 1, 2, 3	ES-33045	5/23
California Easements and Boundaries: Law and Litigation	RE-31506	8/23
California Elder Law Litigation: An Advocate's Guide	ES-33622	7/23
California Elder Law Resources, Benefits, and Planning: An Advocate's Guide	ES-33631	8/22
California Estate Planning	ES-33463	5/23

8.5×11

Update Title	Product Number	Publication Date
California Eviction Defense Manual, 2d Edition	RE-32083	6/23
California Expert Witness Guide, 2d Edition	CP-31685	6/23
California Government Tort Liability Practice, 4th Edition	TO-33136	2/23
California Guardianship Practice 2023	ES-33539	1/23
California Judges Benchbook: Search & Seizure 2022	CR-34184	10/22
California Juvenile Dependency Practice 2023	CR-34124	3/23
California Land Use Practice	RE-33597	10/22
California Landlord-Tenant Practice, 2d Edition	RE-32698	4/23
California Law of Contracts	BU-33617	4/23
California Liability Insurance Practice: Claims & Litigation	CP-39264	9/22
California Local Probate Rules 2023	ES-39667	2/23
California Marital Settlements and Other Family Law Agreements, 3d Edition	FA-35519	1/23
California Mechanics Liens and Related Construction Remedies, 4th Edition	RE-33091	10/22
California Mortgages, Deeds of Trust, and Foreclosure Litigation, 4th Edition	RE-33925	2/23
California Municipal Law Handbook 2023	MI-34044	7/23
California Personal Injury Proof 2023	TO-34151	5/23
California Powers of Attorney and Health Care Directives	ES-33905	10/22
California Probate Code Annotated to CEB Publications 2023	ES-31197	1/23
California Probate Workflow Manual Revised	ES-31567	8/23
California Real Estate Brokers: Law and Litigation	RE-33865	8/23
California Real Estate Finance Practice: Strategies and Forms	RE-33185	1/23
California Real Property Remedies and Damages, 2d Edition	RE-33444	8/23
California Real Property Sales Transactions, 4th Edition	RE-33697	2/23
California Subdivision Map Act and the Development Process, 2d Edition	RE-33254	9/22
California Summary Judgment 2023	CP-34084	8/23
California Title Insurance Practice, 2d Edition	RE-32621	6/23
California Tort Damages, 2d Edition	TO-33513	1/23
California Tort Guide, 3d Edition	TO-32549	2/23
California Trial Objections 2022	CP-32556	9/22
California Trial Practice: Civil Procedure During Trial, 3d Edition	CP-32191	4/23
California Trust Administration, 2d Edition	ES-33304	3/23
California Trust and Probate Litigation	ES-32856	3/23
California UCC Sales and Leases	BU-33473	12/22
California Uninsured Motorist Practice, 2d Edition	TO-33284	7/23
California Wage and Hour: Law and Litigation	BU-34144	1/23
California Will Drafting, 3d Edition	ES-30324	11/22
California Workers' Compensation Practice, 4th Edition	WC-33155	3/23
California Workers' Damages Practice, 2d Edition	WC-33294	9/22
CJER Benchbook: Domestic Violence Cases in Criminal Court, 2022	CR-33765	8/22
CJER Felony Sentencing Handbook 2023	CR-33159	3/23
CJER Mandatory Criminal Jury Instructions Handbook 2023	CR-33109	1/23
Complete Plans for Small and Mid-Size Estates	ES-32927	12/22
Condemnation Practice in California, 3d Edition	RE-31308	9/22

Update Title	Product Number	Publication Date
Counseling California Corporations, 3d Edition	BU-33816	5/23
Crossover Issues in Estate Planning and Family Law	ES-34233	8/23
Debt Collection Practice in California, 2d Edition	BU-32986	2/23
Dividing Pensions and Other Employee Benefits in California Divorces	FA-32386	9/22
Drafting Business Contracts: Principles, Techniques and Forms	BU-30803	8/23
Drafting California Irrevocable Trusts, 3d Edition	ES-32719	7/23
Drafting California Revocable Trusts, 4th Edition	ES-33611	9/22
Drafting Employment Documents for California Employers	BU-34242	11/22
Effective Introduction of Evidence in California, 2d Edition	CP-33235	10/22
Employment Damages and Remedies	CP-34252	5/23
Employee Leave Laws: Compliance and Litigation	BU-30098	7/23
Estate Planning 2022	ES-31604	9/22
Family Law Financial Discovery	FA-33856	12/22
Fee Agreement Forms Manual, 2d Edition	MI-33247	11/22
Fiduciary Accounting Handbook 2022	ES-30025	4/22
Financing and Protecting California Businesses	BU-31898	2/23
Forming and Operating California Limited Liability Companies, 3d edition	BU-30029	12/22
Forming California Common Interest Developments	RE-33611	12/22
Ground Lease Practice, 2d Edition	RE-33088	5/22
Internet Law & Practice in California	BU-33581	7/23
Jefferson's California Evidence Benchbook, 4th Edition	CP-33835	2/23
Neighbor Disputes: Law and Litigation	RE-34071	4/23
Office Leasing: Drafting and Negotiating the Lease	RE-30899	12/22
Organizing Corporations in California, 3d Edition	BU-33424	1/23
Persuasive Opening Statements and Closing Arguments 2023	CP-31593	4/23
Practice Under the California Environmental Quality Act, 2d Edition	RE-33786	3/23
Practice Under the California Family Code: Dissolution, Legal Separation, Nullity 2023	FA-31955	3/23
Privacy Compliance and Litigation in California	BU-33936	8/23
Real Property Exchanges, 3d Edition	RE-33563	4/22
Real Property Ownership and Taxation	RE-30486	1/23
Retail Leasing: Drafting and Negotiating the Lease	RE-33576	11/22
Sales and Mergers of California Businesses	BU-33453	9/22
Scientific Evidence and Expert Testimony in California 2022	CR-30047	10/22
Secured Transactions in California Commercial Law Practice, 2d Edition	BU-33394	1/23
Selecting and Forming Business Entities, 2d Edition	BU-33317	4/23
Special Needs Trusts: Planning, Drafting, and Administration	ES-33746	6/23
Strategies on Appeal	CP-34350	8/21
Trade Secrets Practice in California, 2d Edition	BU-32598	11/22
Trial Attorney's Evidence Code Notebook 2023	CP-31098	2/23
Understanding Fiduciary Duties in Business Entities	BU-30017	3/23
Wrongful Employment Termination Practice: Discrimination, Harassment, Retaliation, 2d Edition	CP-32658	6/23

CEB®

Ensure That Your Legal Know-How Is Always Up to Date.

We recommend that you keep your practice materials current by purchasing regular updates. CEB updates provide the latest developments, rulings, and case law to guarantee that you will be working with the most timely information possible. Our Automatic Update customers also receive reduced pricing on new editions and other discounts.

If you bought this book from a bookstore, you may not be registered as an Automatic Update Customer. Please take a moment to fax us this form at 1-800-640-6994—or call CEB Customer Service at **1-800-232-3444**—to ensure the accuracy of your CEB legal materials.

Title of Publication _____

Product Number _____
      (CEB product numbers can be found stamped or printed on the back cover of all CEB books and Action Guides.)

Date Purchased _____

Name _____

State Bar # _____

Firm Name _____

Address _____

Telephone _____

Email Address _____

Signature _____

As an Automatic Update Customer, updates, revisions, and new editions will be sent to you automatically as they are released with an invoice (including sales tax and shipping). Full 30-day return privileges apply. You may cancel this service at any time.

Auto Update 8.5x11